Advance Praise

"Jennifer Mullan offers a fiery provocation to all of us—especially those called to serve as therapists, practitioners, and healers. The call is to grasp at the root of that which really harms us, those oppressive practices of our training that do more to dehumanize and disconnect than we've known. This book is a remembering of the wisdom of our practices and survival. What Mullan leaves us with, somehow, is everything, each other, and the beautiful and challenging project of creating decolonized spaces of healing and repair."
—**Prentis Hemphill,** cofounder of the Embodiment Institute

"To receive the therapy you deserve, read *Decolonizing Therapy* and insist your therapist read it too. Empowering, worldview-shattering, and necessary for immigrants and people of color."
—**Stephanie Foo,** author of *What My Bones Know: A Memoir of Healing from Complex Trauma*

"All practitioners and therapists would greatly benefit from immersing themselves into the roots of *Decolonizing Therapy*. Dr. Jenn nurtures a space for us to dig deep into rooted, humanizing, reparenting, loving, new world work that bridges the ancient. She invites our humanity and our pain to the table."
—**Shefali Tsabary,** PhD, *New York Times*–bestselling author of *The Conscious Parent*

DECOLONIZING THERAPY

DECOLONIZING THERAPY

Oppression, Historical Trauma, and Politicizing Your Practice

JENNIFER MULLAN, PsyD

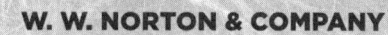

W. W. NORTON & COMPANY
Celebrating a Century of Independent Publishing

Note to Readers: Standards of clinical practice and protocol change over time, and no technique or recommendation is guaranteed to be safe or effective in all circumstances. This volume is intended as a general information resource for professionals practicing in the field of psychotherapy and mental health; it is not a substitute for appropriate training, peer review, and/or clinical supervision. Neither the publisher nor the author(s) can guarantee the complete accuracy, efficacy, or appropriateness of any particular recommendation in every respect. As of press time, the URLs displayed in this book link or refer to existing sites. The publisher and author are not responsible for any content that appears on third-party websites.

Graphics created by Maverick Lumen for Dr. Jennifer Mullan

DECOLONIZING THERAPY is a registered trademark of Decolonizing Therapy LLC.

Copyright © 2023 by Jennifer Mullan

All rights reserved
Printed in the United States of America

Frontis and chapter opener art: (tree and roots) lightsource / DepositPhotos; (background) amtitus / Getty Images

For information about permission to reproduce selections from this book, write to
Permissions, W. W. Norton & Company, Inc., 500 Fifth Avenue, New York, NY 10110

For information about special discounts for bulk purchases, please contact
W. W. Norton Special Sales at specialsales@wwnorton.com or 800-233-4830

Manufacturing by Lakeside Book Company
Production manager: Gwen Cullen

ISBN: 978-1-324-01916-9

W. W. Norton & Company, Inc., 500 Fifth Avenue, New York, NY 10110
www.wwnorton.com

W. W. Norton & Company Ltd., 15 Carlisle Street, London W1D 3BS

10 9 8

For all the therapists, practitioners, root workers, space holders and healers who have contributed to creating spaces of safety, impacting generations to come. For those who guide us on our journey back home . . . back to the Root of our Collective Tree. I see you.

For the Spirit of PEP and my Peppers: We are the abolitionists of traditional therapy and the rooted raging descendants of our ancestral healing. Thank you for trusting me and pushing me to decolonize western therapy. I am you.

For all the past versions of myself, especially young Jenny from around the way. I adore you.

Thank you to all Ancestors who helped bring this book to fruition. I honor you.

Contents

Acknowledgments xi
Introduction 1

PART 1: THE ROOTS: WHERE IT BEGAN

CHAPTER 1   Your (Our) Therapy Is Colonial   39
CHAPTER 2   Emotional–Decolonial Work   68
CHAPTER 3   From Lobotomies to Liberation   99
CHAPTER 4   Diagnostic Enslavement   125

PART 2: THE TRUNK: WHERE WE ARE

CHAPTER 5   From Historical Trauma to Healing the Collective Soul Wound   169
CHAPTER 6   Intergenerational Trauma Transmission: Ancestral Trauma and Wisdom Exist *Together Within Us*   190
CHAPTER 7   Ancestral Roots in Mental Health "From Root to Bone"   214
CHAPTER 8   Collective Grief and Sacred Rage As Expressions of Colonization   238

PART 3: THE LEAVES: GROWING A DECOLONIAL FUTURE

CHAPTER 9   From the Inside Out: Energetic Boundaries   285

CHAPTER 10 Politicizing Your Practice (Is How We Begin to Decolonize Therapy)   316

CONCLUSION Call to Action   366

Practitioner Resources   369

Glossary/Terms to Chew On   395

References   407

Index   435

IRE IONA IPONRI ATIWO ORUN
IFA SAYS: MAY THE JOURNEY OF SELF-DISCOVERY
BRING YOU THE BLESSINGS OF SPIRIT.

Acknowledging & Loving Y'all…

I wrote and read voraciously as a child. It was my world. My grandfather, Benigno Mark, would sit me next to him, the bus would be careening down Flatbush Avenue, and he would quiz me on capitals of countries around the globe, on what I was reading, all while giving me lectures on the value of respect. He would tell me to respect myself, my parents, and my great-great-great-grandparents enough to speak the truth and speak it with clarity. That truth telling was indeed love and one that the world deeply needed from a person such as me.

I know this book is an act of love; because love is, after all, really rebellious.

I give a deep, tearful gratitude to my ancestors who are the shoulders and spirits I do this work for and with: Benigno Mark, Lucia Mark Jimenez, Inocencia Ayarza, Julia Telese, Felicia Tunyon, James Mullan, Sr., and so many others whose faces and spirits I feel, but whose names go unspoken. I honor you. To besties I have had to grieve too early: Raynelle White and Tondra Martinez—I do this for you.

To the lands that cradled me and sustained me while writing this book. Especially the land stewarded by the Leni Lenape peoples. I remember those whose labor was exhausted and exploited across these lands. Those removed from their families, tongues, cuisines, and lands. I honor you. To the constellation of energies that is Decolonizing Therapy. I thank you.

To the spirits and ancestors of the East: To the morning dew, to the essence of spring, the feeling of falling in love, to the condor, to the butterfly, to the morning sunrise, to the eagle and the wind. To Baba Obatala. I welcome you.

To the spirits and ancestors of the South: To the noon-time scorching sun, to the sacred fire, to that which we release and burn away, to the releasing of illusions and fear and loss. To the desert scorpion, snake, energy of resurrection, and the phoenix. To Sango. I welcome you.

To the spirits and ancestors of the West: To Mama Wata, the luminescence of the surrender—the release—the letting go of that which we never had control of. I honor the whale, dolphin, octopus, and shark spirits. The deep depths, dark secrets, and abundance at the bottom of the ocean held under the love of Olokun. Yemaya and the siren song. I welcome you.

To the spirits and ancestors of the North: To the cold white winter earth. To the polar bear, the white barn owl, the desert wolf. To that which must die and leave. To that which we must walk with our ancestors. I welcome you. I welcome you sacred ones, medicine ones, you whose bones lie beneath the earth.

To the rooted nations, to that which holds and sustains. I welcome you. To those from above: to the ascended masters, bodhisattvas, high master teachers, galactic wisdom keepers, archangels, and celestial families. I welcome you.

To Jaguar, I bow to you. To the drum and the conga. To the divine masculine and feminine. Consciousness. To all the divine feminine energies that have been outcasted and minimized. To my queer fore-people. To all who have felt unloved, unseen, too much, and yet not enough. To all who have had to hide their shine; their Knowing-ness. I see you.

Respect, love, libations, and a deep bow for those that paved the paths, built the foundations, spoke with their voice shaking, and for all of those blood and non-blood relatives who took a chance and spoke out. To every elder, ancestor, teacher, activist, and liberator that spoke of the emotional impacts of colonization, no matter the language, the pentameter, or whether or not the words were acknowledged by academia or community organizers—I honor you.

> A deep bow of love and gratitude to the individuals who held and contained me, mind, body and spirit, throughout the manuscript writing process. Those that gently lulled me out of isolation with companionship—a walk through nature, a song, meals, words of encouragement, or an inappropriate laugh:

To my Ace and Mommy, Maria de los Angeles, you are the most magical being consistently loving me back to myself.

To my Dad, Jim, you are my mirror—I am so verbose because of your passion and intensity. What a ride being your kid.

To my baby brother, Mike, "I don't know how to put this . . ." but I appreciate your reminders, cheerleading, and love, coupled with your badass photography.

To Beatriz Villatoro, you complete me, my soul-sister. This and every lifetime in every version of the matrix.

To Aneesa Holliday-Dingle, you are my star, protector, joy-bringer, and oldest chosen family.

To Dr. Lee Vickers, you consistently show me the power of love and light.

To Peter Esgro, you're my shaman brother. Keep nourishing and enlightening this world.

To Venida Rodman-Jenkins, you are unlimited black girl joy! Loyal love in action!

To Maverick Lumen: You are the *VAGUS NERVE* to this DT book. You have been a patient, present companion, and book doula. *Mic drop.*

To Jessa Bonafe, you flew the plane—while we built it. Together we agitate and style on 'em.

To Alisha Sharma, you're my journey-Goddess-sister full of golden light. Thank you for protecting this work.

To Raphaella Sadia Hamidu, you are my Ghanaian-goddess-gardener-womb-shaman! I give thanks to you and your medicine daily.

To Dr. Diana Chacon, for modeling healthy therapeutic boundaries, beauty, brains, and Spirit in one.

To Ruthie Arroyo, your *re*-education planted the seed in me—making this book happen. Thank you *compañera*.

To Dr. Jen Douglas for your reminders to smash perfectionism and your delicious sarcasm.

To Wilkins, wow. Thank you for matching me.

To Gabes Torres and Ji-Youn Kim, you both have been cocreators in perfect harmony, reminding me to remain steady in this liberation work.

To The Swaggy Simon's: Lauren, Ms. Michele, Ashley, and Ms. Pamela Watts, you all gave me space to speak into existence what my soul longed for.

To my Warriors of Light crew, I truly believe we are all decolonizing in our respective elements. Natoya Hall: the Mothaaa of Celestial Knowing, Jen Maramba: the ancestral jaguar, Dr Jacqui Wilkins: the potent plant whisperer, Clare Kenty: the healing holder of realness, and Cian Knight: the gentle giving goddess.

To Shane Cook, bruh, you believed in me and DT from the get. You be up on everythang!

My PEP Fam. You are the definition of community care, "doing the work," and true love: Rukiya Bluford, Charles Yarbrough, Zhane Malone, Maria Parmagos, Brianna Gipe, Zakiyyah Plantyn, Rashad Wright, Kiana Thornton, Ezenwa Wosu, Shayla D. Cook, Wilton Jimenez, Glennifer Braker, Henry Espinal, Shalisha Cook, and so many more.

Gratitude and hugs to the following phenomenal beings; words cannot adequately describe my appreciation for the help, care, editing, ideating, conversating, astrologizing, pontificating, blazing, humanizing, joy-filled moments of care you each have given me:

Dr. Erin O'Neill, Dawn Harrison, Sonalee Rashatwar, Ana Robelo, Dr. Rebecca Vicente, Renee Sills, Toi Smith, Dr. Abisola Gallagher, Dr. Alissa Koval-Dhaliwal, Dr. Alfredo Lowe, Veronica Baker, Krystina Pasteur, Tina Yagnam, Sara andKaytie Brisenden-Smith, Karina Gonzalez- Blaver, Yolanda Renteria, Dr. Yumiko Ogawa, Ruby Warrington, Natalie Miles, Jane Clapp, Layla Saad, Nova Reid, Danielle Cohen, Angelica Frausto "Nerdy Brown Kid," Ebony Janice, Fara Tucker, L Tantay, Monica Monfre, Natalie

Gutierrez, Minaa B., Dr. Mariel Buque, Giselle Buchanan, Dr. Carla Vilches, Ndeye Oumou Sylla, Annick Ina, Estefania Mendevil, Eleri Smith, Jane Clapp, Colin Bedell, Natasha Sandy, Melody Li, Awo Okaikor Aryee-Price, Omisade Burney-Scott, Momma Lucy Rodman, Todd Jenkins, Mr. and Mrs. Benjamin and Sheila Holliday, David Marshall, Luna Lotus Blue, the Romans, the Marks, and the Mullans.

Thank you to my dope literary agent Laura Lee Mattingly for being an accomplice and friend. You're a real one, LL!

Thank you, W. W. Norton team: Deborah Malmud, editor, vice president, and director of Norton Professional Books. Thank you for the vision. Sara McBride Tuohy, Mariah Eppes, Olivia Guarnieri, Gwen Cullen, Lauren Graessle, Kevin Olsen, and Natalie Argentina, thank you all for helping to bring the DT book together. Annie J. Nichol, wonderful and patient developmental editor, for breathing support and care into the work. Janay Nachel Frazier, thank you for the cover art work. Thank you Camille Guy for your detailed editing, clear mind and eye, spiritual insight, and word-smithing. Thank you Dawn Michelle Hardy for your literary prowess and support.

I thank my past and present clients, students who, without your trust, presence, and even intense pain, this work would not be possible. You are the real MVPs. Thank you NJCU students—y'all know who you are; whether six months or six years in that office together, thank you for trusting me, and growing with me, and pushing me to "show up in the world." Thank you for showing me that we can have a relational therapeutic liberatory, yet real-ass relationship with therapist-intimacy that is consensual, boundary-filled, safe, and real AF.

Such love and bows to my companion and goddess-cat: Isis. Every page. Every lifetime.

Deep gratitude to the Intergenerational Ancestors who have informed my work and elevated my world (those living and those that walk in the ethers):

Dr. Bola Cofield	Lama Rod Owens	Dr. Tanya Wilkinson
Dr. Sue Esquilin	Diana Melendez	Ruby Warrington

Dennis Febo
Prune Harris
Baba Sean Gayle
Dr. Na'im Akbar
Dr. Judith Herman
Lisa Oliveras
Isabel Wilkerson
Erika Hart
Dr. Frances Cress Welsing
Paulo Freire
Carl Jung
Anakbayan NJ & NY
Assata Shakur
Dr. Allan DeFina
Dr. Kimberly Richards
Milta Vega
Dr. Peter Donnelly
Ruth King
Steve Campos
Dr. Rupa Marya
Madrina Elemi Gayle

Dr. Ignacio Martin-Baro
Tricia Hersey
Mia Mingus
Nedra Tawab
Roberto & Bonnie Duran
Dr. Connie Wun
bell hooks
Maya Angelou
Dr. Nancy Boyd Franklin
People's Institute of Survival & Beyond (PISAB)
Project Lets
Ta-nehisi Coates
Dr. Patrice Dow Nelson
Ron Chisom
Bonnie Berman Cushing

Toko-pa Turner
Dr. Joy DeGruy
Robin Gorman
Dr. Thema Bryant
Stef Kaufman
Dr. Hector Adames
Maryam Hasnaa
adrienne maree brown
Kelsey Blackwell
Dr. Frederick W. Hickling
Dr. Huey P. Newton
Dr. Maria Yellow Horse Brave Heart
A Course in Miracles
Institute for Development of Human Arts

. . . and so, so many others.

May we continue to alchemize our ancestral wounds into crystal gems of intuition, movement, and (R)Evolution.

DECOLONIZING THERAPY

Introduction

This book is wrapped in deep love and compassion. Its use is not just limited to therapists, but also to body workers, social workers, teachers, nurses, and others. We were trained within and for the System. No matter the oppressive system—we are Gatekeepers (and decently paid ones) in those systems. So, let us begin . . .

My dear fellow colonized therapists,
    We need to not just understand and be aware, but also take activated action.
    It is time that we recognize the historical roots of the disability rights movement, and how mental and emotional health are firmly in the center of this movement. We need to remember that the disability rights movement was founded by queer people, in particular queer, trans, black, brown, and indigenous racialized people.
    May we honor the beauty and necessity of mutual aid in all of its forms, and be willing to recognize the fluidity of human experiences.
    Many of us began this career path with a deep calling to help others, but what we really needed was to help ourselves . . . to locate the root of our need to give and help and triage almost everyone everywhere despite ourselves.
    Many of us began this process of learning, interning, and performing in order to help people. What we were really doing was making ourselves feel better by cyclically caregiving and educating others.
    Many of us began this process honored that so many people trusted

us with their stories and pain, yet rarely did we make the space to tend to our own excruciating stories of abandonment, neglect, and low-key codependency. May we value our various roles, and the abilities of each of us, while we learn from one another. May we find the beauty and necessity in conscious peer support.

My dear fellow colonized therapists,

May we place a high value on the healing power of simply having choices.

May we vow to never again support or participate in coercion or forced treatment.

May we transform together, the mental and emotional health care system.

May we understand that for change and healing to be sustainable and real, it must happen throughout our communities and systems.

May we remember that "I" am not solely the responsibility of each individual seeking help, that engaging at an individual level is unsustainable and inhumane.

May we share power and value reciprocal relationships between people with lived experience and those who are working to support us.

May we engage from a decolonial and anti-oppression framework, meaning that we understand that structural ableism both informs and reinforces other structures of oppression (i.e., racism, sexism, classism).

May we seek to dismantle all forms of oppression, recognizing that our freedom, rights, and liberation must be collective and, therefore, include the most vulnerable among us.

May we learn from the Land, from the Indigenous people of the Land, and engage in reciprocal right relationship with the Land, as well as one another.

As we slowly awaken, undo, and decolonize our mental and emotional behavioral care systems, may we allow for room to not know and to learn from the people we serve.

May we stop calling the people who participate in therapeutic work with us "patients" and "clients." It is so capitalistic and pathologizing.

May we find new language rooted in healing justice and possibility.

May we have fun cocreating new ways of relating and calling in.

My dear fellow colonized therapists,

May we stop medicalizing and pathologizing race and ethnicity while using "multiculturalism" and "diversity" training as a cure-all elixir.

May we continuously learn about the differences between gender identity, gender expression, and sexual orientation.

May we please stop calling the end of therapy sessions "termination sessions"?

May we please have large-sized-fat-affirming chairs that are comfortable for every body in our offices? These are basic accessibility requests.

May we begin to unpack and teach people to live with their trauma more and "treat it" less.

May we ask about folks' migration stories.

May we create genograms and timelines for trauma, abuse, IPV, diseases,[1] and so forth and begin to unpack intergenerational trauma—not just staunch the bleeding.

May we stop insinuating that people under the poverty line need to work harder. Poor people are some of the hardest-working folks I know.

May we talk about colorism, race-based trauma, anti-Black racism, and neoliberalism.

May we work on our own emotional and ancestral shame, guilt, and grief.

May we realize how illness is written on our bodies and the bodies of our therapy participants—through relationships, rituals, and their stories.

May we realize that this process is full of dichotomies and paradoxes. A personal, yet collective journey; a lonely, yet supported journey; a political and healing journey; an abolishing and merging journey; and a practical and scientific, yet ancestral and fluid healing journey.

May we honor that the very nature of the decolonial process is one that seeks to change how we see the world, while living within the world

---

1 A term learned through the work of Louise Hay and Caroline Myss. See the glossary for more on how it is used.

sustainably. Decolonization cannot be intellectualized as it is historical and constantly evolving, within and outside of us.

May we remember that colonial capitalism banks on our obsession with money and "making it," as it has been programmed generationally into us and our lineages. The heart and brain of oppression is class warfare.

May we work on our own grief and honor our righteous sacred rage.

May we make space for big feelings, old teachings, and new ways of implementing our elders' medicines.

My dear fellow colonized therapists,

May we democratize medical knowledge, in particular, the often-exclusive forms of "professionalized" therapeutic knowledge, and recognize that the mental health industrial complex (MHIC) does not have a monopoly on mental and emotional wellness.

May we continue to engage and think globally, and act locally.

May we build on a national level; believe in building strong, grassroots community-based systems of care, while forming international partnerships to undermine imperialistic practices; and support economic justice for previously colonized nations.

May we engage in models of care that shifts tasks and work, and may we be conscious that the work of listening, healing, supporting, and so forth is not limited to those with a particular license or degree.

May we recognize in ourselves the ways that dominant ideas about what type of person is seen as a potential caregiver or healer or professional simply replicates oppressive hierarchy.

May we stand firm in our beliefs that we do not heal or treat; we merely have the privilege of offering support and help.

May we innately know and believe that everyone is capable of healing themselves.

May we seek to resist colonial and commodifying practices of divorcing global indigenous, religious, spiritual, and holistic healing practices from their roots, in particular the roots of emotional and mental health modern-day practices.

May we recognize the power of our ancestors' practices with respect to their historical context and reject cultural appropriation of healing traditions.

In evolution,
Dr. Jenn

The damage the MIC [medical industrial complex] has inflicted on our planet should be enough for us all to dream and invest in building alternatives. . . . What could true wellness and care look like for our communities?
—Mia Mingus (2015)

Transformation has to be politicized, viewed ecologically, and pursued interdependently.
—Gabes Torres (2022)

Becoming aware of our stories leads to grief, but it also leads to validation.
—Lisa Olivera, Already Enough: A Path to Self-Acceptance (2022)

When you are living in a garbage dump, you don't breathe too deeply. This is how it is living in a society polluted with hateful supremacy. Which is why everyone suffocates, and even newborns breathe with a shallowness. We need fresh new air.
—Jaiya John, Freedom: Medicine Words for Your Brave Revolution (2020)

This book is for those of us who tend to the root of things.

The Root Workers.

Those of you who tend to the deeply buried parts of human suffering, society, and the global consciousness.

Those of you who truly embody space holding. The containers. The "sin-eaters." The hope holders. The medicine makers. The soldiers of suffering. That is what I think really helpful mental health practitioners do. We contain and metabolize suffering into possibility. We offer constant shifts in perspective. We help those in pain, deep in their defenses, to consider *choosing* to see it all differently. We provide options and create connections for access. We push, sometimes shove. We hold the fort. We worry. We make sure it's safe, and we water. We water the roots. We prune the leaves. Some of us excavate the bones. We are those who witness and metabolize the pain in society, the shadow parts of the collective.

Historically our names were curandera/o, shaman, priestess, witch, babalawo, iyanifa, santera/o, palera/o, ndi obi, szeptunka, kaiwhakaora, íceach, Bengali Babas, and many other names across the globe that had been reserved for people who help the healing process, outside of the Anglo-Christian gaze. Of course, there are still many practicing, thriving, traditional Indigenous healers listed above; however, the hook of colonialism and white supremacy have created a curtain of silence, shame, or secretiveness around many (not all) Indigenous healer identities.

This is due to safety, legal ramifications, acculturation, internalized white supremacy, but mostly at the root is colonization.

Colonial consciousness has created rules that are not as client-centered as they would have us believe. The medical industrial complex (MIC) has turned healing practices into for-profit practices. Persons who once "healed" now "treat." Persons who once "scanned" now "assess." Persons who once "cleared energies" now "diagnose." This lucrative pivot in practices benefits those at the top of the power hierarchy of these interlocking systems (not the people receiving the care, and sometimes not the providers). So you see, the medical/mental health industries have capitalized on and commodified healers and healing. This in turn has deeply impacted everyone, including our Earth.

White supremacy informs and births white culture that is analogous and difficult to pin down. It is everywhere and tangled within the roots of many things. White culture leans toward individualistic, consumeristic, time-oriented/results-oriented, "professional," de-spiritualized, hierarchical, monotheistic, dichotomous, content-over-process thinking and is quite rageful and violent. This permeates therapy, our clinical education, and how we engage in therapeutic practice. From our session limits, to the theories most valued, to the ways in which supervision is more about accumulating hours than processing super uncomfortable human interactions and natural processes. We live in a society with a myriad of experiences, stories, and perspectives. Our experiences are affected by the media, ancestral trauma, our environment, our families and their stories, as well as by our lived experiences, how we walk in the world, and how we are perceived.

The Root of Dis-Ease

This book is naming the root of disconnect from our bodies, minds, emotions, one another, and Earth. We are affected on multiple levels, and this book seeks to begin the process of reconvergence and reconnection—Individually, Systemically, and Ancestrally:

> **Individually ➔ Internalized White Supremacy** (can look like internalized racial inferiority or internalized racial superiority privilege). It disconnects us from one another, our culture, our humanity, our Earth, global issues that we believe do not affect us, among other things. We have internalized and been fed diets of colonial consciousness throughout our lives, in conscious and unconscious ways.
> **Systemically ➔ Medical/Mental Health Industrial Complex** are systems of profit over health, wellness, and care. Healing is almost never mentioned. Fee services, pathologized treatments, denial of services to poor and migrant communities, attempts to control populations through forced sterilization, to dangerous contraceptives and minimizing the prevalence of trafficked young women of color. To the deep health crisis (including mental health) burrowing itself within the tentacles of late-stage capitalism and imperialism.
> **Ancestrally/Historically ➔ Colonization** has us collectively disconnected, activated, and in deep grief all at once. There is a deep disconnect between therapy services and our history. There is a lack of culturally competent services; minimal discussion or context throughout the educational process for other ways of knowing; minimal awareness

around forced migration, ableism, capitalism, and cultural ways of healing; as well as demonization and erasure of Indigenous healing and practices globally.

Its roots run deep. This book will highlight how the MHIC history and the harm we experience in the present are connected to everything: eugenics, childhood adversity, queer and crip politics, capitalism, colonization, slavery, immigration, war, prisons, and reproductive oppression. These are all systems of oppression.

The Shoulders We Stand Upon

The psychological roots of colonization are embedded in our bodies, in how we problem solve, in how we think about what freedom feels like and looks like. Over the last 20-plus years, I have been deeply enamored and consumed by feeling free and safe in my body. But this has also included my mind. I have sought out teachers and practices with a deep ache in my person; this ache was a hunger. I wanted more; I expected my initiation into psychotherapy and to becoming a therapist would somehow quench this ache. It didn't. It hasn't.

Any of us who studied Freudian psychoanalysis are familiar with the Oedipus complex and the mother wound. It was like psychology and the practice of therapy were not giving me what I needed, psychotherapy became the "good enough mother." But like any healthy relationship, I realized that one practice, modality, philosophy, or person couldn't possibly give me everything I needed; it was not possible.

Along the way I have been exposed to an array of teachers, books, critical theories, and brilliant people who crafted an eclectic and holistic shift in me. I could double the size of this book with the fields, theories, activists-scholars, and free thinkers who have impacted *Decolonizing Therapy*, and on the lands, roots, and people which it firmly stands.

For now I will note that the politicization of my therapeutic practices, and emotional–decolonial process that I am still personally embarking upon has involved the storytelling, scholarship, and activism of: Ignacio

Martín-Baró and liberation psychology, Paulo Freire, Frantz Fanon, Nelson Mandela, Lacanian psychoanalysis, transpersonal psychology, breathwork, Central and North American shamanism, African spirituality, Buddhism, somatic therapy, psychodrama, African psychology, community mental health, Jungian analysis, family systems therapy, Dr. Kimberlé Crenshaw, critical race theory, queer theory, Dr. Joy DeGruy, People's Institute of Survival and Beyond's antiracism work, Ruth King's rage work, Dr. Bola Cofield's Blackness and love work, bell hooks, Dr. Maria Yellow Horse Brave Heart, Dr. Luisah Teish's Black Mother Rising class, Dr. Judith Lewis Herman's Trauma and Recovery course, the organizing of AnakBayan NJ and NY, and countless others. It is so important to remember that we did not arrive here alone or without massive support and companionship.

Mental Health Oppression

Mental health oppression is the systemic suppression of emotional discharge and the invalidation of oppressed people's minds. It is violent, and working as it was intended. It is the attempt to control people by enforcing standards of conduct, thereby invalidating their process, categorizing people into diagnoses, pressuring people "to do something about it," and punishing any attempts at liberation. Mental health oppression oppresses people systematically "forgotten," left out of the equation, and relegated to the margins. What it also does is maintain imperialism, white supremacy, ableism, fatphobia, and transphobia by reinforcing and hiding the function of these very oppressive movements—TO GET PEOPLE TO CONFORM.

Mental health oppression affects people NOT living with mental anguish. It helps to maintain the structures and hierarchies of society by keeping people and their big emotions in line. It is abusive. It is an abuse of power on the part of mental health professionals. It minimizes people's capacity to really believe that they can connect, trust one another, and liberate themselves.

Mental health oppression impedes all liberation movements. It makes people afraid of big feelings and afraid of losing their minds if they were to let go and let out. The largest deceit of all is mind control. This sick syndrome of gaslighting where people are tricked and bamboozled into thinking that overseers/police, politicians, and millionaires are generally trustworthy. We are collectively gaslit into believing that unhoused people and disabled people are to blame for their predicaments.

System Blaming Versus People Blaming

Decolonizing Therapy advocates for stepping out and acknowledging violent systems, antiquated colonial consciousness, and a lack of supportive connective spaces, while deciding how we will divest and heal from them. We are calling attention to the systematic targeting of oppressed communities under the guise of care, health, and safety. Like other oppressive systems, there are many individuals within the MHIC who do good work. You who picked up this book likely went into the MHIC to serve your communities because you wanted to change the system, and provide reliable and safe care to those who need it. You may be an individual who helps many mental health/therapy participants to find loopholes, shortcuts, and life rafts through the river that is drowning so many.

I am not anti–mental health or therapy. I am a critical lover of the field. I was so deeply blindsided and gaslit by a field I believed was in it to heal, but upon entering I immediately saw the sea of disconnect. Three years in, I discovered how deeply unstable the MHIC really was. Five years in, I felt the lack of care for the lives of the people seeking services (likely, it was sooner than that). Seven years in, I realized going into "private practice" or providing coaching of some sort was a way that providers tried to make it out alive and on their terms, and make more money. Nine years in, I was pretty politicized, bone-tired, burned out, and being blamed for my exhaustion. I was carrying a bigger course, case, and group session load than I could hold.

I am not saying that there are no useful or helpful things within the mental health systems. I am exposing the reality that many of us or our loved ones are dependent on the mental health systems because it is "all that we got," while we are simultaneously trying to change it—and ultimately build alternatives to it. Many people that I have served had not wanted to utilize the mental health system, but they had few other options. Still, many of us are fighting for access to current (or better) services within the MHIC.

This book offers no easy, clear answers, and the world and structures we are forced to live in are often unfair and unjust. Similar to our work to resist and challenge capitalism or to create alternatives to the police and prisons, resisting and challenging the MHIC is rife with complexity, and there is so much we need that we don't yet have. This book offers more questions, with a side of possibility. I believe it might be terribly ironic for one person to have all the answers.

I am not blaming white supremacy. I am holding it accountable. I am not blaming the MHIC. I am holding it accountable. I am calling attention to the systemic targeting of oppressed communities under the false pretense of health and safety.

I am holding the institution of white supremacy accountable for the ways in which resources have been poorly and criminally allocated. The ways in which mental health is underfunded across every institution of learning, but inner-city police forces are overfunded. I am holding the institutions accountable for neglect of its people, for creating millions of motherless Black and Brown children, for the violence on all of our women, for the very few options when it comes to our health care needs, and the kind of care we receive (or lack thereof).

I along with you my readers, am demanding change. Except, change needs to arise from within our organizations, our practices, our structures, and work. Our therapy participants can no longer afford to be fearful and distrustful of mental health support. What would it look like to not be fearful of mental health support? What would it look like to be able to trust that the care, interventions, treatments, and support received would not just care for the individual, but would also be care-filled for the larger community and the Earth?

This book reviews a brief history of how colonization is a root core human trauma; the importance of emotional–decolonial process; the history of how mental hygiene became mental health; how this has perpetuated further harm (to therapists and participants); and how the MHIC stole, institutionalized, and created a business, to what present-day therapy is. We will explore what emotional and mental health practices and care could look like outside of theory, while including healing-centered engagement,[2] mutual care, peer support, accessibility, and sustainability.

This book is an ode to decolonial action—a return to the root of the ways that people globally became well, after experiences of trauma—in particular, trauma as colonization. This is a call to connect the MHIC to our political work. This is why we politicize our practices; healing, wellness, health, emotional freedom, and disability are part of liberatory practices. Healing is political, particularly when our ancestral healing practices have been co-opted by mental health fields, then deemed groundless and invalid.

Years of colonization, the demonization of natural Indigenous methods of healing, and the systemic medicalization of healing have created the medical and mental health industrial complexes (Mingus, 2015). Interlocking systems of policies, structures, governing bodies, institutions, rules; as well as legal Ponzi and pyramid schemes where ableism is manufactured, perpetuated, and fed. The MHIC, a part of the MIC, is a massive system with tentacles that reach beyond doctors, nurses, teaching institutions, clinics, and hospital beds. It is a system about profit.

Decolonizing Therapy involves breaking cycles of "because that's how it's always been" responses, feelings of inadequacy and imposter syndrome on the parts of practitioners of therapies, and goes beyond narrow definitions of identity politics. Rather than shout that mental health systems need holistic practices, it may be more prudent to note that seldom do systems that benefit from staying the same actually change without: solidarity, a need for accountability, an understanding of historical perspectives, Indigenous and Black stories, historically marginalized peoples' stories, frontline input on colonial capitalism, an analysis of power, and deep-rooted understanding that therapy alone will not liberate us.

The mental health structures, diagnoses, programs, and solutions that we research and create are not devoid of corporate and financial interest. Yet

---

2 Healing-centered engagement is a term coined by Shawn Ginwright (2018).

the Indigenous and ancestral ways of knowing and healing are demonized, appropriated, minimized, and/or pathologized, and are often seen as not "professional, therapeutic, evidence-based, or peer-reviewed." These critiques on the mental health systems are not a plea to stop all care, instead we are demanding trauma-responsive, culturally full, transparent, anti-carceral, non-ableist care. We all deserve this. Our children deserve this. Our elders deserve this. Future generations deserve this. This book is my offering for more cross-movement, intergenerational, neurodivergent, gender-queer, ancestral, abolition-centered, embodied therapeutic work that actually works, and does not devour.

Throughout, I invite you to continue to ask yourselves:

- What could true wellness and care support look like for one another?
- Are we attempting to change an innately violent field amid an innately violent structure, in the name of keeping our degrees, titles, and cushion of our professions?
- How has colonial violence been embedded within the bodies and psyches of the people we work with; within ourselves; and within the institutions, businesses, nonprofits, and coaching consulting programs we create?
- Who gets to decide what is healthy, healing, and harmless?

Calling You In

If you are a clinician, therapist, social worker, psychologist, psychiatrist, healer, and helper—if your work is to help people feel and be better, in any capacity—this book is for you. But it delves deeper than technique. It delves deeper than naming and pathologizing and creating more boxes. It goes deeper than centering whiteness—whiteness does that all on its own. It goes deeper than "how to . . ." Instead, it is an invitation for the helpers to be helped and held. It is an invitation to create the space to be creative in and to cast big imaginative possibilities for a return to our practices while in the modern world—again and again.

This book invites all readers IN; into your own rabbit hole of healing. Into your own ancestral lineage. Into your own migration stories. Into the history of the original Indigenous peoples of the land you reside on, and explains why naming, honoring, and decolonizing our real estate and our emotional states are key components to liberation (in my opinion anyway).

> *The ordinary response to atrocities is to banish them from consciousness. Atrocities, however, refuse to be buried. Equally as powerful as the desire to deny atrocities is the conviction that denial does not work.*
> *Folk wisdom is filled with ghosts who refuse to rest in their graves until their stories are told. Murder will out. Remembering and telling the truth about terrible events are prerequisites both for the restoration of the social order and for the healing of individual victims.*
> —Judith Lewis Herman (1992), Trauma and Recovery: The Aftermath of Violence—from Domestic Abuse to Political Terror

Taking an emotional–decolonial approach when creating and facilitating healing spaces will help while we are in transition, creating space for what currently IS, while we are questioning, dismantling, and abolishing. It is a shift in perspective. It is a verb—a call to action.

I have been a student and practitioner of psychotherapy—particularly clinical psychology—for over 18 years. I have provided "treatment" as a "clinician"[3] working for and providing services to the community through partial care programs for children and adolescents in a major trauma university hospital; providing "trauma-informed care" to adolescents incarcerated in residential centers for sexual abuse; providing neuropsychological assessments and assisted support techniques around memory and cognition

---

3 I am providing quotation marks around these words throughout the book to acknowledge that this is common Eurocentric shared clinical language that has been widely taught and understood by mental health practitioners globally. However, the quotation marks also indicate that I no longer prescribe to these words, terms, and identities and that this entire book is a journey toward discovery/finding new ways, together, to talk about and come back Home to Healing and Hope. Yet, I recognize that the use of these terms create a shared colonial education that make discussing this work possible.

for people living with HIV/AIDS; and supporting young children living with terminal cancer diagnoses receiving chemotherapy—as well as dealing with their impending deaths. I have organized and advocated on the streets of what are now known as San Francisco, New York City, Chicago, Los Angeles, and Jersey City—screaming and chanting for miles and hours, holding hands and locking arms with hundreds of people to protect those indigenous to the land we stood on, and indigenous to lands globally.

I have sat in small crowded rooms and learned from some of the most brilliant individuals and community organizers for hours, as we processed, discussed, debated, and created plans of resistance and hope for our youth with our communities. I have provided multiple forms of mothering, support, group therapy, counseling, and care to hundreds—maybe thousands—of university students (who predominantly have grown up at or below the poverty level with diverse backgrounds and identities) for over 12 years. These were years spent teaching college students, holding space daily for multiple forms of crisis, and providing triage after sexual assaults, community shootings, deaths, deportations, and food and housing insecurity. Not to mention the unofficial support provided to colleagues who encountered multiple forms of university racism and oppression.

I have cofacilitated a nationally recognized peer education group where I wrote grants, facilitated retreats at the ocean, and provided group psychotherapy and somatic and psychodrama techniques. I have had the honor of holding space for and cofacilitating the LGBTQIA+ support group for students on a university campus for 11 years.

People do not come into any of the spaces I mentioned above truly knowing that colonization—the violence of homeland separation—is a core wound for themselves or their ancestors. When they come into spaces for "therapy," the issues and "symptoms" are camouflaged with issues around sleeplessness, anger, sadness, conflicts, trouble with focusing, not being seen/heard/believed, childhood traumatic events, problems with family, and one of the most common: "taking on too much that isn't mine to take." Usually our time together starts with the aforementioned concerns and perhaps weeks or even a month or so later, the core wounding arises. It can sound like:

- "I just really miss home . . ."
- "I didn't grow up with my dad, and he didn't grow up with his . . ."
- "I don't know why I hate myself so much, I just know that I learned this from somewhere, no matter how many affirmations or cognitive distortions I correct—I do—it's like DEEP, you know?"
- "I keep dreaming, I think it's a dream, about this woman. I feel like she is my great-grandmother or aunt or something, and she keeps showing me her hands in water. These big, big Brown hands—and I just cry and cry . . ."
- "I am so bone-tired. I say the right things; change my hair. I articulate, smile even when I don't feel like it. I am always on time—and they just don't listen to me, and I haven't gotten a raise in over seven years. I feel like I am everyone's go-to, but I am never made the 'boss.'"
- "I don't want to pass this down to my child. I can't. I got to do something . . ."
- "I remember how anxious and fearful I felt as a child to wonder if my mother would be home making tamales after school or whether she would be deported. I still have this anxiety with me today . . ."
- "I don't want to keep making my Blackness the most interesting thing about me. I have so much more to say, discuss, do—beyond just one of my identities. None of my white friends, coworkers, or even my partner asks me about who I am aside from my Blackness . . . even my last birthday party was at a museum with a Black artist exhibit. I should be happy! Instead, I am resentful and disconnected all of the time."
- "I grew up in the religion. I grew up wearing white and attending *misas*. This isn't a fad for me. But, why do we need to hide our identity? Why do we need to hide our traditions? Isn't that the remnants from some slave shit?!"
- "My mom is fine with my identity. My nanna is even accepting of my identity. She said, 'I don't care who ya love or what ya look like, as long as you love, and are loved in return and don't harm yourself.' That is huge, but I feel so unsafe, almost everywhere. I am Black, big, trans, dyslexic, and have a lisp—with a five-o'clock shadow. I feel unsafe, even here, I know you are cool and all, but didn't therapy like say that queer folk had mental issues a ways back? That is still scary, you know?! Like damn, where is a bitch safe?"

- "I can't talk to that white therapist about my OCD. It is sexual in nature. I feel like I will be placed in some straitjacket if I told that therapist how many times I think about sexual things, randomly, without control for no reason, and how anxious it makes me. I don't think she would look at me like you do. I just don't. Is that bad?! Am I being racist?!"
- "I just needed a therapist I don't have to 'be on' for and with. I just needed to talk about my spirituality, my love of my People, my big body—all of it—in peace, without the cis-skinny-white f*cking gaze, man. It is so uncomfortable, even when they are being nice."
- "I wonder if I will ever feel at home. Even traveling, my friends and I only feel emotionally safe to travel in Black, Brown, 'other-identity' countries and states. Otherwise, I feel like I might be harmed—even overseas. It is like my body remembers something my mind doesn't. Is that weird?"

Everything returns to the colonial root. Not just to our parents' parents' methods of coping and surviving—although intergenerational transmission, directly and indirectly, plays a large role—but to the core colonial disconnect. From our cultural and ancestral lineage, the structures and roles that have been tended to, the effects on the land to the emotional and physical adverse and resilient effects on our ancestors and how we are called to see ourselves in a world that projects on us constantly. So the personal is political, and often becomes more conscious and politicized after an analysis of race and class. Can this be the catalyst for deeper global rooted colonial healing? Even if your therapy participants do not SAY these things to you, are their bodies feeling it? Holding it? Cradling it like an unbirthed child? The comments above have all been said directly to me in individual or group therapy. Each time I took a deep breath through my nose, accompanied with a slow nod. I felt my eyes close in deep "Yessss, okay, okay. I see you, I feel you. I hear you." I made deliberate and gentle eye contact with the person sharing. I did not allow myself or the group to shift away from the deep discomfort. Make no mistake—even if no one in the room is white—whiteness is IN the room. Even if colonization is not in the room, it is IN the room. Therefore, some deep-down safety mechanism is ever present in many people of the global majority, in order to protect white people's fragility and feelings.

Instagram accidentally became a space for me to post a lot of what I saw as a result of those I held space for and with. It became a space to process a disconnect from our cultures, countries, spaces disconnected from ourselves. That included a disconnect from seeing bodies, hearing accents, speaking in tongues that are indigenous to us. My Instagram @decolonizingtherapy was lovingly created by my peer education students. I was called to task. They supported me, urged me, voluntold me.[4] Community created *Decolonizing Therapy*. I have just decided to spend the majority of my time watering and tending to the garden that it has become. Daily, I receive messages from people: older career therapists, people interested in possibly pursuing studies around psychotherapy/counseling/psychology, social workers, psychiatrists, lawyers, educators, and professors:

- "Why are we not learning this at school!!??"
- "Please teach a whole year's class on this."
- "Dr. Mullan, please, please help me. I want to help people. I feel I am made for this, to support people going through suffering, but I am so over colonial white education."
- "If I take another diversity equity workshop or class led by another white person, or a person of color trained and supervised by a white person, I am gonna lose it."
- "Thank you, I am leaving the center after 8 years because of this page."
- "YES—Black kids are diagnosed and pathologized on their behavior not their FEELINGS. We aren't seen as human!"
- "My 6-year-old had the cops called on him, Dr. Mullan. He was just tantruming in his first-grade class. He said the teacher doesn't talk nice to him like the other kids. I moved to a 'good neighborhood' for him. So, he can live and be free and play in clean grass. Now this neighborhood is more unsafe than our old hood. Please help me."

---

4 *Voluntold*—originally heard from trainers at People's Institute of Survival and Beyond (PISAB) meaning "I volunteer for you and I am gonna tell you you really should do this."

- "I see a future of something like therapy but it ain't JUST therapy. What do we do?"
- "If I see another counselor or therapist that asks me HOW I KNOW it was about my Indigenous identity, I am going to lose it."
- "Dr. Jenn, I am white. I am an elder. I speak of some of what you share to my colleagues—and some of them want to get it, but their whiteness is so embedded in who they are—the fabric of our personalities—that it is like a disease. I want to thank you for allowing us to sit and writhe in our discomfort. I want to thank you for allowing white people to step up. I am so tired of staying on the sidelines and saying 'Well, I am not allowed to say anything!' It is a cop-out. I am crying. I feel this so deeply. Thank you."
- "I had a great therapist who I loved—woke-ish white woman—and she admitted that she couldn't keep seeing me—that I NEEDED MORE. 'More what?' I asked. She said 'More of you, someone who mirrors you in this new level of your identity and cultural development.' Girl, I hollered and cried; she was right. That was some G-ish. That was love."
- "I thought seeing another WOC therapist would be IT. Instead, this woman truly used all of whitey's tactics and interventions on me. It was disappointing and hurtful to say the least. If she asked about my black-and-white thinking one more time . . . I was going to vomit. I felt like I was performing the whole time—that's too much. I perform everywhere else in life. Naw girl; no, not here. I am not paying you so that I have to perform and articulate and be penalized for being eight minutes late. C'mon that is ON TIME in my family!"
- "I am emotionally disconnected because of my trauma—separation from my homeland and village in Kenya. But the trauma worsened because of the therapy I received the last 10 years. Some were OK. But mostly they did not know how to facilitate healing—it felt like I was . . . broken. That my emotions were too much. They focused on trauma, and never weaved into my ancestors, ritual, and my family; they had been through similar things. My migration was never discussed. I am not blaming mental health—but it made me feel BAD—worse about myself, my body, my African-ness."
- "I swear Dr. Jenn, that my therapist was the therapist from *Get Out*. I left each session feeling like I was losing the POC in me. Like I had to just 'Be

more appreciative. Be less angry. Just hold those boundaries.' Been there, done that. No offense but I am grown. It was deeper. I asked if we could go DEEPER. I don't know if she could have gone deeper, maybe that was as deep as it got!?"
- "Decolonizing Therapy is IT. It is true we exist inside of a capitalistic world. Where even healing from our ancestors has been rigidly and whitely commodified. I am tiredddd and I have been a successful psychologist for over 20 years. Thank you."
- "Dr. Mullan, I decided to write to you. I decided to become a therapist for many reasons that I consider powerful. I am also decolonizing, scaffolding what I am learning as a way to maintain my Indigenous identity and stay connected to my roots. Your page, your experience has helped me so much. You paving the way is such a blessing. I pray that you get blessed abundantly for all the lives you are transforming like mine."
- "Thank you. I am Indigenous. Yet I do not fit/look like the 'Indigenous box.' My mother is Paiute Indian, my father is Black—Jamaican Black. Both are Indigenous people, you know!? I feel like all aspects of how I walk in this world would be useful to my therapy clients, and I am so angry—so angry at how both of my peoples were treated and how we still treat each other. How anti-Blackness just permeates Native identity. I think politicizing and decolonizing is the way . . . and psychology and mental health is the way IN."
- "Thank you for this work. I cry during your posts. They HIT ME so hard. Thank you for saying what I have been screaming inside, and to my homies. This is SO healing for me, like damn."
- "I just want to have space held for my suffering, and be able to connect some of what my people went through to how I feel now. Is that so hard? Why can't regular therapists do this?"

This is not about ME. This is about the movement and the collective need to elevate and evolve in our therapeutic consciousness. It is time to begin the journey toward being part of the solution—to figure out together what "therapy" will look like as we unpack and unfurl from a very white patriarchal, cis, hetero, middle-class, "how-does-that-make-you-feel?" frame of psychotherapy.

Decolonizing Therapy seeks a healing paradigm that is accessible to all. Affordable to all. Implicitly trauma-conscious. Implicitly nonhierarchical. Implicitly pro-Black. Clearly pro-decolonization. Clearly pro-abolition. Clearly pro-fatness. Clearly action centered. Clearly lovingly antagonistic. I desire to have new therapists begin their educational journey (because there are some things to certainly learn) questioning everything, pushing envelopes, disagreeing, pushing policies, and bringing ethics and licensing boards to task. I want to see our new therapists and social workers on the news and on podcasts speaking out for the people they hold space for. I want to see us all ACTIVELY part of the political changing climate. Not silently shrugging our shoulders and saying "There is nothing I can do about that." LIES your teacher taught you! YOU CAN and we can do it TOGETHER (fist in the air).

It's All So Political

There cannot be mental and emotional healing without a politicized framework. Everything is political. The Land we live on. The rivers in the Amazon. Whether your 3 p.m. new "client" has health insurance. Whether health insurance is universal for everyone in the country in which you reside. How the T-shirt you have just purchased was sourced, and by whom or what, and where. How your grandfather, great-grandfather, or great-great-uncle came to the place you grew up in. Whether it is safe to be queer and out to your family. Whether your emotional well-being was considered while growing up. Whether your body feels safe enough to take on a lover—or two or three. Whether you can speak out against microaggressions and covert (or overt) racism in your place of work/worship/residence/in your relationship(s). Whether you will be followed into your corner store. Everything is political inherently. Whether our mother received prenatal care throughout their pregnancy. Whether you grew up knowing your birth mother. Whether you were required to live separately from your birth mother because of mandates or laws from the state. Whether you grew up in various homes or one home in foster care. Whether you are seen as attractive or smart or likable is political. Your skin tone and shape of your body have been made political. Whether you have access to affordable homeopathic, allopathic, or holistic medicine in addition to the medical industrial complex is fucking political. Whether your family has a summer or upstate or lake house is political. Whether you have $9.00 or $900,000 in your bank account is so political. Whether you "pass" as the gender you are—political. Whether small tasks, habits, and purchases feel political or not—is political. Whether this book "just doesn't appeal to you" or you can afford to put it on your bookshelf and never look back at it. POLITICAL.

Decolonizing anything must center on Indigenous sovereignty and land, and we must continuously situate ourselves in the settler-colonial context of Turtle Island and across the globe. Otherwise, the term loses its true meaning and becomes co-opted. Allow me to offer that this journey and movement is intended to center the **emotional–decolonial process**, which I and others believe is essential to take clear action toward physical Indigenous and land sovereignty across the globe. Tuck and Yang's work, "Decolonization Is Not a Metaphor" (2012), beautifully describes how harmful the adoption of the term "decolonization" continues to be across academia and activism.

> . . . adoption of decolonizing discourse by educational advocacy and scholarship, evidenced by the increasing number of calls to "decolonize our schools," or use "decolonizing methods," or, "decolonize student thinking," turns decolonization into a metaphor.

Upon reading this article back in 2013, while just finishing my dissertation around the soul wonder and intergenerational trauma in inner-city youth of the African diaspora, I thought to myself, "yesssssss, AND, there is nothing metaphorical about emotional health." You see, even the article is academic in nature. I love it, and it is also an academic article. Much like how part of my conditioning is deeply academic and steeped in Eurocentric terminology. I am unlearning. I am finding new words in community and in our *plácticas*, sharing and trying on new terminology that resonates with our People and our spirits.

I respect the tone of decolonization as a metaphor, and I stand in front of it crying out: but we don't get there through just policy or leases on land and discussing theory. I believe those of us relearning and better understanding coloniality must embody it, feel it, unlearn it, and heal it. THAT is a deeply emotional and personal process, not just a physical or intellectual one. Our conditioning is psychological and purposeful, and, in my opinion, it IS part of decolonization. For these reasons it is identified as an emo–decolonial process. It requires embodiment of something other than colonial conditioning. It requires community, joy, and remembering ancestry. While the goals of social justice and other methods are needed, they aren't always compatible with decolonization (Tuck & Yang, 2012). This text stands firmly in the belief that along with the rightful regaining of land across the globe, there needs to be an emotional and psychological process unhooking us from these behaviors—even among Indigenous peoples, and people of the African diaspora who were made to come to these lands away from home.

I believe there is a massive space for emotional soul healing to enter and *support* the physical decolonial process. Here I enter, just doing my small part in helping to support the process of decolonization. I think that decolonization becomes a myth, a far-off hopeless dream, unless we support it and nurture it with the internal soul-psyche change in consciousness.

Decolonization is unsettling.

But, so is the often forgotten enslavement and labor of Africans across every continent. Let us not forget the ways that many of us of African descent have had to, and continue to, unlearn the ways of "master." We have had to unbox ourselves emotionally, physically, and spiritually. I believe this is much how the decolonial process works—we need to unchain ourselves: physically, mentally, spiritually, and emotionally. Even the most brilliant academics, activists, and historians may overlook the vital role in emotional and mental health in decolonization. As Renee Linklater contends in *Decolonizing Trauma Work: Indigenous Stories and Strategies* (2021):

> Colonialism, manufactured by settlers, caused a great deal of damage to the Spirits of Indigenous peoples across the globe. It is necessary to declare that the root of the injury has been caused by colonial violence.

Healing and wellness **are a huge part of decolonization**. To forget this is to extract and pull out the presence of the Spirit, ancestors, intergenerational transmission, emotion, and of the fabric of connection that allows us to be here. Our Indigenous shamans, santeros, curanderos, and healers certainly didn't forget.

I have held space for many, many people in sacred circles. I have been held in many sacred Circles, with other Black and non-Black POC, and always we walk away saying, sharing, and noting that change is near impossible if it is not supported by: (a) truly seeing and being honest with one another, (b) unlearning colonial ways, and (c) shifting the socialized brainwashed mind. This IS decolonization.

> TO IGNORE THE EMOTIONAL AND SPIRITUAL IN DECOLONIAL WORK IS TO DENY THE SACREDNESS OF INDIGENOUS IDENTITY, AND OUR ANCESTRAL IDENTITIES—IN CONNECTION TO ALL OF NATURE, ONE ANOTHER, AND TO THE LAND.

As I continue to untangle and air out my own identities, and the life and teachings of my late-departed abuela's life, as an Indigenous Panamanian woman of Maya and Kuna Yala descent; I still deal with the shame of feeling disconnected as a youth—embarrassed even about the Indigenous rites of passage I was asked to undergo. I am still managing and processing the belief that I did not have a right to identify as Indigenous, or even as part Irish and Italian—because I do not look it. I recall a family member saying, "Just tell people what they want to hear." But telling people what they want to hear based on how they racialized and saw me created a disconnect. It made it easier for colonialism and white supremacist practices to burrow themselves in my body, in my beliefs, in my relationships, and on my tongue. Emotional wellness is beginning to be viewed through a decolonial lens.

Over the past 40 or so years, my journey has culminated in this book.

From my racialized bigger body, to having been born to a Black Panamanian mom who is a first-generation migrant. To having been born of an Irish and Italian father, who grew up in the projects. To have grown up working poor. To being a "gringa" when going to Panama. To everyone, sizing me up in confusion when I say "I AM Jennifer Mullan." To my very

Indigenous Panamanian Mayan and Kuna Indian abuela. To my activist communist abuelito. To my Italian grandma, "Nanny" Julie, who was tough as nails. To being bullied for being sensitive, big, smart, and compassionate. To figuring out how to live daily with symptoms and experiences of trauma and/or attention deficit. To never, ever feeling like enough, and yet feeling like too much. To being a great sponge of a student to help deal with the emptiness inside. To understanding how effective therapy cannot be delivered without some form of therapeutic activism.

Why Are Babies in the Water?

I was deeply impacted by a story from People's Institute Survival & Beyond (PISAB) where they likened social workers, counselors, psychologists, nurse practitioners, and psychiatrists to individuals doing their jobs so well and in such thick-glassed silos (social workers doing child welfare; counselors counseling; psychiatrists prescribing meds) that when a baby is in the river drowning—one person gets great at rescuing the baby, then another baby is in the water. They pass the baby to another person; that person gets amazing at swaddling the baby. As another baby arrives in the water, they pass the other baby on again—and that person is great at feeding the baby, etc. etc. As more and more babies are in the water, we become drained—burned out—lonely and isolated—tired and complacent. "We handle constant emotional crises." But that is NOT what mental health practitioners should do—we cannot stick our heads in the sand, consciously or not. Someone has to ask WHY does this keep happening?! Someone has to say, "Why are the babies in the water in the first place!?" And that search and the answer may cost them their job, allegiance to the field, time, etc.

I will weave this metaphor through some chapters of the book.

The Urge to Know . . . Everything

You will have an urge to jump to Part 3, and the HOW. "Let's get to the point."

You will have an urge to intellectualize what you are reading, and not to embody the reflection questions.

You will have an urge to disconnect yourself from painful histories of violence and the effects on our bodies, minds, and emotions.

You will have an urge to speak about what you learn in the book, regurgitate information, and expect that this means you are a "decolonial therapist."

You will have an urge to put the book down, walk away, and choose to not engage. Of course, some of us will do this more than others. Others of us do not have that privilege; our life depends on this work.

You will have the urge to say you don't understand.

You will have the urge to ask others (interns, early-career therapists and social workers), the questions and reflections—yet not engage with the material yourself.

Know that you may do a number of these things. Know that it is okay.

Create a container of compassion and generative curiosity.

But I beg of you, My Good People,[5] to understand that we cannot decolonize therapy as it stands today. We cannot decolonize mental health alone. Our journey is about returning the medicine back into the practice. To re-remember, and cocreate. Together. The goal is healing centered, rather than medical model terminology and pathologizing centered.

The goal of this work has always been to slowly and methodically organize, activate, and politicize the practitioners of this field in order to create something bigger, something older and more ancient, yet newer and more current. To create new ways of relating to people in all mental health facilities, hospitals, community health centers, schools, and practices. If we are not made to feel uncomfortable, how will we change? If we are not asked to look long and deeply at our collective shadow as an industrial complex, how can we be pushed to deeply bring about lasting change?

---

5 My Good People is a term utilized within the Black and Brown communities in the inner cities for years. It is a term of endearment, of community building, and an invitation for our readers to pull up a chair with me—the author, as we are all learning and unlearning and relearning—together. It is important to note that this author does not subscribe to the "good" and "bad" separating binaries.

- We can be in relationship with decolonial inquiry while taking generative action.
- We can politicize our practices and our knowledge base.
- We can reconnect with our native tongues and ancestry, while asking how we are doing or how we have done egregious harm.
- We can want to be activists, but we need to be realistic about our capacity and our passions.
- We can elicit deep inquiry into how the mental health systems have been co-opted from Indigenous healing practices across the world, while stigmatizing and pathologizing Indigenous peoples globally.
- We can honor the pain and violence we have cosigned and helped to incite.

Some of us will handle policy; others will handle care practices. Others will handle managed care; others will handle the Eurocentricity of research we believe "qualifies" as research. Others of us will write, draw, speak what needs to be spoken, and engage in reeducation. Some of us will take to the streets and the social justice centers with others seeking to abolish and transform other systems.

Some of us are freedom fighters who won't have time to write a book, create a social media page, or ever be acknowledged for our dedication to the struggle—to the dedication of holding the world together at the seams.

What This Book Is and What This Book Ain't

What is clear is that this book will be a resource to those interested in decolonial inquiry and reflection within mental health, and those seeking to crush the MHIC and cocreate in its wake.

It can serve as a primer, a deepening, a resource for graduate students in their early career, as well as individuals who have been in the field for years. It can serve as a reminder of what has been done, what needs to be done, and how far we have come.

Not everyone will be at the same level while reading this book. I acknowledge that some of you, My Good People, will feel overwhelmed by some of the terminology, by the titles, by the voice echoed within these pages—that's okay. Feel that, breathe into that, take a moment, and allow the glossary to be your best friend. Welcome. There is no rush, as time is a colonial construct and we are seeking to undo these relationships and old rusty ways of thinking. We have a Glossary of Terms for your ease and reeducation.

Welcome.

Some of you, My Good People, will feel deeply energized and seen by this book. You will be nodding and digesting and saying "Fuck yeah!" Great, good. So settle in and find some places and spaces where you may need to think things through further. I encourage you to engage in the reflection questions and allow yourself to not just **know** it, but **be about it**. *Embody the knowing* and allow the mind to quiet just a few. Allow yourself to NOT KNOW, and be okay with inquiry, and be okay with dreaming up new and ancient ways of space holding.

Welcome.

Some of you, My Good People, will feel like "I know this; okay, okay, what else? What are we going to do about it? I have been sitting with this for two, three, 10 years!" Know that you're not alone. That the work is just beginning for you as well, as our field is old, dangerous, and fickle. This means it is time to come together in a collective group to begin to create a plan for structural change within mental health. I invite you to slow down, my Justice Warrior, and ask yourself when was the last time you allowed yourself to deeply feel? To grieve or to rage? To nap? To not read a book all the way through and "be knowing?!" Perhaps take your time with the emotional nervous system work related to the big feelings of rage and grief folded into Part 2, before jumping into the "What Next?" of Part 3.

Sometimes we are so ready to burn it down, that we burn ourselves down in the process.

We need you here.

Welcome.

I am a critical lover of my field. As a critical lover of the field I have been indoctrinated into, I have a right and a responsibility to hold myself, my fellow healing-fighters, and the field ACCOUNTABLE.

As I have changed, I trust that we all can change. The more we become politicized and expand our analysis,[6] the more that we can shift our thoughts and behaviors into DIVINE HEALTHY ACTION. This is part of "being the change we wish to see!"

The more we divest from Eurocentric white supremacist actions, consciously and unconsciously, the more we can pull what is now known as therapy up by the roots. The more we can prevent massive overdiagnosing, pathologizing, and institutionalizing. The more we do that, the more space people have to figure out what they need. So many of us, when asked in therapy, do not know how to answer "What do you need?" when we are asked with compassion. Because we are exhausted, overburdened, overworked, underappreciated, feeling isolated, mistrustful—all for good, good reasons! Our systems, policies, and governments have shown us time and time again that they are untrustworthy.

We have experienced deep harm. Both as practitioners, and many of us as participants as well, of therapy. This is the primary reason why this book is written in such a humanizing, connective, and healing manner, including affirmations and exercises. Therapists are people too. The fields have extracted aspects of humanity from therapists, ethically binding clinicians to: minimize sharing personal information; follow restrictive, arbitrary rules; memorize treatments rather than build knowledge and relationships; to name a few.

A large aspect of decolonial work is realigning, revitalizing, repairing, and restoring—not just ripping down! How can we do more of what we do naturally, within the context of the clinical and sociopolitical material we have learned? How do we honor that we cannot simply be a blank slate without erasing our existence as clinicians? Furthermore, many of our participants do not desire that of us! The therapeutic relationship has the danger of becoming another nonreciprocal, insecure attachment relationship in our lives. Therapeutic space can be untherapeutic for many people. Hence, this book seeks to create connection with and for practitioners of mental

---

6 My analysis is ever-changing. Part of decolonial work and abolition is constantly unlearning, questioning, and learning. It is learning to love the questions.

health, and create pathways for embodying decolonial energy—political, ancestral, emotional, and community-based.

As Judith Lewis Herman, author of *Trauma and Recovery* (1992), has beautifully explained for us, "the concept of complex posttraumatic stress disorder is prolonged, repeated trauma." She noted the importance of regaining a sense of safety. Safety is a massive aspect of a decolonial journey, as it is often ambiguous and just out of reach. Particularly for people embodying and living with multiple historically marginalized identities. *Decolonizing Therapy* seeks to help practitioners AND participants of therapy to *safely* inhabit therapeutic and healing spaces.

CAN THERAPEUTIC SPACES AND HEALING SPACES COEXIST?

Herman also noted that the second phase involved "active work upon the trauma, fostered by that secure base, and employing any of a range of psychological techniques" (1992). The final stage was represented by an advance to a new posttraumatic life, possibly broadened by the experience of surviving the trauma and all it involved

We are not "losing it." We are not the "problem." The systems are the problem, and we will speak about that throughout the book.

What the systems do not want is for us to trust ourselves. To come together and trust each other.

TRUST YOURSELF. TRUST YOUR INTUITION. TRUST YOUR FELLOW COMRADES. TAKE A BREATH.

We decolonize our therapies to understand that research could never . . . It could never tell us more than what the People, people without access, have to say. That we cannot all be "mentally ill." That psychology tells us, when an environment is toxic, the inhabitants of this environment will eventually either wither and die or assimilate and conform.

My goals are to:

A. Beg of you to begin to turn your internal GPS back online. To look at where you have conformed, regardless of your race, ancestry, identities, letters after your name, or political analysis. You are invited to re-return to conscious awareness throughout the book. You will have these lightning moments of reflection and remembrance. Whether related to your own people's histories, your own educational process, or your own journey with emotional wellness.

B. Rebel. Together. Yes. We get to make decisions based on what people we work with tell us they need—verbally and nonverbally. We get to make decisions on revealing parts of our authentic selves. We may get it wrong sometimes. We may not always be liked. But we may come closer Home to ourselves. Imagine really feeling good about the kind of goodness you bring into the world and the collaborations, healing, and structural resistance you impart.

C. Work on your self-inquiry. Work on YOUR shit. Not your clients, not your students, not world problems—your own material rising to the surface.

D. Invite healing—embodied healing—into your life again. Invite the possibility of healing into your work with others. Invite in the unknown, the surrender, the releasing of control, and the warmth of your lineage.

E. To convey that decolonizing therapy is the process of collective shadow work. It is not an intellectual exercise. It is not a magic theory. It is a methodical and intuitive collective paradigm shift. We also get to accept accountability for how we have been steering the ship and get curious about whether our kin were the captains or the cargoes on these ships—and what this means for us now. We get to turn the ship around together.

We can also decide that ships no longer work for our global community.

All We Need Is Honesty

So, this book is pretty honest. I do not sugarcoat:

- What has happened.
- How it has affected how we have come to see ourselves.
- How it has affected our lineages.

- How it has affected our children.
- How it has affected our relationship with others.
- How it has affected who receives access to services and therapies.
- Who has to settle for "scraps."
- How this impacts people all across the world.
- How this relates to current and past colonization.
- What we can begin to do about it . . . together.

It has been very difficult to write this book because it required a deeper level of honesty with myself, people around me, and my people's history than I had ever experienced before. I had to continue to dive into the stark reality that I was pulling history and the mental health system apart to create a better way. I honor all the ancestral scientists, the healers, the mathematicians, the medicine people, the families, the land, the ancestors of the stolen land from which I have written and to all of their descendants—and mine—who are still here. I see you. This book was written with the support of so many, visible and invisible. So, before we jump in . . . here are the tenets of what those of us emotionally decolonizing our therapy stand for.

Tenets of the Emotional–Decolonial Process
1. The personal is political. The political is personal.
2. We acknowledge that we seek to divest from colonial theories, conceptualizations, and practices of mental and emotional health.
3. Most quality therapy,[7] as it stands, is not consistently attainable or affordable for those who are NOT in the middle class (petit bourgeoisie).
4. Therapy, as it currently stands, is inherently white supremacist.
5. Therapy is an extension of white-bodied supremacy.
6. Systems of oppression like the prison, mental health, and educa-

---

[7] Quality therapy means affordable and accessible, with therapy providers who have the language to hold space for healing-engaged practices, and can understand how identity and class are indeed political—which all affect our well-being and emotional health.

tional colonial industrial complexes thread together/work together to create inequities.
7. All people, regardless of gender, race, ability, or socioeconomic status, deserve access to free healing and quality support services.
8. Current mental health systems have co-opted Indigenous practices across the globe.
9. Grief and rage are healthy responses to colonization and colonial ongoing violence.
10. Energetic boundaries are mandatory in decolonial historical frameworks.
11. We cannot decolonize our mental health or therapy processes because therapy is built on violence, but we can emotionally decolonize our conditioning; form healthier relationships with one another, with ourselves, and with our histories of violence; and learn from our cultures and elders.
12. As we engage in emotional–decolonial work, we will be ushered into a rich life of complex big emotions. This is not to be feared; rather, it is an invitation.
13. Emo–decolonial work is firmly planted in liberation and abolition.
14. Emo–decolonial work is informed and guided by ancestral work and connection.
15. Intergenerational trauma exists in and through us.
16. Historical trauma, intergenerational trauma transmission, healing engagement, ancestral reverence, and the Rage-Grief Axis are all a part of emotional–decolonial work and cannot be rushed.
17. Emotional–decolonial engagement cannot be intellectualized. It begs to be embodied.
18. Unresolved historical trauma, collective trauma, and intergenerational trauma show up in the fabric of our society, and come out in our mental health and relationships.
19. We are all impacted by late-stage capitalism and imperialism across the globe.
20. Community, connection, creativity, ancestral engagement, sensuality,

energetic boundaries, and joy all combat colonial practices and mentality.
21. Part of historical and intergenerational trauma is excavating and honoring ancestral trauma. This includes recentering ancestral strengths.
22. We seek to divest from pathology-centered engagement into an ancestral-healing engagement.
23. We must center healing back into our communities. We must center wellness and emotional consciousness.
24. What combats trauma is abundant collective joy.

Decolonizing Therapy is a deeply intimate process of returning to the root of all things. Confronting the multigenerational impact of colonization and recentering a collective healing process for all Indigenous peoples globally (including the descendants of Indigenous peoples).

Loving On You

I have been told from many people who care for me that working with me is intense. That the work people are called to do with me, in collaboration with me, is an initiation of sorts. If you know anything about initiations, you are aware that they take time, require guides, require an amount of faith, proper planning, surrender, and risk. Meaning we are aware that we are being introduced into a world that will bring about energies of death and rebirth. That we will look at, and maybe feed, our demons—as Tsultrim Allione (2008) beautifully writes in her book *Feeding Your Demons*: "Demons do not occur in a vacuum; they are often inherited. The way to change things is to address the underlying issue, through feeding our demons, what they actually need instead of what they seem to want."

Hence, as you embark on this journey (and it is a journey), take your time, enlist support—real solid, sturdy support—and create a place of refuge for yourself that is multidimensional. Some of the words, inquiries, reflections, and examples will kick up some uncomfortable and even painful material. Therefore, it may be best to engage in some of the practices I have summarized for you in the Practitioner Resources section at the end of this book. There I have included a small array of practices that can support your nervous system, energetic boundaries, spirit or energy bodies, and emotional self. As always, resource in ways that feel good to you in the moment.

For over 18 years, I have had the privilege and honor of supporting children, adolescents, groups, grassroot organizers, college-aged individuals, and elders—living within and amid intense institutional, historical, lateral, racial, physical, energetic, spiritual, and emotional abuse. It has been an honor to support people and the larger global collective to create spaces of emotional wellness, connection, and healing with their pasts, in order to better thrive and stay alive in the present. My practice was deeply impacted by the people I conspired and collaborated with, within, and outside the therapeutic container. This book is filled with anecdotes, stories, and references to individuals who have impacted my worldview professionally, politically, spiritually, and personally. However, all names, identifying facts, and details have been changed to maintain anonymity to any of the fictionalized versions of experiences with the people I worked with in therapy. The hope is that you see yourself in these stories and exchanges.

I trust that this book will serve as a shepherd and a guide to the deep benefits of decolonizing our practices; of understanding how oppressive colonial consciousness and therapeutic practices can be; and how valuable it is to flush neutrality down the toilet in order to make room for the bliss and pleasure of true individual and collective emotional freedom.

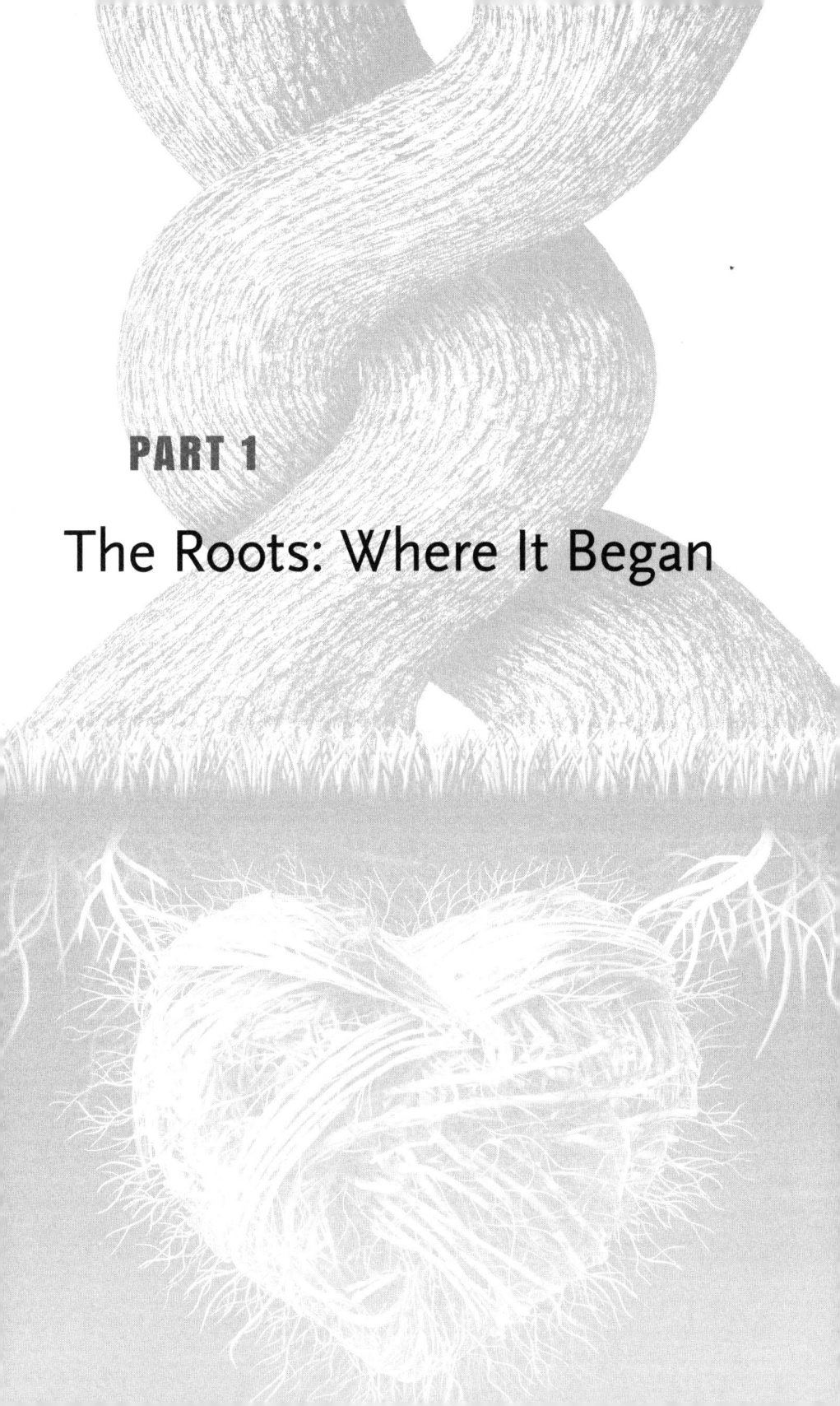

PART 1
The Roots: Where It Began

CHAPTER 1

Your (Our) Therapy Is Colonial

Colonialism and slavery were the foundations of capitalism.
    —Angela Davis, author, professor, and activist (2020);
    interview by M. Moran for *The Observer*

Not only are Indigenous people forced to shoulder the burden of colonialism; we are expected to celebrate it.
    —Tanya Tagaq, Inuk throat singer from
    northern Canada (2017) *[Tweet]*

Every empire, however, tells itself and the world that it is unlike all other empires, that its mission is not to plunder and control but to educate and liberate.
    —Edward W. Said, *Blind Imperial Arrogance* (2003)

Decolonization transforms the consciousness of the colonized through the reclamation of the Filipino cultural self and makes space for the recovery and healing of traumatic memory, and healing leading to different forms of activism. It is an open-ended process. It is a new way of seeing. As a way of healing, it is also a promise and a hope.
    —Leny Mendoza Strobel, CfBS founder and former
    executive director, *Coming Full Circle* (2016)

> *African Americans are the displaced descendants of Indigenous Africans. We never relinquished our relationship to the land of our ancestors, nor did we [forfeit] our inherent sovereignty. The land recognizes our indigeneity to the lands of our ancestors.*
> —Amber Starks (2021) *[Tweet]*

Colonization is the core wound—the separation from Home. The loss of Home means a disconnect from one's primary places of connection, and perhaps safety. Home can be a person, place, state of feeling, or thing. I have heard Home be identified as "a place where people feel like you." Forced migrations, natural disasters, foreclosures, stealing of land, as just some examples, all have a deep impact on the emotional health of individuals. Trauma from individuals and communities experiencing past and present traumatic stress from genocide and deeply entrenched structural violence means navigating ongoing grief, restoring self-community and human-ecological relationships, and generating cultural vibrancy.

Depersonalization, increased disconnect from culture, identity, practices, and a sense of hypervigilance are created from a disconnect from our Home; a fundamental part of oneself was removed and separated, and can create a disconnected and distorted sense of identity—a long-term identity crisis of sorts. There may be a need to assimilate and acculturate. There may be an increase in senses of failure, fear, poverty, political oppression, feelings of abandonment/separation, intra- and interpersonal conflict, exploitation, racism and discrimination, racial profiling, implicit/explicit bias and microaggressions, religious discrimination, shifting of family structures and dynamics, social isolation, separation from family, institutional racism and social determinants of mental health, fear and distrust of the U.S. legal system, fear of deportation—to name a few real-world effects of displacement from our sense and physicality of Home.

Colonialism thrives on isolation, denial, confusion, historical and interpersonal forgetfulness, and separation. Colonialism wants us to question whether it's really relevant to therapy or clinical practice. It wants us to question its relevance or even its existence.

In many professions, political circles, and relationships, to even speak about colonization and its impacts on our well-being and world often sends a person eye-rolling and tuning out. This also serves colonialism's objectives. This is because there is a systematic and purposeful process to colonization; if we aren't actively dismantling it, we are perpetuating it.

But I invite you, My Good People, to tune in, and on. Tune in and ingest tablespoon by tablespoon of truth, no matter how bitter, no matter how difficult to swallow. I invite you to go deeper and more personal with me, one another, and with the experiences of the people for and with whom we hold space. Reading and learning about the histories of colonization allow us, particularly as mental health practitioners, to take part in tending to the collective (global), intrapsychic, psychological, emotional wound of almost, *almost* every country in the world. There is a sacred responsibility attached to participating in emotional–decolonial healing, as it directly corresponds to our ancestries, experiences of ancestral grief and suffering, and that of the people we serve.

Colonialism[8] is an ongoing process, and so is our fight for liberation—for self-sovereignty. We see this from *la isla de Puerto Rico* to the Cayman Islands. We see this in the vast majority of present-day cities and neighborhoods, consisting mostly of POC, that run close to public transportation (gentrification). This book, and my personal life's journey thus far, centers on the understanding and healing of the emotional ramifications, as well as psychological expressions of the effects of colonization on global citizens. Colonization and its intergenerational and historical effects on descendants have typically been seen as something separate from psychological pedagogy. As a clinician, I slowly and painfully came to comprehend the psyche and body record history, as many theories like epigenetic, polyvagal, social learning, narrative, art and drama, liberation, feminist, African-centered, Indigenous, and family systems theories have taught us. The emo–decolonial work is about healing that emotional toll; acknowledging the effects (symptoms) of these violations; and learning how to live in joy, integrating what was and what is today.

---

8 Defined as "the policy or practice of acquiring full or partial control over another country, occupying it with settlers, and exploiting it economically" (Oxford Languages, 2022).

This book is a CALL to ACTION to mental health practitioners, space holders, and wellness workers everywhere. If we are to "treat," heal, and educate the individual, the group, and/or the organization, is it not essential to also include history, life experiences, and cultural traumas? We MUST make it our practice to ask these questions:

> How can we, as practitioners, conveniently step over the impact that colonial violence has had and continues to have on our selves?
>
> How can we, as mental health practitioners (MHPs), step over the impact that colonial violence has and continues to have on the people we are working with?
>
> How can we, as MHPs, step over the impact that colonial violence has had and continues to have on the therapeutic relationship AND the quality and type of healing?
>
> How can we, as MHPs, step over the impact that colonial violence has had and continues to have on our ethics, education, and practices?
>
> How can we, as MHPs, step over the impact that colonial violence has had and continues to have on the people in desperate need of support that do not have the access to receive it?
>
> How can we, as MHPs, step over the impact that colonial violence has had and continues to have on how we educate and raise our children and youth?

Won't you join me?

Colonization As Trauma

Colonization is a psychological and spiritual trauma.

Colonization and its effects are traumatic and can cause continued trauma. There have been numerous definitions of colonization. One definition is the systematic and methodical removal of land, culture, trust (in self and others), family, history, freedom, and Spirit (religion or any form of worship and honoring). Colonial occupation and invasion have been, and continue to be, enough to erode the foundations of many a thriving Indigenous[9] society.

How we understand each other, the removal of our mother tongues, the birth and pillaging of nations, how we have come to communicate with one another, and how we currently have come to hold space and do therapy, have their roots in colonization and our People's resistance to it, all across the world. Colonialism is seen as control by one power over a dependent area or people. Colonialism is when one country violently invades and takes control of another country, claims the land as its own, and sends its own people, "settlers," to live on that land. Colonization has taken place all over the globe through the stealing of lands; the raping of women; the taking of slaves; the breaking of bodies through fighting, labor, imprisonment, and genocide; the stealing of children; the enforcement of religion; and the destruction—or attempts to destroy—spiritual ways of life.

Europe's expansion is remembered as an exploration, and the men who helmed ships that landed in foreign countries were heroes. However, they committed atrocious acts of violence and genocide against Indigenous peoples, including my own family's people—the Indigenous Kuna Yala and Maya people in Panama.

In the 19th century, in what is known as "the Scramble for Africa," European nations such as Spain, France, Britain, Germany, Belgium, the Netherlands, and Portugal took apart and shared the African continent, creating arbitrary borders and boundaries, and claiming land that belonged to the people indigenous to the lands for themselves. This resulted in further ethnic tensions between cultural groups, deeply affecting—and in some cases obliterating—various aspects of Indigenous political, social, economic, and spiritual life. These traditional and Indigenous ways of living were seen as "less than" and "inferior." Again, this is the way colonization moves.

---

9 Indigenous identities span more than just the North American Indigenous Peoples. We honor the identities and experiences of the First Nations, Métis, Inuit, and all Native American Indigenous Peoples and Tribes due to us living on their lands and the history of colonization. However, when discussing colonization as a whole, we must also understand indigenous as any people who originated within a particular place. A native to their lands.

Learning to Decolonize

DECOLONIZATION in the most literal sense is about a return. Returning land back to the original inhabitants. This is a physical return, a stewarding of the land, an honoring of the land, and a relationship with the land. There are also the emotional, cultural, and ancestral aspects of decolonization, such as returning to cultures, traditions, and ancestral knowledge that were stripped away from so many people. It involves a return to a more authentic and deeply felt part of ourselves that allows people to fully assimilate their histories and the lived experience of their families and communities. Setting up these sorts of stakes early in the chapter will help make decolonization feel like an integral part of healing.

Throughout my career I have spoken in front of many audiences full of therapists and social workers, and am often asked (explicitly or implicitly) to make colonization more *palatable, sexy, easy to understand*, and *something people would want to hear more about*.

There is something inherently colonial, violent, and Eurocentric about these requests to essentially make mainstream middle-class people more comfortable as though, once again, history continues to repeat itself. The requests invoke a shudder of nostalgia mixed with nausea for me. There is not a word, phrase, or quote that will make the next few chapters easier on you, My Good People. The constant requests to simplify a complex and ever-changing force like colonization minimizes the longevity and cunning of the colonial chameleon.

Walk with me a moment.

The requests in themselves beg for a watering down of the truth, and quite frankly that is what people who are mental health practitioners need less of—watering down. In fact, colonialism is a subversive force and a purposeful one at that. It involves acts of violence, taking, lying, weaponizing, and creating false narratives—narratives that have stayed tucked sneakily within the fabric of our families, institutions, self-concepts, and "treatment" for decades and have changed the fabric of the world. It involves weaponizing gender and sexuality, exploiting and extracting from our Earth, planting seeds of separation, constructing *race*, creating multilayered Ponzi schemes of economic inequality, gaslighting people who have been victimized, and then, of course, pathologizing big emotions that are merely healthy responses to abusive behaviors. Thereby teaching us, my fellow colonized therapists, how to pathologize big emotions. Colonialism is a root disease, entangled deep into our individual and collective psyches.

The process of deprogramming colonial behavior and our thinking must first go through a politicizing of our therapies. This includes reprogramming our thoughts from the literal matrix—from the beliefs, norms, and ways that we have been socialized to see as "good"—as a global community. Practitioners would benefit from caring about emotional decolonization, My Good People, because this process shows up in our teaching, therapies, and wellness work daily, and because our very well-being continues to be impacted by colonial logic.

Emotional decolonization involves coming to awareness, unlearning, grieving, raging, and divesting (slowly) from the lies we have been told by colonizers, perpetuated by a white-centered lens. The truth is that psychological enslavement (Akbar, 1996) no longer requires a specific oppressor (although there are many); it works all by itself, as it was originally intended. Now, we continue to psychologically oppress and inflame one another and ourselves. This is perpetuated through internalized racial inferiority, as well as internalized racial superiority, gatekeeping, gaslighting, colorism, ableism, and fatphobia, just to name a few. This has been further compounded by our mental health training.

During a meeting with a prospective chair for my doctoral dissertation, I explained to my professor my thesis interest in the intersections within my work with communities (much like the one I grew up in) that felt disconnected from culturally, racially, and socioeconomically responsive and aligning therapy. I listed all the ways that many POC were exhausted and did not trust systems—for good reason. I explained that I wanted to study intergenerational, historical, and racial trauma as root causes of this mistrust of POC and really understand the concept of soul wounding as related to attachment.

> He was one of many white-identifying professors in my small doctoral program. I met with him, with hope, because of his work with communities of color. However, he looked at me with exasperation and said, "Jennifer, please hear me ... politics and psychology do not mix. They do not go together. It is important that you get that through your head."
>
> Needless to say, he was not my chairperson. Thank goodness, my soon-to-be new chair listened to my interests. She handed me a copy of *Native American Postcolonial Psychology* (which I hadn't heard of at the time), and said, "This is gonna bring you to deeper levels of your own people's suffering, and the hope. If you are willing, well then let's get started."
>
> Who knew what I was really getting into. But I am so glad that I did.

My dear fellow colonized therapists, we are not free of responsibility. We have been and continue to be impacted by legacies of colonial violence. Many of us reading this have both legacies of harming and being harmed historically and in the present-day. It is time to make part of **our** work uncomfortable—until it isn't anymore. It is part of our job to help organize and reeducate ourselves, our colleagues, our lovers, and siblings. It is part of our job to activate and advocate healthy counsel to our communities, not as solo martyrs further harming others, but with others. It is part of our job, historically, to care for the wellness of the village and the children, to carry on the stories, to bring insight and understanding to our villages, to distribute aid and healing. It is part of our job to ask whether the children are well and the elders are receiving adequate care. It is part of our job to understand what redistributing resources looks like, and helping to return the land back to the people (across the globe) and to whom it belongs.[10]

The violence of colonial thinking sees Black, Indigenous, and other POC as disposable, and in the words of P. Diddy, it was always all about the Benjamins. We notice how even POC define success under capital-

---

10 We will talk more in Chapter 10, Politicizing Your Practice, about what this might look like, and how we can maintain our health, boundaries, and belief systems while being part of abolishing decrepit, outdated rules that may no longer have relevance in the near future.

ism's terms. The world's wealthiest countries hoard global resources in a never-ending quest for money and power. This is psychological. This is political. This is spiritual. This is cultural. Colonial mindsets continue to highlight the needs of the wealthy, at the expense of the poor and politically powerless.

Therefore, this book attempts to touch your emotional, psychological, and humanitarian selves. To call us back in. This is not a set of practices to engage in decolonial therapy. There is no such thing. Rather this book is a very clear motion toward all of you, My Good People. Come on in; we need each other. We have got to wake up even if it hurts. We have to look at how the Earth's resources are being pillaged by greed, and how the world's caretakers (Indigenous peoples across the globe) are being pillaged and murdered to this day as well. This is more serious than how to do conscious politicized therapy. We are dying and we need one another to engage in emotional–decolonial work. We have to collectively continue to remember to receive the new manual—the new path—to walk the spiral back Home.

So as someone trained as a clinical psychologist; as someone who has engaged in forms of community organizing; as someone who has cofacilitated hundreds of groups, classroom lectures, and student learning; as someone who has unconsciously harmed many, many, many people through my colonial mindset and Eurocentric–supremacist education; as someone who has continued to have been called back Home to my kin's ways; I invite you to take this walk and embark on this journey with me.

Colonialism 101

Colonization and its effects are vast, deep, complicated, and much like a nine-headed dragon. There are hundreds of wonderful historical and political sources I would encourage you to read. Many are cited in the references section. However, this cannot be a book around decolonizing therapy without a general summary (a very general summary) of colonization.

Growing up I learned that in the 15th century, during Europe's Age of Discovery, European countries (Britain, Spain, and Portugal predominantly) pillaged and colonized lands across North and South America. Missionaries felt that it was their moral duty to spread Christianity, and they believed a higher power would reward them for saving the souls of colonial subjects. Additionally, colonizers exploited resources of other countries to benefit their own economies. This was the sort of competition between European nations that would allow the glory of attaining the greatest number of colonies. According to new colonial logic, "a place did not exist unless white Europeans had seen it and testified to its existence." But the kicker is that colonists did not actually *discover* any land. The "New World" (hello Vespucci and Columbus) was not new at all: People had been living and thriving in the Americas . . . forever.

Settler Colonialism

According to Osman (2020): "A settler can be defined as any non-Indigenous person living in a settler-colonial state like the United States, Canada, Australia, or New Zealand." With this understanding, settler colonialism may offer us a different light in which to view colonialism: not as a one-time event in history, but rather as an ongoing process of violence emotionally, spiritually, and physically—that tries to erase Indigenous people—globally. Overall, colonizers did not care that there were people already living on the land. They did not want peace and harmony between cultures; they wanted to utilize and take the land for themselves, regardless of the abundance of resources that could be shared. The goal was to generate wealth for personal gain. There was minimal respect for Indigenous cultures or histories, and instead unspeakable acts of violence became the norm. It didn't matter if the land was considered sacred and communal. Everything, including the Earth, could be bought and sold. Osman (2020) defines settler colonialism as "a distinct form of colonialism that seeks to replace, often through genocide and forced assimilation, an Indigenous population with a new settler population."

The land now known as the United States has committed heinous crimes. As the Center for the Study of White American Culture (2014, personal communication) members have pointed out, the original "affirmative action" was white affirmative action. I recall, years ago, Bonnie Berman

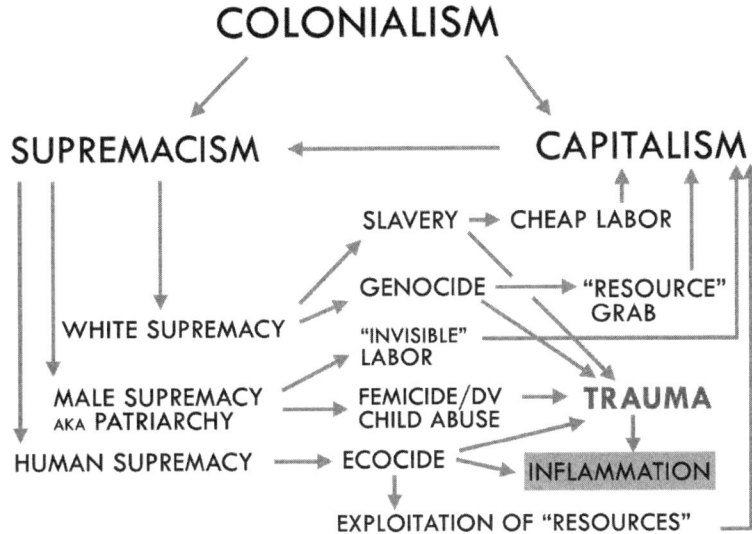

FIGURE 1.1 Colonialism Diagram *By Rupa Marya (2018) presented during her talk, "Health and Justice: The Path of Liberation through Medicine" at the National Bioneers Conference.*

REFLECTION QUESTIONS

- How might colonization affect the exploitation of the Earth and her resources today?
- How do we see this sentiment and behavior impacting the Earth's resources?
- How might climate change and the mining of Earth's resources affect people?
- Who are those most affected by climate change and the mining of Earth's resources?
- How does this impact us individually? Collectively? Generationally?

Cushing (social worker, trainer, and self-identified racist–antiracist organizer for the People's Institute of Survival and Beyond) stating that. I recall being fascinated and astounded that white supremacy had done such a good job socializing Americans that we could not clearly see that white affirmative action existed: The Indian Removal Act; chattel slavery in the antebellum

South; 50 acres, 30 shillings, 10 bushels of corn and a musket; Treaty of Guadalupe Hidalgo; The Naturalization Act; the Tuskegee experiment; The Homestead Act; the founding of American gynecology on enslaved African people's bodies; the Wilmington Massacre; *Brown v. Board of Education*; the Chinese Massacre of 1871; California Genocide; Ocoee Massacre; and the G.I. Bill, just to name a few.

Global Colonization 101

The lived experiences of marginalized POC, particularly and most violently Black Indigenous People of Color (BIPOC), are a mirror for the histories of white America. The insidious nature of systemic oppression AND white-bodied supremacy continue to support the colonization that has bled, and that continues to bleed, exploitative fear, propaganda, grief, and trauma all over the globe.

The effects of colonization have been and continue to be felt across the world. Walter Rodney's research and book, *How Europe Underdeveloped Africa* (1981), meticulously details the impact of slavery and colonialism on the history of international capitalism. Rodney unpacks how Africa developed Europe at the same rate that Europe underdeveloped Africa. We can also see this in the colonization of the "New World"[11] from Columbus's arrival until the Civil War. Colonization can be seen throughout the creation of the "United States of America," in the violence employed against some 13 million Africans and over five million Native Americans who were forcibly made to build and cultivate a society for white settlers under the guise of "liberty and justice for all." Dr. Rodney noted that systemic poverty in what is known as America can be directly linked to European exploitation and resource extraction. The colonization of the *American* continents by European *empires* led to the collapse of traditional Indigenous ways of relating to self and other. The colonization of India (most notably for spices) by the British in the 1600s; the colonization and disruption of Aboriginal and Torres Strait Islander cultures all led to degradation of the traditional

---

11 Please note the New World is Turtle Island/Canada/United States of America.

Indigenous ways of relating to themselves and their environment. The list continues from Turtle Island to the Motherland of Africa.

A current day example of how colonization continues includes the Galápagos Islands of the Philippines. Spain (1565–1898) and the United States (1898–1946) colonized the land and the people of the Philippines. In the 1500s the Philippine people were lied to, forcibly violated, and invaded by Magellan and his forces. These beautiful archipelagos continue to be violated through forced contractualization, industrialization, and the pillaging of lands very rich in resources and minerals (Migrante, 2012).

The Philippines, like the Falkland Islands, Gibraltar, Cayman Islands, St. Croix, Puerto Rico, New Caledonia, and Mozambique are just some of the lands that are still "occupied" today. The United Nations would state that they have dissolved all colonies in favor of self-governance. However, we know there are residual, deep, long-standing effects of colonization, resulting in these areas being called "dependent territories." (We would identify these occupations in 2022 as being under imperial rule, but for the purposes of this book, we will utilize the overarching term of colonization for clarity and convenience. But make no mistake about it, there is nothing convenient or clear about the effects of colonization on our People.) "There are 61 *colonies* or territories in the world. Eight *countries* maintain them: Australia (6), Denmark (2), Netherlands (2), France (16), New Zealand (3), Norway (3), the United Kingdom (15), and the United States (14)" (author emphasis; Infoplease, 2017, para. 4).

Some groups of white-bodied people are also processing the historical trauma of colonization on their lands and lineage. There is a troubling and pervasive history of British colonialism on the Irish people. England's King Henry VII began the Tudor "reconquest" of Ireland and gained the submission of the Gaelic chieftains by promising that they would retain lordship of their ancestral territories. In the 16th and early 17th century, English conquest was marked by large-scale "plantations" in Ulster and Munster, so small colonies of English settlers could form model farming communities on confiscated lands. The result was the establishment of central British control (Roth, n.d.).

Irish culture, law, and language were replaced, and many Irish lords lost their lands and hereditary authority. Land-owning Irish people who worked for themselves suddenly became English tenants. The plantation system eventually degenerated into a series of atrocities against the local civilian population before finally being abandoned. On January 1, 1801, when the Act of Union came into effect and took away any measure of autonomy, the Irish Parliament was abolished and Ireland became part of a new United Kingdom of Great Britain and Ireland (Roth, n.d.).

Soon after, the Irish Potato Famine occurred, and was deemed one of the worst disasters in world history. Famine is neither inevitable nor natural. From 1845–1849, in England's first colony—Ireland—over a million Irish citizens died of famine. O'Grada (1993) concluded that in 1846, Ireland exported over 400,000 pigs and over 30,000 tons of grain to England. The Irish died because they did not have the money to buy food, not because they did not have food.

The Great Potato Famine is relevant, as it is a specific example of how British Parliament created the famine and committed a genocide of the Irish through continued demands for crop exports while the people were starving (Reardon, 1997). We also see this in many parts of the Philippines, with rice and other rich minerals. This is a consistent product of colonization: the land is rich, but the people are poor due to imperialism and contractualization.

In Ireland, the colonizers may not have created the plant blight that infected the crops, but their policies and demands lead to many dying from starvation (O'Grada, 1993; Reardon, 1997; Roth, n.d.). It is also important to note how many of the census and historical records of Ireland have been lost through colonization, as the English kept records differently and forced the Irish to switch to their methods. During war efforts, many Irish census records were ordered to be pulped for paper, leading to a loss of history and family records for many generations (Roth, n.d.). Between the famine and the war, many Irish were desperate for a chance to live. This led to the emigration of over a million people to Britain and North America in the 19th century (Roth, n.d.). Known as coffin ships, the vessels the Irish sought passage on were overcrowded and often not prepared for the long journey to America. Many ships would lose a third of their passengers to disease and hunger before reaching port, and it is said that sharks followed in the wake of the ships.

It may be helpful to note for those of Irish descent, and those working with people of Irish descent:

- How have colonialism, white supremacy, and patriarchy influenced Irish people's current emotional health?
- What are the correlations between Irish people's well-being and generational abuse and colonization?
- What may be some of the intergenerational expressions of what was described above for Irish descendants today?

> **THE LANGUAGE OF COLONIZATION**
>
> Colonization shows up even in how we **speak** of it. Our language is steeped in Eurocentricity and coloniality. For example, should someone state that the Philippines is still under colonial rule, and we identify that Magellan did in fact colonize the people of the Philippines, I most often hear the following question: "Well, then who founded the Philippines?" No one "founded" the Philippines; Filipinos indigenous to the land were there long before our history books opened. Furthermore, is this what native populations called themselves? Even in speaking about Indigenous groups colonialism raises its head. The Philippines is made of numerous tribes with numerous languages and modes of communicating. Even in our conceptualization if "indigeneity," we have a colonized mindset. You will hear me note the coloniality of language throughout this book.

Forced Migration Is a Product of Colonization

Many people are FORCED to migrate, whether they are conscious of it or not. You may often hear phrases such as, "There are more opportunities in America/Britain . . ." or "I came here for a better life." Although these phrases are true to that individual and perhaps to that affected community, there is a deeper root cause to the migration.

Forced migration is a product of colonization. The term generally describes the movements of refugees and internally displaced people (those displaced by conflicts with their country of origin) as well as people displaced by natural or environmental disasters, chemical or nuclear disasters, famine, or development. Colonization changes laws, policies, and cultural customs and affects contractualization and extraction of minerals, as well as farming and the health of the farmers. Army bases are built in the colonized country. Soon the people who were originally in close relationship with the land—the farmers—are forced to turn over land that has been in their family for generations and become laborers. People are forced to work, for little to no pay, on what used to be their land. They can no longer afford the cost, physically and mentally, of colonization. Their crops and resources are used up for trade. Their children are forced to speak in an English tongue, forced to cut their hair, to change their clothing, to change their diction. Beliefs and religion are challenged, demonized, and pathologized.

Soon they can no longer afford the very beautiful natural land that they were in relationship with. One main caregiver may realize that they cannot continue to survive, raise a family, and tend to the community in their Home. For instance, a child or adolescent would live apart from a parent for years, due to forced migration, and then be brought to live with a parent they no longer truly know. Perhaps the last time they saw this parent was years before, and their main connections involved cards or pictures. The attachment at its core is contorted and strained. This shapes the parent, the child, and the generational lineage.

How many of us would want to leave our children, partners, families unless we **had** to? Thus the beginning of separation and migration. We say forced migration because colonization and imperialism are the cause (see next definition). The effect is hundreds of thousands of people migrating and leaving loved ones for years while we "save up enough" to go back, or bring the entire family with us to the "New World." This "New World" being the place where the original colonizers came from. The "New World" often being the places where those violated and colonized are not allowed easy access and entry. This is a vicious cycle. The cost of colonization is too expensive on the family system, the individual and their mental health, as well as on the collective culture.

> **REASONS YOUR CLIENT/STUDENTS/PARTICIPANTS MAY CHOOSE TO NOT DISCUSS HISTORY/CULTURE/IDENTITY WITH YOU**
>
> - If you are white, they may not feel comfortable discussing vulnerable aspects of their identity with you, even if the participant is white.
> - You haven't examined your points of privilege.
> - They aren't aware of it.
> - They're trying to forget/ignore it.
> - They don't remember it.
> - They do not see a connection between their history (ancestry) and their present.
> - They're in crisis.
> - For other reasons they are not comfortable sharing—and that is OK.

The Past Does Affect the Present

The thing is, our past does have an effect on us. We have seen this when being activated by a partner, later realizing we were triggered by an older parental wound. We see this in how teachers may become cross, curt, and respond to a student based on how an older cousin acted in their class five years prior. This is loosely how policy makers and politicians decide who or what deserves the right to receive funding in the next fiscal year. We see this in how survivors of intimate partner violence and many other forms of abuse have involuntary visceral body reactions to colors, smells, names, and places.

Historically, we also witness the shadows of the past hanging over entire racial and cultural groups when we consider the very clear economic, psychological, and physical consequences of the racial profiling and unacknowledged racism in the United States toward peoples of the African diaspora. The murders of Ahmaud Arbery, Breonna Taylor, George Floyd, Philando Castile, Tamir Rice, Eric Garner, Sandra Bland, Muhlaysia Booker, Trayvon Martin, and more are clear examples. Their names and experiences create a visceral emotional reaction of fear, rage, grief, and perhaps hopelessness—if even for a moment—in the soma and psyches of most

Black people. We also see the past affecting the present in the ways that domestic workers (people) are major exports of the Philippines, and forced migration, imperialism, and greed continue to split families apart. We witness this in the way that Deferred Action for Childhood Arrivals (DACA) recipients speak of the fear of being deported—their parents fighting for the American dream and the ways these dreams are dependent on following a set of invisible rules for being as obedient as possible.

The People's Stories

This is an example of the legacy of colonization showing up in a therapeutic setting where a practitioner provides the space for the participant to explore the deepest roots of an emotion. Note this therapeutic dyad has worked together for over six months, and trust has accumulated.

> CLIENT: I don't understand why I keep blowing up! This time it was bad, I smashed the door window when I slammed it shut! I know better. Doc, I keep returning because I have seen some great expensive therapists, and still I keep missing something, something related to this belly of rage. I think I have to admit something deeper than just anger is here! I work myself to the bone [client works as a day laborer] and yet I feel still wired and this sense of gnawing old rage wanting to come out.
>
> PRACTITIONER: I am really hearing you noticing and identifying with your somatic and emotional feelings much more quickly than you did a year ago. I am also really glad you didn't harm anyone or yourself in the process physically. Can you allow yourself to honor that?
>
> CLIENT: I suppose so. You did say that self-compassion was perhaps the MOST difficult to give oneself, and yet the most helpful and healing. Correct! The burning almost aches, ya know—for days afterward. I feel like I just want to crawl back home across the world (Ireland) and sit my head on my mum's lap!
>
> PRACTITIONER: Yeah, emotions show up in our body—they ache. Maybe it is saying something.

CLIENT: It is definitely saying something. My brain can't think my way into "a better thought" or a more rational thought. This is REAL.

PRACTITIONER: It is also super healthy to want to be around a safe person or space when we feel this shame, and fear. . . . Does mom feel like "home" to you?

CLIENT: Yeah, yeah she does (choking up). I miss her. I miss the damp green land. I miss the pubs. I miss my Da. He was a mean man I told ya—angry too, but I miss him still. Argh, it aches.

PRACTITIONER: Can you point to where this rage resides?

CLIENT: (Points at belly)

PRACTITIONER: Might you close your eyes and say aloud what the color/age of this gnawing rage is . . . ?

CLIENT: It feels like hunger . . . a gnawing, raging hunger . . . like I am hungry . . . maybe I am hungry, dammit.

PRACTITIONER: Have you ever felt hunger like that before?

CLIENT: No. Well, yes, a few times growing up, I would feel ravenous and eat a lot. My Da would slap me across the head and my Da would say, "You don't know hunger boy, your great-granddaddy starved almost to death and watched his sisters starve! I felt hunger!" He would say that our people were supposed to go hungry a little for our kin. To not eat so much or so fast—for our people. You know, something about this makes my stomach ache even more.

PRACTITIONER: Have you ever made this connection before? Between your father's rage when drinking, and his violence—and eating—and staying hungry?

CLIENT: Hungry, huh, fascinating. I don't think I let myself really feel or realize it. Maybe it was there in the back of my mind, but I would light a cigarette or have a drink.

PRACTITIONER: Would you like to stay with this feeling further, or would you like to slow it down, or just stop? All are acceptable options. But ask your body what it wants.

CLIENT: I think I want to eat . . . . I smoke cigarettes and drink a bit. I barely really feed myself. You know, it's funny, slowing down never occurred to me. I've been told my whole life Irishmen don't soften up, slow down, we push through like our men did. We push the fuck through. So yah, maybe I will slow down, and think this through. Somehow, I am talking about my ancestry and my Da and being hungry—there is more here, Doc. A lot more here (points to belly).

In this example, I am highlighting how easy it would be to simply focus on the content, and not the process. However, focusing on just the behaviors (of course there is a time and place) continues to feed more colonial mentality, leading to feelings of denying, tolerating, or minimizing historical and modern-day oppression for all people in the room! Individuals (and this may be many of us) affected by colonial mentality seeking support in therapy or being mandated to be in therapy are often not conscious of how the past is exacerbating their current distress and mental health. It is not the role of the practitioner to force our beliefs on others; rather, it can be a beautiful space to get curious and explore. Many practitioners do this already, we say statements such as:

- "I am wondering if it's possible that . . ."
- "Humor me, but I am sensing . . ."
- "I am thinking this is about something else, something deeper . . ."

We also have an opportunity to keep allowing these lines of curiosity and colonial mentality–checking to show up. We can state:

- "How does it feel when I ask you to consider if your great-grandfather's experiences might be mirrored and present in your own?"
- "I think it is valid to desire to look more like _____, but is it possible that desiring lighter skin, a smaller nose, a smaller bottom (more European traits) are forms of internalized racial oppression?"
- "I am wondering if your disconnect and deep agitation with other El Salvadoran people may be related to how and why your parents left El Salvador."

In the dialogue above, the participant is clearly speaking to BOTH his childhood traumas and an underlying belief, "hunger" and behavior that is beyond his capacity to change. There could be a massive connection to the Irish Potato Famine. There could be a connection to his sense of worth, and of leaving Home behind in order to survive.

The root of our disconnect is frequently right under the surface. It requires practitioners to be flexible, reeducated, and to acknowledge colonial oppression as valid trauma.

Even if it isn't immediately clear to you why someone is bringing their cultural or racial identity to therapy, or what importance it may hold in a clinical context, it is our responsibility as practitioners to learn and try to understand how colonization has impacted them. We are holding the frame and the root for when it is appropriate and relevant to ask the questions and insert the references. Some of your therapy participants may never bring up their histories—that is okay. Regardless, as practitioners, it is our responsibility to hold a conscious frame and to create threads of commonality between what was and what is now.

Even though more and more people are coming to recognize the reality of colonization, many make the mistake of believing that it doesn't really impact the daily lives of people today or fail to understand colonization as a daily lived experience. Allow us to take a historical real-world example:

Think about the effect this has on the people you do therapy with. As I provide this historical example, related to the island of Hispaniola and Haiti (*Ayiti* in Creole), in an effort to bring our understanding and (re)education to life, please consider people of Haitian descent who you may have supported and worked with, and/or anyone who identified as Dominican, as well as many Black-identifying people whose family has a history of enslavement across the globe.

As Sutherland writes: "In the 18th century, Saint-Domingue, as Haiti was then known, became France's wealthiest overseas colony, largely because of its production of sugar, coffee, indigo, and cotton generated by an enslaved labor force" (Sutherland, 2007). There were three general groups of African descent: those who were free (est. 30,000 in 1789), half mixed-race and identified as mulatto, who were quite wealthy; those who were enslaved (close to 500,000 people); and those who had run away (called *Maroons*) who had retreated deep into the mountains and lived off subsistence farming.

Despite the harshness and cruelty of Saint-Domingue slavery, there were rebellions before 1791. As Carroll writes: "One plot even involved the poisoning of masters" (Carroll, n.d.; Encyclopaedia Britannica, 2020). Sutherland notes that "the Haitian Revolution has often been described as the largest and most successful . . . rebellion [and revolution] in the Western Hemisphere." Not only did the previously enslaved population emancipate themselves from the shackles of slavery, but they also succeeded in ending French control over the colony (Sutherland, 2007). Toussaint L'Ouverture led a successful revolt and emancipated the enslaved people in the French colony of Saint-Domingue.[12]

Jean-Jacques Dessalines, one of L'Ouverture's generals and himself a former enslaved person, led the revolutionaries at the Battle of Vertières on November 18, 1803, where the French forces were defeated. Former enslaved people managed to stave off both the French forces and the British who arrived in 1793 to conquer the colony, and who withdrew in 1798 after a series of defeats by L'Ouverture's forces (Ott, 1973; WGBH, 1998).

On January 1, 1804, Dessalines declared the nation independent and renamed it Haiti. Also important to note, the name Haiti (Ayiti) is derived from the Indigenous Taíno-Arawak name for the entire island of Hispaniola, which they called Ay-ti, "land of mountains." It was Christopher Columbus who renamed it La Isla Española ("The Spanish Island") when he arrived in 1492. By 1801, L'Ouverture expanded the revolution beyond Haiti, conquering the neighboring Spanish-speaking colony of Santo Domingo (present-day Dominican Republic). He abolished slavery in the Spanish-speaking colony and declared himself governor–general for life over the entire island of Hispaniola.

Of importance, after Haiti's liberation from France, the island nation

---

12 For the purposes of this book, the history of Haiti and their magnificent revolution has been extremely simplified and summarized.

was ordered to pay **$21 billion** in reparations to cover the cost of France's losses during the Haitian Revolution in exchange for its independence. *Please sit with this for a moment.* This calculation included the "cost of lost slaves." Haiti, the "poorest nation" in the Western hemisphere, made **its final payment to France in 1947**. Clearly, Haiti becoming one of the poorest nations in the Western hemisphere is directly related to the colonial and imperial behaviors of France. Once again, imperialism aims at the creation of an empire, and uses military force to do so.

As Marlene Daut (2020) has beautifully noted in her article "When France Extorted Haiti: The Greatest Heist in History":

> What France did to the Haitian people after the Haitian Revolution is a particularly notorious example of colonial theft. France instituted slavery on the island in the 17th century, but, in the late 18th century, the enslaved population rebelled and eventually declared independence. Yet, somehow, in the 19th century, the thinking went that the former enslavers of the Haitian people needed to be compensated, rather than the other way around. (para. 3)

Reflection Exercise
- If you identify as Haitian, have your people's histories been included in your primary and secondary educations? In your therapy or counseling services?
- If you identify as Haitian, what have you been taught about your history?
- Did you know about the Haitian Revolution? (Whether Haitian-identified or not.)
- What effect may knowing about the history of the Haitian Revolution have on people of Haitian and/or Caribbean Islander descent?
- What effect may knowing about the history of the Haitian Revolution have on people of French descent?
- What effect may knowing about the history of the Haitian Revolution have on people of Dominican descent?

- What effect may knowing about the history of the Haitian Revolution have on those whose descendants were enslaved?
- How might this knowledge positively impact your therapeutic work?
- How might this knowledge impact how we view reparations in what is now known as the United States?
- Do you have any reflections on colorism or anti-Blackness after hearing this?
- Why do you believe you may or may not have been privy to these historical facts?

Author Reflection

As someone who was employed as a university psychologist—living in, having grown up, and worked in Northern New Jersey—a good portion of my colleagues and students had ancestry from the island of Ayiti, now colonized and known as the island of Hispaniola. As part of my work as a therapist and community advocate, it was my duty and practice to learn about histories, rebellions, and the level of collective and cultural trauma outside of my own—particularly as it related to the community and students I served. This is an example of politicizing our practices, actively decolonizing what we have been taught (unconsciously or consciously) about Black people from the Caribbean, and in particular Haitians. The process of moving outside of our own range of reference is an act that we intellectualize, but often do not actively engage in. It is also essential to note that it would benefit supervisors, vice presidents, program directors, and others to make space during administrative time, staff, clinical supervision, and process meeting for the sharing and reeducation. For me, not only was unlearning and relearning part of my decolonial process as it relates to clients and oneself, it was essential and clearly made an impact on the people I was asked to clinically work with.

As a therapy practitioner working within the structures of the MIC, I often ask, "How can we make it better? Is there a way to cocreate a system that infuses healing and not just treatment within an unwell and violent structural arrangement?"

How can we create such a system from systemic and structural classicism, racism, ableism, sexism—a new way? This would require decolonial practice. This would require decolonial relationships and decolonial wellness—a return Home. As the medicine is literally within the person and their divine placement within their community, healing must occur from the root (ancestral and intergenerational) up. For if we merely pluck at the leaves (symptoms) each year, the same fruit will grow until eventually the root rots.

We must make no mistake that the arrangement is working the way it was created to. The same way that white supremacy, imperialism, and anti-Black racism continue to work the way they were intended—to keep the vast majority of the population sick and tired. Diagnosis frequently begins and ends with the individual, identifying bioessentialist causes at the expense of examining social factors.

Holding Our Histories

Although some of the information imparted may feel too historical for you or perhaps you are feeling a heaviness, I welcome you to roll your shoulders back, drink water, allow yourself to take deep breaths, and release sounds. Perhaps allow movements—small or large ones—to show up in your body. It is important to note that the more that we honor and allow information to process through us—the more we show up with some parts of the global history—the more we realize how inextricably linked mental health is with experiences and histories throughout the world. Can we work with a Punjabi family whose lineage is that of primarily agriculturists without knowing a bit about and acknowledging the expressions and possible traumatic generational effects of Punjab under colonial British rule?

Learning bits about the people we work with is such a forgotten art. But what I believe is even more pressing is the need to know one's self and one's history as much as possible. It will bring us back Home again. It will make these larger words and intellectual ideas come back Home HERE (pointing to the heart and gut) again. In much the same way, it is the duty of a practitioner to better understand what happens for a person when they are not privy to the truth about their people's history. What sorts of symptoms, behaviors, thoughts, and emotions might arise in a person who is disconnected from Home? Would a person dislocated from their home not struggle with feelings of unworthiness, deep rage, disconnect, and a sense of being an imposter at every turn? That is the insidious and most troublesome part of histories of colonization passed down among our lineages: the level of collective gaslighting and manipulation that permeates our bodies, removing us from any semblance of Home. This return to home within ourselves is the essential work of decolonizing.

Throughout this book, each chapter will offer affirmations for the reader. So often our histories of colonization will have bred a sense of disconnect from our feelings. It was often unsafe; survival was a focus for many of our kin, and there was no real space, politically or socially, to feel and deal. These offerings of affirmation are an invitation to slow down as practitioners. They are an invitation to internalize the root of our disconnect. The affirmations are a start. A place to allow some light, compassion, and healing into a wound of suffering, self-contempt, rage, and/or disgust. It is my belief that we cannot move forward with deep hatred and mistrust in our bodies, and certainly not as we expand and move forward into our ancestral lineages. For some communities, affirmation is easily given to another, and in others it is taboo. Some of us gain affirmation through music, Spirit, or dance; others of us through "I am" statements on a mirror or while looking tenderly at a child or lover. What is clear to me is that as deeply as my lineages have dehumanized and been dehumanized, coming back Home to myself, my roots, my body, and my breath with intentional affirmation has been a necessary and a welcome respite.

Aspects of Emotional–Decolonial Unlearning
1. Colonialism is one of humanity's core wounds.
2. Colonization thrives on isolation and maintains separation.
3. Colonialism is a current-day issue—an ongoing process that parallels the ongoing fight for liberation, universal equity, and self-sovereignty.
4. Colonization is psychological and spiritual trauma, as much as it is a physical one.

FIGURE 1.2 Colonization: A Blueprint *By Natasha Sandy (2022) for her Instagram @rehumanizingourselves*

5. It is our birthright to be free, on our homelands, growing crops, being healthy, and being in relationship with one another.
6. Decolonization is the return of land, to land, and to our sovereign and healthiest selves.
7. Colonialism is a root disease, entangled deep within our individual and collective psyches.
8. Emotional decolonization involves coming to awareness, unlearning, grieving, raging, and divesting (slowly) from the lies we have been told by colonizers, perpetuated by a white-centered lens.
9. We are all part of the problem and the solution. This has been further compounded by our mental health training.

10. The process of colonization is perpetuated through internalized racial inferiority, as well as internalized racial superiority, gatekeeping, gaslighting, colorism, ableism, and fatphobia, just to name a few.
11. Therapists, whom we identify as practitioners throughout this book, are not devoid of responsibility.
12. It is part of the practitioner's job to help organize and reeducate ourselves, our colleagues, our lovers, and our students. It is part of our job to activate and advocate healthy counsel to our communities—informed council.
13. Practitioners are not solo martyrs. It is part of our job, historically, to care for the wellness of the village, of the children, to carry on the stories, to bring insight and understanding, and to distribute aid and healing.
14. Settler colonialism is directly related to and in relationship with our internal sense of self and one another, the political climate globally, our history, our ancestors, and our personal and collective traumas.
15. Forced migration is a product of colonization and is maintained by imperialism.
16. Healing, including the practices known as therapy, must occur at the root of the dis-ease or imbalance: individually, politically, collectively, and ancestrally.

Emotional–Decolonial Practice Offerings
- Be open to learning the history of the individuals, groups, and organizations you are serving. This includes organizational histories, as well as the history of how and why a position opened up in an institution.
- Consider how your history and personal experiences are/could be blocking, projecting, minimizing, magnifying, or gatekeeping.
- It is beneficial to always have the inquiry of: "Where is **my** trauma showing up in this therapeutic relationship?" in your mind.
- Consider the possibility that the root of a person's imbalance and unwellness may come from historical trauma.
- Be conscious of spaces and places of disconnection from feelings.
- A natural expression of colonial harm and trauma is to numb and/or disso-

ciate oneself from overwhelming feelings, especially as it relates to feeling, culture, homeland, and/or identity.
- Consider that perhaps an individual's reactions and responses are healthy reactions, embedded in their mechanisms of survival via their ancestral lineage.

Affirmations
- I honor all treaties, promises, and agreements with myself.
- I work on forgiving myself and my ancestors for the treaties, pacts, and agreements that we have broken.
- I am willing to breathe into where whiteness has closed me up.
- I work on allowing myself space to grieve lands I have never set foot on.
- I am willing to learn my mother tongue.
- It is okay to want to reclaim my cultural identities.
- I trust my sovereignty and intuition.
- I let light in through my emotional cracks.
- I am a child of my ancestors.
- I am willing to learn, and I am willing to unlearn.
- I am willing to accept responsibility for my ancestors.
- I am willing to learn about my ancestry and forgive myself.
- I am willing to live fully in this body.

CHAPTER 2

Emotional–Decolonial Work

she recounts the day
she gave birth to twins—
how one was pulled from her arms,
and bound by the slave trade,
how the other remained
in her arms
but was bound by colonization.
she tells me,
"this is what it means to be
separated at birth."
—africans and african americans
   —Jacquelyn Ogorchukwu Iyamah,
      The Geometry of Being Black (2018)

There's no such thing as neutral education. Education either functions as
an instrument to bring about conformity or freedom.
   —Paulo Freire, *Pedagogy of the Oppressed* (1968/2018)

Home. As of late, I have chewed on the concept of Home. Is it a place, a space, or energy within your body? Is Home within a community, or among your beloved friends? Is Home merely an abstract concept, a movement practice, or a land? I would like to think that this concept—a concept of Home—is synonymous with a deep sense of safety, on all levels: emotionally, physically, culturally, spiritually, racially, energetically, and internally. A place where you feel safe, guarded, protected, seen, loved, and appreciated. At its core, "feeling at home with something" should feel familiar and safe. Yet, during a time of late-stage capitalism—when so many people with racialized and politicized bodies and identities do not get to just feel safe—this is in fact a privilege. Rampant imperialism and white-bodied supremacy is soaked into the very fabric of our political, justice, medical, and educational systems; so the question of Home is also a question of safety for some. Who gets to be safe?

Maybe, just maybe, we should all be asking ourselves whether our therapy is safe and more accurately, "Am I familiar with this experience of constantly inquiring whether this school, room, therapist, date, or job will be safe enough for me to show up, and even survive?"

The Privilege of Safety

As psychotherapists, we learn that safety is paramount in theory and practice. This includes practitioners like Carl Rogers, Bessel van der Kolk, Margaret Mahler, Melanie Klein, Ivan Pavlov, Peter Levine, Erik Erikson, Deb Dana, Marsha Linehan, and the list goes on. Many theorists and clinicians have posited that safety is of importance to the therapeutic container. One of the pillars of trauma-sensitive therapy is learning how to safely tolerate activating thoughts and feelings. The traumas of abuse, loss, separation, famine, poverty, and racism can leave many feeling overwhelmed and disconnected. I have heard clients describe the feeling as "unsafe." With feelings of unsafety arrives a flood of emotions and thoughts that feel as though they might drown us. Therapy can be a guide that feels and has proven to be safe. We can slowly work through and ride the waves of emotion to find neutrality, and even a sense of peace. In the therapeutic container, we should be able to set up a frame for a life that is ready to withstand triggers and deep overwhelm.

But what happens when the therapy room, psychiatrist office, partial care program, social services department, or residential program creates the unsafety? What happens when teachers and outpatient programs police our symptoms of unwellness and imbalance? Who holds the helper accountable? What happens when cultural competence and implicit bias training create more rage and the urge to flee? Or when government officials, policies, and law enforcement create the internal red flags? What happens when the helpers are the source of suffering?

WAYS THERAPISTS POLICE PEOPLE

Treatment plans: The name alone is quite telling. It describes a plan to "treat" the individual or family system that often does not include the input of the individual or family, and usually omits culture, context, and experiences such as disenfranchised grief and cultural, historical, racial, and intergenerational trauma histories. The treatment plan is also seen as a roadmap, predominantly for managed care, is often rigid in objectives, and utilizes *Diagnostic and Statistical Manual of Mental Disorders* (5th ed.; *DSM-5*; American Psychiatric Association [APA], 2013) criteria. It is often seen as pathologizing and quite a burden for practitioners.

Session limits: Although boundaries and limits are often taught as a central piece of the therapeutic process, the reality is that session limits began through and around managed care pricing and limitations. Due to managed care, care and healing spaces became therapy spaces. Support became treatment. The very profession has been created to fit an hourly rate, similar to how an accountant or mechanic charges by the hour. A practitioner's needs are also important. One may require rest, to contact or make referrals, to ground oneself, to take a brisk walk, or to call a loved one! However, even with one's humanity being considered, an hour session usually means 45 minutes. Research does not indicate that 45 minutes a week is enough to support the variety of diagnoses and areas of concern that people seek services for. Many individuals require more time to vent, more time to process, and a bit more space for intervention and practice.

Minimal sharing about self: It is crucial to recall that psychotherapy was co-opted and recreated by cisgender, European males quite interested in psychoanalysis. This method has been part of practitioners' therapeutic conditioning. Be a blank slate. Do not talk about yourself. Do not have anything in your office remotely suggestive, personal, or activating. In Chapter 3, we will explore the roots of mental health further and its proximity to the rise of systemic oppression and white supremacy, along with the MHIC. However, in many cultures across the world, the healer/practitioner naturally would share, when appropriate, with the receiver of support. There was not such a strict code or belief that sharing about oneself would lead to "poor outcomes." This is another example of a symptom of Eurocentric individualistic beliefs effecting and affecting a helping relationship. Therapists can hold a human boundary and share about their world. Additionally, receivers of support deserve to know more about the people who are providing a safe container for them.

Asking students to walk in straight lines in schools: This request begins to create a pattern of behavior and conditioning that mimics detention centers and prisons. It is also a pattern of behavior that is thought to keep children in line, yet this is often not a tactic seen in wealthier public schools. Students asked to walk in straight lines have an expectation placed on them—one that expects misbehavior and disorderly conduct over that of sovereignty, agency, and trust. Many times the students are also punished as though they are in a juvenile detention center (i.e., embarrassment, removal of rewards, isolation, etc.). This is particularly prominent in inner-city and poorer communities.

Note-taking during sessions: I have done it too. There are many reasons practitioners take notes during sessions: (a) to recall a week or so in the future what the participant said; (b) they have many "clients" to serve, and it is difficult to recall everyone's experiences; (c) to create treatment plans and notes later for managed care or to fulfill policy and ethics requirements; (d) some practitioners process by writing. However, writing while holding space for another can also be seen as a form of avoidance and disconnection, perhaps even dissociation. It can be uncomfortable for the participant and feel negligent. Oftentimes, our participants do not feel important; as though no one listens to them. This further exacerbates these feelings of neglect.

Where are "undocumented" children safe? Where can Indigenous and racialized peoples reside in a grounded, tethered, and seen way? Where do fat people get a seat without thinking about chairs prior to attending an event? Where are people truly safe to be and speak of their fluidity and identities?

What is your *Home*, and do you feel a connection?

If our homes have been vandalized, removed; if we have been kidnapped and sold like cattle from a *Home*; if we have witnessed extreme poverty despite excessive labor while *Home*, then can we feel **safe**? Will this lack of safety not produce a set of symptoms?

When did safety become a privilege? It in fact has. Perhaps our sense of safety began long before family systems and our nervous systems. Perhaps Home and a longing for safety have been more about an unconscious nagging, like a toothache coming on, or the beginnings of the flu. For many beings, Home may become a person, or a church, or a pet before it becomes a place. And that's okay. But, yet again, I inquire, what are the effects on a person who cannot or is not "allowed" to return back to a physical place to see other bodies and faces that resemble theirs?

Home is a process of excavation and revelation—surprising us, unnerving us, and uncovering more of us. Not just more of us, but more of who we are, where we come from, what our ancestors needed, and how we survived. I would dare to guess that most individuals seeking support services are not only seeking solace and relief, but a deeper desire to dig up the bones . . . to excavate—to have a Guide, so to speak, to lead them Home. I believe that those bones are the crux of our stories back to ourselves and back to the people we love—back to the origins of our culture.

I recall reading the children's book *Are You My Mother?* and exclaiming aloud to my beloved mother, "Mommy, thank God I know that you are my mother! I would be so sad and lonely without you." Although my response was that of a four-year-old child, there is wisdom in those words. There are so many people who deeply hold Parent/Caregiver/Mother Wounding. So many people never met Mother or had mother energy. Psychologically, energetically, metaphorically, politically—who are we without the cord . . . the tether . . . the deep root of Mother? From Mother Earth, the level of environmental racism and disconnect with our most original mother; to the

Motherland of beloved Africa. In much the same way, what arises in a person when they are not privy to the truth about their people's history? What sorts of symptoms, behaviors, thoughts, and emotions might arise in your body when there is an inherent spark, a KNOWING, buried deep inside your subconscious attempting to re-remind you of your inherent worth and wholeness; yet society has an entirely different and damaging story?

This chapter functions as a synthesis of the emotional damage of colonization, and how it has impacted people and land across the globe. This chapter will set the stage for the book and allow for readers to gnaw on the experience to follow. Whether in one-on-one sessions or within inpatient settings or clinics, it will present the idea that no therapist is above considering the questions that an understanding of these concepts creates. MHPs have a duty and ethical responsibility to inquire and unpack how, why, and where we cause harm, inadvertently or not.

If mental health professionals are to "treat" symptoms of trauma, anxiety, depression, and a vast variety of mental health symptoms, then it is also safe to assume that we have an inherent responsibility to make a connection between the loss and separation of land, identity, language, culture, relationships . . . and an individual's current emotional state.

The People's Stories

After years of deep depressive episodes, Luz entered therapy for the first time in a student therapy group. The group was led by a psychologist, who used a process-oriented and emotionally focused approach. Luz dealt with exploratory work and processed a great deal of her emotions in one-on-one counseling at the university's counseling center. She engaged in retreats, weekly group process meetings, and some identity exploration and development work.

She may not have gotten to deeply explore her identity as it related to her homeland overseas in the Philippines if she had not gotten to explore her identity, ancestry, political climate (in the States and overseas), as well as her permission to feel anger within one-on-one counseling sessions (which the university wanted to keep on a time limit). She had a session where her counselor inquired about her migration story and the floodgates opened.

Her deep struggles with feeling her anger and depression now had roots. It had names, faces, places, scents, temperatures, and energy—much like her symptoms had roots inside of her. As a college student her identity was beginning to be caught up in the depressive symptoms. It appeared that when she began to finally identify where grief was living and why, the grief could be addressed and felt. Luz needed permission to grieve the loss of her entire life in a land that was Home for her.

It was only as she entered community organizing seven years after beginning therapy that she would begin to truly unpack and process how her family's migration experience had been forced; unbeknownst even to them. It would be 14 years after she left the Philippines that she would understand how much late-stage capitalism and colonization shaped her, her beloved country, and her psychological attachment processes. It was not until she was asked about her migration story that she considered forced migration as a form of trauma.

RELEVANT THERAPEUTIC QUESTIONS FOR UNFOLDING A PERSON'S MIGRATION EXPERIENCE

- "What does 'Home' or 'feeling at home' mean/feel like/look like for you?"
- "You mentioned feeling disconnected/out-of-place/displaced a lot last time we came together, when else have you felt this way? Had you ever felt that way when you immigrated to this country?"
- "Would you like to tell me a little bit about your migration experience?"
- "How would you best like to share with me your experience of migrating to this country?"
- "What would make it safe enough to talk about your migration experience?"
- "Can we create a peaceful/safe space for a session or two before discussing your migration story?"
- "Would it be okay if I slowed you down, prompted you, or noted your body language during your sharing, so we can track what's happening for your body?"
- "How does your body feel when you say this?"

- "Would you like to (draw, hold this ball/stuffed animal, look away, etc.) while you share your story with me?"
- "What might you need or want from me when you start to share your experiences with immigration?"
- "Where does your migration experience begin from your perspective?"
- "What emotions are BIG when you think of Home?"

The violence and imperialism intertwined in the migration process of a family is huge. As we witness and experience hundreds of thousands of migrants being forced to leave their homelands due to the workings of imperialism and colonization, we are reminded that families are still deeply affected. Children still long for their caregiver who was offered the chance at a life where they can feed their children daily. Luz's story is not an isolated one.

The vast majority of therapists, when asked if they had been trained to ask about a client's migration experience in social work or counseling programs stated, "No, never." This is not only scary, it is dangerous. The Eurocentricity and privilege of our clinical practitioner-oriented programs focus more on what is defective with the mind, as opposed to one's experience. The belief continues to pathologize the person seeking help.

Colonization and colonial violence had impacted Luz's family. It had impacted her trust in herself. Her symptoms of depression and anxiety, feeling disconnected from others, and low self-concept could all more centrally be connected to colonial mentality—due to the effects of colonization and imperialism on her homeland—more so than they could be connected to "a defective brain." Her brain, body, and emotions were reacting to the loss of her Home. To the dissolution of her family and life in the Philippines. She was not broken or a burden. She was grieving, and eventually through her community organizing, was more clearly able to understand the root of her dis-ease.

Part of the emotional–decolonial frame involved considering Luz's:

- Historical context, including the current experiences of the people in the Philippines.
- Her perspectives/feelings about what her parents understood as the

reason for their migration to the United States, and what her perspective was; as they understood the move as voluntary, she understood it to be forced due to the political underpinnings.
- Her experience with the actual migration and relocation process.
- Processing parts of her life back home that she continues to miss and grieve.
- Her anger at the forced separation her family was forced to endure.
- Processing how her depressive symptoms are connected to her experiences and her family's experiences of political violence.
- Renegotiating her new identities, as a Filipina living in America, with residency, and any other salient identities.
- Finding new pathways toward releasing her resentment and anger, and taking embodied healthy action. For Luz that became activism; finding a community that held intersecting Filipinx identities as she does. Being part of the change was crucial to her well-being and her identity.

Colonization as a Collective Global Stockholm Syndrome

Stockholm syndrome is a psychological response where a person or people held captive begin to identify closely with their captors. They may take on the captor's beliefs, demands, and agendas. There is a great deal of literature that supports the myriad ways that those held captive need to break the psychological bond. As one may imagine, simply knowing that the person is harmful, being told repeatedly that they are harmful, or taking space from the captor and perpetrator are not a quick fix. We have seen examples of this in multiple situations, from one person to hundreds being convinced that a leader or movement will heal or protect or save them.

It is fascinating, because Stockholm syndrome is actually named for a bank robbery that took place in Stockholm, Sweden, in 1973. Four people were held hostage by the robbers for six days; when they were rescued, the hostages attempted to protect the perpetrators, with whom they claimed an "amicable" relationship.

The online resource GoodTherapy connects the symptoms of Stockholm syndrome with the process of colonization: "Stockholm syndrome [sufferers] often experience symptoms of posttraumatic stress: nightmares, insomnia, flashbacks, a tendency to startle easily, confusion, and difficulty trusting others. In much the same way the process of colonization, although very much about land, also contains a deeply ingrained and often taken for granted component—a deeply psychological one" (GoodTherapy, 2016). This process is deeply ingrained in the psyche because much of (though not all) colonization occurred hundreds of years ago. There is a particular type of emotional violence that I am introducing in emotional–decolonial work—it is the decentralizing and decolonizing of colonial mindset. It is nuanced, detailed, and deeply intertwined with colonization, policy, psychology, socialization, culture, and most importantly the Eurocentricity of colonial language.

Emotional decolonization involves the emotional and psychological deprogramming from historical and present-day forms of colonial violence. In other words, this work can help untangle the human emotions from psychological enslavement and programming. This emotional work is an essential component to literal land decolonization.

The Eurocentric conceptual system will eventually implode. It will destroy itself, collectively and individually. We can see the long- and short-term effects in Eurocentric functioning, most notably in participation in late-stage capitalism, ecological racism/ecocide, and that of the psychological collective socialization of people of the global majority. Globally and individually, we can see how individuals living within such an exhausting ecosystem (characterized by burnout, horrible work–life balance, living wage exceeding minimum wage) report an increase of intense exhaustion/fatigue, trauma, anxiety, depression, and a disconnect from our cultures.

Black psychologist and author Dr. Na'im Akbar (1981) describes four categories of mental disorders among Black people based on our disenfranchisement from our cultural structure and sense of identity. Dr. Akbar discussed how Black people's forced assimilation into European culture due to the institution of slavery across the globe has succeeded in an alienation of the Self, and created a collective denial that these experiences of slavery and colonization have an effect on people's psychological and physical health.

It is important to note as we discuss decoloniality and indigeneity that

I am also speaking to all people forcibly removed and affected by the act of colonization across the globe.

Check-In
- What arises in your body when you say or read the term **white supremacy**?
- How does your practice benefit from colonization and white supremacy?
- How do you benefit from white supremacy?
- How did your ancestors benefit from white supremacy (even if it did not have that name)?
- Where are you willing to start to untangle yourself from colonial mentality?
- Where are you more interested in helping your "clients" untangle from white supremacy, as opposed to looking at one's self?
- How do your recipients of care discuss the effects of white supremacy on their emotional health?

We see with Luz's experience how colonization speaks to the root of the dis-ease, the root in this sense of being landless, parent-less, unlovable, and unseen. There is a deep sense of disconnect. I would surmise that to work on the intellectual mind, even stating affirmations and rewiring our cognitive distortions—without acknowledging the ways that our histories and ancestry may have impacted our psychological well-being—is only scratching the surface.

Individuals in emotional distress benefit from all sorts of therapies. Yet, are we not participating in gaslighting as practitioners if we are not acknowledging the infection, but continue to cover the wound?

For example, a mental health practitioner may work on relational issues with a person, focusing on childhood events, abandonment, abuse, attachments, and family dynamics—which are all relevant and can be important. However, if ancestry, homeland, mother tongue, or a disconnect from any of these aspects of culture and current political climate are not discussed, then the therapy is incomplete.

If a mental health practitioner is discussing better boundaries and time management yet not acknowledging that the ancestors of their client were hung for "speaking out of turn," or that time was managed for them on a farm or plantation, or that they currently reside in affordable housing living paycheck to paycheck with barely enough money left to buy food—would these things not take precedence over boundaries and time management? We continue to pick the leaves off the tree, rather than dig up the root.

Author Reflection

For years when working in an inner-city counseling center, skilled and brilliant clinicians around me would state: "We are not doing *therapy*, this is community mental health, not psychology. This is triage! I am holding a bleeding wound. I am not using anything I learned in school!" This got me to thinking, "Well then if we aren't doing therapy, what are we doing?" This is what the community needs. This is what early-career psych students need. This is what social work, counseling, and psychology needs. If our programs aren't teaching how to heal the bleeding wound and we aren't part of dismantling that which creates the wound—WHAT ARE WE DOING?

So, this work, *Decolonizing Therapy*, is about THAT. It centers on all of the people forgotten and abandoned in the name of "real therapy."

The theories we have been taught are good; they provide a base from which to jump. I would dare say that this work is asking mental health providers to dig a tad deeper into the *collective soma* . . . into the soul wound of a person (Duran, 2006).

My Good People, we've been lied to, bamboozled, and told incomplete truths.

Your entire education HAS been a form of colonization. We have been taught to medicalize and treat symptoms, yet we continue to ignore the soul wounds of historical trauma and colonization. We victim-blame by focusing on personal deficiencies and trauma, rather than structural violence. You see, the systems are working exactly as they were intended. When a society is not equipped to hold up an accurate mirror to us, we end up interpreting our reflection according to the available structures and terminologies.

As I will detail in Chapters 6 and 7, Dr. Joy DeGruy, Dr. Bruce Lipton, Rachel Yehuda, Dr. Frederick Hickling, Dr. Maria Yellow Horse Brave Heart and Dr. Michael Yellow Bird, among others, have all shone a light on the ways that large patterns of historical and collective trauma are passed down from one generation to the next through our DNA. This trauma—which manifests in our bodies, psyches, emotions, and personalities—sometimes influences our behaviors in ways of which we are often unaware. This can result in feeling deeply dysregulated when activated. When triggered, our bodies sense and remember this trauma, leading us to have an emotional response such as overwhelming anxiety, fear, irritation, and rage. Oftentimes, our minds are not able to fully comprehend and know where these strong emotions are coming from.

It is within this membrane that colonization lies, often dormant until our levels of trauma and stress begin to increase and drown us in fear, anxiety, and rage. In Chapters 5 and 6, we will discuss the intergenerational trauma transmission process, along with the roots of historical grief and trauma, tying together the charge of therapists with colonization even further.

As a psychologist and ancestral rage and grief worker, I am clear that balanced health is something that invites both comprehending and acknowledging, unlearning, questioning, honoring, and healing. Healing does not include moving on, but it does include creating space for grief, ritual, and pain. For unraveling. For understanding. For the deep dives. It also includes space for deep pain to surface, establishing and negotiating boundaries with others, creating coping mechanisms and rituals that allow for a semblance of normalcy to arise. With the constant spiral staircase[13] of excavating and healing, it is only then that, perhaps, we can choose again . . . that we can see past the pain and deep betrayal to forgiveness. But "moving on" is not quite feasible for many of us who do not have the privilege of ignoring a salient and socially marginalized identity (e.g., body size, gender identity, skin color, accent, and disability).

Many countries, people, and spaces that abuse power (consciously or not) benefit from a forgetful memory that would simply allow communities to not accept responsibility for their ancestors or their own actions, verbally,

---

13 Dr. Alissa Koval-Dhaliwal spoke of the spiral staircase as part of the therapeutic process, whereby we never "finish" working on core issues. Rather, we grow and go up the spiral staircase, occasionally needing to look back to see how far we have come, and perhaps where we still need to travel (personal communication, 2018).

fiscally, through land, etc. This is true since traumatizing colonial incidents are sufficient enough to produce posttraumatic stress disorder (PTSD) symptoms. Dr. Joy DeGruy speaks of posttraumatic slave syndrome (PTSS) and the generational effects of American chattel slavery and the African Holocaust on the minds, bodies, relationships, and mental health of Black people (2005). She also notes the ways in which the land currently known as the United States of America continues to retraumatize the enslaved African descendants. This too shows up in our therapeutic encounters.

Many of us reside on traumatized land. We inherit the trauma wounds, not simply from our human ancestors, but also the land's experiences. This can be viewed from both an Indigenous (people native to a land) perspective and an intergenerational trauma perspective. Dr. Maria Yellow Horse Brave Heart and other Indigenous-identified scholars have provided many trauma researchers with the roadmap to the cords of connection between the soul wound and the epigenetic inheritance. More on that in Chapter 5 on intergenerational trauma.

Decolonization Is Unsettling

Decolonization has traditionally been defined as the process of deconstructing colonial ideologies of the superiority and privilege of Western thought and approaches. Returning and dismantling structures in order to provide a form of return—original land and/or "suitable" reparations. It also speaks to the dismantling of structures that perpetuate the status quo and addressing unbalanced power dynamics. Is not the mental health system a structure that can perpetuate the status quo? Are there not unbalanced power dynamics that may not benefit those being served? (If you are unsure about this, please take special care when reading Chapter 4.) Does a structure that ethically seeks to create wellness perpetuate the true advocacy for emotional wellness? I believe we established that wellness historically embodies loss and pain. Wellness transmutes suffering. Emotional–decolonial work seeks to transmute suffering.

The call for decolonizing education and including Indigenous ways of knowing and being in education was first articulated in 1972 in "Indian

Control of Indian Education" by the National Indian Brotherhood (now the Assembly of First Nations). Decolonization engages with education and mental health at every level. The call to decolonize education also challenged how higher education, research, and publishing are complicit in and, in fact vital, to the colonial oppression of Indigenous peoples and enslaved Africans who built much of the world around the globe.

Decolonization is unsettling, uncomfortable, and messy. Decolonization is a cycle and process of destruction and creation, much like the phoenix accepting its fate. In this way, white supremacy permeates and dictates the education, mental health, medicine, prison, transportation systems, and has created a dis-ease of sorts. White supremacy is a virus. A plague. An ancestral intergenerational curse that sits upon the chests of people and impacted communities yowling for more. It is only when we decide to see the beast for what it is that we can properly address the virus and find solutions. We can find solutions through community. We can find solutions through understanding our history, our People's ways, our traditions, our plant allies, and through reeducation.

When we try to get to the root of suffering through the lens of mental health, behavioral health, and psychiatry, we only skim the surface. The root of anything is full of depth, darkness even, and shadows should we want to authentically identify, understand, and extract. Therefore, even psychology, social work, counseling, and psychiatry are being called to **dig deeper**. To address the ROOT. The root of many people's trauma lies at the feet of histories of colonization, ancestral, and historical trauma. The root of the illness or dis-ease must be found in our histories. The root of the pain and the severing of our healthy attachment, I believe, can be located within our histories and our altered stories.

This is essential because of increasing rates of suicide, depression, murder and overall loss of life due to a loss of connection with each other (and our own humanity). Person-centered. CBT. DBT. Psychoanalysis. Solution-focused. Family systems. Object relations. All of these theories and practices have their place, space, "treatment," and helpfulness. But without an emotional–decolonial frame we continue to elect without context. We shout "BLACK LIVES MATTER," yet institute unstable diversity and equity structures in our hiring without supporting the Black and Brown peoples in our corporations. We speak of capitalism without an analysis. We conflate antiracism work with decolonial work (both needed, but different).

Decolonization is a painstaking process; the introduction to the end of the very systems and ways of being that have come to be seen as "normal." It calls for an awareness of your relative position(s) in your community, your role(s), and your actions. My colleague, Maverick Lumen (personal communication, 2021), would state that this energy of decolonial unpacking, the introduction to the end as a means to a new beginning, would be depicted by the nine of swords in the tarot. Taking ourselves from the nine (the painful awareness) to the 10 of swords (the time for transformation and disrupting the cycle) is the natural next step.

Decolonization is a historical process, generated by the making of history (struggles, strategies, and tactics), which is found in the everyday practice of coordinated human action (McLean, 2017). Decolonization **is** healing. It is a process that is often overstated, misrepresented, misunderstood, and it involves long-term commitment to unpacking, fantasizing, imagining, planning, restructuring, and creating a different way to be. It is clear that many of us will struggle with changes to mental health and other systems. However, the resistance may point to where the privilege resides.

The past few years have exemplified for us that the gift is wrapped within the struggle. The future also lies nestled within the mistakes of our past. Therapists know better than most that the insightful reflective struggle produces an awareness so that healthier decisions can come to fruition.

Decolonization doesn't mean "diversity," it refers to the collective journey toward undoing systemic and individual harm on people, land, cultures, our emotional health, and physical bodies. We are being asked to look at who has taught us, what have they taught, who has it been approved by, and why. Decolonization is a process of asking ourselves: "Whose history is this?" "How do your words and actions seek to address what has been stolen/lost?" and "How we can heal?"

It is our belief that decolonization cannot occur in a silo. It must be examined, studied, and understood. Land sovereignty is essential to the process. This book is about human beings and the psychological and energetic effects of colonization. It is also about how the mental and behavioral health fields are complicit in adding to the violence of colonization (even unconsciously) through our methods of instruction, level of focus on psychopathology, obsession with cognitive–behavioral therapy, and intellectualizing our emotions.

The Mental Health Industrial Complex

The MHIC continues to medicalize spiritual and emotional dis-ease, creating further trauma in the person, at the hands of the MIC (Gallagher, 2016, para. 12). We decolonize our therapy in order to take back our land, our cultures, our lives, and our ancestral healing—which we can find at the roots of many of our helping professions. In decolonizing our therapy, we agree to unpack and stand in solidarity to decolonize and heal every other system across the board. Our liberations are deeply intertwined because colonization and the emotional and physical effects of its malignancy have made us very sick.

For example, for many people who do not have access to high-end private practice therapists and coaches, community mental health and nonprofit group practices are the go-to for mental health needs. These practices and nonprofits primarily employ recently graduated social work, counseling, and psychology students at the rate of $30–50/hour for a 55-minute session, for which the group practice charges anywhere from $150–200 an hour. Often these offices are not providing payment to the early-career clinicians for administrative work, such as notes, outreach, referrals, or meetings. These early career clinicians are often struggling to receive proper supervision, working other jobs to meet their basic needs, paying student loans, dealing with intense vicarious trauma due to the material they are helping to hold, are overworked with 40–80+ cases a month, and move from job to job due to constant microaggressions, burnout, bias, and acts of discrimination. Furthermore, the approved therapeutic methods of early-career clinicians at these kinds of organizations are often confined to CBT and "clinical" modalities that introduce other kinds of problems.

In turn, clients have poor outcomes because there is constant burnout and turnover within the staff. This continues to affect people seeking support and increases feelings of abandonment and mistrust in the

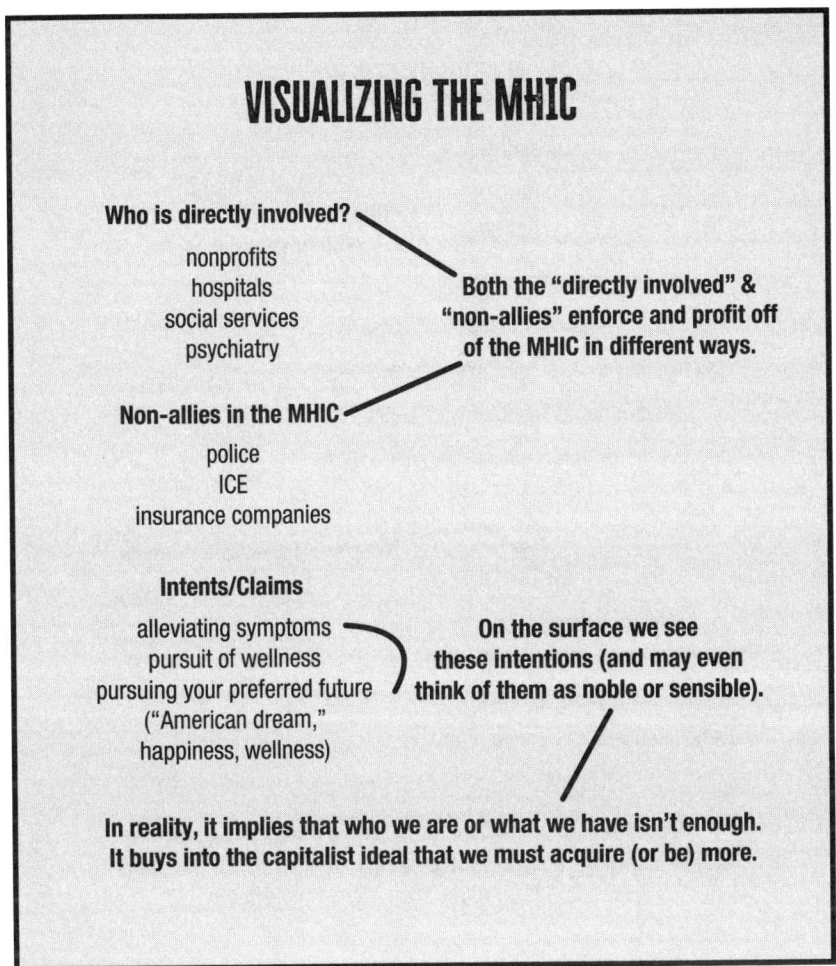

FIGURE 2.1 Visualizing the MHIC *Source:* Original text from a collaboration between Jennifer Mullan, Ji-Youn Kim, Gabes Torres, & Maverick Lumen.

system. With addiction cycles, trauma stops being processed, symptoms arise, violence toward self or loved ones increases. The behavior is eventually criminalized, especially when a person is BIPOC. This is an example of how our fields exploit and perpetuate violence on freshmen as well as the community they should be serving. By forcing the practitioners to work within the narrow confines of the system, they are being forced to

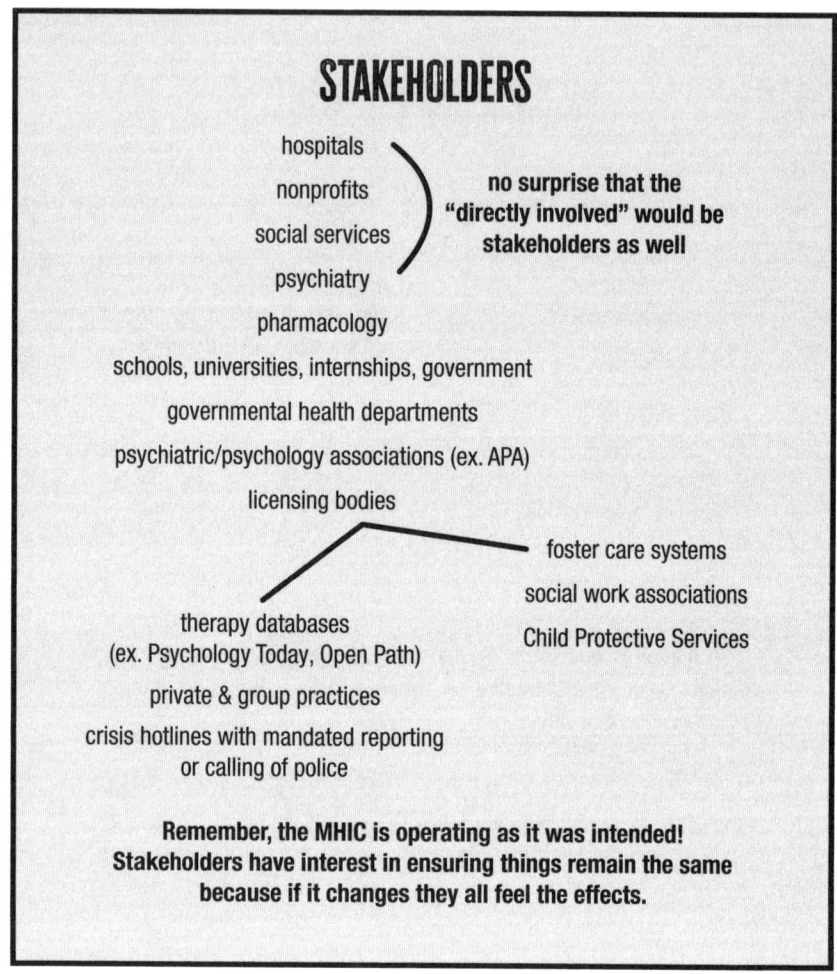

FIGURE 2.2 Visualizing the MHIC: Stakeholders   Source: Original text from a collaboration between Jennifer Mullan, Ji-Youn Kim, Gabes Torres, & Maverick Lumen.

inflict the same harm on the people they want to help that they themselves have received.

Decolonizing is about reclaiming ourselves from exploitation. Part of what makes colonization so violent are the rationalizations of Western thought that "being civilized" requires various prescriptions of what we ought to be. There is a general narcissism and violence in assuming that all people should subscribe to and be aligned with certain systems, and

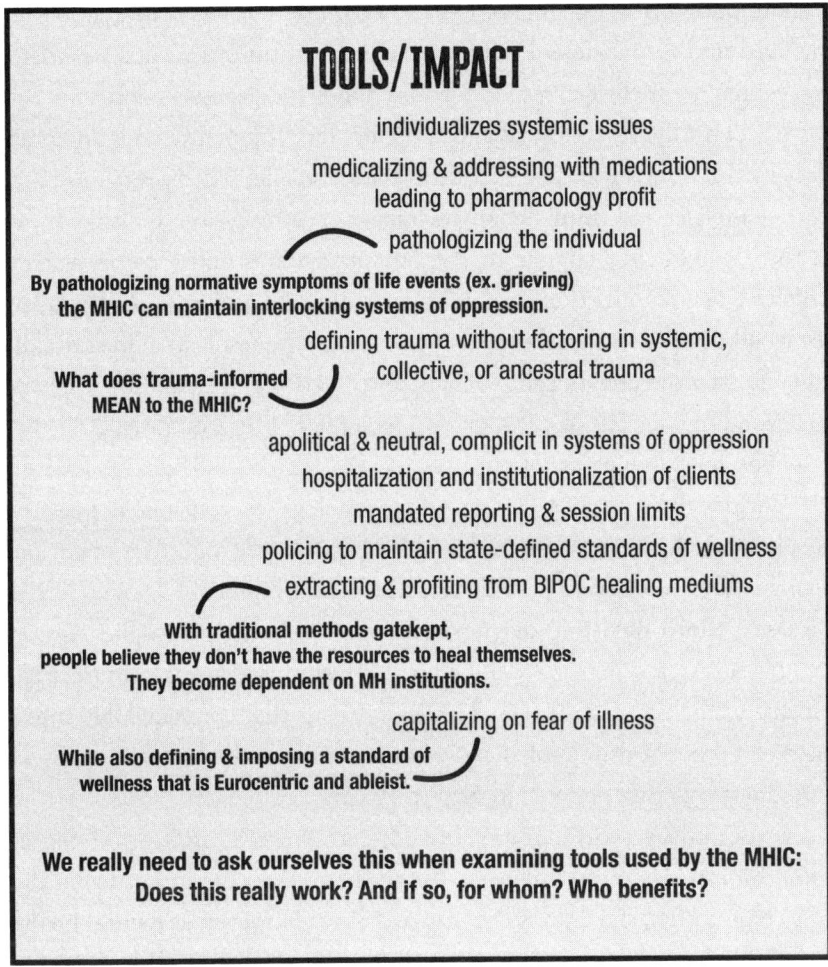

FIGURE 2.3 Visualizing the MHIC: Tools/Impact   *Source:* Original text from a collaboration between Jennifer Mullan, Ji-Youn Kim, Gabes Torres, & Maverick Lumen.

expected to achieve uniform outcomes regardless of circumstance. At the very least, colonization is a violent history that still shows up at the present, requiring sameness, loyalty, fealty to an idea, and a certain brand of humanity.

We work in systems that perpetuate colonial ideals and privilege Western ways of engaging with services. From student services, to child welfare systems, to how libraries catalog knowledge—all are Western and colonial.

Decolonization is an ongoing process that requires all of us to be collectively involved and responsible. Decolonizing our institutions means we create spaces that are inclusive, respectful, and honor Indigenous peoples.

Recognizing the historical and contemporary colonial systems and practices within our educational institutions and broader society requires all of us to self-reflect and think about the impact of colonization. It also requires us to help influence change in the broader systems and societies within which we operate. "Institutional reform must be undertaken on multiple levels, by all peoples in the academic community, and result in a dramatically different structure, relationships, goals, and outcomes" (Pete, 2016). We must go beyond having "decolonization as a metaphor" (Tuck & Yang, 2012) but as a conscious, living part of our lives.

Within structures of sociology and psychology, we continue to hear the people receiving services referred to as *patients*. We are told to *terminate* our sessions. We are asked to provide an ICD-9 (International Classification of Diseases, Ninth Revision) diagnosis, despite the long-term implications of the diagnosis on a person's well-being and future. We are told to *treat* the *patient*. Vilma Santiago-Irizarry (2001) contends that commendable intentions can produce unintended consequences in her ethnographic fieldwork programs for Latinx patients in New York City.

Over and over BIPOC are studied, pathologized, and experimented upon. Our fields are no different. When many theorists in academia discuss colonization, the land is the primary focus. However, as mental health human service workers and people seeking to unfurl themselves from the grips of ancestral trauma, it is essential that we continue to hold the awareness that the process of colonization is, and continues to be, violent and traumatic, and that it affects people currently.

This is visible in the traditional therapeutic relationship. For instance, during my 18 years as a direct services psychotherapist, I noticed the very clear effects of colonization express themselves in what I would call a *Trauma Burger*. The symptom, level of distress, and trauma expressed itself in a very specific manner. It felt cyclical; although they may have not been there before, it also appeared to cause the person a great deal of distress, as though they had done something wrong or they had not cared for themselves properly. The person's insight and self-reflection was high, but their inability to regulate their emotions created more distress than the emotions themselves. Additionally, there was an element of cultural group and/or racial trauma that the individual had been or was consistently exposed to. Therefore, I would note, individuals that (a) presented with intense anxiety, rage, dysregulation, and/or depression, coupled with; (b) a current-day traumatic global event, coupled with; (c) family trauma histories that were political, historical, or cultural in nature, coupled with; (d) present-day cultural, racial, and/or political trauma created this vortex of suffering that was indeed clinically relevant. The person was deeply suffering and unable to find relief with traditional therapy interventions. Therefore the *Trauma Burger* was:

A. Historical/ancestral/intergenerational trauma due to colonization.
B. Childhood trauma or adverse experiences that impacted a sense of safety, identity, trust, and nervous system regulation.
C. Present-day suffering, and possibly racial or political collective trauma, that activated the ancestral/historical/intergenerational wound.

For example, Sherene came into counseling for support with insomnia, night terrors, visions of elders from her family, attention deficit disorder symptoms, loss of interest in her close friend circle, and loss of interest in her career and small business (design and architecture). She was unable and unwilling to consistently keep practices that had been useful during prior counseling sessions when she struggled with depression and anxiety expressions. She identified as Armenian, and was quite aware of the impact the Armenian genocide in the early 1900s had on her family's relationships, well-being, and emotional health. She had also been assaulted by four police officers during a protest. She was dragged away from her organizing pod, and some of her friends were also beaten and arrested. She was beaten with nightsticks and kicked with steel-toe boots, while being pepper sprayed and called names that were racially and religiously bigoted and violent. Her hospital bills were extensive, and she was currently involved in a court case related to the arrest post-beating.

Sherene was also a full-time student, and this was deeply affecting her grades, internship, and self-esteem. She began to experience panic attacks when needing to leave the house or when seeing police cars and/or officers. She began to take cannabis gummies more often in order to cope with the trauma expressions. Her family blamed her for being at the protest, and stated that she deserved the beating. They mentioned how vital it was for "people like them" to stay away from "dangerous situations like a protest" and that she should be "happy that she had rights and was in America." They wanted her to settle down, focus on school, and keep her head down. She also has extensive histories of physical, emotional, and sexual harm from ages 3–7 years old prior to migrating to the States with her immediate family, away from the violent uncle who had perpetrated these acts. By the time she entered our therapy sessions she had been on our university waitlist for three months, on two community behavioral health lists for six and eight months, and had been hospitalized by a crisis response worker twice.

This is an example of how the colonial wound expresses itself in the present-day. This is also an example of how focusing on symptoms, childhood trauma, and cognition alone is incomplete, and at times, even unhelpful. I wish I could state that this story is the minority; however, unfortunately I witnessed it in the majority of the individuals I have supported as a therapist across my clinical career.

Looking at the endeavor as a collective, working together, encourages us to think of decolonization as a reciprocal partnership required for all people to participate in their own internal process, and to further create spaces for safety and collaboration within new interlocking spaces. This means examining how severe psychological distress receives support, and how to support positive transformation and self-determination.

Decolonization is a way of living toward possible abolishment of an antiquated system of care that favors prescribing medications with countless side effects, session limits, and carceral hospitalizations. As Dr. Marya and Raj Patel (2021) beautifully explain in *Inflamed*: "Inflammation itself isn't a disease—it is a sign of a larger problem." They note that our body is part of an inflamed society; and that we are part of an intricate web of activation. Our nervous systems quickly shift from fight, to flight, to freeze; we are collectively witness to intense racial violence; we are literally experiencing ecological inflammation and industrial pollution.

We should not utilize the term *decolonization* if we are unprepared to return land back to the Earth and allow the Indigenous people's stewardship to be in the right relationship with the land. We should also not presume to *decolonize* if we are not prepared to confront capitalism and imperialism, even when it does not affect us and our loved ones. We should also not utilize the term *decolonization* if we are not prepared to unlearn. Decolonization REQUIRES us all to create more sustainable futures; all levels of society must shift and upgrade. Decolonization is not dependent on who gets elected, or what the government sanctions. Decolonization involves imagination, evolution: environmental, economic, and of the human spirit (Renee Sills, 2020).

Fanon (1952/1967) notes that decolonization seeks to create new men. "New men" as in new humans, new ways of being in relationship with one another, the Earth, our bodies, our plant and animal kingdoms, our trauma histories, our virtual spaces, philosophies, core beliefs about ourselves, ancestral wisdom, mental and emotional wellness, and our minds. Our language has to evolve, as does the manner in which we use it. The discord between who we presume to be, how we behave, and the actions we take must evolve. To decolonize is to oppose Eurocentric-Western colonial prescriptions, descriptions, and beliefs—white ain't always right. Whiteness is truly a Western wound. Where whiteness requires silence, decolonization requires revolutions, even small ones.

> **SMALL REVOLUTIONS FOR CARE WORKERS AND SPACE HOLDERS (PRACTITIONERS)**
>
> - Shift to a healing-justice frame
> - Include community/clients/participants in all board meetings and large organizational decisions
> - Cocreate and participate in affinity groups for practitioners
> - Employ peer support

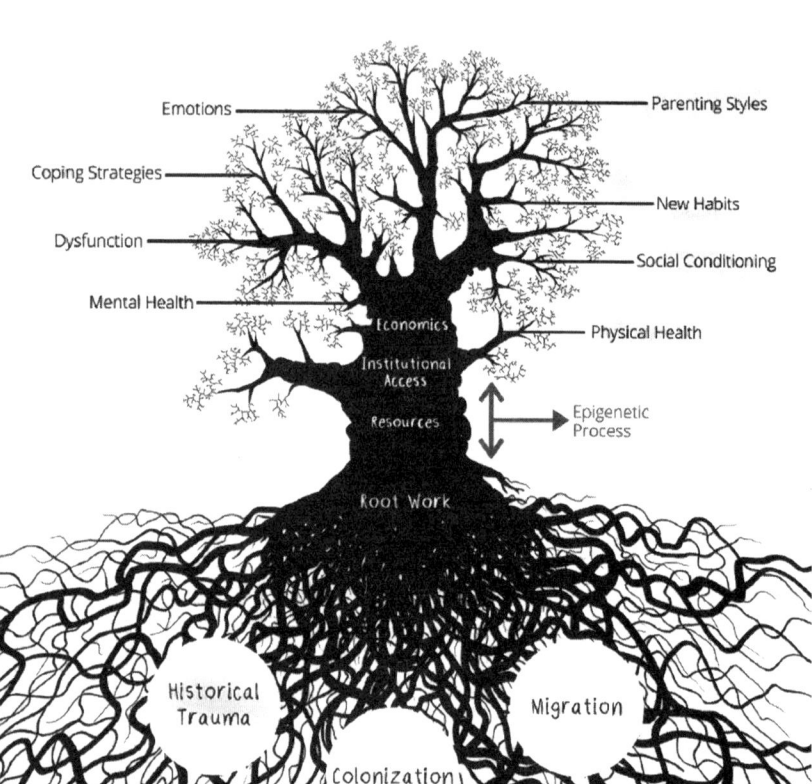

FIGURE 2.4 Intergenerational Tree of Transmission Source: Created by Toi Smith for Dr. Jennifer Mullan.

- Cofacilitate all sessions and groups with community, spiritual, holistic practitioners, and organizations, as needed, and relevant to the participants of therapy
- Facilitate and hold group and circle spaces not related to a problem (i.e., holding circles and consistent spaces for reclaiming joy, for interest in culture, cooking, breathwork, relearning a native language, etc., as opposed to an anxiety or depression support group)

- Encourage peer/therapy participant support
- Discuss the most harmful rules and policies that your organization/practice/hospital/school/board engages in and create coalitions (that includes community) to abolish them and recreate new ways of helping
- Instead of paying consultants, including us, pay for childcare services at your hospital/school/offices
- Engage in outings and activities that do not include a therapy focus for the practitioners
- Provide interns and practicum students and employees 40–50% of the rate/fee, instead of 15–25% of the hourly fee
- Learn from community organizers and commit to creating space for racial identity work, ancestral processes, and political understandings
- Include colonial wounding, historical trauma, intergenerational, and racial trauma in the education of practitioners across the disciplines (while we are creating new ways of supporting and helping people)

Expressions of the Trauma of Colonization

Below is an evolving list of expressions of transmitted colonial pain. This list has been created as a way to remind individuals that much of what we deem a mental or behavioral health issue may actually be a generationally transmitted manifestation of colonization.

This list does not mean that individuals do not and would not benefit from culturally appropriate, politicized, liberation-focused psychotherapies—on the contrary. However, it is essential for the individuals who participate in therapies, and those who provide therapies, to realize the root of the disease. **When we understand the origins, we can begin to release shame, self-blame, feelings, and behaviors of unconscious victimization and fear.** Then the work feels more expansive, more possible, and becomes a process in which we cocreate our wellness plan, rather than be forced to submit to a "treatment plan" we do not identify with.

As someone who is living through and healing historical trauma, I am determined to ensure that others who experience pervasive expressions of this pain create more compassion for themselves. When we can see ourselves as living survivors—descendants of historical pain—then we may begin to comprehend how this pain unwittingly was passed down, creating cycles and patterns in the present. It is then that we can begin to witness them, grieve them, and release them.

Many of us identify as grandchildren of traumatized grandparents, and may have even been traumatized by our grandparents or other members of their generation. Even further, many of us have survived traumatization at the hands of our parents—due to these inherited and transmitted historical traumas. Therefore, the list below is an attempt at identifying how the historical wounds of colonization show up in us today.

Clinically, and personally, I found that long-standing chronic or pervasive expressions (symptoms) that continued despite an array of solid treatment and healing interventions show up as the following thoughts, feelings, and/or behaviors:

- Difficulties trusting oneself (often known as imposter syndrome)
- Perfectionism/high control needs
- Codependence or difficulties asking for help
- Existential anxiety
- Consistent verbalization of statements around existential dread such as: "I do not want to be here" or "What is the purpose of all of this?"
- Often diagnosed or identifies as neurodivergent (which may be extrasensory abilities expanding, or healing taking place and inability to deal with the overwhelm of current environments)
- Symptoms or expressions of mental health diagnoses that are chronic, long-term, and even generational that do not decrease with processing and support
- Difficulties trusting others, and often shutting down as a protective mechanism
- Difficulties feeling safe and regulating in new situations
- Elevated stress and cortisol levels (i.e., can often lead to hormonal imbalances or anxiety attacks)
- A need to "fix" or tend to others' needs over one's own
- Intense sensitivity

- Elevated intuition
- Difficulties concentrating
- Internalization of sacred rage leading to frequent panic attacks
- Seeing or hearing things that others say are not there
- Generational patterns of inability to access, control, or safely express one's rage/anger
- Generational patterns of incarceration
- Generational patterns of addiction (i.e., shopping, food, sex, substances, overworking, etc.)
- Generational patterns of porous boundaries
- Generational patterns of excessive caregiving, despite one's own needs
- Generational patterns of an inability, or lack of space, to grieve
- Generational patterns of financial instability due to land removal, forced migration, forced labor, or enslavement

This is not an exhaustive list, and these are not meant to be seen as symptoms to diagnose. These are not negatives or weaknesses, they just ARE.

Mental health practitioners would benefit from considering whether current diagnoses are manifestations of the above symptoms. It is important to note that these insights are not meant to further pathologize, diagnose, or be a checklist. Rather, the aforementioned insights create the allowance for:

- Unscripted dialogue with client that centers on ancestral knowledge
- Reeducation (for oneself and client) around pathology and diagnosis pros and cons
- Discussion related to Home and land of racial and cultural origin
- Space for migration patterns and stories
- Space for identity dialogue
- Better insight into internal locus of control
- Space necessary to consider a healing plan
- Space to unravel trauma cycles in our lineage
- Space for bilateral learning within the therapeutic relationship
- Space to drive relationships with family with whom we struggle

- Space to dream and create
- Space to cocreate new ways of healing and living
- Space for ritual and or ceremony that is culturally relevant
- Space for somatic or body-based interventions

Throughout the rest of this book, I invite you on a journey to emotionally and intellectually decolonize and politicize our worldview. The emotional–decolonial paradigm shift is one that can be metabolized by all people, but in particular, students, educators, recipients of counseling, social work, psychiatry, and psychology therapy; therapy with the imbued assumption that healing—not medicalizing—is the focus. It is a journey.

It is a journey that Western education systems would benefit from—traveling with humility. The undoing, deconditioning, rehumaning, and reclaiming processes require compassion, humility, multigenerational organizing, and listening to the wisdom of our ancient traditions; while creating a frame for our mental health futures.

Decolonization is a call to remember it was not always this way. It does not have to be this way. Start slow, struggle with meaning, words, and actions. Each day, find out how you can meet the basic needs and legitimate expectations of yourself and others. The struggles of human history are what set the stage and terms for decolonization.

Unpack It With Me Reflection Questions
- Where is Home to you?
- What is your relationship to that Home?
- What is your migration story?
- What is the migration story of your mother . . . father . . . grandparents?
- Have you ever explored your migration lineage in a safe setting?
- Where have you been (forcibly) removed, exiled, or "left out" in your life?
- Where does unlearning and relearning most need to happen in your life?
- What lies have you been told about your ancestors?
- How has this impacted your relationships?
- How has this impacted your choice of work?

- What is your family's relationship to colonization?
- How may that show up for you today?

Aspects of Emotional–Decolonial Unlearning
1. One-size-fits-all mandated reporting where law enforcement criminalizes mental health experiences is dangerous in most instances, in particular among BIPOC people. What are other ways of providing safety within mutual aid and community?
2. White supremacy and whiteness situate themselves in many, if not in all of us, in unique and pervasive ways.
3. All therapists, professors, nonprofit employees, and care workers benefit from white supremacy and poor people—whether we are conscious of it or not.
4. Rescue mentalities among therapists are remnants of colonial consciousness (colonization).
5. Racism, sexism, classism, xenophobia, ableism, heterosexism, and so forth: all affect and impact one another. They all impact and affect each individual differently.
   — Not all Black people grew up poor and in the inner city. Just like not all Black people feel anti-Black racism is a "thing," nor do all Black folks feel they have experienced historical trauma.
   — If we do not know how our ancestors benefited from colonization, then we are unable to fully grasp how our ancestors may have been impacted by colonization.
   — What is occurring outside of our country of residence is just as valid, horrific, and important to our global collective well-being.
   — Safety—emotionally, physically, psychologically, and spiritually—is essential to helping and healing.

Emotional–Decolonial Practice Offerings
- Cultural and historical trauma lead to body and land dissociation. Therefore, it is imperative to begin the emotional–decolonial process with oneself primarily.
- Once a practitioner is in a consistent community of others unpacking their

own biases, histories of harm, and areas of invisibility, then a practitioner is better able to unpack and hold the emo–decolonial lens with another.
- Practitioners would benefit from stepping into consistent curiosity and compassion with themselves and their therapeutic participants.
- It is useful to process how and where removal from the participant's Home, their countries, and lands of origins, or stewardship over these lands have affected them. This can also include how it has or has not impacted their elders and their culture.
- Speak to colleagues and peers working in an emo–decolonial lens about MHPs' relationships to struggle and shame. Both are products of overwork leading to fatigue, as a result of capitalism and colonialism.

Affirmations for Grieving and Reclamation
- I hold my family's lineage with compassion.
- I honor the anger my body holds at how my people have been treated.
- I honor feelings of separateness between my homeland and I.
- I create space to grieve.
- It is safe to grieve for a place I have never been.
- It is healthy to grieve for people I have never met.
- I release family karma that is not mine to hold.
- I can choose to see my experience(s) differently.
- I choose feelings of safety and centeredness in my body.

■ CHAPTER 3

From Lobotomies to Liberation

Heal the root so the tree is stable.
—Anonymous

*Oppression—overwhelming control—is necrophilic;
it is nourished by a love of death, not life . . .*
—Paulo Freire, *Pedagogy of the Oppressed* (1968/2018)

*Certainly there were formations of gender norms and heterosexuality
prior to colonization but what colonialism did was officially establish
the gender binary and heteronormativity. What colonialism did was
criminalize people for transgressing from these gender and sexual norms.*
—Alok Vaid-Menon & Janani Balasubramanian, trans Indian
poets and organizers, Darkmatter (The Cake, 2015)

The question of how to address a human's emotional, mental, or behavioral dis-ease, unwellness, or imbalance has evolved across cultures and millennia, adapting as the understanding of the human condition has changed in the face of advances in theology, anthropology, science, sociology, medicine, and psychology. The history and evolution of mental and behavioral health and treatment is not always a flattering story, but it explains a great deal about how and why the landscape of mental health treatment is what it is today and how to best support humanity through an array of emotional, political, climate, and public health crises.

The root causes of mental and emotional injury lie at the metaphorical depths of history: at the bottom of the Atlantic, within the roots of our trees and crops, on the edge of dry deserts, within our DNA, in our song, and certainly within our dances. Most clearly the energy lies upon and within the bodies of people with colonized histories, as well as (although differently) the bodies of those whose ancestors did the colonizing—both individually and collectively. The root cause of the traumas many of us contend with is caused by colonial violence. This violence was caused and has continued to be perpetrated for over 500 years by governments. Governments have played a huge role in the accumulation and continuation of this historical trauma (Brave Heart & DeBruyn, 1998; Brave Heart, 2003, 2005). The manifestation of policies, interlocking systems, and academic and medical institutions, including the tainted histories of research, have all colluded to keep and maintain these very beneficial arrangements. The question is *beneficial to whom?*

It is important for readers to note that this chapter is only a sliver of our histories as MHPs. There are numerous instances, historical references, and personal accounts of how Western mental and behavioral health practices have let people down, and set people up. We could fill encyclopedias with accounts and stories of deep violence "in the name of science." Many of these stories depict practitioners as the sidekick or the person in history just doing what they were told to do, with the minimal tools offered. Though that may be true, that is also true of those who stood by and watched lynchings in West Virginia, or in the hot sun in Shreveport, Louisiana's cotton fields, or on the logwood camps in Belize. Not taking any action is a political message. This is OUR history too.

Throughout this book, I will continue to invite you into the history, the research, and the experiences of prior therapy participants in order to help us change through embodiment and humanizing.

As practitioners, many of us who proclaim out of the box thinking and practice still place participants of therapy into new boxes. Each time a therapy participant shows signs of resistance, or defensiveness, it would benefit us all to consider the history they shoulder—the memories (conscious or not) of the helpers harming and our history, as helpers having harmed.

I invite those of you with multiple privileged intersecting identities to consider diving deeper. Really allow yourself to feel those feelings. Allow yourself to swallow the bigness of the anger, shame, defensiveness, and incredulousness you may be feeling . . . allow it. Maybe befriend it, in order to become comfortable with what it's been and how we benefit from adhering to traditional psychotherapy methods. Answer the reflection prompts. Call another friend on this journey. Start a book club. Talk to faculty and staff about it. Listen more. Learn to sit without needing to know everything or fix a thing. I know, it is tough.

I invite those of you with multiple oppressive intersecting identities—who know all too well this struggle (personally and professionally)—to consider pulling back. To take this hour outside in some sunshine or on the grass, or to engage in a movement or breathing practice. Throw on some music and dance. Hold your child/nephew/niece/friend and appreciate them. *Take a break.* Maybe skip this chapter all together. This book is a call to action for MHPs, and if we have been the ones calling with no answer, then I implore you to tap out and take a rest.

Roots of Western Mental Health: A People's History

My Good People, this chapter was so difficult to write. For multiple reasons. There is so much I could say (and which I purposely omitted) related to the roots of Western mental health. I could include detailed histories, stories, and examples woven throughout all of our fields: psychiatry, social work, counseling, every branch of psychology, psychiatric advanced practice nurse, etc. But also because I allowed myself to feel and truly embody and synthesize what I have been reading, writing, and even teaching, I asked for support. I moved my body in ways that felt good, and pushed my comfort. I cried and released old experiences. I thought about my own experiences as an early-career practitioner, and above all, I thought of all of the people I had, in good faith, harmed while trying to help. As I mentioned above, this history is merely a synthesis of areas that in my experience as a practitioner, instructor, and participant have often been skimmed over and omitted.

Colonialism, manufactured and caused by settlers, has caused significant damage to the mental, emotional, physical, and spiritual health of both the colonized and the colonizers. In speaking, writing, and processing mental health from a decolonial perspective, it is important that we consider the deep intergenerational effects of colonization on people with significant histories of surviving war, displacement, forced migration, attempted genocide, and enslavement. Therefore, it makes sense that cultural and politicized approaches to *healing*, not just mental health, are essential to healing from the effects of colonization.

For the most part, people with colonized histories have been "diagnosed and treated" through a Western, individualistic, patriarchal, and oppressive lens. Western frameworks of social work, psychology, and psychiatry have medicalized and dehumanized the experiences of BIPOC, and (we) helping professionals have been slowly emotionally calcified—or worst—cut off and euthanized from our own emotions, and polished in an attempt to attain perfection and professionalism. But at what cost? MHPs have astronomical caseloads, impossible treatment plan deadlines, crises to manage, and no consistent processing place to hold it all (without paying a great deal for supervision, which in fact is nearly unaffordable to most early-career practitioners).

Rugged individualism, plans, and symptom checklists all conceptualize an ILLNESS over a PERSON. Much of our humanity, unique perspectives, cultures, ways of Knowing, and personalities are sanded down to apply rapid diagnoses, treatment plans, and termination sessions. All from a deeply medical framework. Western forms of psychotherapy and social work, although well-intentioned, have caused harm. These are a few examples of the ways that Western paradigms do not meet. As Renee Linklater (2020) has beautifully stated, "Indigenous healing philosophies are based on a wellness model, while the medical model is based on illness." Once again I point out, those operating in a colonial system of practicing therapy are holding collective global space for humanity's emotional health WHILE in the midst of evolution and revolution. This is huge. We need some maps.

This chapter is highlighting the need, and collective call to action to our field. We see this call to action and accountability globally to honor the ROOTS of our work, our healing. To simultaneously return and learn, and to integrate while we create and evolve.

Institutionalizing Resistance to Oppression

Modern treatments of mental and behavioral health are most associated with the establishment of hospitals and asylums beginning in the 16th century. Such institutions' missions were to house and confine those they deemed mentally ill, poor, homeless, unemployed, and criminal. Multiple drafts for world wars and great economic depression produced vast numbers of people in need. Individuals were in need of resources and support—food, shelter, medical supplies—but instead were criminalized, pathologized, separated from society, and sent to mental institutions.

Two of the most well-known institutions, St. Mary of Bethlehem in London, known as *Bedlam*, a term that today means "*a state of uproar and confusion,*" and the Hôpital général de Paris—which included La Salpêtrière, La Pitié, and La Bicêtre, which began housing individuals seen as "mentally ill" in the 17th and 18th centuries (Lumen Learning, 2022). As confinement laws focused on protecting the public *from* those struggling with mental health issues, governments became responsible for housing and feeding institutionalized people. Many hospitals and monasteries were converted into asylums. Initially, many scholars believe that the intent was benign; as asylums began to overflow with individuals needing deep care, the people came to be treated inhumanely.

Most people hospitalized were called "inmates" and many were institutionalized against their will. Accounts report individuals living in filth and chained to walls, and some patients were even commonly exhibited to the public for a fee. Mental illness was nonetheless viewed somatogenically, so treatments were similar to those for physical illnesses: purges, bleedings, and emetics, as noted above. As such, "instilling fear was believed to be the best way to restore a disordered mind to reason" (Walinga & Stangor, 2020).

Psychological Enslavement

As a very visceral example, well into the 21st century, Black women in the United States continue to grapple with medical racism and the systemic discrimination that births ongoing health disparities. We have seen how American gynecology was born, with its roots deep into systemic racism birthing massive health disparities for hundreds of years to come. Most notably, we witness the health disparities for Black mothers, where the maternal mortality rates are a staggering three and a half times higher than that of white mothers.

Historian and brilliant writer Deirdre Cooper Owens revealed and discovered the origins of medical racism, that was pioneered by white 19th-century medical men, and thus was deeply intertwined with the institution of slavery. Her brilliant and powerful book, *Medical Bondage: Race, Gender, and the Origins of American Gynecology* is a must-read for any medical and mental health professional. Modern gynecology advanced quite rapidly in the Deep South because the doctors, many of whom were slave owners, had access to Black bodies—particularly Black women's bodies—to experiment on, examine, and "cure" or "treat" diseases and disorders.

Legacies of slavery are intertwined with both histories and ongoing forms of medical racism. This includes early experimentation on communities of enslaved people and continues today in the form of scientific racism. This is evidenced from Tuskegee to race-based diagnostic models and race-based disparities in health care access. The experimentation on Black bodies has been documented throughout the globe. Archives document a British doctor's smallpox experiments on 850 enslaved people in 18th-century rural Jamaica (Owens, 2017).

Additionally, enslaved Black people across the globe held a great deal of knowledge that slavers and doctors desired. Bertrand Bajon, a French physician working in Cayenne envied the "numerous plant cures" known to "Indians and Negroes" (Schiebinger, 2017). Bajon demanded that "for the good of humanity" slaves be obliged to "communicate the plants he [or she] used and the manner in which they are employed." In return, Bajon recommended the enslaved person be offered freedom—but not until "a great number of experiments confirmed the cure's virtue." Once again, this level of exploitation and enslavement is also psychological. The people experimented upon and in shackles are those with the solution. Extortion, manipulation, and gaslighting continue to be part of the psychological violence of colonization, and knowledge created in this period was obtained in the name of the colonial conquest, and to increase power, privilege, and money.

Systematic racial divides in access to technologies, medicines, and critical health services perpetuate health inequalities to this day. It is crucial to ask: What is the legacy of medical racism and how does this discussion relate to the health and wellness of people from the diaspora and our relationship to trust and medical services today? How have legacies of slavery been reproduced in medicine in ways that are facilitating and recreating racial injustice? How have legacies of slavery created diagnostic categories, in the name of profit?

Wealth on the Backs of Black Folks

Much of the wealth of the United States was built on the labor of enslaved Africans. "In 1850, Congress passed the Fugitive Slave Act, which required police officers everywhere in the country to capture escaped slaves and return them to their owners" (Social History for Every Classroom [SHEC], n.d.). Although anyone who was caught helping escaped slaves could be arrested and face large fines, abolitionists resisted the law and continued to support the actions of enslaved people seeking freedom.

African Americans refused to conform to the racist, oppressive nature of the U.S. starting with protests during the Civil Rights Movement that had their anger and rage pathologized and diagnosed as mental illness. This shows how ableism and racism overlap AND how the legacy of racism in psychiatry continues today in the mental health industrial complex.

This atmosphere of fear was created by these heinous acts of psychological and physical violence. This violence resulted in psychological enslavement, to everyone involved in the institution of slavery globally. White people hold guilt, shame, and often an array of internalized white supremacy that impacts one's relationships, identity, and ancestry. There was and is a psychological and generational inheritance attached to the ancestral inheritances of white people, and it is often a heavy burden that becomes like a haunting. Like anything seeking our attention that scares us, it is essential to acknowledge, set boundaries, honor, and excavate the root of the shame. As we know, unexamined shame leads to the perpetuation of violence, as we have seen in the Civil Rights Era and beyond.

A 1968 article in the well-reputed medical journal *Archives of General Psychiatry* (as cited in Metzl, 2010), for example:

> ... described schizophrenia as a "protest psychosis" whereby Black men developed "hostile and aggressive feelings" and "delusional antiwhiteness" after listening to the words of Malcolm X, joining the Black Muslims, or aligning with groups that preached militant resistance to white society.

Race-based thinking and pathologization in psychiatry reformulated schizophrenia in the Civil Rights Era. What initially was seen as "a white woman's illness" quickly became a tool against Black men who were rightfully angry about the oppression and treatment they received. Schizophrenia became a racialized label in the U.S. during the Civil Rights Movement. For example, an advertisement from the makers of Haldol in 1974 show "an angry" African American man with his fist raised in the air and the caption "*Angry and Belligerent? Cooperation often begins with Haldol*" (Metzl, 2010). Today, as reported in the *Washington Post* in 2005, we continue to see bias and racism, although research has contended that schizophrenia has been shown to affect all ethnic groups equally:

> ... Scientists found that Blacks in the United States were more than four times as likely to be diagnosed with the disorder as whites. Hispanics were more than three times as likely to be diagnosed as whites. (Vedantam, 2005)

This "new version of schizophrenia," allowed for incarceration of Black men in prisons and psychiatric hospitals; any anger was attempted to be "diminished" with antipsychotic drugs. It formed a fresh new fear and social aversion toward Black men where freedom of Black people was in direct opposition to white safety and sanity. In this view, resistance could be easily dismissed by medical pathology.

We also see this historically, as enslaved Black people who weren't submissive enough were seen and identified (and classified) as mentally ill and institutionalized, or murdered quite publicly. Indigenous peoples, in what is now known as North America, who went against race-based laws (i.e., arguing with reservation officials/engaging in their spirituality/refusing to relinquish children/speaking their languages, etc.) were and are still categorized, institutionalized, and often incarcerated.

Once again, the medical and mental health fields have been used to torture, gaslight, and overmedicate—further feeding Big Pharma's pockets. Psychiatry has been founded on punishment in the same way our prison systems have been for decades. It was a method of control to ensure BIPOC and/or disabled, queer, mad, and other people were labeled insurgent groups, and their ideas were quelled.

It may be important to provide a specific example when discussing the experiences of insanity with those who have ancestries of enslavement.

Drapetomania and Scientific Racism

On March 17, 1851, at the annual meeting of the Louisiana Medical Association, Dr. Samuel Cartwright presented a committee report entitled, *A Report on the Diseases and Physical Peculiarities of the Negro Race*. It was filled with claims of "scientific racism," and the report also documented a new disease: **Drapetomania**.

Dr. Cartwright, a pro-slavery advocate, had just a year before, in December 1849, at the Louisiana State Medical Convention, been selected to chair a committee tasked with investigating and reporting on diseases "unique to Black people." In the report, Dr. Cartwright contended that Black people were "very different physiologically from white people, possessing smaller brains, more sensitive skin, and overdeveloped nervous systems." "These unique traits," he claimed, "gave Black people an especially high propensity for servitude" (1851). He cited "scientific" evidence and biblical scripture. Dr. Cartwright argued that "the Negro is a slave by nature and can never be happy . . . in any other condition."

It is important to note that Cartwright was making these claims in the mid-19th century. Dr. Cartwright wrote that "if a slave is simply treated kindly and protected from abuse that they will be spell-bound, and cannot run away." He was of the position that it was "natural for white men to be masters" and for "Black people to be in a state of submission" (1851). Such thinking is transparent throughout his work. He described how a planter/overseer must be kind and attend to physical wants—but at the same time not become too friendly—and to not treat one's slaves as equals either, for that would make them run away as well.

Dr. Cartwright invented the term Drapetomania, derived from the Greek words for "runaway slave" and "crazy," to describe a new "curable mental disease." He contended that when infected with this affliction, enslaved Black people were struck with an urge to flee bondage and seek freedom. He further explained that the disease was triggered by enslavers who unwisely treated enslaved people as their equals. Dr. Cartwright prescribed "treatment" such as severe whipping and amputation of the toes.

Upon reviewing Dr. Cartwright's texts and life history, his work resembled that of the Willie Lynch letters—whether fictional or not—the symbolism still haunting, and violently effective. Furthermore, particularly in the 1900s, his having been a scientist and doctor, afforded him more "credit." From these quotes, we can see the infantilization of Black people, enforcing an idea that "they couldn't possibly know what's best for them."

When describing **Dysaesthesia Aethiopica**, an alleged mental illness described by Dr. Cartwright in 1851, which proposed a "theory for the cause of laziness among enslaved Africans." He describes commonalities that he has noticed among free Black people, those on "badly governed plantations" and any person refusing to work for a white master.

Physical lesions: what he described as the outward symptom that will predispose one to the illness. He notes that this leads to the insensitivity of the skin, and no remorse or reaction to pain when being whipped. He then ascribes this as "part of the illness" when it's plain to see that the lesions of toughened and scarred skin are a result of being whipped, and not the cause. However, he argues that because enslaved Africans no longer feel the pain of being abused, they are more likely to not work or will perform their duties poorly.

Throughout his paper, he takes a stance that every behavior is both coming from a place of mischief and this is a disease that causes Black people to not want to work. So, which is it then? It doesn't make sense to propose that it is both an inherent moral failing that exists within a person and a curable disease. But perhaps this is what scientific racism is—tying morality and nature-based arguments to behaviors that come up in response to extreme abuse and dehumanization. It is also important to note that these examples of scientific racism continue to show up in the covert and overt relations, political protests, murders of civilians by police officers, and ideations of Black people today. Once again, the roots and expressions of colonization continue to impact Black people's safety, treatment, and emotional bandwidth today.

It is clear that Dr. Cartwright, among many others participating in this violence, bore what Kwame Anthony Appiah called a "cognitive incapacity" to view Blacks' aggressive demands for freedom as earnest. It is this incapacity that led Cartwright to misperceive Black vigilance as madness (Appiah, 1990). By creating the diagnoses he did (and defining symptoms and behaviors that fell under them) Cartwright could offer ways for other physicians and overseers to effectively contain Black rebellion. Although, Cartwright's medical diagnoses seem absurd or outdated to many MHPs today, when one breaks down his claims to their simplest terms one sees that the racial regime that led him to invent Drapetomania and Dysaesthesia Aethiopica are the same racial regimes that lead modern MHPs to diagnose defiance, hyperactivity, and attention deficit disorders among inmates, students, and Black laborers at higher rates globally.

Malnourished

Another intense example that highlights the term "we are fighting 400+ years of psychological enslavement" is exemplified with *horrific* techniques that doctors used to try and stop enslaved Africans from eating dirt, such as the use of tin masks chained to the floor and iron gags. This barbaric practice was so widespread (since eating dirt was, and is still, an ancestral practice of many peoples) that some plantation owners in West India would display the heads of slaves who had died from it in an attempt to degrade their bodies and discourage others.

Cartwright, however, saw dirt eating as a symptom not a cause, and he believed it was the onset of potentially rebellious behavior. He was called to court at least three times for his medical opinion on dirt eating, and he did believe that it was a "quasi-religious ritual of African origin." However, it was also a "disease of the mind because the ritual only came about from how Black people have poorly managed themselves." He felt that by being enslaved by white people, he thought it protective and benevolent, a way to sustain their mental health as these rituals were stripped away.

Once again colonization is apparent in the belief that African spiritual and religious rituals "need to be stripped away," and in the way that a medical professional's clear racism and bias permeates "treatment," and deeply affects Black people. It is also important to note that Cartwright is not just an example of "one bad man." Rather he is a small sample, a part of a larger whole of beliefs, actions, murders, torture, and dehumanization. These examples are not for "trauma shock value." On the contrary, these are carefully selected examples that unfortunately deeply personify the barbaric nature of scientific racism, colonization, and how trauma from our ancestry continues to permeate in our society and behaviors today. Additionally, Cartwright wrote about the Haitian Revolution—to him it was a "mass outbreak of mental disease"—erroneously stating that if a Black person was "effectively civilized and domesticated, they would be less susceptible to deviant behavior." He degrades what was a major change and freedom for a people as simply the result of illness. We can see that Cartwright doesn't even think it possible for Black people to want freedom nor does he understand the injustice of slavery (Cartwright, 1851).

Myers (2014), the author of *Drapetomania: Rebellion, Defiance, and Free Black Insanity in the Antebellum United States*, also noted portions of his own early career where he described in detail chasing young Black teens through the woods so that they could be brought back to the center where they were strip-searched, abused, kept in isolation, and forcibly medicated. The text notes that had the teens shown signs of any noncompliance or any resistance to the treatment, that they would remain in isolation, and be placed one-on-one with a staff member; while having their education dosages manipulated as the staff saw fit. Upon reading about his experiences working with absconding youths (we would call it going AWOL on residential units), I was struck by the familiarity and parallels between Memphis's treatment of runaway enslaved Africans in the past; Myers' account of that moment chasing teens on his first night at this job; and my own practicum, internship, and early-career psychology experiences. Too much harm under the name of "these are the rules and how to keep the youth, and the unit/hospital safe" (Myers, 2014). Once again, these are all clear parallels connecting our systems of beloved mental and behavioral health.

The Construct and Creation of Race

The construct of race was essentially created to justify slavery and prove Black people were subhuman. This had been "proven" through scientific racism (as explained above) to show the "real" differences in biology between people. Yet the true goal was to justify, normalize, and legalize the systematic dehumanization of enslaved Africans to prove "inherent inferiority."

As we jump ahead over the Atlantic to "The New World" in what was now quickly becoming colonized, the moment that Europeans landed on Turtle Island we begin to see how intertwined colonization is and was with the desire to make money. Making money required creating castes and classification systems. The concept of race as a superficial division of anatomically modern humans (*Homo sapiens*) has an extensive history in Europe and the Americas. The contemporary word *race* itself is modern; in the 16th to 19th centuries it was used in the sense of a nation or ethnic group. Race acquired its modern meaning in the field of physical anthropology through scientific racism starting in the 19th century.

With the rise of modern genetics, the concept of distinct human races in a biological sense has become obsolete. In 2019, the American Association of Biological Anthropologists stated: "The belief in 'races' as natural aspects of human biology and the structures of inequality (racism) that emerge from such beliefs are among the most damaging elements in the human experience both today and in the past."

"The biological concept of human races, as subspecies characterized primarily by physique, has a stormy history" (Bhopal, 2007). Johann Friedrich Blumenbach (1752–1840), the German anatomist and naturalist who established the "most influential of all racial classifications," invented this name in 1795, in the third edition of his seminal work, *De generis humani varietate nativa* (*On the Natural Variety of Mankind*). Blumenbach proclaimed that such people were only separated from other humans by opportunity. This contribution alone is notable.

Blumenbach's central question, one of great interest at the time and still occasionally discussed in science, was whether contemporary humans comprised one or more species (Bhopal, 2007). Plurality of human species (polygeny) was the popular view in the 18th century. However, Blumenbach emphasized the unity of humanity. He saw gradations among humans, but no distinct species or subspecies.

He had, however, developed a concept dividing mankind into five races in the revised 1795 edition of his *De generis humani varietate nativa* (*On the Natural Variety of Mankind*) (Blumenbach, 2022). Blumenbach's concept later gave rise to scientific racism ("Scientific racism," 2022). He did underline that humanity, as a whole, forms one single *species* and pointed out that the transition from one race to another is so gradual that the distinctions between the races presented by him are "very arbitrary."

The consensus after the Second World War—that race is a social construct with minor biological components—is now under academic scrutiny, as illustrated by three advances in biomedical science

I recall Ron Chisom, one of the cofounders of The People's Institute for Survival and Beyond (PISAB) sitting in the middle of a large circle of "professionals" asking us directly how we talk about race in our therapy, in our social work visits, in our classrooms (personal communication, 2011). I remember feeling a different weight on my shoulders, a sense that, upon entering a profession or field, I became PART of that history, part of the problem unless I was working toward a solution with others. The People's Institute taught me that. They taught me how to look at class status critically, earnestly, and honestly, and to understand that race was a construct. Race is hard to explain, never clearly seen, only a footprint to let you know he's been there. Racial oppression on POC is Bigfoot. PISAB really began to help my inclusion of analysis, as a person of color, and my responsibility as a mental health practitioner working with other POC.

What is Race? So what is racism? I recall trainers at PISAB speaking about how we have no "workable" definition . . . that we mix up manifestations, feelings, analysis, and experience. It is essential to have a *working definition* of racism in order to organize a movement to undo it, yet its elusiveness creates confusion. Racism is the glue that keeps this foot in place, connecting all systems. Every system was created by and for people who believed in white supremacy. So every system works on behalf of people who are white, and disadvantages POC. Every system is racist.

The People's Institute's definition of racism is one that was first identified and used by Dr. Maulana Karenga, Black historian and Kwanzaa creator:

RACE PREJUDICE + POWER = RACISM

That is the definition for racism that *Decolonizing Therapy* utilizes, as well. It is essential for people to understand that racism is a branch off of the roots of colonization. There are histories of origins of systemic classification of "races." In the 17th century scientific revolution, there was interest in understanding and classifying all organisms; therefore in the 18th century, Carolus Linnaeus, a Swedish botanist created a system of taxonomy, which was a classification of organisms. Johann Friedrich Blumenbach, German physician and the "father of modern anthropology," published a system of human races correlating skin color/skull size/shape, and noting "white" as "superior" with skull size and shape. Two of the predominant skull sizes and "races" were "Caucasoid" for the largest skull size and later Caucasian race to denote people of the Caucasus Mountains region and Negroid to denote the "Black race." As I recall People's Institute trainers noting, African, called by color, not by place/history, further removed *Negro* from the family of humankind. I recall being deeply touched and affected listening to another Black person discuss this. It felt powerful and freeing.

It is important to note that Blumenbach attributed differences between these human types—such as variations in stature and color—largely to climate. He noted that many plants and animals in northern latitudes are white, especially in winter, and also that humans are all born red. He also stated that "Color . . . cannot constitute a species or a variety" (Bhopal, 2007). He attributed the shape of the skull to environmental factors, an observation that threatened the foundations of craniology but was not properly heeded by craniologists (and possibly by himself). He identified the important role that culture plays in changing the body. Nevertheless, much of his findings became the basis for the classification systems of race, and structured the bones of white-bodied supremacy. Categories are essential and a tool for colonialism, because distinctly divided groups are ideal to control and separate.

Plantations, Policing, and Asylums

Myers (2014) notes that in the 1840s, individuals seen as "good Samaritans" focused on prison and asylum reform had a great effect on Southerners' interest in regulating plantation labor, in particular the management and treatment of enslaved peoples. As a result, Cartwright wrote that slaveholders should take an empathetic approach toward Black folks, especially toward slaves who were newly purchased at the auctions where they first interacted. Whether in the Northern state prisons and asylums or the Southern state plantations, Black was synonymous with "the deviant, the criminal, and the poor" (Myers, 2014).

Europeans started traveling to America to assess and learn about the nation's recent expansion in state-run penitentiaries, new asylums, and the burgeoning Southern plantations to learn about managing deviant populations (Myers, 2014). In 1831, the French sent Alexis de Tocqueville and Gustave de Beaumont to America. Tocqueville made notes on asylums, prisons, and the labor regime of plantations. Myers (2014) noted that mental specialists at the time thought insanity was a part of the process of civilization and that many mental specialists believed that Africans, an allegedly "uncivilized people," were exempt from experiencing madness. It was a common belief that insanity was an effect of civilization, since in the white American and European view, Indigenous and Black people did not come from civilized societies. Contemporaries speculated "either that [Black people's] physiology differed from whites' or that slavery somehow shielded [Black people] from the worries of civilization" (p. 322).

Dr. Sanford Challaie, an official of the insane asylum at Jackson, Louisiana, announced that enslaved people did not "lose their minds" because the laws about slavery provided them protections from making decisions about their present and future desires (Myers, 2014). It was this mindset that led to a salient shift in asylum reform, most specifically the belief that slavery *protected* [Black people] from becoming insane. This belief, sadly, continued to support the stipulation that Black and Indigenous people did not deserve, nor need, mental health care.

The Pathology of Moral Treatment

Moral treatment, as a psychological medicine of the time, implies that society holds a moral obligation for the improvement of people who are not otherwise morally responsible for their acts, nor capable of improving on their own (Myers, 2014, p. 325). Treatment within asylums focuses on reintegrating a citizen back into the community or isolating and holding someone who contaminates the meaning of citizenship. Therefore, Cartwright saw some of his work as finding ways for enslaved people to take up their positions in society as well-cared for and productive laborers.

Philippe Pinel (founder of moral treatment) utilized nonviolent treatment in his moral therapy, while other practitioners, like John Conolly, did not use restraint or violence at the Hanwell Lunatic Asylum (Myers, 2014). Both practiced moral treatment as a foundation (which suggests kind treatment of patients reaps more results). Conolly advocated for isolation and sedation over restraints.

Upon reading about the treatment of enslaved people in asylums, I am reminded of my time working as a mental health specialist in a partial care hospitalization program for severely abused and traumatized children and adolescents. I also had spent time as a doctoral intern in a residential treatment center working with adolescents who had been accused of severely sexually harming other children. I am reminded of the multiple ways in which our treatments and interventions mirrored the carceral system, in that we were immediately trained on nonviolent crisis intervention. However, the "therapeutic hold" often felt violent to the youth being placed in the hold, to the other youth witnessing the hold, and often (even if hours later) to the staff providing the hold. I am also reminded of the ways that children's and adolescents' snacks (food source) were threatened and or removed as a consequence of not meeting the daily points of the behavioral chart. They were also consequenced with a loss of a fun activity, the loss of a family visit, or threatened with behaving—"or else you will get sent upstate"—upstate meaning a more secure detention center for adolescents who had committed a crime. These examples and more are reflective current day examples that are remnants from lunatic asylums and the prison industrial complex. American physicians also adopted moral treatment, especially from the influence of Benjamin Rush, but would still use more violent measures when they determined it would ensure proper patient behavior. Historical research contends that patients who continued to self-injure, engage in defiant or sexualized behaviors, such as feces smearing or masturbating, were often physically assaulted in the name of restraint and modeling "good patient behavior" (Myers, 2014). The consequence often included torturous devices such as straitjackets, electrocution, and flagellation. Myers (2014) describes moral treatment as advocating that any patients who exhibit good behavior and maintain healthy relationships with staff will become participating members of society.

Myers (2014, p. 331) noted in his article that there are four similarities between the themes of the plantation and asylum management. These tenets are crucial to understanding the emotional–decolonial process, and why we must start to politicize our mental health practices today. These four tenets continue to show up and are perpetrated today. Perhaps in 2050 our grandchildren will look back and be appalled at the treatment, classism, racism, ableism, sexism, homophobia, archaic practices, and rigidity of our own Mental Health Systems today. These tenets are:

1. The mandate that recalcitrant or disruptive persons must be separated from their original locations and families and then settled into a neutral, highly controlled environment.
2. The belief that ordered agrarian or manual labor was therapeutic.
3. The belief that absolute authority and dominion of the master or physician was necessary to revitalize the enslaved person or patient combined with the principle of reeducating the patient or enslaved person by means of coercion.
4. The belief that new environmental influences produced new associations, generated new ideas, and shifted the patient's or enslaved person's self-perception.

How do these barbaric and archaic behaviors, policies, and beliefs show up in our therapy today? In our social work? In our educational system? Myers (2014) provides the following examples:

- It was seen as therapeutic to remove [Black people] from the "indolence and torpidity" of Africa (p. 333).
- It was better to remove newborn babies from Black mothers (p. 333).
- White women intervening is what was responsible for the health of Black enslaved people's children, for if they were left with the mother they would die (p. 333).
- "Ordered labor was a critical form of the subtle exercise of power in both moral treatment and with plantation slavery" (p. 336).
- In both plantations and asylums, captives are allowed to have "musical celebrations . . . folk dances, traditional instruments, and sometimes special costumes" (p. 336).
- There should be "limited agency in the allowance of amusement" (p. 336).
- People were kept busy with tasks and labor regardless of how small or repetitive they were (p. 342).
- Repetitive labor and hobbies were encouraged; in fact, the more someone did the same task, the less they would have to be supervised (p. 336).
- "Managing others through the influence of a strong and overpowering personality remained a theme in . . . the physician's ability to exert moral

> influence onto a patient . . . a belief first held by practitioners of moral treatment" (p. 345).
> - In asylums, we see how patients are also treated like children/family members of the asylum superintendent through the use of the words, "Father" and "Mistress" used to refer to superintendents and their wives, to bring the "home" into the institution. Enslaved Africans were sometimes encouraged to call their master "Father," creating gaslighting and emotional violence. This family structure method was a part of moral treatment in asylums, often referring to the institution as "our family" (Bockoven, 1963, as cited in Myers, 2014, p. 349).

Myers provides examples of how absolute power is used in the patient–provider relationship; he notes:

- By presenting oneself as the authority, confident in your treatment method, self, and system, the patient will submit to your authority in the same way a terrified animal would.
- Firm eye contact is used as an example in the animal–patient metaphor.
- The power that both physicians and keepers have; has to be seen as absolute (unquestionable, all-knowing, etc.).

As a result, Rush and Cartwright's work resulted in American asylum superintendents incorporating absolute dominion, terror, shame, force, and physical compulsion among their range of treatment techniques. Physical discipline was an attempt to create shame, fear, and to distract the enslaved African away from their own needs and desires, and instead toward the needs and desires of the "master." Each master had their own techniques for achieving and executing these principles just like each doctor or superintendent might have their own ways of implementing their treatments.

We have seen throughout this chapter how Cartwright, and many others, have implemented forms of scientific racism and moral treatment in his advice for the management of enslaved people because he believed that white men were superior morally—in the same way asylum/prison workers believed themselves morally superior to the "deviants being rehabilitated." However, many asylum workers were determined to not use the same terminology as prisons because they appropriately surmised that hospitals should not utilize such words as "cell" or "warden." This is deeply ironic, as a great deal of the systems that are working today continue to have "many keepers within the walls."

The *Washington Post* had an article (Ruane, 2019) that synthesized how scientific racism had lingering effects, and the ways in which it permeated white supremacy, and therefore shaped how racism shows up today. This article describes how this line of thinking persisted throughout the 18th and 19th centuries and lasts even still today. However, the way it presents has since shifted. We do not see the same overt forms of racism in science, but the legacy of scientific racism has permeated much of the ways our culture is anti-Black and racist. "What Black inferiority meant has changed in every generation . . . but ultimately Americans have been making the same case," said historian, Ibram X. Kendi (as quoted in Ruane, 2019). Ruane (2019) writes that in the time of scientific racism, "Here, enslaved people were beneath even the human desire for freedom. They had to be diseased." There are deep roots in the level of overt and covert racism in our histories, and this continues to manifest itself today.

Who Is Your Master?

Once again I inquire, who is and has the mental health system been working for? Who have we been working for? What does our history show us?

The history of the counselor, clinician, therapist, social worker, psychologist, psychiatric nurse, and psychiatrist is VIOLENT. Separating families. Assisting at interrogations and torture. Drugging the youth and our older adults to "keep them quiet." It may be relevant for us to know the roots of the term *psychiatrist*, as I think words hold power. Alienist may sound like it should mean "someone who studies aliens." It turns out *alienist* and *alien* are related terms, both derived from the Latin word *alius*, meaning "other."

In Latin, *alius* (other) led to the French adjective *aliéné* (insane) led to *médecin aliéniste* (a doctor who treats the insane). This then led, in the 19th century, to where *alienist* shows up in English to refer to psychiatrists at the time (Merriam-Webster, n.d.). *Alienist* is much rarer than *psychiatrist* these days, but at one time it was the preferred term. I find it fascinating that even the etymology of a once-preferred term for *psychiatrist* shows how we have viewed those who disrupt the social norms. That they are the *other* to be feared. As People's Institute (PISAB) trainer and facilitator, Dr. Kimberley Richards would often state, "Sticks and stones can break your bones, but words will shape your reality." Words and language around how we speak about people and our dis-eases have power.

I strongly advise that after reading this chapter that you allow yourself to feel emotion. Engaging in breathing exercises; journal writing; sharing only with a willing person who has a similar analysis and is undergoing or has gone through serious shifts in their racial, political, and colonial identities.

If you are a descendant of Africa: If you were with me throughout this chapter, I ask you to please, find what feels good. Find release. Health-grounded, safe relief. Take a salt bath, listen to music, and sweat it out moving your body in ways that feels good. Wrap yourself up with a big blanket and watch cartoons or anime, or eat some nourishing food that reminds you of childhood joy. Take a walk. Drink lots of water. Connect with your group/class/affinity spaces. Phone a conscious friend. Use sacred medicines of your culture and belief systems to clear energy in your home, body, psyche, etc. Ask for a hug. Play with a pet. Go outside and ground yourself in grass, or water, or rain. TAKE CARE OF YOU. I most definitely had to regroup, and emote, nourish, and move every few hours after writing these chapters. I promise you the next few chapters will get a little clearer and lighter. So glad we are in this together.

If you identify as POC, non-Black: I would advise a mixture of both, ensuring you are not saying, "Well, my People went through. . ." This is not the Oppression Olympics, and that is a tenet of anti-Black racism. Allow yourself to feel the confusion, the sadness, the understanding that anti-Black scientific racism and pathologizing continues to play out in every country across the globe. Period. It is so real and necessary to grieve, to feel, to be sad, angry, guilty, resentful, and unclear. BE WITH IT.

If you are white: Do not just intellectualize this material, allow yourself to feel it. Does your body feel heavy? Are you feeling irritable? Are you needing to release emotion? What are the big feelings arising? Can you be WITH these emotions, and move? Your body, your practices (not immediately of course)? Can you allow yourself to see the blatant projections, perversity, and pathology in this treatment? It was dehumanizing... to everyone, including white people. But, it has been physically and deeply emotionally violent to Black people and their ancestry. Ask yourself—what do I need? Ask yourself how I can stay with this a tad longer instead of immediately rushing to clear and move it.

Aspects of Emotional–Decolonial Unlearning

1. The vast majority of people with colonized histories have been "diagnosed and treated" through a Western, individualistic, patriarchal, and oppressive lens. This further perpetuates harm.
2. Colonialism, manufactured and caused by settlers, has caused significant damage to the mental, emotional, physical, and spiritual health of both the colonized and the colonizers.
3. Colonization has had deep intergenerational effects on people with significant histories of surviving war, displacement, forced migration, attempted genocide, and enslavement.
4. Cultural and politicized approaches to healing, not just mental health, are essential to healing from the effects of colonization.
5. Historically, treatment consisted of instilling fear in order to restore a disordered mind to reason (Farreras, 2013). How may this continue today?
6. Race was created to divide and conquer.
7. Race is a specious classification system that structured and supported the bones of white-bodied supremacy.
8. Categories are an essential tool for colonialism because distinctly divided groups are ideal to control and separate. This continues today.
9. Racism and ableism overlap and work together to perpetuate and fund the mental health industrial complex.
10. Violent terms, such as Drapetomania and Dysaesthesia Aethiopica, alleged mental illnesses, which proposed theories for the insanity and causes of laziness among enslaved Africans. Ironic, as labor is

all that enslaved Africans engaged in. This can be seen today, packaged in behavioral diagnoses, such as oppositional defiant disorder, conduct disorder, and intermittent explosive disorder, all of which are diagnosed significantly more in Black children living in poverty.
11. Western frameworks of social work, psychology, and psychiatry have medicalized and dehumanized the experiences of BIPOC.
12. As helping practitioners, we have been slowly, historically, and methodically taught how to remove ourselves from our own emotions. This is harmful to us, our personal relationships, and our emotional health.
13. Practitioners have been deeply harmed by Western Eurocentric frameworks of the mental health system and there is little regard for practitioners' mental and emotional health.
14. Psychiatry has been founded on punishment—in the same way, our prison systems have been for decades. The criminal justice system colludes with and informs the mental health systems.
15. Psychological enslavement still occurs today, in multiple insidious, covert, and overt ways.
16. The legacy of scientific racism has deeply impacted the lives, and future generations, of Black people globally.
17. Scientific racism permeated much of the ways our culture is anti-Black and racist.
18. Many asylums and forms of psychological and psychiatric practice were born violently on the backs of the survivors of the Transatlantic Slave Trade.

Emo–Decolonial Practice Offerings

- Notice where attachment concerns in therapy participants begin to arise. Be present to the possibility of attachment styles having a relationship and a disconnect stemming from counties and lands of origin, including the effects of settler colonization on Indigenous lands across the globe.
- Get curious about Eurocentric arbitrary rules that encourage conformity, individualism, and not getting critical of possible alternatives to dominant practices. For example, why can't someone work with two separate ther-

apists? Why can't individuals in group work/treatment have relationships outside of the group? Why can't healthy boundary-filled relationships occur between practitioners and participants prior to a 2- to 3-year period post-termination?
- Consistently ask "Who regulates your therapeutic healing relationships, and why?"
- Consider multiple forms of processing emotion and communication that your therapy participant may require. For instance, this may look like engaging in simple physical activities while talking; art; play; role-playing; peer support; journaling; sharing/writing letters or notes back and forth; the use of music and metaphor; the use of animals, or even memes!
- Honor, consider, and invite multiple forms of wellness. Individuals have various needs, ideas, and cultural norms that lead to safety.
- Session limits are arbitrary and can be fluid. Time is a colonial construct. For instance: Maybe a "session" need not be 55–60 minutes once a week. Maybe 20 minutes three times a week, or 60 minutes twice a week is needed.
- Inquire daily about how colonial practices, education, and socialization have impacted the way you engage and "do therapy."
- Challenge the pathologizing of behavior. For example, if you work with children, prior to a diagnosis of ODD, is there a better way to conceptualize and understand what the "acting out behavior" is covering?
- How can we honor science, while honoring the felt sense, experience, intuition, and support sovereignty in therapeutic relationships?
- How did the barbaric and racist treatment of enslaved Africans in the South impact Black Americans and Black-identified people globally, today? How might this show up in your therapeutic containers?

Affirmations for Reclaiming Equitable Healing
- We are not crazy; we have been systematically colonized.
- We can slowly unlearn colonial ways.
- I am proud of myself for creating new paths and stories.
- I am allowed to be angry with a profession I once loved.
- I am allowed to grieve my work as a _____.

- I am allowed to be angry with a profession I still love.
- My needs and emotions are allowed to change.
- I am allowed to humanize myself and my needs as a practitioner.
- I am allowed to love my calling, and rebel against the profession.
- I grieve and take responsibility for the violence my field has engaged in.
- I allow myself space to honor that I am working for a system that has historically harmed my ancestors.
- I am worthy of receiving and providing therapeutic care that honors my practices.
- I am willing to unlearn what harms me.
- It is healthy to do things differently.
- I can choose to see emotional experiences differently.
- It is safe for myself and others to express our suffering in big ways.
- I am allowed to grieve what I have lost, anyway I like.
- It is safe to come out about my religious/spiritual practices and beliefs.
- My feelings are complicated. That is valid and deserves space.

CHAPTER 4

Diagnostic Enslavement

Renaming is a critical part of resistance. It is a reclaiming of vision and the power to name.
— Bonnie Burstow, *Radical Feminist Therapy: Working in the Context of Violence* (1992, p. 247)

Dehumanization, which marks not only those whose humanity has been stolen, but also (in a different way) those who have stolen it, is a distortion of the vocation of becoming more fully human.
— Paulo Freire, *Pedagogy of the Oppressed* (1968/2018)

——— **AUTHOR CARE NOTE** ———

As a person deeply impacted by my ancestors' experiences of enslavement, land displacement, and trauma, I kindly ask all people of the African diaspora to engage in extreme self-care while reading this chapter. Consider even skipping this section. As the author, and as someone of the African diaspora, this chapter in particular raised the most somatic grief and exhaustion in my body. As if I was reexperiencing (just for hours, mind you) the level of hopelessness and exhaustion that the people I was writing about, may have experienced—even a small fraction of these feelings. I found myself feeling a deep sense of grief.

I advise you to:

- Skip the section.
- If you will read it: Read while in nature (at the beach, under a tree, with a loved one, in a collective, with support).
- Have a somatic or therapeutic or healing session after reading.
- Create a white bath for yourself post-reading.
- Read with reverence and closing your energy to any of the intensity of the text you may experience while reading it.

Once again, many of us intellectually KNOW this information, but often hearing and reading it with emotion and couched within a system (Mental Health) that is supposed to support and heal, not hurt, is more damaging and violent. Allow yourself and your body to process.

It is important for longtime practitioners to unlearn and reexamine the ways they were trained, and for those new to therapeutic practices and with fresh eyes on the fields, to have the tools to interrogate their learning spaces and the emotional bandwidth to push for new ways to help. This chapter asks some key questions; many of which I, as author, do not have the answers to. Nor should I. Rather, these questions are provided as a place from which each of us would benefit from interrogating: individually, collectively, politically, and historically.

The Roots of Diagnosis

By now, I imagine that we are clear that colonialism, manufactured and caused by settlers, has caused significant damage to the mental, emotional, physical, and spiritual health of both the colonized and the colonizers.

In speaking about, writing about, and processing mental health from a decolonial perspective, it is important that we consider the deep intergenerational effects of colonization on people with significant histories of surviving war, displacement, forced migration, attempted genocide, and enslavement. Therefore, it makes sense that cultural and politicized approaches to *healing* are an important part of mental health. They are essential to breaking the emotional, structural, and psychological effects of colonization.

The emo–decolonial framework posits that historical emotional injury impacts our choices, thinking, and behavior in the present and presents itself as mental "disorders" that requires a categorization of a diagnosis. Although there can be impactful important parts of diagnosis for an individual feeling alone and confused, there are also many harmful aspects of diagnosis and the diagnostic statistical framework as well. This process fans the flames of pathology and feeds capitalism. It is also incredibly white. Labels, categories, symptom checklists—there is nothing truly *personal* about it. Where are the nuances . . . the contexts, the cultural considerations, the language gap/differences? Where is the space to consider the possibilities and options?

The mental health industrial complex (MHIC) continues to present obstacle after obstacle, utilizing an outdated system of wellness that is void of wellness. Barriers exist from extensive hospital wait lists for counseling, to providing detailed histories to providers (when an appointment is provided), to private group practices that require the motivation to continue follow-up calls and the know-how to advocate for oneself. Most providers are too overwhelmed with notes, sessions, meetings, and vicarious trauma—creating a cycle of exhaustion. Even the most skilled social worker spends hours seeking out accessible services for people struggling to survive, let alone receive access services that are useful and aligned with their values, identities, and belief systems.

I know, I know—any of us who have served in an institution, nonprofit or hospital will be shouting aloud, "With what time Dr. Jenn?! Sure, how, when I barely have time for a health bar at my desk in between clients or a cafeteria sandwich for lunch—never mind read this book!"

My response will be a compassionate nod and grimace. Yeah.

We can do what we have always done and get what we've always gotten.

Or, we can cause an evolution of sorts in our fields.

This evolution in our fields will lead to the cocreation of new pathways in how we support.

New ways of supporting, inclusive of practitioners and participants, creates more equity and accessibility to support care services and health.

More accessibility, equity, increases in support care, and health = a natural remembrance, revival of ancestral ways of practicing, supporting, and tending.

An increase in ancestral ways of tending to emotional health = honoring and referencing the ancestral roots, while establishing sturdy, futuristic ways of being in relationship to our emotional health and one another.

This does not necessarily look like spending 3.5 hours with each new person we encounter, BUT this may lead to drastically changing "Intake Forms." (Can we rename them too while we are at it?) Maybe we can note participants' strengths first? Maybe we can note when they had felt this way before and who they called for support. Maybe we can note if they felt this way PRIOR to being forced to leave their countries, forced to leave their families, or after losing their jobs. Maybe we can offer them a snack and munch on our snack bars together. Maybe we can be human. Maybe if their leg is shaking nonstop and they're looking around quite frantically, we can engage differently—stop writing, offer water, ask if they would like to listen to some music, practice a self-soothing action, walk around the building, color, talk about the Superbowl or manicures, or 90's hip-hop, or WWII. Maybe we could really practice humanization, since so much about living with emotional and mental imbalances are dehumanizing, embarrassing, and painful for so many people.

We Are Part of the Solution and the Problem

We have been taught to medicalize and treat symptoms. I like to call them expressions,[14] as opposed to symptoms. We have been taught to treat, poke, observe, and assess. It is what we are good at. Shoot, I have to consciously UNDO this aspect of my training on my personality.

Unconsciously, we victim-blame, by focusing on personal deficiencies and lack. We measure "normality" against a heteronormative, white, able-bodied, slim-bodied, binary focused, light-to-white skinned, attractive, articulate, and wealthy avatar of a human.

---

14 I prefer to shift the language to expression(s), rather than "symptoms" of an issue. The word "symptoms" denotes a disease or illness. Rather, in decolonial spaces we are also seeking to embody a more humane and natural way of speaking about perfectly normal and understandable expressions of suffering, pain, or unwellness.

Healthy = "balanced mind"
Healthy = "intelligent"
Healthy = "self-awareness"
Healthy = "you have resources to accept my support"
Healthy = "you are consistent with your treatment"

You see, My Good People, the Systems are working exactly as they were intended to keep us separate. When a society is not equipped to hold up an accurate mirror to us, we end up interpreting our reflection according to what's available. Even if the terminologies and labels do not quite fit us.

This is an invitation, for those of us in privileged positions within institutions, hospitalization programs, juvenile detention centers, nonprofits, private practices, group practices, school systems, and residentials, to take a long hard look at how we are DEEPLY COMPLICIT (on even the most basic level) with systemic oppression and how we benefit from it. We police each other. We use LANGUAGE THAT POLICES.

We have been conditioned to believe that inclusive holistic language is offensive language. This is reinforced by rewarding the use of restrictive and medical language. Keeping poor people on a hamster wheel.

But these "symptoms" are often limiting, misleading, and violent. The language—the tongue in which we've been trained to speak—is inherently debilitating, violent, and elitist.

SYMPTOMS
DEFIANT
DEFENSIVE
TREATMENT
TRAUMA
OPPOSITIONAL
TERMINATION
NEEDS ASSESSMENT
NONCOMPLIANT
COMBATIVE
EMERGENCY HOUSING (shelter is not housing)

DIFFICULT CASE (creates false narrative before meeting a client)
HIGHER LEVEL OF CARE
ETHICALLY
EVIDENCE-BASED (synonymous with best "treatment")
QUIET ROOM

Question
Can you find synonyms for these words? Words that can nurture wellness and healing in the therapeutic relationship, as we begin to detangle what mental health has become?

Yolo Akili created a post in June 2022, where he noted: **"I am going to stop using 'marginalized communities' and instead say 'intentionally exploited communities.'"** This post reminded me of the 18+ years where I was forced to utilize harmful terminology such as "disadvantaged or marginalized communities" or "at-risk youth" for grant money in order to continue to receive funding for amazing programming around mental health and intergenerational trauma. Here are some of language reframes to actively shift away from the violence of the phrase "marginalized communities":

- Historically and systematically excluded communities
- Communities targeted for marginalization
- Communities recovering from systematic oppression
- Purposely ignored communities
- Intentionally impoverished as punishment
- Intentionally made vulnerable communities
- Community disinvestment
- Lastly: instead of "food desert" → food apartheid

At the end of the day, the mental health industrial complexes continue to play us all. It is time to wriggle out from under the boot of oppression and climb up the statues of colonial colonizers. Scream at the top of our lungs (PISAB via Undoing Racism workshop, personal communication, 2011)! Because when we are hurting . . . we are angry that we didn't know better. We are frustrated because we are meant to do "good" in the world. We did not sign up for this, yet here we are.

So shall we . . . dig into the past a tad of our beloved professions?

> **GROUNDING REFLECTION QUESTIONS**
>
> (or a pre-survey; I know how much we love a pre-survey in our field):
>
> - How do I feel about the mental health system/industry?
> - What did I believe I was "signing up" for or studying to do/provide?
> - What am I currently providing/giving/doing? How am I servicing others?
> - How does this make me feel?
> - How are mental health providers treated within the mental health system?
> - Does oppression exist within this system?
> - Who is not serviced, excluded, dismissed within this system?
> - Who do I oppress, or exclude, within this system?
> - What do I want to do/provide?
> - What are my feelings about diagnosis and the *DSM*?
> - What are my feelings about medication?
> - What are my feelings about community mental health?
> - How do I feel right now, after responding to these questions?

Understandably, many practitioners and care providers may feel compelled to skip to the "good part." Perhaps that is the chapter on the Grief-Rage Axis for you; for others it may be the chapter on *Energetic Boundaries*, or *Intergenerational Trauma Transmission*. For others it will be the end. "Let's get to the part where you tell me, and show me, how to be a good therapist!"

My response would be to lovingly and compassionately smile and say, "But the bones of a business are always the good part." That is where the work is. As the quote suggests, "We heal the root, so the tree is stable." Or as I have often said in therapy sessions, "How long shall we keep placing Band-Aids on a pustulant and infected wound?" Yes, let's bring healing and well-being work to the forefront in the mental health system. First and foremost, allow us to ask the people most deeply affected by systemic and global oppressions what their needs are, and does this resonate?! If it does resonate, allow us to allow those most impacted to receive the fruits of its labor *first*.

I am tired of our poor, Black, Brown, and queer communities being the "lab rats." I am tired of having most internships and practicum sites starting in the "hood." I am tired of the trial and error energy of our emotional and behavioral health fields trying out new practices and programs, yet never stopping to investigate the root of the dis-ease. Never stopping or having enough time to inquire "Why are so many poor Black and Brown people living in big cities, massively 'diagnosed,' exhausted, dealing with various addictions, and feeling deeply unwell?" Now for many of you reading this, with an analysis, this is obvious. Systemic inequities. But there is something almost clinical and cold about saying that. It cuts off humanity at the knees. Many people are dying emotionally and physically because of the ways that mental and behavioral health professionals are conveniently "just focused on doing my job." But I ask, "What exactly IS our job?" "What did we desire to help with?" "Are we helping?" "Who are we helping?" Sometimes I do wonder if we are helping our egos—ourselves—or are we helping those most deeply impacted?

When we talk about and interrogate the mental health industrial complex, we are making the historical political. We are making the political, personal. We are making the personal part of the process. Perhaps, that has been part of the "problem" with how we have been educated and trained to follow the rules, stay in line, obtain many certifications (i.e., ABPP, LCSW, PhD, LPC, MFT, PsyD, LSW, MSW, etc.). The way that this mental health system works is much like the prison industrial complex, the transportation system, the school-to-prison-nexus (pipeline), and the medical industrial complex, and so on (more on these systems and the MHIC in Chapter 4). Our systems interlock. Collude. Benefit from one another. Benefit from keeping therapists and social workers, and so forth *trained and in their lane*. The cold part is that many of us do not realize this until we are in the midst of a professional decision—making a huge decision between our integrity and intuition; and our allegiance to the system that feeds us.

The Violence of Diagnosis

I worked on a partial care unit for children and adolescents for 3 years at a prominent hospital, while obtaining my master's on the weekend in the city. I loved it . . . eventually. Initially, I had such a deep visceral reaction my first month on the unit. My first few months might even be identified as traumatic. The crisis was intense; the level of violence in the stories of the youth I held space for was unbelievable. Sometimes the youth were not even aware or able to recall their trauma histories. At times, I felt grateful for the brain's mechanism to protect and dissociate.

At 23 years old, I loved working on a team making decisions together, arguing various points of view. We had relationships with the crisis staff, transportation staff (super important things always happened in that van), psychiatrists, clinical social workers, psychologists, colleagues who were mental health specialists like me—who I just simply admired. I remember my supervisor saying I was a sponge. I drank it all up. This included the traumatic material as well.

After my nervous system simmered or I began to become numb to the level of intensity, the drama, and trauma; I started to feel jaded and a bit frustrated with the whole system, not just our unit. Even the word "unit" made me think of both the police station, and a hospital (granted we were in a hospital), but I wondered (in my novice mind) *"How do kids feel about coming to the hospital for support with their emotions?"* Their classmates back at school knew they left class early, got into a hospital van, and knew they "acted out in class." There had to be a better way. We were helping them; why did it feel like they were being punished for what had happened and was happening to them?

As conscious as we could be . . . as connected to the surrounding community and inviting to the "hood" as we could be for a hospital unit, still Black and Brown youth were primarily diagnosed with behavioral disorders—diagnoses that followed them . . . for a long time. Still, lighter-skinned kids would be believed a tad more, heard a tad more, and definitely complimented on the instances of "good" behavior more. Still, staff who would have days of "I just can't do this today," or "I can't work with this child anymore; it's too much . . ." were seen (unsaid of course) as "not as strong" and would not be promoted as often. Still darker-skinned kids were generally receiving diagnoses of conduct disorder and oppositional defiant disorder.

I remember coleading the latency-aged group, welcoming them at the door with music and smiles as they came in from school. Of course, they were generally deeply upset to be here, yet they felt safe enough to express their emotions with us. One youth, who I secretly adored because he was so honest, bold, and rightfully angry shoved the door hard, and it slammed against the wall causing a big bang. Many of the youth jumped. Some began crying. Some ducked behind the table. Two grabbed my hands, another my colead's waist. One youth ran to the corner and hid; another attempted to lock themselves in the bathroom. Meanwhile another attempted to run away out of the room. Two other youth began cursing at the youth who slammed the door shouting, "Are you dumb!? Why would you do that? You are gonna hurt somebody! You could've hurt Ms. Jenn's hand! You have a serious problem!"

We helped deescalate the situation, and process the situation. We had the space to ensure the youth did not have "his points lowered." But I thought to myself—this is it . . . this is trauma personified. Some of us fight; some of us flee. Some of us freeze. Some of us have no choice but to hold space despite our reactions. Some of us hold onto what feels most safe in the room or the world. Some of us are just in our feelings, not thinking about how our actions might impact countless others. I kept saying to myself that the level of rage and deep grief that the youth are displaying in spaces where they feel least in control and least seen, must be deeper than what they've experienced. Don't get me wrong, what many people experience is DEEP ENOUGH and we are allowed REACTIONS UPON REACTIONS. However, the deep-rooted sadness, the weariness, the despair, the heaviness—sometimes I would look into an 8-year-old child's eyes and see elders. I could feel the messaging and voice of their ancestors, "Well, I guess it's always gonna be that way." Or "Well, that's how it's always been done, Ms. Jenn." So weary.

Then we would begin to hear from the family members or caregivers, and would receive similar messaging. I always found myself focused on what was NOT being said, not just the "storyline." I would hear a feeling of legit struggle for freedom, whether or not the person realized it themselves. Freedom from the systems, from the scrutiny, from the intergenerational pain, from medication (self-administered or prescribed), and from the constant labor. Emotional and physical labor. The labor it takes as a POC to just survive in a wealthy, able-bodied, hetero, white world.

I felt as though mental health practices were "the best of what we had" but not enough. As a POC, working predominantly with other POC, I believe it is safe to say that we are tired of getting "just enough." It is truly depressing in a clinical and metaphorical sense.

At the Root of Our Depression Is Colonization

We spent a chapter talking about settler colonization, for good reason, because many of our lands, or the return of our lands, have become a distant aching for the fullness of our Home, that was described in Chapter 2. This ache for Home manifests itself in the present. This can look and feel disorganized and result in confusion, lethargy, apathy, loneliness, and even a dissociative quality can arise (to use colonial psychology terminology). This is much like the chemical imbalance that psychology and other fields call depression.

The feelings are real. It is happening to you if you feel it permeate every part of your life, experiences, and lenses. But we are not depression. We are not these set of symptoms in a text. Yes, what we are feeling is an accumulation of hundreds of years of acquisition from our bloodlines. This is not a curse. This is where it's at, here and now, with us because many of us have the privilege of having the space, time, and energy to acknowledge, feel, label, name, and process our emotions. If you're reading this, then yes, you are privileged. We have the generational bandwidth and responsibility, and perhaps—even with social media and grassroots organizing communities on the rise (they've always been there)—we have the support to work this through. We may have the words, the consciousness, and the space to unpack what our ancestors could NOT.

Perhaps instead of feeling like something is "wrong with us" or the people we work with, we can acknowledge that we are here to unpack 400 plus years of psychological enslavement. We are here to unpack the pattern. Perhaps we are here to build into our lives spaces of nonwork and rest; to be reunited with communities that are family; to relearn our Mother Tongues, if forgotten or never taught; to be more creative and silly, to utilize our joys with our craft; and to be nurtured back to health. It is time to be returned back to where colonial states separated us from . . . HOME. We are here to reform healthy attachments and spit up the emotional poisons of colonization from our relationships and how we see ourselves. Maybe some of us are here to reconstruct old belief systems and outdated ways of "curing what ails us."

Various diagnoses throughout the years have been used to affect public law and policy by dictating immigration and citizenship laws. For example, the first federal immigration act of 1882 which prohibited entry to the United States of any ". . . lunatic, idiot, or any person unable to take care of himself or herself without becoming a public charge" (Immigration Act, 1882). The wording is absolutely atrocious and quite telling. In 1907, legislation added "imbeciles, feeble-minded, any mental abnormality ever . . . which justifies the statement that the alien is mentally defective" (Immigration Act, 1907). "Alien," meaning people of different races and ethnicities, which was conflated with mental illness in the eyes of immigration authorities in the early 20th century. That bias still persists today, both consciously and unconsciously.

"An interpreter at Ellis Island noted, 'over fifty percent of the deportations for alleged mental disease were unjustified' based on ignorance on the part of the immigrants or the doctors and the inability of the doctors to understand the particular immigrant's norm or standard" (La Guardia, 1948/1961, p. 65). The 1924 Immigration Act started a national quota system to restrict immigration of people from ethnicities, ethnic origins, and races that were "undesirable" based on **diagnosis**. By the 19th century, people born out of the States occupied "an unusually high percentage of patients in mental hospitals and asylums." In fact, 80% of the population in the

New York City Lunatic Asylum between 1847 and 1870 were immigrants (Grob, 1972). Eugenics movements and scientific racism attempted to prove the inherent supremacy of the Anglo-Saxon and was what informed both psychiatric practice and immigration policy.

Again, scientific racism has sought to prove the biological superiority of whiteness. Current-day mental health systems seek to prove what is socio-culturally superior, through the descriptions of humans in the *DSM*. The people described as "normal and healthy" are very Western people. Medicalization and rugged individualism support late-stage capitalism through pathologization of big emotions and attempting to medicate big emotions that are a result of the suffering from systemic inequalities and lateral violence. We cannot diagnose without context. We cannot separate human emotions and experiences from the social context they were created, and exist within. This is the path and the invitation to the part where we are innately unlearning and relearning.

Tools of Colonization

This is where real reform can happen. We can evolve outdated colonial diagnosis into a new emerging field of collective-empowerment, which encompasses our history, practices, and emphasis on therapists' own emotional health, as well as the full spiritual breadth and humanity of all therapy participants. Diagnosis, although it can be a tool, like all tools that aren't adequately supported and based on guides for context can become weapons. They become as dangerous as the trauma we are attempting to get better from.

They're expired.

I know this is difficult to swallow, as our whole lives, student loan debt, and our resentment, and even exhaustion are built on these fields. While it may be that the fields did the best they could with what was heard, seen, and acknowledged at the time and maybe . . . just maybe . . . some of it was even "revolutionary" for its time—I am not convinced. The MHIC is expired, fungus filled, soggy, incompetent, and even harmful. Starting with diagnosis, it needs to go.

I know many people I have served would say that they were never given

OPPRESSIVE, INACCURATE, VICTIM-BLAMING MENTAL HEALTH LANGUAGE	ANTI-OPPRESSIVE, TRAUMA-INFORMED, RESPECTFUL MENTAL HEALTH LANGUAGE
MALADAPTIVE BEHAVIOR	SURVIVAL STRATEGIES
HOMELESS	UNSHELTERED
DRUG SEEKING	RELIEF SEEKING
DIFFICULT CASE	ACCOMMODATION REQUIRED
DEFIANT/COMBATIVE/ DEFENSIVE/RESISTANT	ASSERTIVE, SELF-ADVOCATING
NON-COMPLIANT	DOES NOT CONSENT
MENTAL ILLNESS/DISORDER	HEART/SPIRIT WOUND
ADDICTION	PHYSICAL DEPENDENCE
EVIDENCE-BASED, PEER-REVIEWED	PRACTICE-BASED, CLIENT-CENTERED, CONTEXT and NUANCE-SPECIFIC

FIGURE 4.1 Oppressive, Inaccurate, Victim-Blaming Mental Health Language versus Anti-Oppressive, Trauma-Informed, Respectful Mental Health Language
By Natasha Sandy (2021) for her Instagram @rehumanizingourselves

an opportunity to discuss the diagnoses given to them by a practitioner. That is why I enjoyed doing therapeutic work at a university; we were not mandated to create and use ICD-9 codes and pathologize what arises from trauma. Some people I have worked with would say that I may have brought up a set of symptoms or expressions as we spoke about a particularly abusive parent or lover as a way to understand that something "deeper, more profound, is there." I am not always proud of how I have managed sessions, crises, or individuals whom my colonial education dictated were "deniers" or "resistant." Yes, absolutely there are deeply wounded people in the world who should not have access to others while the former are in an unconscious or unnecessarily violent, traumatized, or completely inhumane state.

There are individuals I have supported who had said, "I am so grateful I understand depression better—how it shows up in my body, as a Dominican man (for example) with my trauma history—and if I didn't take (insert antidepressant medication) for a year, I might not be alive and in love today."

So, I want to honor and acknowledge that individuals have benefited from understanding a set of symptoms that have impacted them, and they are not alone. Yet, just because diagnosis is "what we have," it doesn't mean it's what we now need.

Human suffering is not black and white. Neither is the mental health system. While we are understanding and learning from what has been done, what we continue to do, and who we continue to leave out of mental health conversations . . . in the meantime, people need support—sometimes BIG support, around their pain points. Sometimes the safest way is to manage the pain, while we allow a person to return to their bodies. After people return to their bodies and feel that they are in their "right mind," they can make decisions about what they need and how they want to heal—and most importantly the ROOT of that dis-ease. **If we do not examine and honor the root of the suffering, such as colonization and dehumanization, we will continue to experience the same suffering over and over and over without a map.**

Capitalist Causes of Suffering

Diagnoses are capitalism's attempt to quantify human suffering. Otherwise we would not need to know, *so, for whom are diagnoses and treatment plans effective? Whose lives?*

For the lives saved, how many have also been smashed? How many poor mothers have been institutionalized? How many POC have been targeted and kept in institutions, prisons, behavioral schools, or out of jobs and promotions because of inadequate mental and emotional support? Because of an inadequate and incomplete mental and behavioral health care system? Sure, having a tidy, neat guide like the *DSM* supposedly makes things "easier," but for who?

Psychological pathology is the study of the causes, components, courses, and consequences of psychological disorders (Holmqvist, 2013). These are generally characterized by what is "abnormal and dysfunctional." So, we might say that the *DSM* and looking at abnormalities creates a set of standards and creates normality around mental health. Is that exactly true? Many communities, cultures, and families still mistrust the MHIC. So many POC have been overdiagnosed, misdiagnosed, or not provided support at all. They were told they have the tools to "get through it," were sent away, "See you next week," and suddenly they didn't.

> **WAYS THAT THE MHIC EXPLOITS PEOPLE WITH "EXPIRED OINTMENT"**
>
> - Schools, from elementary to universities, do not prioritize mental health, student physical health, nor disability services (unless you're an athlete).
> - Brief treatment is provided as an option in many mental health settings, rather than increasing mental health services in most educational and outpatient settings.
> - Mental health first aid is not a priority nor taught to teachers, transportation workers, nurses, and so forth.
> - In-home therapy is often treated as a lucrative business, where individuals without mental health degrees create in-home services.
> - Child and adult group homes are underserved, understaffed, and under-resourced.
> - Inpatient residential units and hospitals (treatment centers) are often given more money to treat mental health rather than direct community assistance to help prevent trauma from happening.
> - Individuals living with mental and emotional pain ("severe mental illness") that disrupts their daily lives and basic needs often have their rights revoked and are simultaneously prevented from having a voice in their own healing or treatment.

Racial trauma is so often pathologized, rather than acknowledged or integrated into an empowered healing paradigm. Advancing beyond individual-level approaches to coping with racial trauma, psychologically and sociologically, for BIPOC folks is essential. Research has shown that

POC have been inappropriately pathologized by being incorrectly diagnosed with mental illness based upon a psychologist's or psychiatrist's lack of understanding of the context in which a person of color has lived (Suzuki et al., 1999).

To push the point further, psychological tests and diagnostic systems used by MHPs to make diagnoses have been "constructed and norms have been developed and standardized primarily on middle-class, white persons of Euro-American origins" (Dana, 2005). In constructing tests and diagnostic systems, BIPOC have been excluded, underrepresented, or not matched with white people on vital demographic variables (Dana, 2005). Therefore, these tools should not be considered accurate with BIPOC. Research points to countless ways where expressions of racism and reactions that a BIPOC may display are not a form of mental illnesses but extremely healthy, understandable, logical responses from living with and experiencing chronic racism, which include: race-based traumatic stress, or racial trauma; racism-related fatigue; anticipatory-racism reaction; and racism-related stress/distress.

As DeArth-Pendley (2012) notes, nearly every psychological theory taught in colleges and practiced in clinics in the U.S. was derived by psychologists and psychiatrists who shared a white, Eurocentric culture.

> *All mainstream intelligence and personality tests administered in U.S. public schools, detention centers, prisons, courts, the military, jobs, and clinics were designed by white practitioners. Furthermore, assessment software programs used to guide parole decisions . . . are based on theories of crime and deviance developed by white practitioners and authors.*
> —Gina DeArth-Pendley (2012) *"Racial Disparity and the Pathologizing of People of Color in Mental Health Diagnoses and Psychological Assessment"*

Actions Over Apologies

In 2021, the APA Council of Representatives recently apologized to BIPOC for their role in "promoting, perpetuating, and failing to challenge Racism,

Racial Discrimination, and Human Hierarchy" in the Resolution (Auguste et al., 2021). Although this is a step toward acknowledgment of perpetuating and upholding white supremacy over hundreds of years, this apology arrives quite late. Over two hundred Black psychologists in the late 60s formed the oldest independent ethnic group: the Association of Black Psychologists (ABPsi). The protests—to engage in less harmful practices; to commit to equity and diversity as a priority, better yet as a public health issue; to commit to taking a stand against bigotry and institutional oppression; to acknowledge the historical and current-day harm that psychology has engaged in—had not been heeded.

This apology omits the depth needed to truly identify and make amends for how the fields of psychology and psychiatry colluded with the state to suppress rights as well as personal and political freedom. Chapter 3 briefly reviews some of the heinous crimes of psychology and psychiatry, such as the involvement and collusion with the criminal justice systems to create and maintain state hospitals that "often disproportionately and indefinitely confined Black people in particular" (Auguste et al., 2021). These histories, however much they attempt to be buried, led the former president-elect of ABPsi, Bobby Wright, to conclude that the "discipline had historically been leveraged to wage war against Black communities" (Auguste et al., 2021).

Auguste et al. (2021) note in their article, "Why the APA's Apology for Promoting White Supremacy Falls Short," how the Central Lunatic Asylum for the Colored Insane, the first state psychiatric hospital for Black people, forcibly institutionalized thousands of Black people in Virginia beginning in 1869. Hospital archives revealed that Black people were taken from their communities and enslaved on the belief that freedom produced mania and forced labor was an adequate treatment. This is cultural, historical, and intergenerational trauma. This creates a deep self-hatred, and a dissociation from the self, community, and family. These are crimes against humanity—in particular against Black people.

This is a representation of what people of the global majority frequently experience: *"Our experience does not matter until white America says so."* This is deeply emotionally and psychologically toxic and replicates the power dynamics seen across history, which leads to racial trauma and a plethora of physical issues (see adverse childhood experiences [ACEs] score and trauma's effects on our lifespan).

Although the article notes that "psychology cannot harness its potential to disarm and dismantle racism without addressing its own history of racism and support for human hierarchy" (APA, 2021), the *DSM* still exists and harms millions of people. Standardized testing is still psychologically supported and continues to impact students of all ages and races. Juvenile detention centers still exist and incarcerate Black and Brown youth, while treating and trying them as adults. Although the apology was stated, what actions have begun to create news ways of healing and helping?

The APA apology article also went on to state that since its "origins as a scientific discipline in the mid-19th century, psychology has . . . contributed to the dispossession, displacement, and exploitation of communities of color . . . psychology, rooted in oppressive psychological science to protect whiteness, white people, and white epistemologies . . ." (APA, 2021). Psychology developed under these conditions, helped to create, express, and sustain whiteness, continues to bear their indelible imprint, and often continues to publish research that conforms with white racial hierarchy (Cummings Center, 2021; Helms 2003; Luther et al., 1996; Santiago-Rivera et al., 2016). Upon reading this, I feel sickened from the years of being told I was being "ridiculous, too political." I feel sickened when I think of the youth I "treated," and how unprepared I was as an intern and early-career psychologist. I feel sickened when I think of all of the student loan debt that I and countless low-income and working poor/poor students, who desperately wanted to enter the field (in particular, sought-after doctoral programs that were providing full scholarships for roughly 3–6 students a year) and were not accepted, incurred. I think of the psychologists we lost; who dedicated their lives to this struggle within such a racist white supremacist field.

Although the field of psychology is merely one example, it is one that I am comfortable speaking on, as I was trained within these structures. However, counseling, psychiatry, social work, psychoanalysis, Jungian analysis, family systems, etc., all have a role and violent history of experimenting upon and deeply hurting all people, particularly Black folks globally.

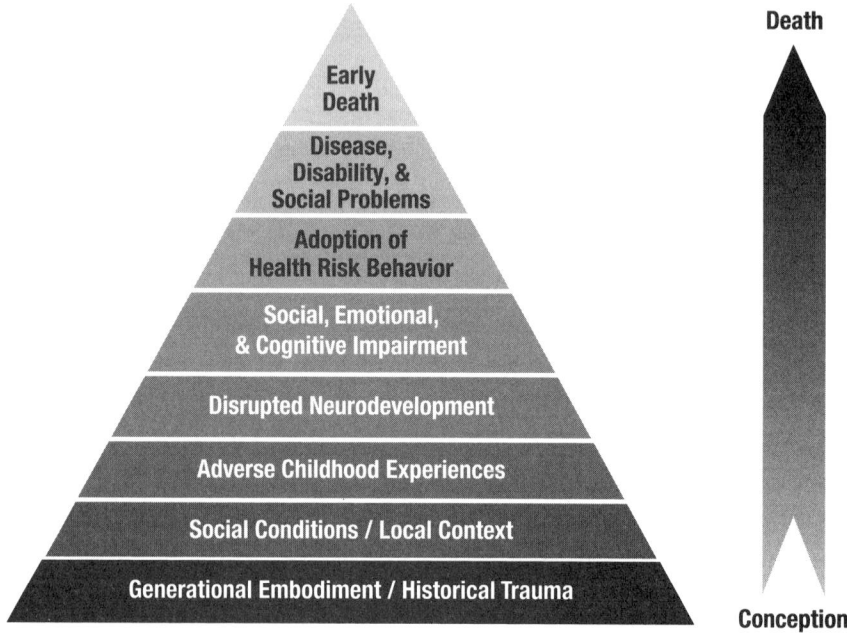

FIGURE 4.2 Mechanism by Which Adverse Childhood Experiences Influence Health and Well-Being Throughout the Lifespan   Source: From the Centers for Disease Control and Prevention & Kaiser ACE Study (2021).

Once again, the APA acknowledged the saturation and birth of psychology on the backs of white males, many of whom contributed to scientific inquiry and methods that perpetuated systemic racial oppression, including promoting the ideas of early-20th century eugenics. And still, intelligence testing, ableism, *DSM* personality diagnoses have all been adopted by the field of psychology and used systemically to create the ideology of white supremacy and continue to deeply harm communities of color.

Frankly, when I read *The Willie Lynch Letter and the Making of a Slave* and other historical forms of gaslighting, emotional oppression, and mind control, I am reminded of the heavy hand that psychology and psychiatry played in maintaining and creating vulnerable populations that were then named as "at-risk" populations. I wonder which came first: psychology, or slave owners who created psychological frameworks. Perhaps they are one and the same.

As we know the ongoing harm still continues, as this book is birthed in the wake of the grief and rage related to the deep harm our fields have and continue to cause, in the name of "science, research, and safety."

The Violence of "Normal"

There is a deep-rooted history of pathologization that the DSM has had. The DSM has undergone many revisions and many of the revisions have highlighted how pathology and diagnoses have increased. Rather than parsing out the overlap, inclusion of trauma, the root of the issues, or the array of symptoms, the DSM continues to lengthen the categorizations, thereby creating more space, dialogue, and white Western teaching, centering white cisgender male and individualistic forms of "sickness." In other words, "the more diagnoses, the more treatment I need."

What is more concerning is that the APA and other associations have continued to justify expansion because of "empirical evidence." Empirical evidence is often another way of speaking of Eurocentric evidence, with predominantly white people as samples. Bias may occur in selection of the sample, language, detection of treatment effects, performance of the study, and reporting of outcomes—each of which may increase the size of the observed effect. Across the past five decades, psychological publications that have highlighted race have been rare. Although they have increased in developmental and social psychology, they have remained virtually nonexistent in cognitive psychology (Roberts et al., 2020). Most publications have been edited by white editors, under which there have been significantly fewer publications that highlight race. Lastly, many of the publications that highlight race have been written by white authors who employed significantly fewer participants of color.

Additionally, systemic inequality exists within psychological research, and systemic changes are needed to ensure that psychological research benefits from diversity in editing, writing, and participation. Furthermore, the DSM-5 has been criticized for allowing **the pharmaceutical industry to have an unhealthy influence on the revision process** and increasing the tendency to medicalize patterns of behavior and mood that are not considered to be particularly extreme. What is not discussed is the increasing link to drug companies as diagnoses get uncovered in the medical industrial complex as well as the financial ties between *DSM* panel members and the pharmaceutical industry (T. Smith, 2012). The trend highlighted is one of matching diagnostic labels to a drug's reaction to a person's biology and mind, thereby creating a more expedited pharmaceutical pipeline, and the FDA approval of that drug with profitability and ease.

The interests of Big Pharma and the medical and mental health industrial complexes are often not aligned, as pharmaceutical companies often have the goal of bringing in more profit, and supposedly the MHIC attempts to ease suffering. With that said, there is an over-medicalization of pathologizing psychiatric disorders and an overreliance on medicalized "quick fixes," with a sparsity of more holistic, artistic, cultural, and somatic-based practices that would allow for more communal mutual support and individual agency. According to the APA, antidepressant medications classify as third "in pharmaceutical sales worldwide, with $13.4 billion in sales last year." Additionally, antipsychotic medications generated $6.5 billion in revenue (Sharfstein, 2005). Wiley (2004, as cited in T. Smith, 2012) has even noted that a complete and full understanding of the problematic ways in which diagnosis has been used, as well as the bias involved in the creation of these categories, seems essential to the education of any competent and ethically minded therapist. Yet it is largely missing from the education of many professionals. I believe we are hearing the cries of many individuals from within the system, attempting to uproot and change the system. And not just the mental health systems, as all systems are inextricably linked. Additionally, T. Smith (2012) notes that the APA (2000) has stated that a mental disorder is "considered a manifestation of a behavioral, psychological, or biological dysfunction in the individual" (p. xxxi). The APA also noted that both deviant behavior (e.g., political, religious, or sexual harm), and any forms of oppression and inequity between people and society, are not considered mental disorders.

One of the many reasons this is problematic is the language. The language itself creates pathology, division, and it IS inherently political. Psychological language is jargony, classist, and often continues to keep the therapy participant on the outskirts, unclear of what a set of symptoms and terminologies signify. It also has roots in Latin, and the European medical model, which further reinforces a disconnect between many individuals who may or may not have the educational background, vocabulary, or emotional bandwidth to parse out what is being said.

It is also problematic because the *DSM* does not distinguish the difference between psychiatric distress and differences caused by behavior in opposition to social norms (T. Smith, 2012). There's been a lack of research into how people have been affected by the pathologizing of the *DSM*, whether from diagnoses that used political affiliation, religion, or sexuality as the basis (Lev, 2005, as cited in T. Smith, 2012). Smith describes how the overuse of medications affects a person's behavior, and their perception of whether the behavior is seen as "normal" or even problematic within their life. Furthermore, the continuum of severity and impact related to the problem is frequently dismissed. Therefore, the medical and mental health fields, and pharmaceutical companies, all benefit from prescribing medications that control a person's behavior. Once we control millions of people's subjective experiences of their behavior and begin to label and treat it as problematic, we can begin to control society's view of what "healthy and normal should be," rather than acknowledging the range of humanity's expression. This is not to shame individuals whose lives have been exponentially safer and improved due to psychotropic medication, rather this is an introduction to allowing more choice, and language around options, and freedom to choose.

This leads us to simply ask, "What is normal, and who gains from creating definitions and continuums of what is considered normal?" Social services and clinical settings seek to define what is an outlier and what is normal. "Normal" is, of course, determined by the society who is judging the behavior and the person engaging in the behavior. For example, queerness was once pathologized as well and has since shifted into being more socially acceptable. However, "normal" has a history of being tied to white, Western, cishet men in a capitalist view. "Normal" looks like a traditional cisgender marriage, it looks like two children (biologically born to their parents), it looks like a slim body, it looks like happiness, and it looks like being middle to upper class. When we unpack "normal," it truly leaves so many of us and the therapy participants out. For centuries, we have had the idea reinforced to us through social beliefs, politics, policies, and the media that heterosexual, cisgender people are the "norm" and that anything other than that is perceived to be "different." It is difficult and takes diligence, and often a true shift in perspective, to see it differently because we have been socialized since birth. These beliefs become second nature. All around us, in television shows, fairy tales, in our places of worship or spirituality, in movies, in storybooks, and online, there are projections of these societal norms. For a teenager who is nonheterosexual or non-cisgender, an environment where they don't feel represented can have detrimental effects on their learning, their relationships, their self-esteem, their mental and emotional health, and their sense of self-worth. Heteronormativity and cisnormativity also impact heterosexual, cisgender children. These kids are growing up in environments where boys and girls are segregated for sports, bathroom use, and lines in classrooms. Certainly, there are parts of the world where these socializations are being challenged and smashed; however, for most people they remain in place.

The Western conception of what is "normal" deliberately excludes the experiences and pain of POC. Because it cannot see the root of that pain, it turns it into a disease or a disorder, inflicting further harm and sustaining the cycle of colonization. The "ideal" human described is a Western one, one who fits the above identities. In this way, the *DSM* is incomplete, misogynistic, racist, and classist.

As an example, someone may be diagnosed with obsessive–compulsive personality disorder because their ruminations pervade every area of their lives. However, I have worked with individuals having just immigrated to the States over the past 3 years. They have communicated that their prior therapist had diagnosed them with obsessive–compulsive personality disorder, and as I continued to get to know the individual all I could see was a person still deeply healing from trauma. Having experienced bombings, brutal training in a military, losing both parents and two siblings, not hearing from their partner of three years, and being forced to migrate from her homeland—all while watching the destruction from oceans away. Yes, there were obsessive behaviors, but these were expressions of historical and current-day colonization that were activated, occurring, and quite valid. If

ANY diagnosis was to be offered and discussed—a trauma one would be appropriate. In no way would OCPD be appropriate nor culturally or politically competent.

In the same branch, workaholism is rarely seen as an "obsessive" or problematic issue. In fact in colonized countries, it is encouraged and often applauded. Hence, "normal" is heavily influenced by the capitalist values of Westernism today.

It is essential that we consider that social failure is considered a personal failure. For example, gender dysphoria puts the onus on the trans/gender nonconforming (GNC) person rather than the society and people around them who are failing to accommodate them because of strict adherence to the gender binary. It was only in 2013, that the APA removed "gender identity disorder" from the *DSM-5* and replaced it with "gender dysphoria." In 2018, the World Health Organization changed "transsexualism" to "gender incongruence" and moved it to the chapter "Conditions Related to Sexual Health" (Fitzsimons, 2018). These are attempts to end the pathologization of "transness." However, transgender oppression is still alive in how it oppresses any person who challenges gender norms within society (whether intentional or not, and whether they identify with transness or not) (T. Smith, 2012).

Another example arises with individuals living with ADHD. Critics of ADHD see it as nothing more than a list of all the behaviors that annoy teachers and require extra attention in the classroom. Rather than understanding why the classroom isn't serving children expressing these behaviors or helping them learn in ways that suit their needs—rather than insisting that everyone's brain is the same—we medicate the youth in order to have them fit the classroom standards, of sitting still, being quiet, only speaking when being spoken to, and interacting minimally.

Just as scientific racism sought to prove the biological superiority of whiteness, modern psychiatry seeks to prove what is socioculturally superior. Despite it not being explicit in its racial and classist alignment, we know it works from within a capitalist, colonial, and racial system. Therefore, those who do well in these systems are "superior" and *those who struggle have failed*. We are forced to constantly readjust and fit a society that is already failing us all.

The Violence of Individualism

Medicalization is the process by which nonmedical problems become defined and treated as medical problems often requiring medical treatment ("Medicalization," 2022). The term *medicalization* first appeared in sociology literature and focused on deviance, but it soon expanded to examine other human conditions. With individualism and medicalization, we separate human emotions and experiences from the social context in which they exist and are created. Medicalization often concerns new diagnoses, "based on a widened understanding of human situations that usually benefit from medical involvement. It, thus, widens the boundaries of medicine. Overdiagnosis, instead, starts inside of medicine, addressing the problem of people receiving a unbeneficial diagnosis" (van Dijk et al., 2016).

As an example, the cultural obsession with diagnosing the U.S. President Donald Trump as narcissistic or sociopathic reflects the social anxiety to label him an aberration rather than an inevitable product of the racist, classist, patriarchal world into which he (and all of us) have been socialized. As I have noted prior, society itself is a depressing experience systemically. We have been deeply socialized to believe various experiences fall into the "norm" and various experiences are "abhorrent and wrong." These beliefs create disconnection between us displaying violence as protection, deprivation of needs/cultural connection/social togetherness and so forth. Unsurprisingly, depression and anxiety spiked among Black Americans following George Floyd's death—however, collective sadness, fear, and anger should be the expected response to state murder (Fowers & Wan, 2020). Yet, psychological discourse and treatment disavows and individualizes these conditions. Instead of adjusting, we as a society are pathologizing, placating, and gaslighting those of us harmed by them. Societally, we are repelled by counseling and therapy, yet we unconsciously and collectively pathologize state murder. bell hooks describes this as a form of "psychological terrorism"—one that both silences anti-racist protest and dissent in any fashion, and encourages "the masses of white folks, and other non-Black groups, to see Black people as insane when they discuss their victimization" (hooks, 2004; Kanji, 2020).

Once again, the emo–decolonial process invites us to the seat of evolution, while revolutionizing. We cannot create new societies or ways of supporting without evolving emotionally as a collective of people on Earth. The MHIC has not evolved or revolutionized; instead, it has valued neutrality, while failing to acknowledge the level of violence and anti-Black racism involved in its history. As I discuss in future chapters, "Black rage" is almost seen as an affliction, something to "be alarmed about." We offer anger management classes. (If I saw another anger management class at the university, I was going to burst.) However, there is no effort beyond the class to fix the rage and manage the rage, to understand the root of that rage, OR to successfully delve into the unhealthiness of white rage and how that is expressed.

Instead, the solutions to "Black Rage" were incarceration, individualization, medicalization, and pathologization.

Tell me, is it truly possible to treat racism, or any -ism with psychotropic medication?

Is it truly possible to treat racism, or any -ism with talk therapy? As my colleague Maverick Lumen (personal communication, 2021) would state, "I would say that mental health systems, as they are today, are akin to hiring someone to mop the floor, while having another hold an umbrella over our head so that we can never be inconvenienced by the hole in the ceiling." If you could see me now, you would see me snapping my fingers.

Capitalizing Off Suffering and Sadness

Diversity across gender, race, sexuality, and disability have a legacy of bias and increased pathologizing (T. Smith, 2012). I would add that the fields of psychiatry, social work, and psychology have also helped to reinforce racism, ableism, sexism, homophobia, and classism. Smith also supports the belief that modern-day bias in the MHIC and MIC can be traced to roots of racism, ableism, sexism, homophobia, and classism that has shown up in how diagnoses have been designed and assigned.

Human suffering is minimized and the *DSM* continues to decontextualize. The brain is powerful; yes, but our brains are not "broken." They are responding accurately to the environment around them. Research has shown that the effects of trauma can be intergenerationally passed on through epigenetic mechanisms, such as methylation. Childhood trauma has been associated with alteration in methylation patterns in human sperm, which may induce intergenerational effects. There is increasing evidence that epigenetics may play a role in the pathophysiology of psychiatric disorders, such as major depressive disorder, psychosis, and addiction. Epigenetic changes occur in response to environmental changes but may also be heritable, which modifies genetic expression directly and indirectly (Rege, 2021). In the broadest sense, epigenetics can be considered as "heritable memory"—an adaptive and dynamic process that ensures proper genomic function through the expression of gene-related activity (Jaenisch & Bird, 2003). In other words, experiences during an individual's life modify genetic expression—directly and indirectly (Lacal & Ventura, 2018). More on this in Chapters 5 and 6.

We know that ADHD medications can create instability in the body, inducing a need for more dopamine, therefore, requiring higher levels and increasing dosages as time goes on. We also know that antipsychotic medications are marketed as a cure for excess dopamine that triggers psychosis; but, they can induce drastic chemical and neuroanatomical shifts that worsen psychosis over the long term, including disrupting motor functions and basic body functions. A lot of research on the adverse effects of psychotropic medications is often not funded for the aforementioned reasons. The MHIC continues to collude with Big Pharma.

Additionally, antidepressants are marketed as a cure to serotonin deficiency. They can repress joy receptors and create a slew of adverse side effects, including suicidality. This is not a plea NOT to take psychiatric medications that may assist you or have been assisting you. Rather, once again, I am laying out that under capitalism, health must be earned, and the inherent value of individuals comes at a price.

The brilliant Dr. Ayesha Khan and Jesse Meadows (2021) have broken down some of the differences between modern and a more decolonized psychiatry. It is a beautiful expression of how modern medicine, in particular the medical and mental health industrial complexes, were created to justify colonization and sustain and feed capitalism, not to help and heal. They also note in their Instagram post that it clearly exemplifies a colonial "divide and conquer" strategy, while keeping practitioners compliant. One of the "tools" is isolation. Keeping practitioners and participants of therapy isolated and in some ways lacking community support. Making individuals easy to control and manipulate via propaganda. It is also so much easier for practitioners to gaslight participants this way, too. In isolation, a participant can't turn to people on either side of them to see whether their experiences are collectively felt.

We are clear that all modern systems—health care, transportation, education, media, and mental health—were all built to maintain power and control over the masses.

TABLE 4.1 Differences Between Modern Psychiatry and Decolonized Psychology

Modern Psychiatry	Decolonized Psychology
Colonial white hegemonic, capitalist system	Indigenous, Black and Brown collectivist, culture-based
Pathologizing (disease, disorders, defects)	Focus on how oppression and the environment impacts individual and community health
Profit-driven focus on medication and selling individualistic solutions	Holistic, systemic, community-led solutions, and a diverse support network
Isolating learned helplessness	Decentralized
Client reliant on provider	Client reliant on community/family/external support

Source: Adapted from Khan & Meadows (2021).

Gaslighting and Capitalism Fatigue

I grew up saying, "let's call a spade a spade . . ." So, I will utilize this term to shine a light on what we may not want to admit or speak of. Let us call a spade a spade. Every system, business, and structure that has pretended to care about its practitioners has some self-reflection and analysis to engage in before stating that they are providing equitable and fair labor—when what is usually desired is uninterrupted labor. Burnout is a form of political and corporate gaslighting on the psyches of industrialized, colonized people globally. Burnout and deep exhaustion are not a reflection of your self-care practices, rather a reflection of a failing system, as a whole.

We speak about burnout and exhaustion, as if it is the fault solely of the person experiencing this. **Burnout is an expression of late-stage capitalism.** Burnout is not a failure of our self-care routines. Burnout is not a reflection of being irresponsible or overly involved with your students or cases. Let's call it what it is: capitalism fatigue. The bone-deep exhaustion that no amount of vacation can really cure. It IS dangerous to one's emotional health. Our exhaustion and frustration is healthy, "normal," natural, and even protective. It is our body screaming, "time out!"

When a community mental health center, a hospital, or a school has insufficient resources, the directors and supervisors are forced to push more "cases" and work onto the employees beneath them. This is how midlevel management colludes. Knowing that upper management continues to gaslight and lie to its employees, directors, and supervisors (yes, even well-intentioned ones) continue to shovel the shit onto the shoulders of those already carrying and shoveling the burden. Yes, burnout can eventually begin to hack at our nervous systems, but it cannot magically be "cured" through manicures, day spas, two-week-long vacations, and therapy sessions. It is a systemic issue; even though capitalism would really like us to believe that expensive pampering can cure us of slow soul death.

In North America, many of us are indoctrinated to believe that hard work means waking up extra early, arriving early and unpaid, never complaining, and leaving after hours, and also being underpaid. This is a Eurocentric, deeply white supremacist way of thinking, and it is straight ableist. It does not consider someone's mental, physical, and emotional capabilities. Nor does it consider whether they have children to care for, older relatives to take care of, or hobbies to tend to. It does not consider offering space to dream, create, or simply partake in a longer lunch or even a nap.

I recall years upon years where I unconsciously did the labor of 4–6 individuals at an institution in which I was employed. Because of my conditioning, the belief that doing more somehow provided me with a feeling of satiation, as though "I am worth something—look at how much I can juggle," but it was an internal victory. "I must be okay if I can manage all of this." Then there came the pressure from the outside, the gaslighting: "A group like this would benefit from having a WOC facilitate it." "We need the cofacilitator to be a MHP and a POC." "Jenn, I really am asking you to think about how much the students appreciate you."

I provided individual, couple, and group therapy; did crisis management; applied for and completed quarterly grant work, as well as annual renewals; and cofacilitated Lesbian, Gay, Bisexual, Transgender, Queer (LGBTQ) support groups. I coordinated a peer education group; supervised work-study students; and supported the peer educators in their growth and in navigating higher ed. I taught two grad-level courses per semester; provided workshops for the counseling center in which I worked; participated in student affairs committees; and was on a coalition, in a primary role on campus, to raise awareness around anti-racist and anti-neoliberal policies and initiatives for students and workers. The students I worked with had massive amounts of deep developmental and community trauma, barely had enough resources or support, were dealing with food and housing insecurity, and were often—understandably—deeply enraged and depressed. Managing substance abuse issues. Flashbacks. All understandable. But nevertheless, there was not enough support and staffing available to support all of our students.

At one point, we had a waitlist of 99 students, no new counseling staff support, yet there were somehow new HR roles, new deans, and new professors. No one paid attention to our students, or our own mental and emotional health—until the pandemic hit. Magically, our center was supposed to provide a myriad of services and answers.

Even while attending things like therapy, acupuncture, support group, and Zumba, walking at lunch, seeing all the necessary health physicians, getting to sleep by 11 p.m., and setting boundaries, I could not wake up in the mornings. I felt irritable, alone, apathetic, enraged at the lack of funding, and deeply disconnected from my personal life. At the time, well-meaning colleagues and friends would tell me to "do less," or call me into their offices to remind me to "take care" of myself. I would often run into the bathroom and cry or want to punch a wall because I felt trapped. No one understood that I needed a part-time job. My salary alone was not enough to cover living expenses, student loans, and self-care. I would be told to stop getting my hair colored every six months, or to see my healing practitioner or coach less. Meanwhile these were the spaces, actions, and individuals that—for the moment—kept me sane. Kept me from "losing it."

Now, I am well aware these are privileged problems, but I share in transparency, My Good People, because many of us "professionals" are just a paycheck away from broke. In fact, these comments that were meant to educate and soothe me, further alienated, depressed, and enraged me. They were classist and even racist. Once again, I was being blamed (the individual) for not keeping up better boundaries. Meanwhile, we were gaslit and compared to one another constantly. Most importantly, I deeply desired for our students to receive a really healing, creative, collective, trauma-engaged frame. I wanted our students to receive the best experiences possible, involving their emotional well-being while immersed in colonial education. No one would dare critique the entire system, unless it began to not benefit THEM. I was raging and fighting for the working-class staff who were taking out our garbage multiple times a day, shoveling the parking garage during snow storms, and checking our students' temperatures.

Self-care is not a "cure" for burnout because it is deeper than you or me. This is, once again, a root issue. Therefore, the root of the issue is the businesses, corporations, schools, and policies that keep us stressed, sick, tired, and too overwhelmed, to question these struggles—let alone organize together and take action.

You cannot self-care or self-love your way out of systemic oppression.

Community care is beautiful (more on that in Chapter 10), yet it is not the antidote for systems that continue to kill us. The mental health fields were created to support and justify dehumanizing the less productive for a more profit-driven society.

For instance, the five-day-a-week, 40-hour, 9 a.m.–5 p.m. "American" workweek began as a way to protect U.S. workers. In 1890, the U.S. government began tracking workers' hours, and they found that the average workweek for full-time manufacturing employees was a whopping *100 hours* (Ward & Lebowitz, 2022). Many individuals have been conditioned to see working around the clock as a kind of status symbol. While many people claim to be working 60- or 80-hour workweeks, much of that time isn't very productive. In general, research suggests that humans can handle working 60-hour weeks for three weeks—after that, we become less productive. Again, the more we work—the more we are exhausted and overburdened—the less time we have to experience joy, be in the community, advocate for change, or ask for what we need. The relentless grind also desensitizes us to our own needs, which makes it that much harder to advocate for ourselves or our coworkers.

It is also important to note that individuals at or below the poverty level are often working 60+ hour workweeks that span six to seven days a week. Once again, when we have discourse around the 5-day/40-hour workweek, we are often speaking of and to the middle class, and not including individuals living at and below the poverty level.

UNPACK IT WITH ME REFLECTION QUESTIONS

- What theories and paradigms for wellness did you study?
- Who taught you these theories?
- What were their identities, did they include culture, race, and identity in all theoretical discussions?
- Name the top three theories that inform and guide your practice. Are they all founded by cisgender, white, senior men?
- Was "Healing" discussed or included within your studies?
- What is your relationship to the *DSM*?
- What is your relationship to psychotropic medications?
- What is your relationship to the mental health industrial complex?

- How have you been, or currently are complicit, with the current mental health industrial complex?
- Where might you have NOT made space for other ways of knowing, including spiritualities in which you may not have been educated?
- Where is your own conditioning (from white supremacy) impacting your resistance to change?
- What can you do, and what will you do, this year to reclaim and dismantle pathologizing behaviors?

Resistance As Insanity

> *Between 1618 and 1620, about 50,000 enslaved people—many of whom had been prisoners of war—were exported from Angola. An estimated 350 of these captives were loaded onto a Portuguese slave ship called the* São João Bautista *(more commonly known as the* San Juan Bautista*).*
> —Olivia B. Waxman (2019)

The summer 2020 public murders of George Floyd, Breonna Taylor, and Ahmaud Arbery, amid the pandemic and the consistent protests across the United States that have followed may have taken many Americans by surprise. For others—especially those who are Black, Indigenous, and People of Color, and those coconspirators in the struggle—the murders at the hands of the police (or those acting on their behalf) served as yet another visceral and historical reminder of the long history of violent racism and inequalities that ignite calls for justice, abolition, and change.

We also saw expressions of this visceral reaction for BIPOC, particularly Black-identified people, spike intensely following the public aforementioned murders. This IS "normal." Yet, society openly pathologizes, then minimizes, and then supports the pathologization. Intense reactions—such as insomnia, irritability, moodiness, crying, intense emotionality, and feelings of deep hopelessness—are all normal human emotions. Public trauma that creates suffering in the global collective and mirrors historical and cultural trauma of

American chattel systems of slavery (and Caribbean and South-Central American enslavement) is allowed space for grief. For widespread grief. For the kind of grief that shuts a person down and consistently can wire a nervous system up.

In my fantasies, global communities of MHPs rose up to demand a rested state for people of Black-identifying ancestry—reparations of sort. I imagined us holding hands (virtually or in person) marching and shouting, "That is enough! LET US REST! LET US GRIEVE!" Writing this, I become emotional, because there is so much history to clear out and process, and as research tells us—sleep is restorative, and helps us to heal more quickly.

But alas, instead what occurred were countless interview requests, an increase in diversity and equity workshops, and keynotes. Black folks were suddenly promoted, hired, and listened to in positions where they had been silenced for years. They were also singled out, asked to engage in more labor, asked to present at workshops around antiracism efforts, apologized to, cried on, asked for solutions. Then all too quickly, there was again silence and slinking back into corporate shadows. This is abusive. It is a perfect example of the issues with traditional white allyship (including white-passing POC allyship). So, we see a massive increase in the use and need for mental health services—naturally. Black people desire more therapists who not only look like them, but can "feel them," feel me? Many BIPOC continue to sit comfortably on the throne of white supremacy as tokens, enjoying the capitalistic benefits. But Black people are desiring not to overexplain their grief, rage, and expressions of trauma to the helpers.

1. It is exhausting.
2. It incurs more emotional labor.
3. It feels and is unsafe.
4. Historically (and clearly currently) our big feelings have gotten us murdered.

Clarity and Community as Key

Those of us who hold space for and work with Black youth, especially youth who live in poor, segregated neighborhoods, often have aggressive responses to youth (or adults) who react strongly, have big feelings, become irritable, do not "color inside the lines," and/or have trouble concentrating. This behavior is often seen as problematic and maladaptive.

Research is highlighting what communities of color have known for eons, that intense behavioral expressions are rational responses to their environment and helps to keep them safe. Noni Gaylord-Harden, a clinical psychologist at Texas A&M University, proposes just that: "That instead of focusing on these behaviors—identifying them as pathologies to be punished or symptoms to be treated—policy makers need to recognize them as adaptive and work to change the inequitable environment that produces them."

Adam Harris's (2021) article, "The Burden of Being 'On Point'" in *The Atlantic* beautifully highlights how in 2016, Gaylord-Harden—who was then a professor at Loyola University of Chicago—wondered what those findings might mean for Black boys. How did they experience, as Ta-Nehisi Coates (2010) describes in "A Culture of Poverty," needing to be "On Point" or else one was "next." In using a therapeutic lens, we see how aggressive behaviors are a form of "physiological hyperarousal—the body's heightened response to trauma." Being vigilant to one's surroundings, assessing threats, assessing escape routes and potential allies, as well as enemies is common in segregated neighborhoods.

Harris notes in his article that one surprising development was that "cautious avoidance tactics" were not protective enough for youth trying to avoid violence. The ones least likely to be victims of violence (whether from police, peers, or others) were both vigilant and able (or at least willing) to respond with aggression to threats (Harris, 2021). This points us to what is vital to understand that the "drivers of violence—poverty and economic insecurity, unemployment, lack of resources, especially now during the pandemic . . . as such—are the solutions to preventing violence." Systemic and structural needs of communities can be found in creating affordable housing, peer support groups at no cost, jobs that pay a living wage, more accessible mental health services, and better-funded schools. As Harris (2021) beautifully states: "The solution is to change the environment that produces such trauma."

Today, studies show the disproportionate number of students of color who are diagnosed with disabilities (intellectual, emotional, or psychological disabilities) in comparison to white peers are "due to the bias in testing, ethnic and linguistic differences, and large issues of institutionalized racism" (Blanchett et al., 2009; Donovan & Cross, 2002; Ford et al., 2006; Harry & Klingner, 2006). African American students are 3% more likely to be classified as having an intellectual disability. It seems it is time to begin to remember that perhaps our work is not so far off from the plans and policies of asylums or plantations.

At some point in my career, I googled the 50 Most Influential Psychologists/Therapists/Social Workers. The reality was that all were white and the majority appeared to be cisgendered white men in their formative years.

TABLE 4.2 Founding White Practitioners in Psychology and Their Theoretical or Assessment Contributions

Theorists–Practitioners	Theories	Ethno–Cultural Groups
William James	Functionalism	White Euro-American
Edward Thorndike	Learning Theory	White Euro-American
John Dewey	Educational Psychology	White Euro-American
Francis Galton	Psychometrics	White Euro-American
Edward Titchener	Structuralism	White Euro-American
Harry Stack Sullivan	Interpersonal Psychology	White Euro-American
Wilhelm Wundt	Foundationalism	White European/German
James McKeen Cattell	Intelligence Theory	White Euro-American
Sigmund Freud	Psychoanalysis	White European/Jewish/Austrian
Carl Jung	Analytic Psychology	White European/Swiss
John Watson	Behaviorism	White Euro-American
B. F. Skinner	Behaviorism	White Euro-American
Aaron Beck	Cognitive Theory	White Euro-American
Abraham Maslow	Humanistic Psychology	White Euro-American/Jewish

Theorists–Practitioners	Theories	Ethno–Cultural Groups
Melanie Klein	Object Relations	White Euro-American/Jewish/Austrian
Carl Rogers	Humanistic Psychology	White Euro-American
Viktor Frankl	Existential Psychology	White European/Jewish/Austrian
Max Wertheimer	Gestalt Psychology	White European/Czech
Heinz Kohut	Self-Psychology	White Euro-American / Jewish/Austrian
Salvador Minuchin	Family Systems	White European/Jewish/Russian/Argentinian
Murray Bowen	Family Systems	White Euro-American
Georg von Békésy	Sensation-Perception	White European/Hungarian
Lev Vygotsky	Cognitive Development	White European/Belarusian
Howard Gardner	Multiple Intelligences	White Euro-American
Jean Piaget	Cognitive Development	White European/Swiss
Mary Ainsworth	Attachment Theory	White Euro-Canadian
Robert Yerkes	Army Alpha and Beta Intelligence Tests	White Euro-American
Raymond B. Cattell	16 PF personality test	White European/British
David Wechsler	WISC and WAIS Intelligence Tests Wechsler Memory Scales	White Euro-American
Alan S. Kaufman	Kaufman Intelligence and (K-BIT, K-SEALS, K-ABC, KAIT, K-TEA series)	White Euro-American
Hermann Rorschach	Rorschach Inkblot Test	White European/Swiss
Aaron Beck	Beck Depression and Anxiety Inventories	White Euro-American
James N. Butcher	MMPI Personality Tests	White Euro-American
Theodore Millon	MCMI personality test series	White Euro-American
Richard Woodcock	Woodcock-Johnson Cognitive and Achievement Tests	White Euro-American

Theorists–Practitioners	Theories	Ethno–Cultural Groups
Thomas Achenbach	Child Behavior Checklist series	White Euro-American
Nancy Bayley	Infant Development Scales series	White Euro-American

Source: "Racial Disparity and the Pathologizing of People of Color in Mental Health Diagnoses and Psychological Assessment," by G. DeArth-Pendley, 2012, pp. 3–4.

As I learned from a variety of professors, clinicians, and community organizers, I was always irritated that they were not talking about what the dope director in that community mental health center was doing or how Instituto Familiar de la Raza in the Mission District of San Francisco was holding *plática*[15] and *limpias*[16] and Mayan readings for their families in addition to psychotherapy. They were not talking about how therapists like Socorro Reynoso are creating community healing spaces that are "designed to mimic a home . . . because home is where we learn, home is where we love, home is where we hurt, and home is where we heal" in Inglewood, CA (Soco Rey Therapy, n.d.). There they also decorate the space with different arts and stories that represent the lived experiences of those using the space to help the clients ground into their own strength and power. Or how Steven Campos, Robyn Gorman, and Dennis Febo have been intertwining social work, community care, and abolishing the juvenile detention complex for youth in New Jersey for over 10 years. What about Nadia Lopez, who left Mott Hall Bridges Academy that she founded and was principal of for a decade due to lack of structural support in education (McMurdock, 2022)? She shifted gears to be

---

15 *Plática* in Western terms is a "chat, or small talk." The term *plática* is used very often to denote a transfer or communication of information, usually in a group setting, where an elder is providing education to others. *Pláticas* are known and understood throughout Latin America and the Caribbean.

16 *Limpias* are practices used to cleanse the spirit. *Limpias* are an Indigenous folk healing method that comes from the Caribbean and Latin America, usually based in curanderismo or African traditional practices. It means to "clean or cleanse." In Western terms, it is a spiritual energetic cleanse, using specific medicine tools (e.g., basil, copal, sage, egg) to heal the unseen levels of energy and consciousness. Often, they are used to rid the body of difficult emotions.

a leadership coach in 2020 after she developed kidney disease from the stress of the profession. Today, she still sees the impact of the same system failing other principals and educators of color as they seek mentorships with her.

As a student, I did not want to just hear about the individuals who were funded fully and supported. I wanted to hear about those whose name has echoed on the lips of families for years in our communities. I wanted to know more about what my supervisors and professors had done to "help people" in real time—not just in quantitative research studies with massive N samples and big ole z scores. I wasn't interested in just peer-reviewed articles. I wanted to know what peers and participants of services felt and said about the people who did not fit a white, middle-class, "well-articulated" version of healing.

Aspects of Emotional–Decolonial Unlearning
On the *DSM*, diagnosis, and symptoms:

1. The *Diagnostic Statistical Manual* is an expired way of viewing the kaleidoscope of human experiences, beliefs, and expressions.
2. The *DSM* is inherently political in that the set of symptoms provides no context, can harm, creates division, and has pathologized differences.
3. Diagnoses are capitalism's attempt to quantify human suffering. Capitalism hurts everyone and dehumanizes everyone.
4. Historical emotional injury impacts our choices, thinking, and behavior in the present, and presents itself as mental "disorders" that require categorization of a diagnosis.
5. Diagnosis can be a transient, fluid, helpful tool in the short-term, but it is not meant to box people into categories for the long-term.

On how the bounds of "therapy" are changing:

6. "Good-enough treatment" is no longer acceptable on the part of practitioners.
7. Our fields are evolving and expanding to fit the needs of people and will lead to the cocreation of new pathways in how we support (in and out of therapy offices).

8. New ways of supporting, inclusive of practitioners and participants, create more equity and accessibility to support care services and health.
9. An increase in ancestral ways of tending to emotional health = honoring and referencing the ancestral roots, while establishing sturdy, futuristic ways of being in relationship with our emotional health and one another.
10. Helping professions need to cease using language that polices.
11. Emotional and physical labor should be paid and paid well.

On the binary of normal versus deviance:

12. "Normal" leaves out the vast majority of the world.
13. All mainstream intelligence and personality tests administered in U.S. public schools, detention centers, prisons, courts, the military, jobs, and clinics designed by white practitioners should be abolished.
14. All theories of crime, pathology, and deviance developed by white practitioners and authors should be abolished.

Emo–Decolonial Practice Offerings
- Notice frequently, if not always, how historical events have impacted your therapy participants' worldview and nervous system.
- Instead of symptoms, consider utilizing "expressions." For instance, Mohammad's loss of appetite, irritability outbursts, and fascination with the news are an expression of their historical trauma and current racial trauma.
- Find ways to speak of and work with more humane and natural ways of speaking about perfectly normal and understandable expressions of suffering, pain, or unwellness.
- Consider not utilizing diagnosis at your centers.
- Consider leaving options available for higher-income earner-therapy participants (and anyone else) to donate to a fund for individuals unable to meet the rate for therapy support.
- How might more accessibility/equity create increases in support, care, and health?

- Inquiring about ancestors is much like inquiring about second-generation family dynamics, histories, and systems.
- Invite remembrance and the revival of ancestral ways of practicing, supporting, and tending to your work.
- We have been conditioned to believe that inclusive holistic language is offensive language. This is reinforced by rewarding the use of "restrictive and medical" language.
- How might you (still be) utilizing punishment—in the form of diagnosis, more treatment, medication, removal from place of residence, restricting visitation, limiting food, and so forth—as a form of control?
- Create new ways of understanding another, without the means and use of assessment.
- Invite discussion around how therapy participants might be affected by historical and current global events.

Affirmations
- We are allowed to talk about and engage in healing.
- It is safe to talk about the harm within my field.
- It is safe to think outside the box in my field.
- Science and research are not the only beneficial parts of our fields.
- I am allowed to struggle with the language, practices, and histories of my field.
- I am entitled to change my mind about what feels important.
- I am doing my best to create safe and equitable health for all people and bodies.
- My practices include history, all identities, accountability, and creativity.

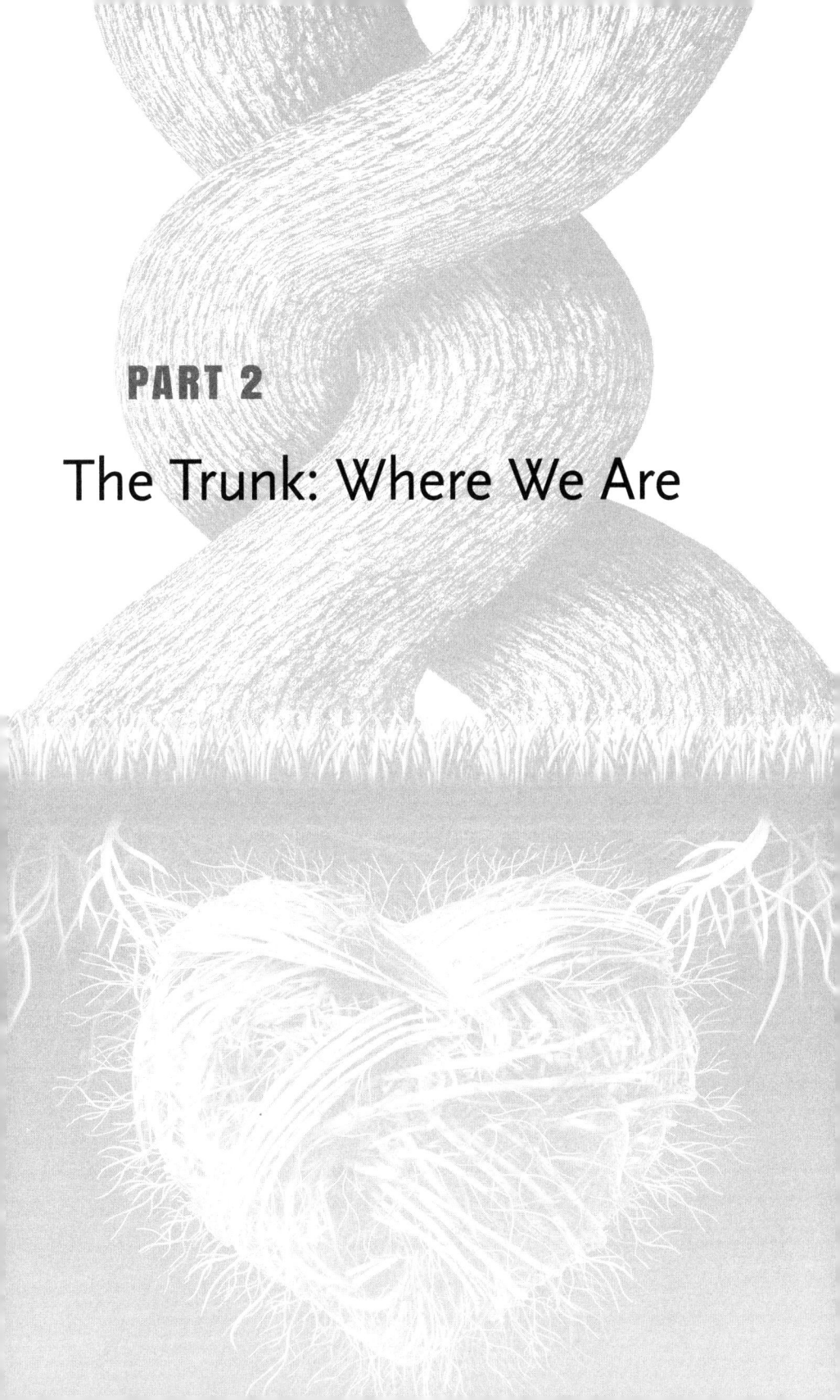

PART 2
The Trunk: Where We Are

CHAPTER 5

From Historical Trauma to Healing the Collective Soul Wound

It's important for us to know our history, because we are carrying it.
—Maria Yellow Horse Brave Heart, PhD (2005)

Like it or not, the ways of our parents and ancestors are with us, even when we don't know them, don't like them, or don't remember them.
—Ruth King, Healing Rage (2004)

Over 500 years of contact between the original peoples of the Americas and settler nations has produced extensive displacement and disconnection. Colonialism, manufactured by settlers, has produced a great deal of damage to the spirits of Indigenous Peoples. It is necessary to declare that the root of the injury has been caused by colonial violence, which was significantly enforced by governments through legislation and institutions. We are now in a process of healing from this historical trauma.
—Renee Linklater, Decolonizing Trauma Work (2014)

There is still an abundance of babies drowning in our rivers. There is an abundance of helpers, healers, and therapy workers who are deeply struggling to pull our babies from the rivers of historical and current violence, while having trouble staying afloat themselves. Knowing about decolonization and engaging in workshop series or readings, is helpful and essential, but is not nearly enough. We must get real. We must get messy . . . gritty; we must show up with humility and be willing to *not* know everything. We must be willing to learn from people whom our education system has conditioned us to overlook. We must be willing to sit in basements with youth organizers 15 years younger than many of us—learning.

The truth is we cannot decolonize anything without *getting curious* and doing our part to learn about the history of the land we reside upon, the history of our original homeland (if we are settlers on the current land in which we reside), and have a more emotional–social worldview around how their experiences affected the way we view the world today. It is my belief that we cannot dismantle, smash, decolonize anything without unlearning—without understanding our role, our kin's role, how we have been conditioned, where we continue to participate in the socialization of others, and where our wounded parts lie (shout out to internal family systems). On top of this, we have the duty to begin to RELEARN what was never taught, discover why it wasn't taught, how we have been harmed by this collective gaslighting, and where it shows up in our decisions, policies, and relationships today—here and now.

We must be willing to investigate the ways that we have been gaslit by the very educational and mental health systems for whom we took on student loan debt. A large part of the longitudinal process of decolonization, for healers, helpers, and therapy workers, is *identifying* and *being truthful* about the emotionally manipulative and violent parts of our training and education. That perhaps, we HAVE been in an *Intimate Organization-Partner Relationship* with institutions, schools, practices, and a field that we have wholeheartedly dedicated our lives to. What makes this exchange even more dehumanizing is the level of trauma that many of us have reactivated from our histories and absorbed from therapeutic work. We have become sick, disengaged, overwhelmed, and have even perished from it—with no compensation for our emotional, unacknowledged labor. For racialized people, this is a recipe for disaster, pulled from the playbooks of our histories through colonization. Additionally, this carefully constructed and intergenerational system of exploitation also deeply impacts the psyches, relationships, and identities inherited by white-bodied people. People who have come to be known as white have also lost a great deal from these arrangements.

> **TRADING IN HUMANITY FOR COMFORT**
>
> NAMING WHITENESS AND DIFFERENTIATING THEM FROM WHAT IT MEANS TO BE A HUMAN BEING IS A NECESSITY . . .
> WHITE SUPREMACY INSIDIOUSLY TRICKS WHITE PEOPLE . . .
> INTO BELIEVING THAT WE ARE SUPREME SIMPLY BECAUSE WE ARE WHITE, [AND] THAT THE END OF WHITE SUPREMACY WOULD MEAN AN END TO OUR OWN SURVIVAL.
> —Greg Elliot (2016), "10 Ways White Supremacy Wounds White People: A Tale of Mutuality"
>
> This is part of the internal, and eventually external, work that white people can begin to embark upon in order to experience less guilt, shame, and minimization of one's historical and personal effects on the present day.

Begin at the Beginning: Understanding Historical Trauma

What is essential about decolonization is rehumanizing ourselves and one another, and acknowledging our capacities. If we do not talk about this, the cyclical violence continues. The mental and behavioral health industrial complexes, as they stand, condone the violence of mass genocide historical trauma.

Further, the MHICs do not seek to change a thing, including how many practitioners are accessible to people. A large part of our own decolonial unraveling is to admit the truth about the dehumanizing one-sided relationship many of us have had with the educational, mental, and behavioral health care systems that we joined with optimism, energy, passion, an intrinsic affinity for, and the hope of helping people be well . . . to heal. But the mental and behavioral health systems should not be confused for healing. Therapy is not necessarily synonymous with healing. This is extremely important because psychiatry and psychology were part of the colonial assault (Linklater, 2014). Should we be interested in the business of healing, it may be beneficial to start at the beginning, or as much of the beginning as we are consciously aware of.

You may be wondering, either:

A. How is it that I have not heard of historical trauma and its effects on my body and mental health?
B. Why haven't I learned about colonization, historical trauma, and its effects, as well as treatment options in my clinical education? Is this new to our field?

To which I would then respond:

A. Because the education, mental, and behavioral health systems are set up this way to keep the general public in the dark—specifically related to atrocities and events that seek to bring racialized and colonized peoples together. Division and secrecy are tools of the oppressors.

OR

B. See the above response. Decolonial work in mental health is NOT new to our fields.

Historical trauma within mental health has emerged from, and has been rooted in, Indigenous experiences and worldviews. Indigenous peoples' trauma across the world has changed since colonization created a climate of systematic oppression, violence, and abuse. At its core, historical trauma is intergenerational trauma experienced by a specific cultural group that has a history of being systematically oppressed.

Historical trauma:

- Is present-day developmental/racial/global trauma, superimposed upon a traumatic ancestral past, creating additional trauma and adversity.
- Impacts spiritual, psychological, emotional, and physical health.
- Is an active accumulation and reverberation of trauma across generations.
- Can affect the well-being and biology of descendants who have not directly experienced the traumatic events, and can lead to symptoms of trauma in the descendants.
- Symptoms can manifest as depression, rage (more in the following chapter), fixation on trauma, vacant self-esteem (DeGruy, 2005), racist socialization (DeGruy, 2005), addiction, spiritual emergency/crisis, and difficulties with change.
- Is people coming into systems of services and support from communities who have been subjected to historical trauma may experience triggers with the systems that are retraumatizing and dehumanizing.

> **QUESTION FRAMEWORK WHEN LOOKING AT HISTORICAL TRAUMA**
>
> INDIVIDUAL:
> - How has this child/adolescent/caregiver/person/couple/family been impacted (from an exo-systemic lens) by colonization and/or (attempted) cultural genocide?
> - Is there possible historical trauma in this child/caregiver/person/family's life?
> - Is there unresolved grief and/or rage affecting their well-being?
> - How does historical trauma show up in how they claim their identities?
>
> COLLECTIVE:
> - How has historical trauma affected their relationships?
> - How has historical trauma affected how they see themselves (i.e., worthlessness, vacant esteem, etc.)?
> - How has it affected how they have been parented and/or parent?
> - Where does white-bodied supremacy and oppression show up in how they (unconsciously) engage with children?

- How does the historical trauma show up in their community?
- How do the effects of historical trauma affect their identity and how they show up in the community?
- How does the historical trauma impact their relationship with their youth/children, and how they are treated?

HISTORICAL:
- What did our elders and ancestors *KNOW* that we may have forgotten?
- Where is there resilience and strength in the individual, community, and system?
- Will learning/talking more about their history and forms of collective trauma and triumphs strengthen them?
- Will it lessen over-responsibility, guilt, and shame?
- How has historical trauma impacted our relationship to ancestry?
- How has historical trauma impacted our relationship to the land we live on?
- Has it impacted their relationships to religion/spirituality, particularly spiritual practices that experience anti-Blackness and anti-Indigenousness (i.e., Ifa, Lucumí, Vodou, etc.)?

The Soul Wound

Eduardo Duran (mixed-race Opelousas/Coushatta descendant) was among the first to utilize the term *soul wound* to highlight "spiritual injury, soul sickness, soul wounding, and ancestral hurt," in *Healing the Soul Wound: Counseling with American Indians and Other Native People*. Some research literature emerged from Israeli studies on posttraumatic stress while Eduardo was seeking further discourse on the *soul* in trauma studies literature. Knowledge of the soul wound has been present in "Indian country" for many generations. It suggests that these concepts all present the idea that when trauma is not dealt with in previous generations, it has to be dealt with in subsequent generations.

To clarify, Dr. Maria Yellow Horse Brave Heart conceptualized the soul wound as historical trauma, contending that historical trauma is defined as what happens when an ethnic group is traumatized over an extended period of time, including forced assimilation and cumulative losses across generations. This loss—or grief as we discussed in the prior chapter—involves language, culture, and spirituality, which contribute to the breakdown of the family kinship networks and social structures. The historical legacy and the current psychosocial conditions contribute to ongoing intergenerational traumas.

An example of intergenerational trauma transmission would be the level of trauma and generational symptoms and struggles among the Lakota people, a group of Indigenous people from the greater Sioux Native American tribe. Dr. Brave Heart frequently speaks of the suffering from impaired grief as an effect of cumulative, massive group trauma associated with tragic events. The Wounded Knee Massacre, assassination of Sitting Bull, and the forced removal of Lakota children to extermination camps[17] for Indigenous children are but a few examples of massive group traumas experienced by the Lakota.

During the late 19th century, when most First Nation and Indigenous peoples were confined to reservations, the federal government engaged in a cultural assimilation campaign by forcing thousands of Indigenous children to attend boarding schools, under the belief that "Native people would not succeed unless their traditions, habits, and beliefs were eradicated" (EJI, 2014).

According to the Equal Justice Initiative (2014), more than 400 day and boarding schools were built, and people indigenous to North America were forced to attend these schools, forbidden to speak their native tongue, forced to renounce belief systems, and forced to abandon the fullness of their identities, including their names. The Equal Justice Initiative notes: "many children were leased out to white families as indentured servants" or murdered (Equal Justice Initiative, 2021). In what is now known as the United States of America, parents who resisted the removal of their children

---

17 Term sourced from Andrea Landry of Indigenousmotherhood.com via an Instagram post (@indigenousmotherhood) calling people to be more accurate in how they describe the genocide of Indigenous peoples on Turtle Island.

to boarding schools were imprisoned and had their children forcibly taken from them or murdered. The Equal Justice Initiative (2021) notes that over 15 Hopi Indians were incarcerated in Alcatraz Island for refusing to send their children to boarding schools in an act of resistance. The actions were consistent with ensuring that their future generations would not be subjected to the violence and abuse of the boarding schools, thereby breaking generational patterns and curses. The boarding schools were violent—filled with sexual trauma, overcrowding, below-standard medical care, little to no food, and little to no healthy attachments and affection. By the 1930s, most off-reservation boarding schools were closed.

This summary is a **small fraction** of what was stolen from the spirits and souls of Indigenous peoples across Turtle Island and what is now known as the Americas. Even still, many North Americans find ourselves believing that colonization is a Western issue. Similar dehumanizing and violent processes can be seen across the globe: from the imperialist plundering of mining, extrajudicial killings, and the militarization of the communities of the Indigenous Lumad People in the Philippines; to the systematic mass murder and ethnic cleansing of over one million ethnic Armenians from Anatolia and adjoining regions by the Ottoman Empire and its ruling party, the Committee of Union and Progress, during World War I resulting in the Armenian Genocide; to the militarization, colonization, attempted erasure, forced displacement, torture, rape, and murder of the good people of Haiti.

I could go on with hundreds, if not thousands, of forms of forced Indigenous land displacement—land that belonged and does belong to the original people.

Dr. Maria Yellow Horse Brave Heart (Brave Heart, 2003) and Eduardo and Bonnie Duran, authors of *Native American Postcolonial Psychology* (1995) were three of the first Indigenous scholars to have raised my level of consciousness as a young doctoral student related to historical trauma. Their discourse around the "cumulative emotional and psychological wounding over the lifespan and across generations, emanating from massive group trauma experience" spoke directly to that of my own—and to that of many of the Black and Brown identified people I served, who lived at or below the poverty level.

As the discourse around mass collective group trauma expanded, research began to unpack and look at the African American experience of generations of slavery, segregation, and institutionalized racism, that in turn has contributed to physical, psychological, and spiritual trauma (DeGruy, 2005). For many of us, living through and bleeding out, the wounds of colonization (i.e., forced migration, slavery, genocide, holocausts, etc.) daily reminders of racial discrimination can exacerbate individual responses to trauma. Reminders that reactivate the soul wound as the pain inflicted is not just that of a mental-emotional nature. The trauma is visceral and somatic—within our soma and cellular memory. The trauma is epigenetic, deeply affecting how we socialize, attach, move, think, and our personality. It is a SOUL WOUND, yet we insist on keeping the wounding "scientific and quantitative" in order to be credible and tangible.

Although the soul wound was originally identified for the experience of Indigenous people affected by historical trauma, as many Indigenous, Black, and Brown researchers have noted, many of our people with histories of collective and cultural violence have experienced the effects of the trauma, and it is important to honor the universality (with some marked differences in types of trauma) that our people have experienced. The agreement leans toward dismantling the "divide and conquer" energy that white supremacy has laid on our laps. Although the soul wound may manifest and look different for various cultures, what is clear is the thread of disconnect from the sense of the self—or in culturally relevant ancestral terms, the soul.

In hundreds of therapy sessions with People of Global Majority[18] (PoGM), what I had continued to note was the connection to the term *soul, community, your people, energy;* whether or not someone was "spiritual," or "politicized." Words like *self* and *identity*, did not land and connect in the same manner. Therefore, I believe as we continue to create politicized care workers and healers, noting the terminology and language that resonates with whom we are serving and holding space for is more important than psychological jargon.

18 People of Global Majority is a term that embraces the power non-white people have as being the majority of the world's population.

Generational Legacies: Posttraumatic Slave Syndrome

It is quite interesting how family systems theory has taught us that individuals exist within and from systems. In order to treat an individual, you must understand the system within which they grew. In the 1950s, psychiatrist Murray Bowen developed the Bowen Family Systems theory, which essentially views the family as an emotional unit where family members are intensely emotionally connected. Keeping with this example, Bowen noted that patterns develop within the emotional system, and each member's behavior impacts the others' behaviors. Depending on the specific family system, the theory suggests that these behavioral patterns can lead to either balance or dysfunction of the system—or both.

Stay with me please, as I further push the metaphor: So even when disconnected from members of the family, the theory suggests that one's family unit still has a *profound* impact on their emotions and actions!

Many of us take for granted that our family patterns, relationships, and behaviors have an impact on how we operate. Take a moment. Take a deep cleansing breath. Now, although glaringly obvious, somehow therapy has persisted all these decades by avoiding a deeper dive and larger discussion of the indelible effects of our ancestral histories on our mental, emotional, and physical health and the intergenerational transmission of historical and racial traumas.

Although traditional mental health models ask us to look within, and to alter or shift our thoughts for a more "stable outcome," the fact remains that Freud, Charcot, Ellis, Bandura, Fitz, Klein, Mahler, Rank, Linehan, and others all sidestepped a fundamental truth—that there are and continue to be deeply impactful effects of settler and emotional colonization that have been passed on to us. That history has played a role in producing negative perceptions, images, and behaviors. That trauma can upset our equilibrium and sense of being, and—if it is severe enough—it can distort our attitudes, beliefs, and relationships, thereby producing unwanted consequences. If a person repeatedly and systematically experiences severe trauma (especially at the hands of other human beings), then these unwanted consequences and reverberations are augmented exponentially. If a person repeatedly and systematically experiences severe trauma, as does their Land and their ancestors (specifically at the hands of other human beings), then these reverberations are further exacerbated, potentially leaving a person feeling incapable, incompetent, disconnected from their Source and themselves, and holding a great deal (understandably) of rage, grief, and numbness.

Dr. Joy DeGruy's legacy work (academic work) on PTSS connected complex and developmental trauma with the impacts of generations of slavery and oppression on descendants of the Transatlantic Slave Trade for many of us of African and Black descent. Her work highlighted not just the current-day racial oppression that people of the African Diaspora endure, but the direct and indirect methods of transmission of trauma on an ancestral-multigenerational level.

PTSS exists "when a population has experienced multigenerational trauma resulting from centuries of slavery and continue to experience oppression and institutionalized racism today." (DeGruy, 2005). This is compounded by a belief (real or imagined) that the benefits of society in which they live are not accessible to them, prompting feelings of vacant esteem, ever-present anger, and racist socialization.

Ron Eyerman, professor and African American scholar, explored the theory of cultural trauma in his classic book *Cultural Trauma: Slavery and the Formation of African American Identity*. He noted that the "trauma" in question is "slavery, not as an institution, experience—but as a collective memory, a form of remembrance that grounded the identity-formation of a people" (Eyerman, 2002).

As the research and life experiences of Dr. Eyerman and Dr. DeGruy suggest, when allowing oneself to absorb the magnitude of the trauma that descendants of enslaved Africans hold, it is not necessary to experience being a slave; however, 246 years of chattel slavery in what is now known as the United States of America (this does not include the years of enslavement throughout Central, South America, and the Caribbean) "guaranteed the prosperity and privilege of the South's white progeny." Dr. DeGruy defines PTSS not as a way of further pathologizing, attempting to "use the master's tools" such as the *DSM* categorizations, but rather as a way to identify the direct relationship between the experience of being enslaved and the current-day levels of oppression—such as excessive police violence—of Black Americans. We also know that through research conducted on other groups who have experienced structural and systemic oppression that characteristics such as self-doubt, shame, guilt, intense aggression, and unaddressed grief and rage are all symptoms of survivor guilt (Danieli, 1998; DeGruy, 2005; Yehuda & Lehrner, 2018).

Dr. Yael Danieli, founder and director at International Center for Multigenerational Legacies of Trauma in New York City, noted in the world-renowned book, *Intergenerational Handbook of Multigenerational Legacies of Trauma*:

> The intergenerational perspective reveals the impact of trauma, its contagion, and repeated patterns within the family. It may help explain certain behavior patterns, symptoms, roles, and values adopted by family members; family sources of vulnerability as well as resilience and strength; and job choices through generations. Viewed from a family systems perspective, what happened in one generation will affect what happens in the older or younger generations, though the actual behavior may take a variety of forms. Within an intergenerational context, the trauma and its impact may be passed down as the family legacy even to children born after the trauma.

Likewise, the effects of unresolved psychogenic trauma on Indigenous and Aboriginal people, have been described by the Aboriginal Healing Foundation as:

> The effects of trauma are not resolved in one generation. When trauma is ignored and there is no support for dealing with it, the trauma will be passed from one generation to the next. What we learn to see as "normal" . . . we pass on to our own children.

PTSS, cultural trauma, historical trauma, and the *Soul Wound*—among other names for generational legacies of trauma due to colonial violence—provide us context as we seek to understand the correlation between the mental health field, psychotherapy, and why it is essential to politicize our clinical and behavioral health practices (while we are in the process of dismantling larger structural systems of oppression). It is clear to me that the physical act of returning the Land to the Indigenous people across the globe, will not happen without there first being a deep shift emotionally. Late-stage capitalism is a siren among the deep waters, calling to even the most "WOKE" of us. With that said, the first stage (phase) of *Decolonizing Therapy* addresses *History*. For mental health workers, this includes understanding how global colonization, historical trauma, intergenerational trauma transmission, and forced migration show up in ourselves and those we support. The key question remains, "How is the legacy of trauma transmitted in this person, family, community, and/or ancestry?"

Questions to consider and process for ourselves and when working with individuals whose history is correlated with the trauma of colonization:

- Have their People/Ancestry experienced slavery, forced displacement/migration, war, attempted ethnic cleansing, genocide, or mass killings?
- What symptoms do you believe may have been exhibited?
- Has the violence occurred on multiple levels (i.e., body, psyche, relationally, etc.)?
- Were the effects of these traumas ever addressed (individually or globally)?
- Do these traumas continue today on an individual and societal level?
- Are there places, spaces, or monuments dedicated to grieving and processing these traumas? Where?
- Is there a legacy of trauma? If so, how does this arise in who we are working with—for them?
- What else are there legacies of (i.e., fighting back, justice work, healing work, creating safety for others, etc.)? The key is to also identify and label the strengths as well.

Note: These questions are inspired by Posttraumatic Slave Syndrome, which is the work of Dr. Joy DeGruy.

Leaders of the Movement Toward Collective Healing

I am saddened to state that recently I have heard of the late Dr. Frederick Hickling's (May 2020, Rest in Power) life's work related to global decolonial mental health. He spoke of the postcolonial Jamaican government and helped to facilitate the deinstitutionalization of many patients who resided at Bellevue Hospital. Dr. Hickling also spearheaded many innovations within mental health and psychiatry related to public policy, instituting systemic changes that resulted in more wellness, emotional and mental hygiene, and freedom for many incarcerated Jamaicans. He also created local policies instituting systemic and criminal justice changes, including recreating a community mental health center and taking the lead in creating structures of wellness, instead of institutionalization, by helping to bring patients from diagnoses of acute psychosis to being discharged and living successful lives.

Dr. Hickling was clear and verbose about the mental health challenge for descendants of African people enslaved in Jamaica. He would frequently contend that creating a blueprint for the decolonization of global mental health would assist in helping to shift the narrative and intergenerational experiences and impact of over 500 years of colonization and oppression for Jamaicans living within the carceral psychiatric institution.

Dr. Hickling's legacy of decolonial mental health activism is yet another reminder of the power of the mental health community of service providers and the essentialism of placing therapeutic community action behind our services. As helping professionals, many of us witness the tentacles of historical trauma show up with human services programs. These programs are intended to provide support, accessibility, and resources to a wide range of individuals, including members of groups who may experience historical trauma. Instead, what often occurs is a replication of the historical trauma experience. There is often not enough time, money, and resources.

As my colleague Ji-Youn Kim—a brilliant decolonial counselor for collective liberation based in stolen Musqueam, Squamish, and Tsleil-Waututh territories (so-called Vancouver, Canada)—states:

Therapists Perpetuate White Supremacy By:
- Maintaining power dynamics between therapist and client by positioning therapist as expert.
- Framing systemic oppressions and experiences of oppression as politics, belief systems, and perceptions.
- Overemphasizing individual choice and self-responsibility.
- Avoiding topics of race and how it plays into the traumatic experience.
- Dismissing appropriate emotional responses to oppression such as rage.
- Positioning racial trauma as past events, not an ongoing experience that will continue to happen.
- Equating cultural competency and values for diversity as a safety for BIPOC.
- Maintaining neutrality in discussions of oppression and avoiding taking a stance. By being mindful of unresolved grief and distrust of majority groups or government programs, human service providers can more readily deliver programs to reduce family stress, child abuse and neglect, substance misuse, mental health challenges, and domestic violence. (Kim, 2020a)

It is crucial to be clear that therapy, as it stands in this space paradigm and time, is NOT a substitute for systemic and structural change. I am clear that the mental, educational, and behavioral health systems will need restructuring in order to maintain wellness, accountability and fluency, as the collective world begins to create new ways. But first, this politicization, this revolution, this decolonization must be within.

The aim of this book, and my existence, is not to provide an entire dissertation on historical trauma, again. Rather, it is to wake up (snap) and galvanize the current societal collective to incentivize those of us already doing important and therapeutic work with the option of learning from all of our ancestors, those living and not of our ancestral bloodline as well. They continue to lay out the map for our future. Decolonization is not about getting stuck within the mud of our historical traumas. NO! Decolonizing includes reclamation. Decolonizing includes land sovereignty. Decolonizing includes liberation from mental, physical, emotional, and financial slavery. Decolonization includes us, here, now, and preparing for the pivot and shift of the near future, everywhere from education, to criminal justice, to health care, to housing, to mental and behavioral health.

Countless scholars, elders, community organizers, clinicians, peer counselors, ancestors, and clients have pondered, throughout the years, that rather than diagnosing and pathologizing a person and grouping their symptoms into a disorder to "track and treat," what would it be like to consistently and collectively create a holistic approach? A WHOLE approach that looks at the entire person, their spirituality, their ancestral history, their health as opposed to deifying the *Diagnostic Statistical Manual of Mental Disorders* (DSM), which was mostly created by older, male, white-identifying psychologists and psychiatrists who impregnated the *DSM* with their white supremacist biases.

Many, many holistic, ancestrally guided, and decolonial approaches have been passed down, created, and are currently being utilized. From the departed brilliant Jamaican psychiatrist Dr. Frederick W. Hickling's (2019) work as executive director of the Caribbean Institute of Mental Health and Substance Abuse (CARIMENSA), University of the West Indies (his contributions of Jamaican psychiatry to decolonizing global mental health have been tremendous), to the power and cultural bridges of Dr. Michael Yellow Bird (2014), "Healing Through Neurodecolonization and Mindfulness." Dr. Yellow Bird is an Indigenous scholar and activist, citizen of the Arikara (Sahnish), Hidatsa, and Mandan tribes in North Dakota. To the necessary brilliance of Black Trans medical exercise specialist, physical therapist assistant, and educator, Ilya Parker, founder of Decolonizing Fitness, LLC. As our bodies, all bodies, must also find a place to "land," to find health and safety as we shift our paradigms while creating space for trans and nonbinary people. To the vital consulting work of Ta7taliya Nahanee, Squamish CEO and consultant of Decolonize First, who engages social change through interactive workshops and workbooks for youth! To Sonalee Rashatwar, a self-identified nonbinary, fat futurist, therapist, and social worker; cofounder of Radical Therapy Center in Philadelphia, PA. Sonalee reminds us that colluding with fatphobia is unethical and a continuation of colonization.

To the ever-necessary Nap Bishop, Tricia Hersey: performance artist, activist, theologian, community healer, and founder of the Nap Ministry. Tricia reminds us all that rest can be an act of resistance. That rest can be powerful and transformational, and that exhaustion is NOT liberation.

All of these beings and more are needed. We are engaging in political work. Our very identities and bodies are political. Our slow deaths on capitalistic company time are political. Whether we have a passport or clean running water is political. It is all political, despite the false belief that politics and therapy should not mix, promulgated by my former graduate school professor.

You—here, reading this dreaming up countless possibilities with me; with your colleagues; where we get to bring together what we do, and do it without the cost of our mental, emotional, and familial health—are indeed so political.

The People's Stories

Charri was a 19-year-old student when she entered the community mental health clinic. She was brought to the clinic by her two best friends who had concerns because she was in a DV (domestic violence) relationship. Charri denied the relationship being violent; however, she did note that her partner frequently spoke of taking their life if she left them. A few months into the weekly sessions, Charri began to have intense migraines. She also identified having many tasks on top of being a full-time student, working two part-time jobs, and picking up both of her younger brothers from school, as she lived in the family apartment with her mother. As sessions continued, Charri spoke of her mother's relationship with her biological father, who had left the home when she was a child. She noted how her mother frequently made her feel unworthy, ungrateful, and incompetent. Interestingly enough, she also had a string of supervisors and bosses who frequently made her feel "needed and like a phenomenal worker," who then months later suddenly "removed their mentorship, kindness, and affectionate supportive gaze" from her, leaving her feeling unlovable and as though she had done something wrong.

As time went on, Charri began to note the pattern and theme with her politicized counselor. They worked on a timeline and genogram that looked at the maternal line of her family and their relationships with one another—and toward their respective partners. She noted a clear line between the responsibilities of the women in her maternal line, abuse histories, neglect from the paternal line, mistreatment from resentful and overworked mothers, and medical ailments that could not be explained by doctors, much like her migraines. The women also overworked, had poor boundaries, and were frequently expected to "cook, clean, serve the man and family—at all costs," much like her Dominican Caribbean culture dictated.

As time went on, the insight and connections between the women in her family and to themselves continued to be helpful but did not "move or shift" the migraines and Charri's experiences. Together the politicized counselor created a three-part ritual for releasing historical stories that involved music, singing, journaling, mantras, burning what no longer served Charri, and creating "expectation plans" with her mother. They also worked with a somatic practitioner in the office to help provide Charri with a more conscious embodiment when engaging and setting boundaries with her mother (which was unheard of culturally). Simultaneously, Charri began to take a nonuniversity community mixed-method course on the Dominican Republic, Haiti, and the island of Ayiti. She began to learn about how her great-aunts and grandmother were explicitly affected by Trujillo, the dictator. It is said that Trujillo's fixation with women "led him to place a subordinate in charge of selecting the most beautiful young girls in the country for him to deflower." He engaged in many barbaric acts toward women, and she began to better understand the relationship of strength and stoicism that her mother and grandmother engaged in.

Needless to say a year later, Charri was attending sessions monthly in a collective group setting with other Caribbean, Black-identified people who had experienced ancestral historical harm and were reclaiming their identities and rewriting new stories with their loved ones.

This is an example of historical emo–decolonial healing work. It is possible. Trauma is multigenerational and intergenerational. It is a psychological wounding that is physical, emotional, spiritual, and which accumulates over time. Historical violence impacts as many as three to seven plus generations removed from the externally induced trauma. Traumatic "blood memory," as many Indigenous communities note, is the experiences of those before us becoming in our psyches and physical bodies.

Therefore, even though the word "trauma" has roots in Western contexts, with an emo–decolonial approach it is essential to name this and—as with everything we are naming in this book—it is essential to find new ways to articulate the circumstances that stem from colonial and psychiatric violence. In using Western trauma terminology, this book is referring to a person's or people's response to an injury, not the psychiatric diagnosis. In this way, this book is seeking to divest from using psychiatric colonial terminology that implies that the individual is responsible for the response, as opposed to holding the larger systems appropriately accountable for our dis-ease and suffering.

If the whole experience of therapy is to take a look at where the imbalance exists, and then to create steps to abolish spaces and practices impeding optimal health, then we are morally (forget ethically) bound to one another. Morally bound to be our siblings' keeper. Morally bound to take serious action toward the collective liberation of all people and all of our descendants. As my *abuelito* would remind me, "We do it—and better—for the seven generations before and after us."

Aspects of Emotional–Decolonial Unlearning
1. Decolonial work is not new.
2. A large part of the longitudinal process of decolonization—for *healers, helpers, and therapy workers*—*is identifying* and *being truthful* about the emotionally manipulative and violent parts of our training and education.
3. Historical trauma has emerged and been rooted in the worldviews of Indigenous peoples globally.
4. We are not meant (as practitioners) to hold, be, and heal each participant of therapy alone.

5. White supremacy tricks white people into believing that they are supreme simply because they are white, and that the end of white supremacy would mean an end to white people's survival.
6. Not all therapy needs to be inside an office.
7. All of your skills are, and should be, translatable to other fields, peoples, peers, and so forth.
8. Practitioners of therapy and our specific expertise are necessary, important, and help keep others safe—when not utilized as punishment or a weapon for structural oppression.
9. All people, at all socioeconomic levels, citizenships, identities, and abilities deserve solid, multigenerational, and multiplicitous methods of healing.
10. Historical trauma **is** an active accumulation and reverberation of trauma across generations.
11. Historical trauma can impact the well-being and biology of descendants who have not directly experienced the traumatic events and can lead to symptoms of trauma in the descendants.
12. Mass collective group trauma was originally explored with what is now North American Indigenous peoples and Jewish peoples.
13. Daily reminders of racial discrimination can exacerbate individual responses to trauma.
14. Daily trauma reminders can reactivate the Soul Wound.
15. The trauma is epigenetic, deeply affecting how we socialize, attach, move, think, and our personality. It is a SOUL WOUND, yet we insist on keeping the wounding "scientific and quantitative" in order to be credible and tangible.
16. **Therapists perpetuate white supremacy by** maintaining power dynamics between therapist and client by positioning the therapist as the expert.
17. **Therapists perpetuate white supremacy by** overemphasizing individual choice and self-responsibility.
18. **Therapists perpetuate white supremacy by** equating cultural competency and values for diversity as safety for BIPOC.

Emo–Decolonial Practice Offerings

- How does whiteness wound you?
- How does whiteness wound your therapeutic practices and ability to engage in healing?
- How does classism wound you?
- How does classism wound your therapeutic practices and ability to engage in equitable healing?
- How does classism wound who receives your healing/help?
- Define and bring into the therapy relationship your definition and distinctions between healing and helping.
- The word **trauma** has roots in colonial and Western contexts.
- Engage in conversations with participants about which and what they prefer and why.
- Invite our forms of wellness, helping, healing, and perspective into your practices.
- Take the space and time to process how cultural and historical trauma show up in the therapeutic space and participants.
- Take the space and time to process how historical trauma has affected how they have been parented and/or parent.
- Take the space and time to process how historical trauma affects a community.
- When a participant is experiencing low self-worth or feelings of not being enough, ask them, "What did your elders and ancestors KNOW that you may have forgotten?"
- Inquire: "Where is there resilience and strength in the individual, community, and system?"
- Notice whether your lineage and history may be impacting the therapeutic relationship.
- Inquire: "Will learning/talking more about their history and forms of collective trauma and triumphs strengthen them or disorganize them at this time?"

Are there other ways to identify deep soul harm that are more comfortable to a participant than the word "trauma"?

■■■■ CHAPTER 6

Intergenerational Trauma Transmission: Ancestral Trauma and Wisdom Exist *Together Within Us*

Decolonizing invites us to stretch our diagnoses back to a time when the concept of the self mattered less than the relationships upon which our lives depended, from the microbes inside of us, to the world around us.
—Dr. Rupa Marya & Raj Patel, *Inflamed:*
  Deep Medicine and the Anatomy of Injustice (2021)

No man can put a chain about the ankle of his fellow man without at last finding the other end fastened about his own neck.
—Frederick Douglass (1894)

When European settlers first came to this country centuries ago, they brought a millennium of intergenerational and historical trauma with them, stored in the cells of their bodies. Today this trauma continues to live on in the bodies of most Americans.
—Resmaa Menakem, *My Grandmother's Hands*
  Racialized Trauma and the Pathway to Mending
  Our Hearts and Bodies (2017)

Your ancestors outnumber your fears. Feel your power.
—Jaiya John, *Freedom: Medicine Words for Your Brave Revolution* (2020)

AUTHOR CARE NOTE

My Good People, please notice your body as you embark on this chapter. As mental health professionals we are not often invited, nor do we often accept the invitation, to take breaks and take care of ourselves.

Regardless, I ask you to please breathe deeply, drink lots of water, hum, move, sing, and listen to music while reading. Take care of your energetic, ancestral, and psychological health.

Mention of possible assault in the chapter, as well ancestral generational trauma.

We pick up things from one another. Unconsciously, inadvertently, socially, culturally, energetically, we pick up mannerisms, body language, habits, and sometimes even the same taste in partners as our caregivers. There is information in the patterns and the choices. There can be liberation in our choices, spaces where we can choose to unhook from a disastrous pattern. The opposite can also be true, where we keep falling down these deep rabbit holes—crevices really—of unconscious drives and patterns. I have heard people I have worked with identify these crevices and patterns of self-loathing and addiction as "black holes of yearning," a constant craving of sorts.

At an East Coast university, where I would provide individual, couples, triage, and group psychotherapy, I would provide copies of the poem "My Autobiography in 5 Short Chapters" as students walked out of the therapy room door after a particularly difficult and trying session. I walk down the same street. There is a deep hole in the sidewalk. I see it is there. I still fall in . . . it's a habit. In those sessions, we explored themes of self-trust, self-compassion, addiction, and family cycles. It was here, in these sessions, where ancestral intergenerational material materialized. It is my belief that when we get curious about these consistent gaping crevices, these holes in the sidewalk, we begin to wake up—to our own shit. Our caregiver's shit. Our People's shit. Especially our historical shit. Even countries have to awaken and experience a reckoning to their own systemic and structural shit.

And it hurts.

Hence the term "WOKE." Being "WOKE" is easily co-opted like most good things. But "staying WOKE" isn't easy, fun, or deserving of badges. Rather it is a slow painful process of self-realization and introspection. It is a peeling of layers, and with each layer comes more inquiry, confusion, shedding, grief, and even deep rage.

Decolonizing is an awakening, a deep digging—as I have described in Chapter 1—and the decolonizing process examines the roles of our histories, identities, our ancestors' decisions, and what we will do about it.

Walk with me, I want to share a personal story.

In late 2007, I was a doctoral student residing on Chochenyo, Muwekma, Ohlone territories, in what is now known as Oakland, California. At the time, I was deeply immersed in my doctoral studies, having just completed my coursework and required practicums. I was preparing for an APA internship across the country—while dissertation writing—and deeply involved in grassroots organizing. I had just come out of a deeply intense practicum experience working with individuals who were incarcerated for violent sexual crimes, where I had experienced a great deal of lateral violence. Working closely with such deep trauma and sexual violence, I was beginning to experience what I call "The Numbing." That period in a human service worker's life, where extreme violence, trauma, and tragedy feels . . . okay. Normal. Even exciting. There was also a great deal of trauma bonding among doctoral students and clinicians around the amount of trauma we could withstand, and the intensity and crisis of the communities we worked with. Looking back, I see this as part of the violence in the clinical mental health initiation process and socialization of "no trauma or story is too much for me!" At the time, I minimized having little emotional responses to deeply violent situations. That conditioning is violent in itself.

One night I exited the BART train station very late and walked the 15 minutes home as I usually had. Mind you Ubers and Lyfts would not be a thing until 2011–2012. I experienced being cyclically followed home throughout the entire 15 minutes of my walk one dark winter evening (myself walking, and the person slowly circling, speaking to me, and following me in their car). As I took a route I assumed the follower would be unable to access, I neared my apartment building and the follower pulled into an empty driveway and exited their vehicle.

I had a deeply visceral experience of rage (more on the sacredness and healthiness of rage in the next chapter). I screamed at them, cussed, tore at my jacket, walked toward them as though ready to physically fight. The Call was heard. Suddenly many, many individuals popped their heads out of their apartments, some running downstairs with bats. Some people screaming "LEAVE HER THE FUCK ALONE" from their windows. Gotta love Oakland. I was supported. The person became scared, apologized profusely, and ran into their car.

Stunned, I ignored the caring community inquiries about whether I needed support, wanted to call the police (no thanks), and what my name was. I felt nothing. I remembered nothing for four days after that experience. The next thing I recalled was a conversation and somatic exercise in my Spiritual Mother/therapist's chair days later.

Dr. Bola Cofield was my healing lifeline, a Heart Medicine Woman, transformative studies scholar, and self-identified Black Buddhist. She asked me how I was feeling and I continued to say "fine."

"What's going on in your body?"

"A tsunami, but it doesn't reach me—it is just a roaring nothing."

"Can you recall what your body felt like as you saw the follower exit their vehicle?"

"I felt like a cat. A cat that was going to be trapped. It isn't rational, but it felt powerful, and I felt powerless."

Now we can reasonably say that screaming in rage is a healthy response to being followed. It is . . . and, if my healer–therapist would have stopped there, I would not have picked up on the changes in my body temperature during the venting, the level of out-of-body rage, the frequency of these fight-or-flight rages, the increasing anhedonia after rage releases; I would have missed it. The intergenerational legacy that I had never agreed to carry nor had I known I held.

Interestingly, as I unpacked aspects of my own family's intergenerational trauma, my mother randomly shared a story about my grandmother (my dad's mother) in Italy, as a young girl being deeply abused by her father and stepmother—being placed in a chest as punishment, without food or water for days.

She stated, "Your grandmother once told me that when they opened the chest, she would leap out like a cat—scratching, screaming, spitting—ready to protect herself, but not herself. She said her worst fear came true—being confined." I nearly choked on my water.

Decades later I was unconsciously reliving and reviving aspects of my grandmother's sadistic abuse history. Furthermore, as ancestral work often does, the spiral unfurled to reveal story upon story of violent situations of extreme domestic and intimate partner violence upon my three aunts (grandmother's daughters) and numerous violent and dangerous rage stories related to my father, who has always embodied his righteous rage, in his words, "in an unhealthy and unsafe way."

Although this and further personal details did not suddenly clear me of angst or my visceral rage in various situations, it did allow for a connection that became a turning point. In understanding that my rage had an origin and that the reaction was deeper than a "trauma response," there was a cracking open . . . a pain and a feeling of freedom, that perhaps the healing could begin now.

The Study of Trauma Transmission

There are many hypotheses regarding how trauma is transmitted between generations, and numerous theories involve biological, intrapsychic, behavioral, social, and familial forms of transmission. Recently, the focus of trauma has expanded from individual impact to the generational impact of trauma. This transmission of trauma begins at the interpersonal level (i.e., from a parent to their child), and expands to the intergenerational level (i.e., a generation of parents to a generation of children), thus impacting an entire group or culture. As related to the psychological community, intergenerational transmission of trauma has only recently (early 2000s) been seen as a phenomenon related to oppressed populations due to the lingering impact of colonization—although Indigenous and Aboriginal scholars have created discourse and scholarship around this for centuries.

What we do know is how intergenerational trauma is passed down through changed DNA. Rather than trauma damaging the gene itself, it changes how the gene is expressed. Epigenetics are changes to how our bodies read DNA, rather than alterations to the DNA sequence itself (Wolynn, 2016; Valeii, 2021). Therapists have been able to learn from cellular biologists, like Dr. Bruce Lipton, and utilize the epigenetic theory to look at how trauma and suffering from prior generations and family members (like a parent or grandparent) are passed down.

It is also understood that these epigenetic changes and "transmission of trauma might be influenced by cultural, psychological, or socioeconomic factors" (Valeii, 2021). When we have children who experienced trauma, we know that it was more likely that they grew up with a parent who expressed instability, distance, anxious attachment, or other trauma-influenced behaviors, thus contributing to another generation being affected by trauma as their children grow up. Valeii writes about how children exposed to early trauma (including in utero, and prior to the age of three) and exposed to community and intrapersonal violence and food/housing insecurity are more susceptible to inflammation and early death.

Inflammation is an expression of this generational or historical trauma. We know that the body has the capacity to heal wounds—it is just part of the body's innate brilliance. But the modern world has impacted much of the body's natural ability to heal. Many physicians, such as Dr. Rupa Marya, have pointed to the correlations between inflammatory disease and more serious health concerns, such as cancer and inflammation, leads to a host of diseases. Yet, many cultures throughout the globe also understand that generational trauma and epigenetic theory cannot account for what the soul has experienced. (More on the ancestral spiritual aspects of trauma in Chapter 7.)

In my dissertation, *Slavery and Healing the Intergenerational Soul Wound in Inner City African American Male Youth of the African Diaspora*, I describe the effects of historical trauma on Holocaust survivors and survivors of the Japanese internment during World War II:

Numerous theories regarding the intergenerational transmission of trauma have been proposed (Baranowsky et al., 1998), and the information related to these mechanisms have since increased to encompass multigenerational transmission effects (i.e., on the grandchildren and great-grandchildren of Holocaust survivors and the children of parents who are survivors) of neglect, sexual, emotional, and physical abuse (Gardner, 1999; Watanabe, 2002).

Shosan's (1989) studies on Israeli descendants of individuals who survived the Holocaust suggest that not only is trauma passed on intergenerationally, but also it is cumulative. Therefore, there is a process whereby unresolved trauma becomes more severe each time it is passed on to a subsequent generation (E. Duran, 2006).

Once liberated from enslavement or imprisonment, survivors manifested what can be seen as a cluster of PTSD symptoms. These symptoms are often referred to as *survivor syndrome* and include chronic or recurrent states of anhedonia, dissociation, depression, anxiety, psychosomatic conditions, intense anger, and survivor guilt (Niederland, 1964).

During World War II, Japanese Americans also suffered immense historical trauma at the hands of the U.S. government. During the years 1942–1945, approximately 120,000 Japanese and Japanese American individuals from the West Coast were forcibly removed from their homes and incarcerated in internment camps due to government fears of treason and espionage (Nagata, 1993, p. 67). The Japanese, culturally referred to as the *Nisei* in Japanese, were forced to live in sparse conditions without food or adequate shelter. The *Nisei* were left to fend for themselves with an experience of helplessness, deprivation, and health issues. Yet, the major groups of survivors, the *Nisei*, generally do not confront the implications of the trauma within themselves or with their own children. In many respects, the *Nisei* have been "permanently altered in their attitudes, both positively and negatively, in regard to their identification with the values of their bicultural heritage; or they remain confused or even injured by the traumatic experience" (Miyoshi, 1978; Nagata, 1993, as cited in Mullan, 2012).

After the horrific experience of incarceration in the internment camps, the *Nisei*, brought forth a generation of children, referred to as the *Sansei* in Japanese. The *Sansei* were reported to have experienced a pervasive sense of silence in the family having been transmitted the trauma of their parents (Nagata, 1993; Yoshikawa, 2005). The *Sansei* children were left to struggle and hold the deep historical wounding which they were forbidden to discuss. This pervasive sense of silence became a source of resentment toward many of the *Sansei's* parents. Research corroborates the conclusions, that much like the children of Holocaust survivors, the *Sansei*, whose parents had been exposed to a traumatic experience like the internment camps, express an elevated level of emotional vulnerability (Nagata, 1993; Yoshikawa, 2005, as cited in Mullan, 2012). According to Nagata (1993), "trauma may directly or indirectly affect the children victims of trauma victims; the multiple pathways of its effects create a variety of consequences." (Mullan, 2012)

Many of the Sansei experienced the impact of the silence around the emotional vulnerability and the trauma of the internment camps. Nagata (1993) and Miyoshi (1978) report that many Sansei-identified people are quite upset about the injustice and feel negative experiences in their own lives are related to the trauma of the internment camps. There are a variety of feelings that research has correlated to the trauma of the camps, such as low self-esteem, loss of Japanese culture, experiencing the unexpressed pain of their parents, and so forth:

It was concluded that traumatic stress has lifelong consequences even in the presence of efficacious coping strategies. When confronted by personal traumas, the children of the Japanese internment camps were more likely to exhibit severe behaviors such as substance abuse and suicidal ideation . . . (Yoshikawa, 2005).

Abdullah (1994) asserts that the African experience in what is now known as the United States, but appropriately known as Turtle Island, meets the criteria for PTSD. Dr. Leary provides a list of some conditions that may promote the emotional traumas that justify the diagnosis of PTSD:

- A serious threat or harm to one's life or integrity.
- A threat of harm to one's children, spouse, or close relative.
- Sudden destruction of one's home or community.
- Seeing another person injured or killed as a result of an accident or violence.
- Learning about a serious threat to a relative or close friend being kidnapped, tortured, or killed.
- Stressor is experienced with intense fear, terror, and helplessness.
- Stressor and disorder are considered to be more serious and will last longer when the stressor is from another human being. (University of Texas at Austin Liberal Arts Instructional Technology Services, n.d.; Abdullah, 1994; American Psychological Association, 1994; DeGruy, 2005, as cited in Mullan, 2012, pp. 83–84)

Considering that the American Psychological Association (American Psychological Association, 1994) considers any one of the above stressors enough to cause PTSD, one can imagine the embedded levels of trauma for enslaved Africans who survived the Middle Passage from Africa, as well as those Africans who survived the atrocity of U.S. chattel slavery. Therefore, we can extrapolate the immeasurable amount of PTSD symptomatology evident in those Africans who survived a lifetime of slavery. There were no counseling services readily available to freed slaves after the Civil War (DeGruy Leary, 2005;

Ginzburg, 1988; Gutman, 1976; Pinderhughes, 1989). Most traumas were never addressed, nor did the traumas cease. People of African descent experienced daily physical assault; however, equally impactful and concerning was the daily psychological assault brought upon their psyches and souls. (Abdullah, 1994; Danieli, 1998; DeGruy Leary, 2005; as cited in Mullan, 2012)

Robert Carter (2007) coined this process "race-based traumatic stress," and due to the violence on Black and Brown bodies throughout 2020, amid the pandemic, it is more commonly known as racial trauma. It refers to the psychological distress associated with experiences of racism.

Research has supported that Africans in the United States have faced four distinct periods of trauma, including the European conquest of Africa established in 1442, the physical enslavement period (1619–1865), the postphysical enslavement period (1865–1954), and the period in which the U.S. federal government and private sectors responded to modern African American movements, such as the Montgomery Bus Boycott, Juneteenth, creation of the NAACP, the Black Power Movement, and Black Lives Matter. . . . Research points to the fact that African Americans continue to bear the scars of each of these historical and cultural traumas.

As I state in my dissertation: "While intergenerational trauma started as exclusively the study of the Holocaust survivors and their offspring, it soon became the catalyst from which to understand the psychological symptoms and treatment infecting other ethnic groups," such as the descendants of First Nation Indigenous People, descendants of the Transatlantic Slave Trade (across North, Central, and South America and the Caribbean), descendants of individuals who survived the Japanese internment camps, and many, many more people who have been exposed to various forms of structural and systemic violence (Mullan, 2012, p. 91).

People develop ways of coping by "managing." Dutch psychiatrist and PTSD scholar Bessel van der Kolk spoke about how utilizing these "managers" have helped people to cope with the trauma, as well as the feelings of not being wanted and not being seen. He notes in his Master Series on Exploring Intergenerational Trauma how we often can't control these

> **GENTLE AND SUSTAINABLE WAYS TO HEAL INTERNALIZED INTERGENERATIONAL CURSES AND TRADITIONS**
>
> - Talking about your spirituality, political stance, gender identity, despite others' comfort (as long as it is safe).
> - Disagreeing without emotion.
> - Disagreeing with emotion.
> - Challenging colorism.
> - Acknowledging and giving up some of your privilege.
> - Verbalizing your discomfort with violent colonizer holidays (such as, Canada Day, Independence Day, Cinco de Mayo, Thanksgiving, etc.) and if attending, providing a brief understandable explanation of the problematic nature of the day historically. Love and compassion are always welcomed.
> - Spending time with chosen family and friends on "family holidays."
> - Choosing to not be present at events where your abusers are welcome or may be present.
> - Spending time with elders.
> - Spending time with youth.
> - Creating a friend-culture of forgiveness and humanity.
> - Not standing for fatphobic comments (nor internalizing them).
> - Stepping away from one-sided relationships.
> - Compassion, compassion, compassion for your inner child.

"managers," and when they are working overtime, they have a life of their own, eventually standing in the way of our current lives. What would conceptualizing intergenerational trauma transmission appear like within transformational justice circles, within group support services, within residential placements for adolescents, and within disability justice circles? What would addressing the legacy wound create more space for?

Emerging trends in psychotherapy and psychiatry are now co-opting what many people on the streets have been stating for the past 50 years—that histories of war, colonization, fascism, genocides, holocausts, wars in the name of God, and forced displacements impact the family and social history as a part of the whole picture. War, domestic violence, enslavement, kidnapping, sexual trauma, suicide, and epidemics can send waves of distress (which can lead to trauma) that can cascade from one generation to the next.

Although this section acknowledges the cumulative effects of historical and intergenerational trauma, and how this arises for many racialized people as racial trauma—as a form of structural violence—it is essential to note that we as a society and as helpers can point to the wound, while pointing to the truth that healing IS possible. Healing these multigenerational wounds requires healing strategies designed to address the soul wounding—the core wounding, and part of this process involves addressing the colonial wounding in the room.

Politicized decolonial work does not benefit from keeping anyone stuck in the past or painful present. It involves honoring emotions such as grief, rage, and deep longing, and how this has shown up for generations in our lineages. Therefore, this book is advocating for acknowledging the root causes of our understanding of trauma and advocates for us to engage in the cultural journey home toward healing. We are not broken beyond repair; we are awaiting to be reminded that we can return Home. *Acknowledging the embodied legacy of oppression and colonization is not at odds with healing, but is an essential step on the journey toward healing.*

Modes and Mechanisms of Transmission

Repetition is the language of the abused child.
—Richard Rhodes (1990)

The following will attempt to serve as a quick synthesis and distinction between direct versus indirect trauma transmission, and how trauma is communicated. Trauma transmission is highly complex and affected by many variables. As Auerhahn and Laub note: "Many children pick up on the defensive structures of traumatized parents. Additionally, the children intuitively absorb the repressed, dissociated, and warded off trauma that lurks behind the aggressive overtones found in many adults' parenting styles" (Auerhahn & Laub, 1998; Mullan, 2012).

The Aboriginal Healing Foundation Research Series prepared a report in 2004 on *Historic Trauma and Aboriginal Healing*, noting that "over time, the experience of repeated traumatic stressors become normalized and incorporated into the cultural expression and expectations of successive generations." This is often a complex process as "trauma manifesting as culturally prevalent will not necessarily and readily be identifiable as a specific or individual disorder" (Wesley-Esquimaux & Smolewski, 2000, p. 3).

Trauma transmission is often conceptualized into two mechanisms: direct and indirect (Baranowsky et al., 1998; Kellerman, 2001; Lichtman, 1984; Rowland-Klein & Dunlop, 1998; M. Weis & S. Weis, 2000). Direct and indirect mechanisms of trauma have been used in reference to symptom development, transmission content, and communication. Direct transmission of symptom development refers to children acquiring symptoms similar to those of their traumatized parents. Indirect transmission refers to a child's development of symptoms as a result of living with a traumatized parent. Direct transmission also refers to the traumatized parents' overt discussion of their traumatic experiences with their children (Baranowsky et al., 1998; Kellerman, 2001; Rowland-Klein & Dunlop, 1998). In this context, indirect transmission refers to covert, nonverbal communication to the child about the parent's traumatic experiences. Direct and indirect transmission can take place within the same family.

There are various theories of transmission of trauma:

Biological theories of trauma transmission address physiological vulnerabilities for the development of psychological disorders that are passed from one generation to the next. A growing body of research suggests that trauma (e.g., from extreme stress, starvation, oppression, and/or colonization among many other things) can leave a chemical mark on a person's genes, which can then be passed down to future generations.

Epigenetics is an emerging and evolving part of research that studies how environmental influences impact and effect gene expression, and how this expression can be passed onto future generations from prior ones. The genes children inherit (from their biological parents) can provide developmental information (Lehrner & Yehuda, 2018). According to a recent psychiatric article, "Epigenetic Modifications in Stress Response Genes Associated with Childhood Trauma" (Jiang et al., 2019), we are learning that the effects of trauma can be intergenerationally passed on through epigenetic mechanisms, such as methylation. This shows us that alterations in methylation patterns do have intergenerational effects. "Specifically, childhood trauma has been associated with alteration in methylation patterns in human sperm, which may induce intergenerational effects" (Jiang et al., 2019).

Intrapsychic mechanisms of trauma transmission "have also been proposed as unavailable for internalization," and researchers have proposed that the psychodynamic concept of projective identification explains trauma transmission (Mullan, 2012). I described the process in my dissertation as follows:

> Rowland-Klein and Dunlop (1998) state that this process involves the projection of one's own denied internal experiences onto another in such a way that the other person actually assumes the feelings and behaviors projected onto her. For example, a parent who experienced abuse as a child may be unable to accept and integrate the traumatic experiences. Therefore, her inability to tolerate feelings of anger and sadness related to her abuse is impaired. As a result of this impairment, she projects those disavowed feelings onto her child. The child then adopts those feelings as her own in an effort to connect with and understand her mother. The child then displays symptoms of anger and sadness, as if she herself had been abused despite having no actual direct experience of the trauma. The child then becomes a vehicle for expression of the emotional experiences that the parent finds unbearable (Gardner, 1999; Maker & Buttenheim, 2000; Rowland-Klein & Dunlop, 1998; Weingarten, 2004). Projective identification is hypothesized to be an indirect transmission mechanism occurring at an unconscious level, without explicit communication about traumatic experiences. (Mullan, 2012)

Additionally, researchers have identified repetition compulsion as another psychodynamic conceptualization of how trauma is transmitted. Repetition compulsion refers to the unconscious patterns that a person reenacts with an intimate other(s) in their lives. Unresolved conflict is compulsively repeated as a means of mastery over traumatic events.

For example, a father who has a history of abuse by his own father may be hesitant to set limits on his son because he is uncomfortable with the potential for aggression in his discipline. The son, then without limits, begins acting out in controlling and aggressive ways toward his father. Therefore, the father feels victimized by his son in ways that are reminiscent of the abuse he suffered by his father. In this way, trauma is indirectly transmitted and happens because the child's developmental needs are overshadowed by the father's traumatic past. Additionally, the process of projective identification can be used in individuals' repetitions. The repetitions may also be carried out through unconscious choice to engage with others similar to the original perpetrator.

Attachment mechanisms of trauma transmission are part of the intrapsychic psychodynamic theory. John Bowlby first developed the concept of attachment, which refers to the "reciprocal, enduring, emotional, and physical affiliation between a child and a caregiver" (James, 1994, p. 2). Attachment has been conceptualized as a process, which begins in infancy and childhood but continues into adulthood. It is through the attachment relationship that a child develops the capacity to regulate emotion, cope with stress, and navigate interpersonal relationships. Problems in the attachment relationship are often noted as influential in the intergenerational transmission of trauma. In particular, Danieli, Yehuda, and colleagues suggest that the transmission of trauma attachment patterns may be responsible for intergenerational patterns of child maltreatment.

There are four main types of secure attachment: secure, insecure-resistant, insecure-avoidant, and insecure-disorganized. Children will use attachment relationships as a "secure base" from which they can venture out and explore their environment.

The attachment relationship can significantly influence the experience of trauma (James, 1998; Weingarten, 2003) and can serve as a safeguard or heighten the child's vulnerability to the detrimental effects of trauma. Securely attached children who have a single, possibly traumatic, encounter may feel adequately comforted and contained by their caregivers. However, children who experience multiple traumas, such as chronic abuse, particularly if perpetrated by a significant attachment figure, may be at greater risk for the development of mental health symptoms (James, 1998). When children experience neglectful, unpredictable, and frightening responses from caregivers, they may become particularly anxious, irritable, or withdrawn (James, 1998). Maltreated children are the most commonly classified as having an insecure-disorganized attachment style, out of the three types of insecure attachment (Bar-On et al., 1998; Carlson et al., 1998; C. Zeanah & P. Zeanah, 1989). The child's experiences in relationship to her or his caregiver are internalized and then utilized to facilitate and comprehend future relationships and steer interpersonal behavior.

Hence, transmission occurs because early experiences are carried forth to the next generation through these internalized models for relationships (Bar-On et al., 1998; Carlson et al., 1998; C. Zeanah & P. Zeanah, 1989). Of particular significance is abusive patterns frequently referred to as "cycles of abuse," which may be perpetuated through attachment relationships.

PTSD often impairs interpersonal functioning; hence interferences in the caregiver's adult attachment may occur. Parents who are currently affected by trauma-related symptoms may have problems in creating secure attachments with their children. As a result of the hyperarousal symptoms, parents afflicted with PTSD may behave in frightening or frightened ways with their children, as indicated above, in turn also producing difficulties in attachment.

Under-responsiveness can also occur as a possible result of disruptions in attachment styles. Additionally, parents struggling with the symptoms of PTSD may be more focused on their own distress, as opposed to the needs of their children.

The attachment styles as a mechanism of transmission are relevant to the trauma of colonization, as colonization breeds disconnect from self and others. One might view individuals who have experienced lifelong forms of oppression and systemic violence as having "insecure-disorganized" attachments styles, collectively, as a People—due to the level of gaslighting, internalized oppression, gatekeeping, and eventual mistrust with the systems (more on the mental health and other systems in Chapter 7). However, a less pathologizing frame instead of "insecure-disorganized" might appear as skeptical, mistrusting, and having trouble honoring one's intuition and/or observations; it is crucial practitioners understand that this is a strength that is often painted as a deficiency in the MHIC.

Also of interest is how cycles of maltreatment have often been observed to skip a generation. It is thought that this may be due to problems in the attachment relationship. In other words, although the majority of parents abused as children do not go on to perpetuate abuse with their own children, their attachment experiences are nevertheless affected by the abuse they suffered. Additionally, based on the premise that attachment relationships are transmitted, it seems quite likely that their children may also experience difficulties with attachment. Therefore, the social learning theory, much like the attachment theory, speculates that the intergenerational transmission of trauma is based on early experiences with caregivers.

The Family Systems Perspective of trauma transmission may reveal the impact of trauma and repeated patterns within the family. It can be argued that children feel indebted to repay parents for the care and nurturance they received, and that for many families, this repayment takes place in the next generation through care provided to children. Researchers have speculated that trauma is passed down from generation to generation in the form of "debts," "entitlements," and "legacies." Maltreatment can hamper this process and create an imbalance in family relational "ledgers." These authors also argue that repetitions occur in the form of "invisible loyalties" in that children are compelled to maintain family connections by recreating that which they received.

In the case of **collective trauma**, Danieli, Yehuda, and colleagues have agreed that children are often filled with a sense that they need to change or reverse the agony of previous generations. It appears that the children often take on their parents' trauma and their grandparent's unresolved traumas and stress as their own. This often continues into a journey that is not always conscious to the mind, which leads to a pursuit for relational connection and truthfulness. We can imagine that the ownership of trauma and agony filled with grief, confusion, and rage can create confusion around intergenerational boundaries. In other words: *What is mine? What belongs to my family? What belongs to my ancestry? What belongs to my culture?* The confusion and blurred boundaries in such a lifelong and often stress-induced emotional journey can recreate traumatic effects for the second generation and inadvertently continue to perpetuate violence.

Boundaries in families with traumatized parents are often noted to take excessive forms in which roles within the family are inappropriate or blurred. Roles can become reversed and children may adopt a parental function. The parent, through conscious or unconscious mechanisms, may exert pressure on the child to attend to parental needs. The child may also sense fragility in the parent and adopt a caregiving role. Such a child seeks to preserve the good, nurturing aspects of her or his parent by relieving parental burdens. While traumatized parents may appear fragile to their children and in need of protection, the opposite can also be true. Traumatized parents are frequently noted to be overprotective with their children. Indirect messages regarding safety in the world, or lack thereof, are consequently transmitted indirectly. Children may be left with elevated levels of anxiety and mistrust. Hence, functioning in day-to-day activities and relationships may be difficult.

Behavioral mechanisms of trauma can be exemplified through **social learning theories**, which hypothesize that children are socialized to behave in particular ways, based on modeling. By observing their caregivers and particularly their parents, children learn behavioral strategies. Danieli, Yehuda, and colleagues have discussed the purpose of social learning theories as explanative mechanisms of intergenerational transmission of trauma. These authors suggest that children may learn parents' trauma-related symptoms and begin to exhibit similar behavior. Social learning mechanisms of trauma transmission are, therefore, direct.

Social learning theory has received significant attention as it relates to cycles of maltreatment (Macfie et al., 2005; Newcomb & Locke, 2001; Solomon et al., 1988; Weingarten, 2004); roughly a third of maltreated adults will continue to perpetuate, knowingly or unknowingly, the cycle of maltreatment with their own children (Macfie et al., 2005; Newcomb & Locke, 2001; Weingarten, 2004). Some authors suggest that parents repeat the parenting strategies they learned or were modeled to them in their own childhood with their own children (Macfie et al., 2005; Newcomb & Locke, 2001; Solomon et al., 1988; Weingarten, 2004).

As previously mentioned, intergenerational trauma transmission is also affected by the parents' present level of trauma-related impairment. Having a parent with PTSD significantly increases the risk of trauma transmission. Parents struggling with PTSD symptoms are likely to be anxious with their own needs and may, as a result, be incapable of fully attending to the needs of their children. Overall, residing with a parent or caregiver who is struggling with PTSD can create a very stressful and anxious home environment. There may be higher levels of familial conflict, which in turn can trigger symptom development in vulnerable children because the effects of a healthy and supportive relationship are lacking.

Global and Indigenous Perspectives on Trauma

Effects of trauma may manifest itself into feelings of fear, anxiety, rage, helplessness, and may potentially result in such maladaptive[19] behaviors as alcoholism, family discord, and high suicide rates. When discussing symptom-oriented problems in communities of color, many Indigenous healers and clinicians in psychological communities speak of ideas such as "spiritual injury, soul sickness, soul wounding, and ancestral hurt" (Duran, 2006). Many psychological literature reviews omit or do not conceive of the word *soul* in connection with providing mental health services. However, Eduardo Duran and Dr. Maria Yellow Horse Brave Heart have been some of the primary clinicians (albeit not the only) in the Indigenous communities to introduce the oral traditions and use of the term *soul wounding* to reflect a spiritual ailment as a collective in the community.

Healers of psychotherapeutic, Indigenous, Native, or shamanic orientation agree that the symptoms of trauma almost always arise in response to

19 Maladaptive: Term referring to behaviors that cause people who have them physical or emotional harm, prevent them from functioning in daily life, and/or indicate that they have lost touch with reality and/or cannot control their thoughts and behavior (also called dysfunctional) (Soicher, 2023).

an external stressor or a combination of stressors; most of which are clearly identifiable and severe in nature. Unlike nearly all other mental-health disorders which separate the question of etiology[20] from diagnosis, the first *DSM-IV* (APA, 2000) diagnostic criteria for both PTSD and acute stress disorder required that the person was exposed to a traumatic event. Similarly, the contemporary shamanic literature contains long lists of symptoms and causes of *soul loss*, including incest, physical abuse, war, accidents, rape, major illness, surgery, and death of a loved one. Both trauma and soul loss imply external stressors. Even in cases where the source of the psychological distress is understood to be an intrusive spirit, this being is described as having appeared at a time when the person was in a weakened emotional and physical state.

Trained psychotherapists and shamans acknowledge varying degrees of severity in complex trauma or soul loss. There are psychological terms for some of the variables that tend to increase stressor magnitude. Therefore, the possible severity of PTSD, complex, or intergenerational trauma response include sexual victimization, intentional acts of violence, degree of unpredictability or uncontrollability, extent of combat exposure, and the grotesqueness of death.

Among shamanic healers in what is now known as North America, there are several recurring metaphors or ways to conceptualize sickness and healing that are analogous to what is called "complex trauma" in psychology. Perhaps the most widely used construct is that of soul loss (Villoldo, 2000). In an appendix entitled "Culture-bound syndromes," the *DSM-IV* (APA, 2000) acknowledges that soul loss may be related to major depressive disorder, PTSD, and somatoform disorders, and that the practices and symptom patterns described as soul loss throughout Latin American cultures are found in many parts of the world. In neo-shamanic, as well as in many Indigenous shamanisms, the idea of soul loss "is that whenever we experience trauma, a part of our vital essence separates from us in order to survive the experience by escaping the full impact of the pain" (Ingerman, 1991). Psychotherapists' and shamanic healers' methods agree that the

---

20 Etiology: The causal description of all of the factors that contribute to the development of a disorder or illness (Soicher, 2023).

transformation of trauma in individuals is inseparable from healing trauma in the larger sociocultural matrix.

It is relevant to note that although the aforementioned material can be reflected under culture-bound syndromes in the *DSM*, the manual is deeply pathologizing and static in nature. The culture-bound syndromes are most often not given adequate attention during classes and practicums. It is oversimplified, and there is a great deal of misdiagnosis, especially as related to relatively normalized experiences within a culture. Again, the *DSM* also has been constructed and created under systems of white supremacy and under colonial beliefs which "normalizes" that which is Eurocentric, cisgender, able-bodied, neurotypical, heterosexual, and "pleasant," as the standard for mental and emotional health.

There is wisdom embedded in our blood and bones. There is wisdom embedded in the rawness of our rituals, services, ceremonies, and traditions. There is wisdom embedded in the wound. Unlike modern Eurocentric mental health practices and the paternalistic attitude of the *DSM*, the meat of the emo–decolonial journey is allowing people to experience themselves as fully capable of knowing what they need. Lived experience is vital wisdom! There is wisdom in beginning to come Home to oneself and in the experiences of our elders and teachers. People have what we need to heal. We are inherently whole. This knowledge can emerge and inform our healing.

Aspects of Emotional–Decolonial Unlearning

1. Therapists perpetuate harm by dismissing appropriate emotional responses to oppression, such as rage.
2. Therapists perpetuate further harm by "positioning racial trauma as past events, not an ongoing experience that will continue to happen" (Kim, 2020b).
3. This transmission of trauma begins at the interpersonal level (i.e., from a parent to their child), and expands to the intergenerational level (i.e., a generation of parents to a generation of children), thus impacting an entire group or culture (historical or cultural trauma).

4. Moderate experiences of stress during pregnancy have a cumulative and heightened effect across generations (epigenetic research).
5. Politicized decolonial work does not benefit from keeping anyone stuck in the past or avoiding the painful present. It involves honoring emotions, such as grief, rage, and deep longing, and how these have shown up for generations in our lineage.
6. Trauma transmission is often conceptualized into two mechanisms: direct and indirect.
7. Attachment extends way beyond the four types, as Bowlby suggested; we are not considering our attachment to Land, cultural identity, country, etc.
8. The attachment relationship to caregivers can significantly influence the experience of trauma and can serve as a safeguard or heighten the child's vulnerability to the detrimental effects of trauma.
9. The attachment styles as a mechanism of transmission are relevant to the trauma of colonization, as colonization breeds a disconnect from self and others.
10. One might view individuals who have experienced lifelong forms of oppression and systemic violence as having "insecure-disorganized" attachment styles, collectively, as a People due to the level of gaslighting, internalized oppression, gatekeeping, and eventual mistrust of the systems.
11. Children of traumatized parents and caregivers are often filled with a sense that they need to change or reverse the agony of previous generations. This is not necessary.

Emo–Decolonial Practice Offerings
- Give up your privilege. It can be incredibly powerful to engage in a small act during the therapeutic encounter that can shift the power dynamics and the participant's energy (e.g., exchange chairs for once; answer questions about yourself; be honest about not knowing something, etc.).
- Consider speaking about your spirituality, political stance, and gender identity when appropriate (as long as it is safe for you).

- Challenge anti-Black racist unconscious thoughts. Yes, even if you are not Black. (Gently of course and when therapeutically relevant.) Anti-blackness, too, can be passed down intergenerationally through role modeling.
- Creating an environment (wherever that may be) that is not fatphobic (e.g., ensuring chairs can hold and contain all bodies).
- It makes perfect sense to pull out cardboard or poster board during a session and help your participants visually see where their parent's experiences and beliefs could be impacting them. Drawing and doodling are encouraged.
- Get into the habit of asking your therapy participants: "Is this yours?"
- Create a small workbook with the participant related to what they might do when feeling overwhelmed by ancestral material and historical experiences.
- Create a backpack audio meditation or breathing exercise for your client to use (e.g., with permission, record audio on their phone reminding them of things such as: "Take a breath. Take a walk. Excuse yourself. Ask for clarification. Cuddle your cat. Pick a card from your Oracle Deck. Ask yourself 'Is this my sadness?'").

Affirmations
- I allow myself time to slow down and engage in intergenerational self-inquiry.
- I am committed to compassionately abolishing the settler within.
- I allow myself to feel the full spectrum of emotion that arises during moments of conflict.
- I am allowed to choose the generational treasures over the trauma, from moment to moment.
- I practice compassion with my descendants.
- I don't have to hold or heal anything in my generational line.
- I practice nonjudgment and empathy with my kin.
- I take accountability when needed.
- I treat my family with empathy and invite intergenerational collaboration.
- It is safe to create space between myself and my kin.
- It is safe to speak to my ancestral team and ask for guidance.

- It is safe to set boundaries with ancestors without guilt.
- I am allowed to set limits and enforce my ancestral, intergenerational, historical, and familial boundaries without guilt.
- I remember that hierarchy is another form of white supremacy and internalized superiority.
- I take time to self- and intergenerationally regulate, instead of transmitting.

CHAPTER 7

Ancestral Roots in Mental Health "From Root to Bone"

The different human peoples did not evolve out of a common ancestor; they were each born out of the womb of their own homeland. We appeared in different parts of the world at the same time. Each group was as much a part of their environment as the other animals and plants of the region.
  —Eliot Cowan, *Plant Spirit Medicine* (2014)

At the onset of the Civil War, our stolen bodies were worth four billion dollars, more than all of American industry, all of American railroads, workshops, and factories combined, and the prime product rendered by our stolen bodies—cotton—was America's primary export.
  —Ta-Nehisi Coates, *Between the World and Me* (2015)

How to gather your ancestors: Make offerings. Pour water. Start with your tears. Burn the plants. Kneel to the earth. Grow silent and still. Find your true heart. Open it. Remember your true soul. Remember peace. Speak to them. They will speak to you. Listen. When you see wind moving the trees, those are your ancestors dancing on the leaves. Cry joy. If you want to hear your ancestors clearly, prepare a space for them: inner quiet.
  —Jaiya John, *Freedom: Medicine Words*
    for Your Brave Revolution (2020)

Spiritual Roots

Prior to the *Diagnostic and Statistical Manual of Mental Disorders* (DSM), hospitalizations, and therapy sessions, there were clergy, curanderas, shamans, santeros, dervish/a, hajah, and healers, just to name a few. There still are. They are here. We are here. Bridging the world between the human in this body on this Earth and the other. For thousands of years, various types of healers held physical and literal space for individuals impacted by emotional maladies and harm.

Many of our ancestors often held a supernatural view of abnormal behavior and saw it as the work of evil spirits, demons, gods, or witches who took control of the person. According to Restak (2000), the aforementioned type of demonic possession often occurred when a person behaved in ways that countered or was seen as delinquent or opposite to the religious teachings of the time. Restak (2000) noted that "Trephination is the earliest example of supernatural explanations for mental illness from as early as 6500 BC." This procedure was supposedly facilitated by cave dwellers using a stone instrument known as trephine. This instrument was used to remove a part of the skull, as it was thought that the "evil spirits could escape," therefore placing a stop on the person's "mental affliction and returning them back to normal." Abuse the body badly enough, and the spirit will want to leave it.

Until the early 19th century, psychiatry and religion were closely connected. Religious institutions were responsible for the care of the mentally ill. A major change occurred when Charcot and his pupil Freud associated religion with hysteria[21] and neurosis. This created a divide between religion and mental health care, which has continued until recently. Dein (2010) has noted that "psychiatry has a long tradition of dismissing and attacking religious experience. Religion has often been seen by mental health profes-

---

21 Hysteria: Term used by the ancient Greeks and Egyptians to describe a disorder believed to be caused by a woman's uterus wandering throughout the body and interfering with other organs (today, referred to as conversion disorder, in which psychological problems are expressed in physical form) (Soicher, 2023).

sionals in Western societies as irrational, outdated, and dependency forming and has been viewed as resulting in emotional instability."

In 1980, Albert Ellis, the founder of rational emotive therapy, wrote in the *Journal of Consulting and Clinical Psychology* that "there was an irrefutable causal relationship between religion and emotional and mental illness." According to Canadian psychiatrist Wendell Watters, "Christian doctrine and liturgy have been shown to discourage the development of adult coping behaviors and the human-to-human relationship skills that enable people to cope in an adaptive way with the anxiety caused by stress" (Dein, 2010). In its most extreme, all religious and spiritual experiences have been labeled as psychosis.

It is only in the last several years that attitudes toward spirituality and religion have changed among mental health professionals. In 1994, "religious or spiritual problems" were introduced in *DSM-IV* as a new diagnostic category that invited professionals to respect the patient's beliefs and rituals (APA, 2000). Recently, there has been a burgeoning of systematic research into religion, spirituality, and mental health. The evidence suggests that, on balance, religious involvement is generally conducive to better mental health. In addition, patients with psychiatric disorders frequently use religion to cope with their distress (Dein, 2010). But what of people who also utilize spiritual practices as a form of managing their mental and emotional health symptomatology?

The biggest differences between Indigenous and Western approaches to mental and emotional healing is that Indigenous approaches seek to integrate the mind, body, nature, and spirit, rather than continue to split and further dissociate, as Western mental health practices often can and do. For Indigenous practitioners, and those of us who have learned and are relearning and remembering from our lineages and teachers, holistic is not "New Age." The practices lumped within that category are mostly derived from ceremonies and rituals that have been co-opted and appropriated into watered-down treatments—that have stolen the healing spirit from our ancestry and robbed these rituals from their context—the place and people who created them. Balance and holism are intertwined with ritual, safety, being naturally trauma-conscious, and often quite raw. But for Indigenous practices globally, spirit and ancestors are not dismissed and ignored in the diagnostics of a person, family, or community's wellness.

Examination of prehistoric skulls and cave art from as early as 6500 B.C.E. has identified surgical drilling of holes in skulls to treat head injuries and epilepsy, as well as to allow evil spirits trapped within the skull to be released (Restak, 2000). Early Greek, Hebrew, Egyptian, and Chinese cultures reportedly used exorcisms in which evil spirits were cast out through prayer, magic, flogging, starvation, having the person ingest horrible-tasting drinks, or noisemaking. It is important to note that exorcisms continue today, and in no shape or form are less valuable than many current-day treatment methods (Giordan & Possamai, 2016).

This is not to suggest that drilling holes in skulls and flogging, for example, should return. On the contrary, this is a part of our history that was attempting to figure out the causal relationship between the mind, spirit/the spiritual, and negative thoughts/behaviors/beliefs. In the same vein, some of these practices are still utilized, but perhaps a tad more evolved.

CARE NOTE: Please be mindful of your capacity as this story contains highly graphic content and descriptions of harm. The purpose is not to dramatize or sensationalize this therapy participant nor their story, but to highlight the dangers of our current systems from the experiences of those who have experienced the harm; to provide clear examples of the types of institutional, criminal justice, mental health, educational, and psychiatric violence individuals undergo (yes, even now); AND how these systems overlap and interact with one another causing further harm and mistrust.

Also, this story is for every practitioner ever who has had to hide. Come out, come out, come out wherever you are, this is for you.

The People's Stories

Zola hesitantly began bi-weekly sessions at the community center reporting on their intake form, "I am living with the effects of trauma from the psychiatric and mental health systems. I am afraid to be here." At 27 years old, self-identifying as Arab (Palestinian) and South Asian (Punjabi), nonbinary, and demisexual, they had been institutionalized 13 times, 10 of which were against their will.

Zola had experienced the violent effects of psychopharmacology, noting that they have felt as if they reside within a "fuzzy numb haze" most days. They frequently reported not wanting to be alive, and they felt most people who said they loved them did so out of obligation. Zola also shared that their medication has been changed numerous times over nine years leading to horrible side effects. They experienced the violence of not only the mental health and health industries, but that of educational and criminal justice systems as well. They had been handcuffed roughly 10 of those 13 times—once they were tasered in a cafeteria at the university they attended. Zola had been arrested twice; called "a crazy Indian chick"; sexually harassed (verbally and twice physically) five times in an ambulance and in the back of a cop car; and sexually assaulted by staff at the psychiatric center roughly five times. They were also assaulted and sexually harmed three times by other individuals residing at the hospital.

Our therapeutic container involved years of various modalities—many helpful and many unhelpful. Eye Movement Desensitization and Reprocessing[22] (EMDR) proved very helpful in minimizing the subjective units of distress and the "bigness" of their emotional reaction when activated. Because of EMDR's similarity to electroshock therapy (which they were terrified of) when using pulsars (my modality) and EMDR's connection to what feels like hypnosis for some individuals, Zola understandably took space and time to warm up to it.

What Zola continued to note was most healing (not just helpful) was the space to explore what they named "Know-Knows"—meaning their intuitive and spiritual ways of knowing and seeing the world in a clairaudient and clairsentient manner. When Zola and I allowed ourselves to open up into

---

22 EMDR (Eye Movement Desensitization Reprocessing) is a therapy technique that allows a person to focus on the memory of trauma while also being stimulated bilaterally via eye movements (EMDR International Association, 2022).

the realm of their family—known and eventually unknown ancestors—and how they survived and then migrated to the United States, I observed that their affect, mood, communication, and interest in being well and healthy dramatically changed.

We immersed ourselves in stories from their family of healers, which their culture called davishas, and ways that they would read tea leaves, seeds, and irises. We processed violence in their family's lineage the best we could, and acknowledged how colonization literally beat the "Know-Knows" out of their women-identified family members. Some of the women-identified people in Zola's family were hung, sexually harmed, and murdered publicly—and horribly harmed in private by men-identified family members. I helped to normalize the fear of fully "coming into and out," in both their gender and intuitive abilities.

We created ceremonies for releasing and grief. I also slowly made, researched, tried, and tested referrals to Zola when appropriate: grief doula, a queer midwife for Arab youth, a nonbinary support circle, etc. Once, we walked to the football field (clearly this took a great deal of processing, timing, and support from other colleagues so we would not be arrested or harmed), and both of us screamed at the top of our lungs until we felt full, then ran upstairs feeling free, expansive, and rebellious.

Yes, even I felt these things. I felt like I was HEALING something in myself and my lineage while helping Zola. It felt important, and I clearly felt the gratitude from Zola at not being "in it alone." I also felt that when we engaged together, they felt less alone and more "useful" in some ways. Many therapy participants want to find ways to have a healthy impact on their practitioners too. As time went on, Zola would enter sessions during this period ready and clearer than ever about what they needed.

Some sessions contained sporadic grief rituals; other sessions felt more political in nature (such as when global and societal events affected the world and their family overseas). Some sessions required over an hour of somatic grounding, centering, and feeling big things. Some sessions we painted, and Zola cried or just said nothing. Some sessions they recounted dreams, and a few even included me and events in my life. Although they may not have known the details of how spot-on every dream was, I often would affirm their accuracy because it was so accurate. I never had to set strict boundaries; instead I would have honest conversations about my healthy boundaries, my personal limits, or what I was or was not ready to share.

At times this would disappoint Zola; other times it was a nonissue and they understood. Zola grew to understand the validity of my needs and those around them. We began to form an energetically healthy relationship that extended far beyond that of the office or room. Our therapeutic relationship was applicable in many areas of their life. I felt it deeply healthy that Zola understood I was not to be her main and only healthy attachment, and that I also would not "disappear" on them.

Zola began to accept healthy boundaries with more ease from their loved ones, and began to slowly set boundaries with others. They began to ask for what they needed 50% of the time, which was a huge shift for them. They did not look down anymore when having casual conversation, and apparently their friends felt the difference in Zola too. Honestly, my relationship with Zola allowed for me to better understand and surmise that boundary setting for many people of colonized backgrounds was a bit more complex than for white people, mainly because of the deep rooted unconscious fears tied up between survival and people pleasing. They taught me to notice when imposter syndrome, boundaries, and professionalism were code words for "being as unassuming, white, articulate, and nonemotional as possible." Zola did not SAY these things, I implicitly heard and understood them and eventually learned it through them and other participants of therapy.

Zola did not go on to be institutionalized or hospitalized again, to my knowledge. They have gone on to obtain top surgery, and their mother and sister have supported their transition. I wrote a letter in support of their surgery and their emotional capacity to handle such a deep change. Their "breaks with reality" continue to make so much more sense when we looked back and reviewed all of the ways that "modern mainstream society," Zola's culture, and their Eurocentric internalized beliefs made them demonize their own abilities, body, identity, and capacity to form healthy relationships.

We both cried when I was moving on from the Center. With permission, they email me from time to time with important life updates, they follow *Decolonizing Therapy* on Instagram, and will occasionally leave a quick emoji or "YASSSS Dr. J." I never feel violated. Instead, the human in me, who held space for the human in Zola, feels seen.

I find that this is an evolution from beyond therapy into the realms of emotional–decolonial healing.

This is what I believe is a modern-day evolution from our ancestral ways in community. Although super simple sounding—it is not. Our practices need to start somewhere, and I believe this story is an example of a healthy shift and start.

Decolonizing Therapy challenges the institutions, policies, and structures every step of the way. It places people over profit. People over systems. Peoples over boards of psychology/social work/counseling and psychiatry.

Decolonizing Therapy also chooses the health, healing, and evolution of the practitioner over these systems. Primarily we care about the well-being and emotional stability of people over arbitrary rules and structures seeking to keep us small, unwell, and insecure.

Stolen Spirits of Healing
It is also essential to note that many cultures across the globe innately and intrinsically include spiritual and or religious ways of not only Knowing, but healing (as described in Chapter 3). Although mainstream psychology, psychiatry, and social work have awoken to the benefits of spiritual ways of understanding the world and have started to explore and acknowledge the positive contribution spirituality can make to mental health, there has also been a great deal of appropriation and stealing of Indigenous and cultural practices from around the world. Some research explores the association between spirituality and mental health as an attempt to understand the mechanisms through which great change, healing, and benefits may occur. The mechanisms most often discussed are our internal and external locus of control, neurobiological mechanisms, social support, the ways in which we cope, and how our external environment are modeled; these are all salient. Whereas many cultures (important to note that many of these cultures and peoples' homelands have been colonized by either the United Kingdom or United States) are not capitalizing or consumerizing ancient healing practices.

For instance, although deeply effective, emotional freedom technique

(EFT) tapping's "origins lie in ancient Chinese medicine with the development of acupuncture—a healing technique that uses needles on the energy meridians or energy pathways, a term used by practitioners of this method" (Carrington, n.d.). Additionally, a prior client, who identified as an Indigenous Peruvian woman, noted that her ancestors used a form of "tapping with rocks" in the Amazon on various meridian points to relieve psychological, spiritual, and physical ailments. However, energy psychology and heart-assisted therapy often do not acknowledge the roots of the technique nor provide compensation or credit to the communities from which they have been extracted.

Another example is the gross appropriation of Maslow's hierarchy of needs. Ryan Heavy Head and Narcisse Blood researched how their people, the Siksika (Blackfoot), influenced Maslow (American psychologist and philosopher best known for his self-actualization theory of psychology) to utilize the teachings received while spending six weeks living at Siksika (Blackfoot), in the summer of 1938 (Ravilochan, 2021). While there, Heavy Head and Blood describe how Maslow restructured his theories and beliefs about self-actualization (the term he used for it). This can also be seen through the juxtaposition between how American ideals focus on individuals and solitary ways of actualizing, and the Blackfoot communal practices that ensure everyone thrives together (Ravilochan, 2021).

These are just two examples of a long list of ways that the mental health industrial complex has appropriated and co-opted, without compensation, credit, or reverence for culturally specific practices that are held sacred by many. Ultimately many Indigenous cultures across the globe have for centuries managed issues of mental dis-ease through spiritual and religious mediums (although not always safely or humanely).

Clearly, the root of modern-day Western psychotherapy derives from the roots and practices of Indigenous people across the globe. Our mental health practices have been co-opted and diluted by mainstream Eurocentric patriarchy practices and beliefs—by boards and checklists and an array of initials, deciding and determining whom or what is deemed "a professional and ethical mental and behavioral health practice." Meanwhile, many, many of the practices and beliefs that our beloved fields have engaged in for the past centuries have been, to put it simply, barbaric.

Like the Indigenous healer, the psychotherapist must help the client to think in the most rational way possible, finding methods to alter or restructure self-sabotaging beliefs and negative self-talk. While the shaman uses their spirit guides to give directives regarding their client's behavior, the psychotherapist instructs clients by quoting proverbs, biblical parables, and dichos—maxims representing the distilled wisdom of the community. The shaman's source of knowledge is said to be outside themselves, the healing comes from the Otherworld through our connection with nature, ancestral spirits, deities, and so forth. By contrast, the therapist's knowledge is represented by the quickness with which they can associate culturally based proverbs and metaphors with the clinical issue at hand, thus describing a rational and effective way for the client to behave.

However, it must be stated that the Western mental health industrial complex is deeply discomforted by African-derived practices, in particular root work (i.e., Ifa, Santeria, Vodou, Candomble, etc.). Part of the fear resides in deeply embedded anti-Black rhetoric within all cultures and ethnicities. Anti-Blackness renders people of African descent categorically unacceptable as human beings, irrespective of their intelligence, character, competence, creativity, or achievements. In *The Souls of Black Folk*, W. E. B. Du Bois described double-consciousness as the constant self-perception of the African and his community against the backdrop of white supremacy. Du Bois argues that this gaze is damaging to the Black person's psyche, causing it to "turn on itself" as internalized Euro-American racism creates anxiety that eventually destroys Black confidence in African ways of knowing (Du Bois, 1903; Allan, 2019).

Possessed
Part of what a colonized education does is erase. It erases our memories by omitting them. In much the same way I was taught about the Boston Tea Party, and I can STILL recite the Gettysburg Address, and the Preamble by heart. Yet everything I know about the Kingdom of Kush in Nubia, or the Kayapo people of the Amazon (peoples of my own distant heritage) come from my own rigorous reeducation, post-education in systems.

To understand the connection between healing and religion, it is essential to understand how illness, health, and healing have been synonymous with mental and emotional health throughout time and are deeply anchored in the worldviews of different religious traditions.

In speaking about emotional decolonization over the past 10 years or so, my work has always returned back to the roots of mental health and healing. According to Lumen Learning's *Abnormal Psychology* online course (2022), prehistoric cultures often held a *supernatural view* of what they identified as "abnormal behavior." It was frequently seen as the work of evil spirits, demons, gods, or witches who took control of the person. The course notes that this form of demonic possession often occurred when the person engaged in behavior contrary to the religious teachings of the time. Which is quite fascinating, as this mirrors much of the way that the MHIC operates today: punishing and pathologizing acts of resistance to the "norms." We see this in conversion therapy today, and how homosexuality was only removed from the *DSM-I* and *-II* in 1973 (Drescher, 2015; Human Rights Campaign Foundation [HRCF], n.d.). What the "modern world" sees as normal has limits, binaries and boxes to adhere and conform to—or else.

The Westernized approach of pathologizing and othering neurodivergence or mental illness is in fact based more in superstitious anxiety than a sophisticated or "civilized" attitude toward difference in behavior or cognition. When we are honest about our fields and how pathology is a major aspect of our training, we can see that our need for people to adhere to some kind of "normal" standard isn't about science or mental health or addressing the needs of any individual. It's about the comfort of conformity and the fear of difference.

Part 2 of this book has outlined how modern psychology others mental illness. To further realign our fields with the honoring of holistic ancestral practices, it is important for practitioners to note how often culturally based practices, that have been used to address mental or behavioral issues in countless different cultures across the globe, have been maligned. It is only in the past decade or so, that researchers across a range of disciplines have started to explore and acknowledge the positive contribution spirituality can make to mental health. In fact, for many of us, "spiritual" is who we are, rather than something we "practice or do." Participants of therapy have also identified the ways in which spiritual activity can contribute to mental health and well-being, and recovery. We can't deny the research and lived experiences of thousands of people whose lives are positively impacted by expressions of spirituality. There is also sufficient research to support that spirituality can be an integral part of managing and living with healthy emotional states and well-being. However, what I am describing is rooted in the past, yet not as clear as the present. As an example, Alcoholics Anonymous is an excellent example of a therapeutic group support system that incorporates a Higher Power and has successfully helped millions of people overcome addiction.

It is vital to note that addiction recovery spaces also engage in gatekeeping and operate under the impact of oppression and colonization. Individuals like Carolyn Collado, author of *Answering the Call of the Ancestors: A Recovery Guide in Times of Reckoning and Revolution* provide lived experience on their experiences healing and coping from substances and generational connections.

Possession of an individual, land, or space by demons or spirits has been documented throughout history, for hundreds of years, throughout numerous religious, political, and historical texts (Reid, 2019; Smith, 2010). For example, Dr. Richard Gallagher, board-certified psychiatrist and a professor of clinical psychiatry at New York Medical College, has written a book about demonic possession in the United States. Over the past two-and-a-half decades, he has provided over several hundred consultations and has helped clergy from multiple denominations and faiths to filter episodes of mental illness—which represent the overwhelming majority of cases—from possession (Gallagher, 2016). He posits that it is an unlikely role for an academic physician; however, he notes that he does not see the two aspects of his career in conflict. He states in a *Washington Post* article, "As a psychiatrist, I diagnose mental illness. Also, I help spot demonic possession" (Gallagher, 2016). He noted that the same habits that have shaped what he does as a professor and psychiatrist—open-mindedness, respect for evidence, and compassion for suffering people—"led me to aid in the work of discerning attacks by what I believe are evil spirits and, just as critically, differentiating these extremely rare events from medical conditions" (Gallagher, 2016).

There are, and have been, historical ritual practices performed by various shamans, elders, curanderas, mediums, imams, gurus, witches, and priests that are often similar to what much of the West calls psychotherapy. The practices of talking to another and holding space in order to support, relieve trauma and internal suffering; create space for practices—ritual singing, dancing, and chanting; body or meridian tapping; and inhabiting one's own body with healthy supportive massage and touch have all been associated with relieving stress, increasing health, and creating better individual and community outcomes. These practices have been well-documented in hundreds, if not thousands of papers, case studies, and collective storytelling among communities that speak of the practices of African Spirituality, such as Ifa, Santeria, and Vodou, as a mental healthcare system within practicing peoples globally. From Espiritismo and Santeria being a healthy gateway into child and family services among Puerto Rican families on the island and across the states; to Santeria as mental health support for practicing Latinx people living with cancer (Sandoval, 1979); to Ifa divination and culturally competent intakes in mental health responsiveness (Bascom, 1969); to Indigenous Yoruba psychiatry (Pérez, 2013); to the belief in Vodou that "Loas are responsible for many aspects of health, especially mental health" (Haiti Outreach Ministries, 2020).

I find myself at odds with practitioners who minimize "prescribing" sunlight, *limpias*, a visit to a craniosacral therapist, a chiropractic adjustment, or a visit with a spiritualist of the person's cultural background—yet much of energy, transpersonal, and heart-centered psychotherapy reside on the shoulders of these holistic ancestral practices.

At times, symptoms of anger, fear, worry, and sadness are believed to contribute to physical and mental illness. Despite the irrational, prejudiced, and Eurocentric Christian-American propaganda that these practices are "bad," it is clear that once again white-bodied pathology has left its mark on cultural and spiritual beliefs practiced by others, particularly when "others" are Black and Brown people of African Indigenous descent. Vodou is not used by its practitioners to do harm; it is not only a religion, but also a healthcare system that includes disease prevention, health, and well-being promotion. Health is perceived as being in harmony with the spirits, the environment, and with others. Vodou gods were, and continue to be, perceived as powerful and protective.

There are, no doubt, better, more robust books on the historical overview, benefits, and current practices related to Indigenous African Religions and other Indigenous religions and practices that would and do benefit humanity's mental health globally. It is also essential to note that African spirituality has been and continues to be colonized and subjected to anti-Black racism across many countries. Part of the power and beauty of our knowledge of colonialism on the African continent is ensuring that we do not create pathology and illness, where there are really workings beyond (some) of our scope.

Ceremony

Ceremony has been an integral part of healing within cultures globally, particularly to people indigenous to a land and their descendants. Ceremony brings community, oftentimes prayer or an aspect of honoring, acknowledgment of an issue, elders, and the magic and gifts of what we (our ancestors or spirituality or practices) already know. It is important to note that ceremony, ritual, and this entire chapter may bring discomfort to white-bodied people or those disconnected from the roots and cultures of their ancestry. That is okay, and normal. It is expected to be defensive, have fear, or feel disconnected from that which we do not know or in which we do not participate.

Practitioners do not need to engage in healing ceremonies if this is not comfortable to them; however, agencies, practices, schools, centers, and hospitals DO have an ethical responsibility to provide access of these ceremonies to those who do. I often consult with large nonprofit organizations and universities, and the first thing I often hear when I mention ancestral knowledge and the healing power of cultural resources is, "But we don't do that here. How will we find someone who does this? I have to ask Legal, I don't know." My response is usually, "Sure, ask Legal. There are hundreds of community resources in your clients' community who are willing, able, even 'certified' in their own businesses to engage in this supportive work. Your job is to be the bridge and help them access what they need. On your grounds or off." So often, MHPs are so deeply conditioned that it is difficult to see past the conditioning and layers of possibility.

There is a belief that we learned from Western psychiatry, psychology, and neuroscience that imprints from childhood affect our personality patterns (usually identified as personality disorders in the *DSM*) that may endure for a lifetime. However, the beauty of reflecting on your ancestry, culture, and family patterns is gaining insight into the gifts and challenges we have inherited. When we act to heal ourselves, many spiritualists across many cultures believe that we also are healing harmful legacies of our ancestors and future descendants. I have sat in many *plática* and teaching circles where we were told that we are impacting and helping to heal "seven generations before and after us."

Ancestral Support

It is important to note that our ancestors are both separate and inseparable from us. By elevating our ancestors' collective spirit, we in turn raise our own vibrations and awareness. What is crucial to note is how the unfurling of generations of gnarled roots of historical and intergenerational abuse can cause a resurgence or aggravation of past trauma, those of our own of our family. It is essential to work with practitioners who spiritually, politically, and therapeutically can provide support; this may not be the same person. However, in these moments your practitioners of emotional support should have a fair understanding of your practices, and have little to no judgment around them. In other words, if you find you are losing your grounding and center, then the dial must be turned down on the ancestral or ceremonial work and practices until the emotional balance is more grounded. Finding an ally or a spiritual buddy early on in ancestral work is also very helpful.

I could write an entire encyclopedia on ancestral veneration, healing, ceremony, accessing traditional teachings, shamanism, Buddhism, and African spirituality as they relate to the elevation and support of our emotional and mental health; alas, this book is unable to hold this at this time. However, what is vital to note is how mainstream Eurocentric, colonial mental health seeks to compartmentalize, despite theories that say the opposite is more helpful.

For example, are expressions of trauma really so different from those of anxiety or depression? Meanwhile, the cultures of Indigenous peoples globally are that of connection and making meaning from connections between nature and the human experience, between one another, and between generations. Even world-renowned trauma therapist and psychiatrist Bessel van der Kolk (2006) acknowledged that "there are other treatment options besides CBT, exposure, and psychopharmacology that are rooted in other traditions and that are practiced in different ways in virtually every culture across the globe."

Many cultures, specifically cultures of PoGM, have robust practices for veneration and support. What is crucial for all people globally to recall are that the most psychologically influential of the ancestral line are often those beyond the reach of remembered names; they may be forgotten by name, but known to history. We know this as their impact vibrates through shared culture, historical identity, and body-level epigenetic influence. For example, the legacy of European colonialism over the past six centuries has been challenging, violent, and exploitative for much of the globe. This period continues to reverberate and inform many white people's experiences of ancestors in the present (Foor, 2017). Even so, it is essential to the health and healing of white-bodied people with European lineage to also remember those who lived before this violence with different stories. Our perception is important to our relationships.

The Youth

Children in particular have very rich spiritual lives, whether or not we know it or acknowledge it. I recall reading *The Secret Spiritual World of Children* by Tobin Hart in my Child & Adolescent Psychopathology and Grief course in graduate school, and I felt seen. It felt important, especially given that I was interning at a massive children's hospital on a floor where small children were living with stage IV cancer and dying. My work was to support them through this transition, through chemotherapy, and to support their parents. One of the biggest questions caregivers would ask was, "What do I tell them about the afterlife?"

After working with the children and hearing all sorts of stories and experiences of the spiritual nature, I knew that children often already KNEW. I would ask caregivers to first ask the child about their beliefs and experiences. The stories I heard from children reminded me of the beauty of the spiritual world. I would hear things like: "A big man with muscles and wings and rainbows said he will be waiting for me next Tuesday to go up to the playground! I can't wait to see my new friends in heaven!" The child did pass on the following week. Or, "When I die next month," (this was casually stated), "I want to come back as purple roses!" Needless to say these things DID occur a month later, and their parents found a purple-fuchsia colored rose months later!

Many people view children as being more intuitively open to the other world because of their more recent arrivals. Whatever our beliefs, my experiences with self-identified "non-spiritual" children and families has shown that sometimes our beliefs need not affect our experiences.

Other books that impacted my worldview by mental and medical health providers have been: *Woman Who Glows in the Dark* by Elena Avila and Joy Parker; *Women Who Run with Wolves* by Clarissa Pinkola Estés; *Root and Ritual* by Becca Piastrelli; *Jambalaya: The Natural Woman's Book of Personal Charms and Practical Rituals* by Luisah Teish; *Many Lives, Many Masters* by Brian L. Weiss; *Second Sight* by Judith Orloff; and *Anatomy of the Spirit* by Caroline Myss—just to name a few.

Many Western MHPs present historical/ancestral trauma as a kind of pathogen that gets passed down through generations, and which MHPs can either perpetuate by pathologizing in all the common harmful ways OR disrupt by adopting these decolonial practices to make it possible for people to find a path toward healing. It doesn't necessarily have to be in this place in the text, but if that resonates with you, that could be a useful perspective to bring in at some point.

I will end by sharing something a spiritual teacher once told me:

> Psychological and spiritual crises will happen in a person's lifetime. We can support them as a community, treat them like human beings,

and the crisis may take 4–8 weeks, or even six months. Or we could place them in a hospital or institution, and they are affected and on psychotropic medication for life. We choose how we want to proceed over the next 50 years as a global community. (B. Cofield, personal communication, 2005)

I would like to believe that decolonized strategies are not outlined by Western notions and boxes; but by reviving and reopening our practices and perceptions to global Indigenous wisdom (without appropriation) such as the importance of love, prayer, community learning, multigenerational rituals and gatherings, storytelling, and more. More on this in Chapter 10.

Please note that the following story includes discussions of death and dying.

The People's Stories

Pia came into the community mental health center dying. She told the therapy group that she had been frequenting over the past three years, that under no uncertain terms should anyone be unclear about her impending death. She shared that she had made peace with the fact that her body no longer could hold the vibrance of her spirit, and that her leukemia had spread. Over the past three months her body increasingly withered in front of us. Pia is of the Shinnecock Indian Nation and Afro-Ecuadorian. Her spirituality—including monthly *danza* ceremonies—was extremely important to her. Throughout her last months in group, which she insisted on attending, she exemplified a deep sense of peace, bravery, anger, and frustration at her body, and demonstrated the wisdom of a teacher and sage. She held space for other group members as they grieved her, which I found to be terribly brave. Finally, her individual therapist and I—whom she shared many conversations with related to loss and death—cocreated a "Dying Death Wishlist" (her choice of words, not ours).

Pia requested for us, if we were able, to come to her bedside and speak about the group (with their permission); to eat as if we were having lunch with her, whether or not she could eat; and to engage in some mutual ceremony practices as she transitioned—if we could. In fact, my colleague and I could and did. We also ensured support for each other before and after the visits to Pia. We also gave as much support as we could (taking turns) to Pia's grandmother, mother, and two siblings. We arranged aftercare for her family prior to Pia's transition, and we helped her mother enroll the children in grief counseling prior as well.

The day before Pia transitioned into Spirit World my colleague and I visited her. We brought marigolds, cinnamon, sage, copal, lime, sea salt, and basil. We also wore and brought various ceremonial Indigenous articles from our personal families. We included her grandmother and one of the siblings (the others chose not to participate). Together we washed her hands and feet, her sibling painted her nails (all Pia's requests). We sang and played her favorite songs, we prayed together—we cried together.

We created a space for *ofrendas* (offerings placed on a home altar) when she transitioned, as per her directions, and hung four bunches of basil tied together by string. We lit incense. We brought groceries and fresh fruit for her grandmother and mother. As relatives entered, they added their own *ofrenda* in the form of a poem, fruit, crystals, and toys in remembrance of Pia. We were asked to stay the night the first evening (my colleague did, I was unable to do so at the time). We were seen and we felt, and continue to feel as though we were and are an extension of Pia, and part of the family.

Not all people receiving therapeutic healing work with us will have such clear desires, instructions, or presence of mind to consider their needs upon dying; nor will they want their practitioners involved as they transition. Many will not know when they will transition. However, this story is an example of what is possible when we reintegrate and allow our duties and presence as caregivers to be a reflection of what our "professional ancestors" provided: presence, compassion, space to grieve, and ritual as ceremony.

Grief Rituals and Ancestral-Healing Inquiries

Below are some inquiries that practitioners may ask themselves in relation to their role in end-of-life grief rituals, death, when a therapy participant passes on in their care, processing loss, or existential climate anxiety. These inquiries invite practitioners to consider when working with people who are actively transitioning:

- What might be some of the differences between traditional psychodynamic and cognitive behavioral theories and that of a decolonial and ancestral framework? What are their relevance to healing and therapy?
- What might transitioning clients need from me? How can I help support their process and where they are?
- How can the community support the family and loved ones, prior to the transition?
- What might sessions that include regenerative themes of repair, healing storytelling, and geopolitical awareness while discussing grief and loss within your therapeutic practices feel like?
- Identify what people, places, and identities are most vulnerable to climate anxiety and climate change, and why.
- Identify how legacies of oppression, displacement, enslavement, and genocide connect to how we support death today.
- Provide grief rituals that promote healthy expressions of grief and ancestral resilience.

Blood and Earth

With basic human rights and Earth's resources being siphoned and extracted without permission, it is safe to say that we are amid a collapse. One of time, space, structures, identities, and a collapse and dismantling of expired collective socialization. This includes racist socializations. white supremacist decisions that have once been taken for face value and digested/assimilated are now being investigated, challenged, and resisted. With collapse comes unbelievable grief. With collapse comes cycles of relishing, clearing, and welcoming what was. Most structures globally are not inherently "bad," as the very energy of the "bad" binary creates a deep separation between "us" and "them." Rather, we might assert that many structures, policies, and governmental systems, including the mental health industrial and medical industrial complexes, are cruel and violent—Unjust. Inadequate. Severely lacking. Causing death, gaslighting, imbalance, and cyclical diseases. Many ancestral traditions would also support that these adjectives describe roots of "evil." That which needs to be cleared, cleaned, exorcised, and which will eventually tip over.

So, the physical collapse and shift of a society usually has the prerequisites of an equally powerful, and emotional, revolution. Once again, in beginning the slow, excruciating at times, and freeing process of decolonizing, we remember with relief that our forepersons (instead of forefathers) have gone through emotional, global, and structural periods of revolution before—and nature consistently does as well. We remember to focus on the basics:

- Caring for one another in tangible ways.
- Healing (emotionally/physically/energetically) practices.
- Creation and preservation of our art (i.e., storytelling, dance, sensual pleasure, painting, etc.).
- Inclusion and advocacy for basic human needs and rights, and the right of wellness for all.
- Ancestors. What we have been shown (historically) has sustained us, and how to call upon their wisdom in tangible ways.
- Relationships with the Land, animals, plants, our bodies, each other, and our selves—such as our emotions and mental faculties.
- We ensure that our communities consistently tend to, and include, children and youth, elders, those who cannot care for themselves, and those who are in deep pain (including grief).

Perhaps the current systems are too restrictive for the future.

Hence, this book and my life's work centers on the decolonial process, because although systems and structures function quite differently across cultures and continents, our mental, emotional, and behavioral health processes and practices will NEED to be fluid; adaptive; sturdy; accessible for anywhere, at any time; humane; holistic; ancestral; and multigenerationally and culturally accessible to all. The diversity of our practices will be our strength as we embark on an unclear future. However, what is clear is that we cannot imagine what our world will be like in 10 years; therefore, may our mental health practices and practitioners be fluid, love-centered, flexible, humanizing, fun, accessible, and liberatory. Truly this is the core of the decolonial root.

Aspects of Emotional–Decolonial Unlearning
1. Prior to the *DSM*, hospitalizations, and therapy sessions, there were clergy, curanderas, shamans, santeros, darvish/a, hajah, papaloas, healers, etc. There still are.
2. Until the early 19th century, religion, spirituality, and psychiatry were closely connected.
3. For thousands of years, various types of healers held physical and literal space for individuals impacted by emotional maladies and harm.
4. Many of our ancestors across the globe often held a supernatural view of abnormal behavior and saw it as the work of "evil spirits, demons, gods, or witches who took control of the person."
5. (We) acknowledge that not everyone's faith is situated within the framework of a religion.
6. We believe that healthy beliefs, outside the realm of science and psychology, are real.
7. Stress can cause hallucinations.
8. Spirits and presences are a common occurrence for many non-white cultures, even more traditional or conservative religions.
9. We do not believe that experiencing otherness or psychic phenomena constitutes a schizophrenic or psychotic diagnosis. That is cultural bias, harmful, and even racist.
10. Healing has been stolen from our wellness practices because they often include rituals or beliefs that white culture does not often understand or has lost.
11. The biggest difference between global Indigenous and Western approaches to mental and emotional healing is that Indigenous

approaches seek to integrate the mind, body, and spirit, rather than dissociate the three.

12. Prioritize people over "shoulds" in the field, as long as people are not being harmed.
13. It is healthy and normal for people to work through their misconceptions and fears around their own process of relearning, or participating in ceremonies, healings, ancestral work, cleansings, and so forth to assist alongside our therapeutic work.
14. We accept and believe individuals when they speak of religious and spiritual trauma. Unfortunately, many individuals have experienced violence at the hands of religious and/or cultural institutions and their leaders (i.e., pastors, priests, *babalawos*, etc.). It is important that we honor and work with religious trauma appropriately.
15. We cannot imagine what our world will be like in 10 years; therefore, our mental health practices and practitioners would benefit from being fluid, flexible, humanizing, fun, accessible, and liberatory. There is no other way to be decolonial.

Emo–Decolonial Practice Offerings

- It is appropriate to talk about spirituality and religion, contrary to popular belief, within sessions.
- Notice where anti-Blackness shows up in your reactions and beliefs around how, who, and what Black, Caribbean, and African cultures worship, celebrate, or honor.
- Practitioners' holistic practices, intuition, abilities, and/or other ways of knowing are welcomed, as long as they are safe, consensual, and desired by the participant, and not exposing the participants to harm in any manner.
- Ceremonies and rituals provide people with closure, celebration, and the possibility of healing (birthdays, showers, weddings, quinceañeras, baptisms, and bat/bar mitzvahs are often more widely accepted).
- Reimagine creating supervision pods from people, practitioners, and participants in your community. Normalize receiving consultation and supervision that is reciprocal, honest, and holds everyone accountable for their interventions and therapeutic relationships.

- When appropriate, consult, invite in, and work with practitioners from various spiritual and ethnic backgrounds, modalities, and belief systems.
- Read and learn about what you do not know, particularly if you are working with specific cultural populations. It is your responsibility to open yourself up to the knowledge without appropriating. Often the fear of appropriation can keep us from celebrating and learning about our differences. There is a difference between celebration (without appropriation) and appropriation.
- Notice if you—consciously or not—regard, trust, or follow white-passing or Eurocentric religions' spirituality over Black/African/Caribbean religions and spiritualities. It is important to check our unconscious bias.
- If a participant reports hearing voices or seeing things, take a breath, and ask more clarifying questions. "Do you recognize the voice(s)? Do they arise only during times of stress? Are they asking you to do anything to yourself or others? How do they make you feel? Did anyone in your family also hear people/voices/spirits? What perspective does your religion/belief system/spirituality/lineage have around hearing and seeing things others don't see or hear? How does this make you feel? How does it feel to share this with me? Do you have concerns about sharing more intimate aspects of what you experience? How can I ease some of this worry? Do any activities or practices help or worsen the experiences? How long and how often have you experienced this? Are they spirits/ancestors/unrecognizable, etc.?"

CHAPTER 8

Collective Grief and Sacred Rage As Expressions of Colonization

The rage of the oppressed is never the same as the rage of the privileged.
—bell hooks, killing rage (1996)

The pain and hurt that created our rage are desperately searching for liberation.
—Ruth King, Healing Rage (2004)

And the thing about white colonist fear and rage is that I have nothing to do with it—but my body becomes a receptacle for this unmetabolized woundedness. At the end of the day, I find myself not just hauling my trauma, but the trauma of whiteness.
—Lama Rod Owens, Love and Rage:
The Path of Liberation through Anger (2020)

Ultimately wherever there is fear, there is the base instinct to protect what we fear losing. And if we aren't attentive to where fear is functioning as it relates to grief then we are constantly enacting those dynamics, causing harm to ourselves and the people around us.
—Breeshia Wade, Grieving While Black:
An Antiracist Take on Oppression and Sorrow (2021)

Grief is what's going on inside of us, while mourning is what we do on the outside. The internal work of grief is a process, a journey. It does not have prescribed dimensions and it does not end on a certain date.
—David Kessler, Finding Meaning: The Sixth Stage of Grief (2019)

Rage is the battle cry of the silenced; therefore, raging is liberating.
—Dr. Jenn

I can go inward instead of going off.
—Gabby Bernstein

Our global collective of humans are not fond of grief nor rage. They are seen as dirty words. Words that perhaps each of us individually attempt to dodge, weave, and duck away from, hoping for respite and space away from it. Rage and grief both are pathologized throughout the mental health profession. We are socialized and colonized to diagnose intermittent explosive disorder, conduct disorder (in children and adolescents), and oppositional defiant disorder (in children and adolescent) (5th Ed.; *DSM-5*; APA, 2013). This is especially overdiagnosed in Black children, and these are behavioral diagnoses. Additionally, grief is frequently diagnosed with major depressive disorder or dysthymia. Any form of dissent, disagreement, or protest has historically been pathologized and treated as problematic. This has been and continues to be passed down in our conditioning societally. Once again, colonization and Eurocentric value systems have their fangs in a range of healthy human emotion.

This chapter will explore the multiple ways that grief and rage are mirrors of each other—openings and entrances to the ways in which microaggressions and microassaults begin to activate our childhood wounds. On an even deeper level, as the prior chapter on intergenerational trauma transmission and research exemplified, our ancestral and historical trauma can be activated. This occurs most particularly during and after societal events, such as the murder of an unarmed Black man simply jogging (Rest in Power, Ahmaud Arbery); or when an autistic Black Dominican teenager leaves school without notice from any adult, and is found dead (Rest in Power, Avonte Oquendo); or when the remains of over 1,500 children, babies, and youth are found across what is now known as Canada in mass burial sites across "residential schools" which were really schools of extermination (Rest in Power, all of the children who were violently taken too early). Many of our emotional reactions are intensified by historical material literally being unearthed as this is being written. We are not "staying stuck in the past," we are actively impacted by our past, in the present.

History Is Written Within Our Bodies

Historical trauma is real. *It is both of the past (what happened to our kin) and the present (how this manifests in our bodies, minds, and spirits today).* Therefore, it makes sense that this collective trauma, which feels like another attempt at cultural genocide, continues to be unconsciously transmitted by society and the people functioning in this matrix around us. This includes our caregivers' behaviors and beliefs, our education system's lessons and expectations, and the generalizations and prejudices related to how you identify and walk in the world. Therefore, when our bodies appropriately tell us that there is a threat, we generally listen. Sometimes, we act before thinking when our parasympathetic nervous system signals for us to respond. Threats to the body activate the sympathetic nervous system and the fight, flight, freeze, and fawn responses. Whereas the parasympathetic nervous system helps the body return to baseline after any events that activate it (Cleveland Clinic, 2019).

One of the solid takeaways I felt in my body after my weekend Movement for Trauma workshop with Jane Clapp was that reoccupying the body (after trauma) is and continues to be a political act. Since the body has historically been a point of violence for people with colonized histories, it is no wonder that "trusting your body" can feel so difficult. When there is the possibility of danger and we are faintly reminded of some far-off time of being *hunted, betrayed, and/or cornered,* it *feels, smells,* and *shows up like survival.* What many of us understand and diagnose as dissociation is actually a healthy and quite "normal" experience of the body protecting us.

There is research to suggest that dissociation is a spectrum and that many people—particularly for people with colonized histories—detachment from our physical bodies is not only a coping mechanism, but a form of bodily intelligence and safety. Many people are often conditioned to push. Push on our farms, on the plantation, to complete the railroad, to finish the roofing on the top of this building. We can often witness this when we perform beautifully and calmly in crisis, even thrive in crisis. I grew up hearing "Save the drama for your momma!" But now I can often be heard stating, "The trauma has you addicted to the drama" instead. We know through much of modern Western psychology that living with traumatic memories can lead to a daily struggle to discern between what is profoundly physical and psychologically terrifying and what may be a reaction from past experiences. We can see that drama was frequently seen as the "storyline," and it is addictive. I would tell my peer educators, "That's the story line; do you want to stay hooked, or can we go deeper?" Drama is addictive when you live in a traumatized state. Change and uncertainty can elicit a fight–flight–freeze response triggering emotions from childhood and our youth—and from our historical ancestral experiences.

If our therapeutic providers are not explaining that family, cultural, and collective histories (which I call *ancestral trauma*) prior to our birth can be contributing to our dysregulated states, then what are we doing? Rage and grief—on an individual, collective, and ancestral level—must be explored when we are learning to metabolize the trauma stuck in our soma and affecting our psychology.

When conflict occurs, physiological reactions course through our bodies, one such reaction being stress in the brain (Patel, 2020). Sometimes this stress lasts for long enough that the hippocampus is impacted, which results in brain fog. Patel writes: "Brain fog refers to the inability to think rationally and usually occurring when in conflict" (Patel, 2020). This can become part of daily life when emotions aren't resolved or acknowledged, leading to frequent memory loss.

Teasing apart stimuli and emotions is not an easy task. Emotions come as reactions to stimuli that our brain interprets, starting with the amygdala (Patel, 2020). When conflict occurs, cortisol levels instantly go up, and overreaction is common. We often describe feeling hot or can feel our blood pumping when we are angry; this is related to cortisol and the amygdala's reactions.

There are two pathways to a reaction that occur in the amygdala: confront the entity (fight) or shut down (flight). The reaction is rapid initially, and we become startled immediately. It is only afterward that we digest the event. The thalamus gland in our brain receives the emotional stimuli. When clinicians say our emotions sit at the surface, they are received in the sensory thalamus. Our reaction, the initial sting, is felt in the amygdala. The amygdala is hijacked, forcing us to become disoriented in a heated event. In the heat of the conflict, our neural pathways, located at the prefrontal cortex, shut down immediately, preventing us from intaking information in a coherent format, while establishing a perception of what the other individual said, and trapping us in the "I'm right and you are wrong" mindset.

While the brain is under conflict, the body is reacting. Both the brain and body are experiencing multiple emotions including anger, fear, hurt, disappointment, and many others. At this moment, people excuse their feelings/reactions by blaming others and pointing fingers, while being angry at themselves for how they reacted (Harris House, 2016).

The People's Stories

"Dr. Jenn, I'm a keep it 100. I've gone to mandated anger management classes, to so-called 'meditation classes,' to all these therapists and stuff, I know how to do diaphragm breathing, to check my thoughts, to look at the facts, to walk away—I know to identify when it is a FEELING, not FACTS . . . and all I know is that once I feel disrespected, once I feel that 'I am being played,' I feel not safe. Not good. A deep old feeling comes up like vomit, and then I go off. The fuck off!

"I know my pops was like that, he was murdered 'cause he was a hothead—my auntie told me. I know my brother Upstate [prison] is like that; my moms told me. I know I been like this since a kid; I was always in trouble for breaking shit and fighting in school. They sent me to a 'therapeutic school.' But, Doc, that place wasn't therapeutic, man. Whatever therapy is—whatever therapy 'sposed to feel like 'twasn't it man.

"There wasn't a fucking thing THERAPEUTIC about embarrassing me in front of everyone, asking me to sit still, knowing damn well I can't, calling the cops when I raise my voice . . . might've well have stayed in juvie [juvenile detention center] cause it felt like I was always being watched.

"But what those therapists and interns didn't understand or ask me about was the deep-ass sadness, man. That pain. Like pain that can't even be all mine, man. I feel so deep, ya know? Like an abyss that makes a person feel paranoid, man. I wasn't paranoid until I dealt with white teachers locking me up. I wasn't fucking paranoid until teachers and therapists who looked like me and even related to me hung their damn heads telling me the same damn thing, 'Sorry, gotta follow the rules, if we don't report this, I'll get in trouble; they already see me as trouble.' [shaking head].

"So, you do this rage therapy thing right? Well tell me this, why we always so hungry??? Why our People so hungry—we talk about anger but not RAGE—I feel like this is something right here. Rage is a hunger—but it's like that hunger comes through as wanting to mess something up?! It is like there is this hunger that can never be fed, and like there is an itch I can never fully scratch. Like I feel like it's down there deep, and every time I let this THING out of me—for good damn reasons mind you—I feel a bit more ME, and a lot LESS LIKE ME too [voice shaking].

"Actually, to answer your question, I feel a lot more connected or something [long pause] to my pops and my brothers, like we all were trying to say something. We were all trying to just EAT—feel me? We were just trying to survive something swallowing us whole. Like I am talking for them—'cause they voiceless and deathless . . . No one wants to be a damn ghost, man. I mean, we been voiceless, and man that's enraging. I am fighting for them and me and everyone I lost; and everyone who supposedly died for me to be free. I don't feel free.

"What's free? What's free when you Black, poor, ugly, and grew up

in the hood in 'Murica? I know that I sound looney, man. I am not—I am not. I am crystal damn clear, Doc [voice shaking]. It's like there is this scheme; and dark, poor people all over the globe are IT, like in tag you know, we are IT. And I'm not having it. Everyone in me ain't having it. It's like a blessing and a curse, know what I'm sayin', Doc?"
—*22-year-old college student, self-identifying Black, cisgender male*

I did know what he was saying. I do understand how deeply ingrained survival felt in my body and how deeply many people who are descendants from the African continent feel a deep disconnect from ourselves, Home, and from others who smile at things and didn't grow up with the trauma of overt and covert oppression behind every corner. I understood as best as I could and at the same time I could not identify. It was important for me to also acknowledge that I was not a dark-skinned, heterosexual male, growing up with carceral intergenerational trauma where my father, uncle, and brothers were incarcerated. I could hold it with him as long as he would allow me to do so. More importantly I FELT the words, as did he. I heard the layers of historical trauma, cultural trauma, racial trauma, the righteous rage, the deep grief, as well as the anxiety of *still* not having the "right" coping mechanisms to survive and thrive, despite years of "therapeutic interventions" swimming in his words.

His story and many, many, many others are why a change is essential and inevitable in the mental health field. It is *incomplete*. It is *incomplete*, and that *lack of completeness* is dangerous, and exploitative because we (helpers, healers, and therapy providers) are not being taught the truth to those we sit with. We are not being honest about the root causes of current-day pain— likely because we are uncertain how the past collides with the present, and that, My Good People, affects everything. I have no doubt that this book will be *incomplete* as well, as is the nature of decolonial work—always evolving and outgrowing.

Although I stand with privilege as someone who holds a doctorate in clinical psychology (among other privileges), my experience growing up in Hudson County, NJ, was a great deal closer to that Brother's story than to the stories I listened to in my graduate programs or among my colleagues.

I could not relate to many academics and clinicians. Frankly, I still do not want to. I often wore many masks not only to navigate the coursework, microaggressions, and structural obstacles/oppression, but also the need to somehow figure out who I am and how I fit here in order to survive the institution. So many BIPOC people are exhausted when we embark on obtaining graduate degrees because we have so much backend learning to do. I learned to articulate when I speak, removed question marks at the end of my sentences, and minimized my passion and "outside voice."

Growing up, I was surrounded by multiple forms of community violence, rage was often coupled with substances, which usually equaled danger. Many people around the globe understand and live with emotionally and physically unsafe environments, and our expression of this pain varies per person, per family, and sometimes per culture. I did not realize until I was deep into my 30s that many of us living under constant threat, whether societal or familial, live with an internal barometer, giving us advantages when navigating the world.

Now, hear me out. Not an equitable or accessible advantage—but an "I see things around me more clearly than you realize" advantage. What do we call that? In my hood we called it "hood-wise," other places call it being "street-smart," and in other spaces it's known as the "school of hard knocks." However we choose to interpret this *deep survival knowing*, it has saved me on many occasions, and allowed me the ability to read a room—whether a boardroom, group room, or a party—quick, fast, and in a hurry.

There is so much wisdom in the struggle. I am not glorifying it. Nothing is glamorous about hunger. But I am honoring the concrete jungle as a space that raised me and honoring that there is wisdom in all cultures. I liken my relationship to the inner city to the scent of a Sunday kitchen— love and understanding wafting from your auntie's safe, loving, comforting bosom when she hugs away your fears; or the tough-love monologues and stories of days of old from one of your eldest, fastest talking uncles. Familiar, wise, full, and brilliant. Everything you needed and didn't know until you had it.

For many children, there is an instinctual knowing. Things that we picked up and understood at a young age, the main one being that *safety* trumped everything. Being safe meant (a) thinking critically and reacting; (b) staying really still and waiting until the storm passed; or (c) getting the heck out of there. Or a combination of the three. Many of us who grew up with developmental trauma made micro decisions constantly that related to our safety. This usually involved caregivers or places in which we were supposed to be safe, such as:

- Your father is drunk in the bathroom of a small apartment for over 10 hours; he is not responding, nor will your mother ask him to move. You are needing to utilize the restroom. Do you: (a) hold your pee, (b) pee in a bucket, or (c) leave the house and find a bathroom.
- A caregiver is screaming and blasting loud music: (a) stay in your room, lay low and hope the rage doesn't turn on you, (b) leave the house and find a way to numb yourself, or (c) tell them to lower the radio and that you are trying to do homework.
- Another student at school is bullying you physically and on the internet. They are sending pictures around that you have shared with them when you were friends: (a) tell a teacher or counselor you trust, risk being seen as a snitch, and be the subject of further bullying, (b) "Puff up," "Handle it," and "Do what needs to be done" to be seen as someone not to be "messed with," or (c) ignore it, it is not worth it.
- A teacher continues to say a student's name wrong. Her face and body language change when speaking to that particular student who does not know the answer to a question: (a) speak to a counselor or a caregiver, tell them the teacher does not "like" the youth, and is possibly discriminating against them, or (b) behave as if it does not matter, or (c) shout your correct name pronunciation the next time the teacher says it incorrectly.
- A colleague continues to cut you off during meetings; they apologize, yet continue to speak after you have been cut off. They also take what you share and change the language, yet present the same information you have. This happens a lot. You (a) attempt to do the adult thing and address the situation, (b) get used to it, or (c) get up and walk out of the room—you feel deep rage and/or insecurity.

These examples of decisions often have multiple options. However, when we are in a consistent state of fight-or-flight—when our nervous systems are unfortunately used to scanning our environments for threats and when the world as a whole begins to feel deeply unstable (specifically for your gender, race, culture, etc.)—alarm bells sound. Options feel more and more limited when we try to find a way of navigating the situation.

Many BIPOC whom I have held space for have an intimate relationship with rage and grief. More times than I care to count, I often dismissed the reptilian brain response of fight–flight–freeze, and the somatic component to trauma locked in the body, as well as the link to familial and historical material because it was not something I could receive supervision on, speak to my professors about, or gain clarity around—on top of just beginning to unpack my own People's colonized histories. It was easier to diagnose and discount it as pathology based on my training as a psychologist.

RECOMMENDATION FOR THERAPEUTIC WORKERS, HELPERS, AND HEALERS

Consider reciprocal supervision that "serves who you are serving." Intergenerational supervision that is cyclical, works. Meaning, an "early-career politicized helper" can engage in supervision/consulting support with a practitioner who has been in the field for some time. There is an energetic exchange where each is serving the other. Perhaps more experienced workers may feel "they do not need supervision," yet I would say this is a dangerous mindset. This evolution from therapy into politicized healing work needs and desires being in a constant practice of humility. More established/experienced practitioners, in particular, might need a little accountability in challenging themselves to embrace a more politicized approach to their practice. Providing mentorship and receiving feedback/new information from early-career folks who may be closer to the pulse of political awareness allows for reciprocity and constant evolution. Mental health practitioners who have years of experience need burgeoning "early-career" workers as much as they need you! I would recommend meetings every other week, and there would be a rotation between the early-career workers providing feedback on new trends, research, and areas to receive further "training" and do more reading in; and then following the session the mature MH Practitioners would provide supervision and know-how, and so forth! It is a win-win, and allows mature therapists to check their power, privilege, and anhedonia around therapy.

The People's Stories

"I know, I know I should be over my mother already, but every day I wake up and it feels like she *just* passed away. That can't be normal! It's been 10 years, Dr. Mullan. Ten years and I feel stuck. I am failing all classes; my professors don't have any more patience for me. They think I am making excuses. They ask if I am still seeing you, as if three sessions will erase the pain of losing my mother at 9 years old. I have trouble cleaning my room, leaving the house or car most days, and just building basic friendships. I am afraid everyone I love and care about will leave. That they will die. Then, on top of all of this my homeland—my people—are dying. We are being murdered; it is a genocide, and no one wants me to talk about it. Who am I kidding? I don't want to talk about it. Because if I do, I won't be able to close the dam back up. I will just keep crying and crying and crying—for my mother, for my home, for my people, and my little cousins back home."

Stages of Grief?!

> *Grief . . . really just love. It's all the love you want to give but cannot. All of that unspent love gathers up in the corners of our eyes, the lump in your throat, and in that hollow part of your chest. Grief is just love with no place to go.*
> —Actually Jamie (2014)

Grief is a natural and primal response to loss. I would also add that grief is a natural and primal response to having deeply loved, cared for something or someone, and its loss. It's the emotional suffering you feel when something or someone you love is taken away, desecrated, or your experiences deeply minimized. The pain of loss can feel overwhelming, can be numbed, neutralized, projected, repressed, and released.

Individuals can experience individual, familial, community, and/or global grief. Humans and animals grieve. Marc Bekoff (2000, 2009), an American biologist who spent his time researching emotions in animals including grief, published findings that observed a grief experience in wolves, chimpanzees, dolphins, whales, giraffes, and elephants, among others. For example, elephants are known to communally recognize a deceased relative similar to how they greet a newborn—by collectively touching its corpse or old bones like they would touch a newborn's body, and possibly wailing.

Grief impacts each of us differently on multiple levels of our being. It can impact us:

Mentally: Impacting our brain function, processing, memory, cognition, brain capacity/space/energy, and our mental health. Countless psychologists and neurologists describe *Grief Brain*, where judgments and memories feel foggy and unclear. Neurologist Lisa Shulman (2018) describes in her book *Before and After Loss: A Neurologist's Perspective on Loss, Grief, and Our Brain* how grief is an intense emotional state that just knocks an individual off of their feet and comes over them like a wave. Grieving does not necessarily have a time frame, contrary to popular belief. McCoy defines grieving as "what happens as we adapt to the fact that our loved one is gone, that we're carrying the absence of them with us" (McCoy, 2021). We will feel grief, virtually forever, as it is a natural response to loss. Hence, we may posit that cultures that have grief rituals and conversations, regardless of whether there has been a specific loss present throughout early stages, also rear children who process and cope better.

Physically: Affecting our physical energy levels, various parts of our bodies, our nervous system, and our biological functioning and physical health. People grieving have been known to experience pain in various parts of their bodies, or phantom pain—most specifically back, chest, and knee pain, and migraines.

Emotionally: Affecting our emotional range, expression, and at times, the ability to express emotions at all. Grief can wash up older emotions we believe we have dealt with as well as stir up an array of new emotions that have never been felt. Grief most commonly is pathologized as depression.

Spiritually: Affects our understanding of our spiritual beliefs, for some of us this is positive and increases connection to a source outside of our own. For some people, anger arises and it creates feelings that a spiritual source has abandoned or left us or loved ones.

All of this makes up a full-body, full-being experience we have after loss. There are numerous historical markers that may have led to the millions of misconceptions about grief.

- The way that capitalism and the work system allots for only one "paid" day to one week for grief.
- The little time allotted to "feel and deal" after a global crisis/war/natural disaster.
- How globally and collectively we have conflated "moving on and being strong" with no longer feeling grief.
- How the global media sensationalizes and memorializes whiter, able, thinner bodies over the loss of bigger, darker, and disabled bodies. How death and war are "normalized" in specific parts of the world (i.e., African continent, India, the Middle East, and Central America as opposed to North America, Australia, and Europe—the whiter-bodied per capita countries).
- Colonization and its effects have also shaped grief.

- What are ways that you have noticed that grief has been affected by historical experiences?
- What is your relationship to grief?
- How have you been socialized to grieve?
- How have you as a MHP been taught to engage with or "treat" grief (if at all)?
- What are your culture's beliefs about grieving?
- Where can you create more space to grieve currently, and what would this look like?

Grief is not only about death; it can be about life. It can be about surviving, when thousands of others have not. Grief can look like apathy or devastation, longing or resentment. Grief is the great chameleon. Taking our emotions on a roller coaster ride, convincing the human body, mind, and heart that it is resolving itself only to create another tumultuous tangle out of what we thought was "just fine."

Many MHPs are taught the five stages of grief: denial, anger, bargaining, depression, and acceptance by Elisabeth Kübler-Ross and David Kessler. They posited that not everyone will experience all five stages, and one may not go through them in a particular linear order. Grief is different for every person, so one person may begin coping with loss in the bargaining stage and another person may find themselves in denial or anger. Some individuals may remain for months in one of the five stages but skip others entirely. Although the stages of grief are useful and have assisted many people in the grieving process, much like much of present-day psychotherapeutic frames, it is incomplete.

Alica Forneret (n.d.) beautifully stated, "We study and prep for so many other things in life, grief should be one of them." It is said that before her passing Kübler-Ross stated that she regretted writing and speaking about the five stages of grief in such a linear manner. Although it was important for her to give a voice to those that were dying, and to provide those suffering as they watched their loved ones pass away, she acknowledged that the stages may have provided a narrow definition of grief. Kübler-Ross noted "many people believed the stages to be both linear and universal." She identified five *common* experiences, not five *required* experiences. Whether applied to the dying or those left living, they were meant to normalize and validate the intensity and range of emotions that individuals might experience in the tsunami that is loss, death, and grief.

Suffocated Grief

I can't breathe. I can't breathe. I can't breathe. I can't breathe. I can't breathe. I can't breathe. I can't breathe. I can't breathe. I can't breathe. I can't breathe. I can't breathe. I can't breathe. I can't breathe. I can't breathe. I can't breathe. I can't breathe.

> *I CANNOT BREATHE.*
> —Said by almost all people living in Black bodies

Emotionally, physically, mentally, and spiritually. WE CANNOT BREATHE.

Whether we are speaking of literal hands, nightsticks, or nooses around our necks. Whether there are machetes at our necks. Whether there are accusations and threats. Whether heavy ancestral traumas and curses are curled around our behaviors.

Dr. Tashel Bordere (as cited in Crowther, 2019), assistant professor in the Department of Human Development and Family Science at the University of Missouri-Columbia, researches grief and loss among African American youth. Her publications have focused on Black youth affected by homicide, gun violence, and race-based trauma. Dr. Bodere "identified the term *suffocated grief* to describe when normal grief reactions among marginalized populations are not only dismissed, but punished" (Fenton, 2020). She notes that Black youth are more likely to have their "normal grief reactions penalized, or they're misinterpreted based on the lens that people are using to decide about whether they get to grieve." Research and lived experience has demonstrated that Black youth are disproportionately placed in classes for special education and behavior issues, in lieu of offering support or adults in caretaking roles misunderstanding that many of their behaviors are tied to normal grief reactions. What we are not taught (personally or professionally) about grief reactions are the quite normal symptoms of being distracted, sleepiness, regressive or "acting out" externalized behaviors, as well as bursts of anger and irritability. This is also true for adults; however, children and teenagers have a biologically lessened impulse control.

Disenfranchised Grief

Grief that people experience when they incur a loss that is not or cannot be openly acknowledged, socially sanctioned, or publicly mourned.

Dr. Bordere suggests this can happen for a number of reasons that, for the most, fall into one (or sometimes more) of the following categories:

1. The loss isn't seen as worthy of grief (e.g., non-death losses).
2. The relationship is stigmatized (e.g., partner in an extramarital affair).
3. The mechanism of death is stigmatized (e.g., suicide or overdose death).
4. The person grieving is not recognized as a griever (e.g., coworkers or ex-partners).
5. The way someone is grieving is stigmatized (e.g., the absence of an outward grief response or extreme grief responses).

Dr. Kenneth Doka is known for coining the term *disenfranchised grief*—encompassing grief for a loss that doesn't fit within social or clinical expectations. For example, if you're experiencing deep grief over pregnancy loss, the loss of a pet, or the death of a celebrity whom you didn't know personally, some people might think it's not comparable to the loss of a spouse, child, or parent, and they might dismiss your grief.

It's painful when others don't understand your grieving or don't believe that you're really feeling the loss that you are. Disenfranchised grief is more common than you might realize, and it increases the trauma of a loss.

Disenfranchised grief is generally grief that is not usually openly acknowledged, socially accepted, or publicly mourned. One's grief is "disenfranchised" when their culture, society, or support group makes them feel their loss and/or grief is invalidated and insignificant. This can occur when:

- The death is stigmatized (suicide, overdose, HIV/AIDS, drunk driving).
- The relationship is seen as insignificant (ex-spouse, coworker, miscarriage, pet).

- The relationship is stigmatized by society (same-sex partner, systemic racism/police shootings, white supremacy, ex-spouse, coworker, miscarriage, pet).
- The loss is not a death (dementia, traumatic brain injury, mental illness, substance abuse).

> **SPACES WHERE BIPOC MAY EXPERIENCE DISENFRANCHISED GRIEF**
>
> Violence to our ancestral lands can destroy our ability to feel human. Places help us know who we are and help us find meaning in our lives.
>
> Old family traumas may lead to a form of family disconnection similar to individual soul loss, which requires a reconnection with the ancestral soul.
>
> Healing the wounds of the ancestors themselves, which have been transmitted through the generations. Many tribal traditions have ceremonies for healing the ancestors and believe the ancestors call out to them for healing help.
>
> Enslavement, genocide, domestic violence, sexual abuse, and extreme poverty are all common sources of trauma that lead to intergenerational trauma.
>
> A lack of support services, such as adequate politicized therapy, also worsens symptoms and can lead to transmission.
>
> **LONG-LASTING RESPONSES FROM TRAUMA RESULT NOT SIMPLY FROM THE EXPERIENCE OF FEAR AND HELPLESSNESS BUT FROM HOW OUR BODY EXPERIENCES THAT FEAR.**
> —Rachel Yehuda

Black parents have had to express to their children, specifically their sons, about the increasing dangers of police encounters and police brutality.

The APA notes that these shared fears among the Black community can lead to distrust among an outside group (in this case, among white police officers).

Healing and Living With Historical Unresolved Grief

Once a person has been assaulted in a genocidal fashion, there are psychological ramifications. With an individual's loss of power comes despair, which is merely a caricature of the power actually taken from a people (Duran, 2006). At this point, the self-worth of the individual and/or group has sunk to a level of despair tantamount to self-hatred. This self-hatred can be either internalized or externalized. I believe Dr. DeGruy's posttraumatic slave syndrome paradigm offers a similar view with the concepts of racist socialization and vacant esteem.

Posttraumatic slave syndrome explains the etiology of many of the adaptive survival behaviors in Black communities throughout the diaspora. It exists as a consequence of multigenerational oppression of Africans and their descendants resulting from centuries of chattel slavery, followed by institutionalized racism which continues to perpetuate the injury. This results in what Dr. DeGruy (2005) identifies as M.A.P.:

- M: Multigenerational trauma together with continued oppression
- A: Absence of opportunity to heal or access the benefits available in the society; leads to
- P: Posttraumatic Slave Syndrome

As discussed in Chapter 5, the key patterns of behaviors reflective of a person living with PTSS can be: *vacant esteem,* along with feelings of hopelessness, depression, extreme feelings of suspicion, and perceived negative motivations of others. Violence against self, property, and others, including the members of one's own group, that is, friends, relatives, or acquaintances; and *racist socialization* (internalized racism) and an aversion for the members of one's own identified cultural/ethnic group; the mores and customs associated with one's own identified cultural/ethnic heritage, and the physical characteristics of one's own identified cultural/ethnic group.

As Eduardo Duran notes in *Native American Postcolonial Psychology* (1995), "When self-hatred is externalized, we encounter a level of violence within the community that is unparalleled in any other group in the country..."

Drs. Brave Heart and DeBruyn (1998) synthesized the experience into "Six Phases of Historical Unresolved Grief" for Native American Indian and First Nations peoples:

1. **First contact:** grieving was pushed aside in the face of genocide and shock. First contact led to colonization where trauma from the introduction of disease, alcohol, and events like the Wounded Knee Massacre.
2. **Economic competition:** sustenance loss (physical/spiritual).
3. **Invasion/war period:** extermination, refugee symptoms.
4. **Subjugation/reservation period:** confined/translocated, forced dependency on oppressors, lack of security.
5. **Boarding school period:** tearing apart families and communities. Language, religion, and culture stripped away and prohibited. Leaving a lasting legacy of identity confusion and parenting struggles in the children that went through such schools.
6. **Forced relocation and termination period:** religion is still prohibited, and many are moved to urban areas. Racism increasing in systems and the settlers around Native peoples. With relocation there is further loss of self-governing community.

Eurocentric Western culture has historically only legitimized grief for immediate nuclear families in the current generation, military, and natural disaster losses. This may also serve to disenfranchise the grief of Indigenous peoples across the world over the loss of ancestors and extended kin, as well as animal relatives, traditional languages, songs, ceremonies, and dances, in particular the freedom to do so without persecution and fines. Religion is still prohibited, and many are moved to urban areas.

Dr. Hickling, Global Father of Decolonial Mental Health (in my perspective) urged Jamaicans to "own our madness . . . if we are to develop as an independent and free people." The "madness" or pathologized hysteria, is really a form of emotional liberation from historical grief. Dr. Hickling proposed that the mental health challenge for descendants of African people (enslaved in Jamaica) is to reverse the psychological impact of 500 years of

European racism and colonial oppression and to create a blueprint for the decolonization of mental health. And he did so. From the dismantling of the colonial mental hospital and the establishment of a novel community mental health initiative, to the successful management of acute psychosis in open medical wards of general hospitals, to a reduction of stigma and the assimilation of mental health care into medicine in Jamaica. In his paper "Owning our Madness," Dr. Hickling (2020) wrote:

> Successful decentralization has led to unmasking underlying social psychopathology and the subsequent development of primary prevention therapeutic programs based on Dr. Hickling's psychohistoriographic cultural therapy and the Dream-A-World Cultural Therapy interventions. The Jamaican experience suggests that diversity in GMH must be approached not simply as a demographic fact but with postcolonial strategies that counter the historical legacy of structural violence.

When a society disenfranchises the legitimacy of grief among any people, the resulting intrapsychic function that inhibits the expression of grief effects is shame. The grief is covered by a deep shame that impairs relationships with self, others, culture, and community. The sacred is extracted, and instead the grief and rage replace—or attempt to replace—the deep loss. The deep collective and communal loss.

It would be easy to ask mental health providers to simply become "more culturally competent and sensitive." However, it appears that we are at a delicate and auspicious point in the revolution of the mental health field. In decolonizing therapy and mental health we are acknowledging the role that mental health professionals currently play in the unconscious gaslighting and violence against the people and communities we work with AND how we have been complicit historically.

So, you may sit in your office or work within the community, and FEEL as though your praxis is liberated; yet is it? If we are searching for a means to a more decolonialend—just as we ask our clients to trust the process, to slow down into the enormity of the loss and trauma—this book begs you to slow down into the enormity of what we are being asked to do (and what we are requesting of our clients). Researching cultural genocide and the extermination of Indigenous peoples and how our people were impacted, or how we have impacted others across the globe, IS ROOT WORK. It IS ancestral work. It IS political work. It IS healing work. It DOES include mental wellness. Some elders have said to me, "we are only as well as our darkest stories." Therefore, the more that we acknowledge, integrate, and somatically honor and embody the massive losses of lives, lands, and culture from European contact and colonization, the more we can begin to free ourselves of the legacies of complex historical trauma and unresolved grief . . . across generations.

Drs. Brave Heart and DeBruyn coined the term *historical unresolved grief*, which is the grief that accompanies the trauma; and they are clear that this contributes to higher rates of suicide, homicide, domestic and intimate partner violence, abuse, and other social and collective issues among Native Americans, First Nations, and Alaska Natives. Historical unresolved grief contributes to a lot of the "pathology" that Western psychiatry and psychology categorize. However, it is crucial for institutions of higher education, and even earlier, to acknowledge that these "pathologies" are not merely a defect on an individual or culture. Rather, they originate from loss of land, lives, and vital aspects of Indigenous culture due to colonization. Losses can range from human and animal life, land, starvation, militarization, attempted annihilation, purposeful spreading of disease, policies, and blocking access to basic needs.

Survivors of many forms of genocide, and their descendants, may naturally experience an array of emotions that may arise as symptoms often seen as problematic. Many of these symptoms are simply expressions, such as intense rage, silence, and deep grief. These collectively lead to psychic numbing, anxiety, impulsivity, nightmares, guilt, shame, self-blame, difficult familial relations; as well as elevated levels of heart disease, and gynecological and hormonal imbalances. These symptoms are quite familiar; they appear as attention deficit disorder, PTSD, anxiety, and depressive disorders, among others.

Often survivors feel a deep responsibility to undo the pain and ancestral past. Another common feature of people who have survived historical atrocities is a sense of not wanting to continue the lineage or procreate.

Some people often believe that a way to end the cycle is by ending genetic lineage. Often, these are not conscious feelings.

This book is not suggesting that you as a practitioner, or as a recipient of care, are obliged to clear generations of historical and ancestral pain. Rather, I am inviting you to acknowledge it. Witness it. Find ways to begin to unpack and release it, because nothing recreates more cyclical intergenerational trauma than suppression and avoidance. Disenfranchised grief (in the context of Dr. Brave Heart's work) is a deep grief and loss that for a variety of socially acceptable and unconscious reasons cannot be openly acknowledged or publicly mourned. I believe this may arise when we attempt to utilize "cultural competence" as a way to generalize treatment and interventions with specific races and identities. This "cookbook approach," as a prior professor of mine had called it, leaves a great deal to be desired as it frames various races and cultures as: "stoic, aggressive, primal and animalistic, unable to display grief, shame, having little ability to mourn, or show pain." Or other groups as "loud, clinging to ancestral history and pain, and creating victim-centered storylines that 'everything is due to historical trauma.'" These generalizations are dangerous, racist, violent, and minimize the kaleidoscope of human experience.

Disenfranchised grief "intensifies other emotional reactions. Without rituals and methods to process it, grief is not resolved. For Native Americans, the continual loss of relatives and other community members greatly factors into their expressions of what is commonly labeled as depression by clinicians. Without proper acknowledgment of death and loss as the cause of these large emotional reactions, people will become more disconnected from themselves overall" (Brave Heart as cited in Smith, 2012).

Things We Are Allowed to Feel Enraged AND Sad About:

- White supremacy
- Having had a colonized education
- Social inequality
- Unfair distribution of wealth and power
- Abuse of power

- Histories of violence in the name of mental and behavioral health
- Colorism and anti-blackness
- Transphobia and violence
- Forced migration
- Abuse of children and elders
- Appropriation of resources, culture, and ritual
- Economic inequality
- Being gaslit
- Medical abuse and anti-fatness
- Accumulated racial trauma
- Imperialism masquerading as *help*
- Accumulated ancestral trauma as a result of colonization
- Our bodies as capital
- Undocumented people in concentration camps
- The spell of capitalism[23]
- The politics around wellness
- The industrial complexes
- Having been abused
- Being told what to do with your body
- Minimizing our trauma
- The loss of Home
- Longing for lost ancestry and culture that our parents did not pass onto us

In my personal and therapeutic provider experience, rage and grief have taught me to address the root of the wound. This is why this book and my work is about intergenerational soul wounding and the violence of colonization. Understanding our past can inform, liberate, and bring joy to our future. We can experience more spaciousness and trust in relationships; there is an embodiment of our adult selves—less apologizing, more of an inclination for self-inquiry, improved conflict mediation, improved communication skills, less guilt and shame, more patience with family members,

---

23 "The Spell of Capitalism" is the work of, and a phrase coined by, Toi Smith.

and the ability to take a wider view of historical trauma stories and their impacts on family (this does not negate abuse and harm), as well as a deeper sense of health and vitality. Healing benefits us all on a massive level.

A large part of unraveling and decolonizing the MHIC is making room for complicated and often ostracized emotions, like unrelenting, unresolved grief and intense, raw rage. Trauma occurs when humans' solutions repeatedly do not work . . . when our goals are consistently blocked.

With grief, we are addressing mourning, individually and collectively. As our prior chapters on historical and intergenerational trauma detail, grief is deeply held in our bodies, as is rage. I often tell people that grief and rage are two sides of the same coin. Some individuals are more readily able to access (willingly or not) deep grief, sadness, and depression. Others are more prone and more easily able to access a deep vibration of anger, rage, and righteous indignation.

However, each are:

- Valid
- At times nonverbally communicated
- Older than our lifetime or generation
- Dependent on numbing or silencing the other
- Dependent on space, time, and multiple modalities to compassionately unpack

Gabor Maté (Psychotherapy Networker, 2021) said this on "Understanding Grief as the Antidote to Trauma":

> Trauma is not the same as suffering, trauma is not the same as pain, trauma is not the same as fear. Those are natural responses to events from us when we get stuck somehow around those events and their impact on us. So, I dare say that I do see a lot of awareness in the world. That's why George Floyd need not be traumatic. And the people who are out there marching and demonstrating and taking an action, or supporting those who do, they will not be traumatized because they're responding to something very painful and very cruel and very unjust.

Almost unspeakable. But they're responding to it actively with a sense of agency. So that's the whole point. If you respond actively, with a sense of agency, this will not have been traumatic.

With unresolved and disenfranchised grief, a person coming into therapy may assume that their rage outbursts when drinking are the main problem. What they may have not realized is the DEPTH of the pain—how the root of the pain is embedded deep under the surface, perhaps deeper than this lifetime. We discussed intergenerational trauma transmission in more detail within Chapter 5. However, in over 85% of the people I have had the honor of holding therapeutic space for, intense symptoms that do not lessen and improve over time (even with the use of multiple relevant modalities) is largely intergenerational and/or historical in nature, "confuddling" clinician and client.

The People's Stories

I worked with Sia for over three years. Sia's father drank excessively and was aggressive verbally. As undocumented migrants from Ghana, her parents frequently arose during our sessions in relationship to their impact on Sia. She noted that her mother was often silent and emotionally absent—even negligent—except for constantly feeding her. Reminding her to eat, critiquing her slender figure and minimal nourishment. As our time and relationship expanded, Sia began to reveal aspects of her life outside of the therapeutic container. This is to say that at first she frequently attempted to show herself in a "favorable light" during our sessions. As time went on, Sia began to reveal the ways in which her drinking and cannabis use "took her over." She often stated in sessions, "Oh that part of me—that's my dad right there—cruel, aggressive, ruthless, and reckless, and I don't give two fucks when I am in it." We would discuss the depth of her anger and eventually Sia was comfortable identifying her uncontrollable outbursts as rage. As we became more familiar with her inner rage child, I began to inquire about her mother's relationship to rage. Naturally Sia assumed her mother did not have one since she often was "meek and easily stepped on." This was an opportunity to begin to unpack her parents' personalities prior to migrating to North America.

One day while processing all this, Sia realized that after forcibly migrating to the States over 20 years ago, her mother did not speak "good-enough English." Her father began to drink more excessively. Her mother would not leave the house due to fear of being deported, and she placed all of her focus on food. Because her mother said "You might forget Ghana, but Ghana will not forget you. Your belly will not forget where Home is."

In unpacking further, Sia began to map and outline with me her personal, familial, and historical trauma history (which I call a SSTT; see Chapter 10 and the Resource Section for an example). This happened seamlessly—we did not intend to create a SSTT—it simply happened. It was a natural progression to see how her life was impacted and even unconsciously being led by unaddressed or unacknowledged familial patterns. It helped us both to visually SEE the pain and how it morphed. In this timeline, we not only identified trauma moments in years and Sia's age, but also helpers. Who helped Sia survive and get through another day when things were most difficult, as well as what Deb Dana calls "glimmers" (Dana, 2018). What are some of the memories that glimmered and shined and felt healthy, despite the depth of the disconnect? What helped her keep on keeping on? Sia began to have a different perspective on "her issues," as her language shifted to "our issues with alcohol," "my family's inability to deal with . . ."

As time passed Sia acknowledged that connecting not just her addictive cycles with drinking, but the experience of being allowed to release her rage in a socially acceptable manner—although embarrassing while drunk—connected her with a sort of power. This further opened her to understanding the deep powerlessness she had been feeling; and not just her but very likely her parents as well. Sia was able to connect her family's history of forced migration, historical trauma, unresolved grief, and even rage to her parents, herself, and her lineage. I believe it is also crucial for me to note that at this time the center in which I was working with Sia pushed for us to maintain 3–12 sessions because of our waitlist. This is important because of how structural oppression operates to place the blame and apply pressure on the practitioners to do more with less, or to place a Band-Aid on the wound and keep it moving because other people need us, rather than advocate for more practitioners, funding, and support to meet the demand of the population. Toward the end of our time together, she would frequently report, "I don't know how people 'heal trauma' in their lives without looking at their cultural and family history!"

I sit here writing this for us all, pondering the same inquiry, Sia.

In traditional psychotherapy, taking three or more months to process family history, intergenerational, and historical trauma is often not encouraged, and is seen in some places as a luxury. What is so crucial about Sia's experience is that the space allowed her to open doors and memories, and conversations with family on her own time.

Traditional therapy is often so Eurocentrically oriented and facilitated, that even time is seen as profit/money/a valuable commodity. Especially for PoGM, there always feels as though there is not enough time, or too little time, or one is not "on time!" When engaging with topics as sensitive as migration, substance abuse, rage, and grief, making space and time IS part of the process. It is key!

Traditional psychotherapy and clinical work focus on outcomes, plans, objectives, billable hours, and quantitative change. Perhaps there is a place for all of this. However, the majority of the PoGM innately and intrinsically engage quite differently, even if it is deeply buried. Many of our cultures took days to wash clothing, to honor a wedding, or the birth of a child. Life was meant to change and slow down when dramatic life changes occurred; hence the power of ritual.

Three months before Sia graduated, we prepared a small ceremony together to close out this period of her life, to create a practice to allow her to honor her inner rage child, to create more space to play and even whine and eat cereal and watch cartoons, because she was always made to clean or cook, instead of just rest. The ceremony was powerful with poetry read, a scripture that represented her grandmother, music from her people's tribes (she had to do some asking and research), a plate of food from her mother's delicious dinner the evening before, water, and some artwork. Sia sang, and I played a small song. We held hands and smiled and took deep breaths. I think we both felt not alone in the room. From my understanding, she is sober and has been for over six years. Frankly, even if she still struggles with the ghosts of addiction today, Sia has engaged in powerful work that has allowed for healing over intellectualized treatment. She has created a new line of inquiry and possibility in her life, and the lives of her descendants.

Collective Trauma

In Jack Saul's beautiful book *Collective Trauma, Collective Healing: Promoting Community Resilience in the Aftermath of Disaster*, he moves us into the "I" and "You" of things. Into relationship and connection. Into disconnection and community. We often talk about "collective trauma" these days as if everyone is impacted by everything.

Maybe.

And maybe we are so on the brink of newness, and of remembering the ancient, while creating the future—and having the privilege to process what is . . . that we are feeling it all. Grieving it all. Enraged at it all.

Erik Erikson (as cited in Saul, 2013), a Eurocentrically renowned developmental psychologist, noted that collective trauma is the:

> . . . blow to the basic tissues of social life that damages the bonds attaching people together and impairs the prevailing sense of communality. The collective trauma works its way slowly and even insidiously into the awareness of those who suffer from it, so it does not have the quality of rudeness normally associated with "trauma." But it is a form of shock all the same, a gradual realization that the community no longer exists as an effective source of support and that an important part of the self has dispersed. . . . This work asks us to consider how our bodies and mental health are impacted by collective experiences, and how collective experiences create a sort of container; reminding us that we are not completely alone.

Glorious Righteous Ancestral Sacred RAGE Is Healthy and Necessary

One of my teachers, Ruth King, birthed a glorious book—a manual that saved my life literally and figuratively, *Healing Rage: Women Making Inner*

Peace Possible. (In my experience, this work can be extrapolated to all people and identities, not just women-identified persons.) I had the pleasure of attending her Healing Rage retreat in the early 2000s in Berkeley, CA, as a doctoral student. The concepts, including the Rage Disguises and Inner Rage Child Altar, changed my life and how I practiced therapy. *Healing Rage* starts out reminding us that:

> Rage is an oppressed child emotion housed deep within our body, mind, and spirit . . . and we will refer to her as our inner Rage Child. We tend to react to our rage child as an emotional enemy to be eliminated, a fire to be feared . . . our rage child is a natural resource of misused energy, and she exists whether we acknowledge her or not. Daughter of our traumas, the twin of our shame, the burden of our denied histories, the foreign language of our emotional pain, and the wisdom that helps us heal. (King, 2004)

That is a definition I hope mental wellness begins to firmly stand behind. Despite all of the deep, deep rage and grief I encountered throughout my years as a university counselor, intern within trauma treatment centers, mental health "specialist," special victims therapist, crisis response coordinator, adjunct professor, and client of numerous services, never once had I really heard a supervisor or professor HUMANIZE and get to the root of the rage/grief cycle. This makes me sad, weary, and quite clearly, that this is unconsciously intentional (purposefully a paradox).

As long as we do not humanize and address rage and grief as two sides of the same coin, we can continue to pathologize (and profit from) symptoms of depression and what we perceive as violent behaviors, such those as seen in the *DSM-5* (APA, 2013): oppositional defiant disorder, intermittent explosive disorder, bipolar disorder, and conduct disorder. We can then go on to say if an individual moves through the school-to-prison-nexus-pipeline that they HAVE or ARE antisocial personality disorder—and if we are feeling "politically correct," we can say they are LIVING WITH APD.

Rage and anger are often considered one and the same, but they are distinct experiences. Both rage and anger are emotions that we feel and may or may not express. Anger is more associated with a current injustice, disappointment, or dislike—someone says something ignorant and your first impulse is to set them straight, or a driver cuts in front of you without signaling and you shout out in the safety of your own car. These are forms of anger—they come and eventually we get over them and move on. Those finding themselves in a perpetual state of anger wear defiance—one of six disguises of rage.

Rage, on the other hand, is an accumulation of anger—an experience that is fundamentally rooted to something older and more personal, often a childhood experience that shamed us, or a child living in a chronic atmosphere of fear. With rage, we feel more shaken, confused, and often paralyzed in fear. Our experience feels foreign, frightening, and intolerable. In fact, when in a state of rage it is often that an an older, inaccessible memory wants to emerge but we can't allow it, and this is often an unconscious process that haunts our lives. According to King, the primary job of rage is to keep us from reexperiencing intolerable shame.

Rage is a deeply misunderstood emotion. It is often seen as selfish, violent, arrogant, narcissistic, and domineering—even dangerous, reckless, and inappropriate. Societally, we have been indoctrinated to see rage as something that only "uneducated people do." If we are really real about it, we have collectively associated rage with predominantly racialized bodies—darker bodies, bigger bodies. Some of us may liken rage to addiction cycles, to young children without "adequate-enough parenting," and even to "disordered behavior" in children and adolescents.

What fascinates me is that we fail to witness our conditioning in these beliefs. We have failed to note the ways in which our collective conditioning has landed many of us in energetic strainers. Places where we are hiding, minimizing, and attempting to change and discard parts of ourselves.

Has folding our true selves up like an origami ever been USEFUL to anybody?

Has sweeping away deep pain mounted with injustice ever lightened someone's load?

Individually, we may have our own experiences with rage. Rage may scare us, and make some of us feel small. Whether we grew up around physically and/or emotionally violent caregivers; emotionally violent experiences where we are bullied, left out, ignored, or chastised, all of these experiences are important in helping us to better uncover and unpack our honest relationship to rage, or as I call it our Inner Rage Child and Ancestral Rage inheritance = our *Sacred Inner Child*. We ALL have rage within us, and each of us internalize or externalize this rage based on a number of factors such as environment, culture, history, social identities, personality, and so forth.

Additionally, collectively, we have been shown countless images of darker bodies across the globe engaging in acts that we associate with rage. "Breaking and entering" into storefronts. Screaming and chanting in a "mob." We hear "raging" and "riots" in the same headline, without context, without humanizing the bodies and the root of the rage. There are healthy reasons for raging. There are perfectly healthy explanations for why a group of people (NOT A MOB) would demand justice and freedom. The release of rage is in itself an ancestral bellow for safety, justice, and a demand to be heard. By definition, rage is that which cannot be quieted or minimized. It is not an experience that "comes out of nowhere." It has been HERE, buried deep, and it is not requiring space and restitution.

Ancestrally, many of our ancestors' main focus was surviving. Fighting to extricate oneself from enslavement, fighting for Indigenous land across the globe. Fighting to keep the family, literally together. Fighting to stay hidden and safe. Fighting to leave a deeply colonized country for more opportunity. Fighting to bring your children over with you. Fighting to stay alive. To stay alive. Just like many of my clients have said, "Dr. Jenn, if I allow myself to feel THIS—this deep well of never-ending grief and rage . . . what then?!" Yes. I ask myself the same question. I admit to the people I hold space for that sometimes my grief and rage scare me too. But I also share with them that what scares me more than slowly releasing this riptide of grief and rage—this rollercoaster—is what will happen to me and my descendants if we do not begin to address this eternal aching. What will happen to my mental and emotional fabric if I do not use the intellectual and emotional privilege and consciousness I have? As my friend Tiffany Roe says, *Feel. Deal. Heal.* We have no choice but to do it. We do have a choice on when, how, at what rate, and who supports us. I have frequently told my students, "We can deal with it now when we have agency, or we can wait to let it deal with you, and that will usually happen at the most inconvenient time."

This is where our rage enters stage left. Cloaked in a dark cape, naturally, likely with fangs or a stream of curses. Raging people are frequently painted as "Bad People." I dislike binaries very much. Binaries cause stagnation and confusion. If rage is "bad," then what is "good"? How can any emotion we are all given access to express be inherently wrong? Ruth King's work acknowledges that whether our Inner Rage Child is the *Defiant* and *Dominant* externalizer of rage (as we often imagine rage to be); or whether our Inner Rage Child is an internalizer, using *depression* (not clinical depression) or *dependence* as a survival disguise; all rage is valid. Or when we cannot stand to tolerate or absorb the full totality of the trauma, attempting to disguise and mask our deep seething rage (often unbeknownst to ourselves) with *distraction* and *devotion*. Either way, no matter the Rage Disguise, it begs our attention. Much the same way our roots, history, ancestry, and lands—collectively, psychodynamically, familially—are calling out for a collective witnessing.

This naturally brings me to also consider how whiteness and rage rarely come together in clinical work, social work, within a school child's study team meetings, and in the media. I believe that the omission of the two words themselves are a metaphor of white rage at work, doing what it does best, hide.[24]

The polarization of a rage or grief, fight, flight, freeze, or fawn response, is not only an unconscious attempt to sidestep danger, but also a strategy to maintain a semblance of connection or—as psychoanalysis would deem—maintain attachment.

Psychology serves capitalism by diagnosing rage as:

- Defiant
- Rebellious
- Resistant
- Dominant

---

24 I am aware that the book *White Rage* exists by Carol Anderson, as it should, and I am told it deals with the racial divide and Civil War, which is important. I would also like to read a book looking at the historical and current pathologies tied to white-bodied supremacy, and what I identify as Caucasity.

- Oppositional
- Uncontrollable
- Unmanageable

Our patterns of rage are passed down through the transmission of our ancestral intergenerational trauma. We have absorbed it, learned it, and may model it. There are different types of rage responses: flight, fight, freeze, fawn. They are deeply connected to our nervous systems and to our lineages of trauma, and they are also connected to our nervous systems, our stress responses, and biological mechanisms. Our nervous systems and biologies are deeply impacted by our lineages of trauma. As stated earlier, inflammation is often a byproduct of generational trauma. These are also commonly known to be fear responses. There is a connection between rage and fear. Both are instinctive, primal responses that can be very hard to distinguish when feeling threatened or in moments of heightened stress.

Our Inner Rage Child is not the problem. They are simply a childhood and historical stream of intrapsychic, somatic, emotional, and biological emotion lodged deep inside of our bodies, fighting for their lives and fighting for their right to be seen. The problem lands with our collective and individual denial of our Sacred Rage's existence. If we disregard our rage contribution to our healing, we can begin to distract ourselves from our Sacred Inner Rage Child because it is not safe to see, feel, or express them; yet our fear of rage negatively impacts the integrity of our lives or exiles/disavows a sacred part of ourselves that exists to teach us something important.

King notes that our challenge is to learn to embody the fierce energies of rage without storylines, shame, blame, or revenge. To develop such a presence with rage that we can witness it come and go without urgency or repulsion. Our first priority is to take care of our own pain. We each have a Rage Child within us that, when triggered, hurts, calling us to attend to our own pain. What's problematic is the overidentification with our thoughts and feelings. Left unchecked and unprocessed, our rage can habitually betray our nature by harming others and ourselves.

I recall Ruth stating in the Rage Retreat weekend that by the time we are 12 years old, we are well armed in our Disguises of Rage. They are the result of both childhood trauma and a rage inheritance—the unresolved rage of our parents and ancestors that we carry out of an unconscious loyalty to them.

We relive what is unfinished through our Disguises, and these Disguises continue to rule our adult lives until we transform them. While Disguises have played a significant role in our survival, they interfere with our healing. We perceive these expressions of rage as being safer and more acceptable than the truth they pretend to hide. Awareness of our Disguises of Rage is healing and often comes as a revelation and a challenge. It is crucial that we engage in a process that reacquaints us with our basic goodness and cultivates our capacity to embrace the ignorance of the world and ourselves with tenderness. As *Healing Rage* notes, "disguises are our rage child's armor—the coats we wear year-round to cope with the chill of life, even on a warm day."

Rage can also slide into places of people-pleasing and look like we are being "Good." The truth is that our rage is deeply connected to our shadow self. That aspect of our Beingness that is NOT SOCIALLY cool. That's what I am interested in. That slithery, sneaky, intense, needy, power-hungry, lonely, irritable, cruel, raw, and hungry-ass part of a person—that upon inspection—is just a "tantruming" and a traumatized child.

We do rage work so that we can take responsibility for our actions.

We do rage work so that we can honor where we perpetrate.

We do rage work so that we can re-parent ourselves.

We do rage work so that we can be honest about where we DON'T want to feel better, and be curious about why that might be.

We do rage work so that we can bring relief to the seven generations before and after us.

We do rage work because in our "mess" we can show up more clearly.

We do rage work so we do not harm ourselves or others.

I highly suggest picking up and working through King's glorious text. As a recap, King synthesizes the six main disguises of rage that we THINK keeps us safe, when in reality they hold us hostage. Her book contains an amazing self-assessment to help individuals better understand their primary salient Rage Types:

- Dominance—You control to avoid being controlled. You distance yourself from others and abuse power (unconsciously or not) to manage your terror of tenderness.
- Defiance—You use anger to divert your need to be loved, often by your perceived enemy.
- Distraction—You avoid intolerable feelings of emptiness by filling yourself and your time with self-defeating diversions.
- Devotion—You take perfect care of others, sacrificing your own well-being to avoid knowing and receiving what you deeply need.
- Dependence—You stay financially insecure and emotionally distressed. You deny your personal power out of your fear of losing love.
- Depression—You would rather disappear than disappoint others. You shut down to avoid overwhelming feelings of grief and rage.

Disguises attempt to hide what we fear, but they have a way of creating more fear in our day-to-day lives and in the lives of others. With Disguises, we convince ourselves that we are in control of a chronically frightening life, one we would prefer to accept as normal. Yet Disguises are symbolic of what is ungrieved, blocked energy that constricts the heart and all matters of the heart. Disguises are ambassadors of the past—old stories of rage that require our loving attention.

We have unconsciously, or consciously, created aspects of ourselves that are still craving control and the release of rage. Whether through the resentment embedded in devotion, or in the passive–aggressive expectations buried in dependence. Some of us distract ourselves so we don't have to sit with losses, and some unconsciously have a thick dark blanket of depression as a way to punish oneself (and maybe others) so we don't have to DEAL or HEAL. So, we don't have to experience or examine what we are so fucking enraged about.

We often categorize rage as raw, primal, and violent expressions of emotion. That's part of it, but not the whole story. It can be slow and seductive, too. You can't cage your Sacred Rage Child. You can't chain our ghosts. You can't shush our howls. Rage expressions are resourceful AF and need to be seen and heard.

> Inquiry first, shall we? These may be some helpful inquiries when engaged in situations that bring up fear or anxiety in you . . .
>
> - Who is enraged?
> - Why?
> - Is anyone unsafe?
> - How are we conditioned to feel when experiencing someone's rage?
> - How did your People(s) express their discontent and rage?
> - Are we projecting . . . ?!

Let's pull back and look at some history. Throughout the 50s, primarily discontented housewives were diagnosed with schizophrenia. Rosenthal notes that the anti-racist revolts of the 1960s "prompted the *DSM* to change its description of schizophrenia from primarily depressed moods to hostility, aggression, and delusions of persecution" (Rosenthal, 2016). Feel that? Take a breath, boo.

What that means is from "white suburban housewives" to "rebellious urban Blacks," Black Americans are around five times more likely than white Americans to be labeled "schizophrenic" when looking at those in American psychiatric hospitals (Schwartz & Blankenship, 2014). **This is an indictment of how diagnosis was only ever meant to subvert and control.** I say this on the heels of stating a fact: that psychiatrists and psychologists have pathologized the protests of enslaved and "extremely political" people. "Rebellious women" have been lobotomized and labeled as hysterical (thank you, Freud), and our fields have and still continue to "convert homosexuals." The nerve, and the violence!

As capitalism beats most of our asses into a perpetual state of crisis, parents are less able to meet children's emotional needs, and many school systems contribute to children's distress by passing them through metal detectors and confining them in closed rooms for long periods to memorize information that has no connection to their lives. When children protest by "acting out and up" we help to label them as mentally disordered and their parents as inadequate.

It is important that we apply a lens to critically analyze the fields we so love and protect. Because the people for whom many of us hold space are not receiving what they fully need. I am sure many of us are sick and tired of being another "good-enough caregiver" in their lives, with not nearly enough adequate funding, counselors, or resources. I am lovingly inquiring whether we are healing OR treating people? Systemically. Because frankly if we focus only on individual "good" therapists at the expense of acknowledging how the history of this field has and continues to cause harm, we once again play into Eurocentricity and neoliberal expressions of "we are doing the best we can with what we've got."

COLLECTIVE HISTORICAL TRAUMA
+ INTERGENERATIONAL TRAUMA TRANSMISSION
(CONSCIOUS OR UNCONSCIOUS)
= THE BIRTH OF THE RAGE-GRIEF AXIS
(ANCESTRAL RAGE + COLLECTIVE GRIEF)

I call this the **Rage-Grief Axis**, as it is the intimate and fluid dance between our Rage Inheritance (what has been accrued from our parents and our family intergenerationally) and the understandable feelings of deep rage at boundary violations, lack of safety, and a mix of disenfranchised and unresolved grief (Brave Heart & DeBruyn, 1998).

This can usually be seen within a person, place, people, or culture, and it is not always conscious or socially acceptable to discuss. We see the minimization of rage and deep grief in many cultures around the globe. It is also important to note that there are countless cultures that honor, sit with, and allow the rage and/or grief to devour them whole. The Rage-Grief Axis are essentially two sides of the same coin. One side needs a release—physiologically and emotionally—and the other requires the space to rest and grieve. To be with the difficult emotions, rather than display them. I once had a professor state that *"grief is anger turned inward,"* and this really highlighted much of my experience as a clinical provider related to the Rage-Grief Axis.

Ruth King noted that "Rage is the child of Trauma and Shame" (King, 2007). Lama Rod Owens noted that "rage is a deeper, more dissociated expression of anger, yet similar" (Owens, 2020). Dr. Brittney Cooper encouraged ". . . All Black women to embrace their Rightful Rage and use it as a tool, allowing for 'Eloquent Rage'" (Cooper, 2018). I read this and I can breathe. I can sink into a space in my body where I nod in knowing that I am not alone. I hear the honoring and respect tied into discourse around rage and this feels important, and timely collectively.

I believe that Rage is Sacred.

Sacred is not a word we often allow into our mental health spaces. It is often relegated to the margins as being "too religious." It is my understanding that sacred refers to that which is deserving of veneration. Meaning that the rage that many of us feel—or do not allow ourselves access to feel—IS TO BE HONORED, VENERATED, SAT WITH, LISTENED TO, CALLED IN, and deserving of SPACE and WITNESSING. In the work I have facilitated for others and for myself, I am clear that rage is simply misunderstood or deliberately misconstrued as a tool for fear mongering. When Sacred Rage is managed and activated appropriately and safely—when we see our rage as a barometer of our boundaries being crossed repeatedly and historically—then we begin to breathe into and create what true Rage Care can begin to look like.

Aspects of Emotional–Decolonial Unlearning

1. Rage and grief both are pathologized throughout the mental health profession.
2. Therapists are taught to pathologize grief (i.e., depression, prolonged grief disorder) and rage, especially in Black youth (i.e., intermittent explosive disorder, oppositional defiant disorder).

    Anger management classes have their place in psychoeducation, and they can communicate that emotions like anger and rage are always dangerous and must be muted, rather than better understood and befriended.
3. Psychotherapy's pathologization of grief and rage, unconsciously and consciously, creates a culture of dishonoring, ignoring, and/or having few role models and processes for healthy release.

4. The nervous system tries to protect us at all costs. Threats to the body activate the sympathetic nervous system and the fight, flight, freeze, and fawn responses. Whereas the parasympathetic nervous system helps the body return to baseline after any events that activate it (Cleveland Clinic, 2019).
5. Rage and grief are healthy emotions.
6. Reoccupying the body after traumatic events is a political and decolonial act of resistance.
7. Grief impacts us mentally, physically, emotionally, and spirituality.
8. Colonization has impacted how we look at grief, and how we allow ourselves to grieve.
9. Colonization has impacted how we look at rage, and how we allow ourselves to release our rage.
10. Grief is not only about death; it can be about life. It can be about surviving.
11. Responding actively, with a sense of agency and purpose toward violence or injustice, can help minimize the impact or possibility of trauma.
12. Healthy releases are not always attractive.
13. Rage is an oppressed child emotion housed deep within our body, mind, and spirit that deserves space and redirection.
14. Society tends to react to rage as an emotional enemy to be eliminated. In reality, those who feel deep rage are keepers of collective repressed rage.

Emo–Decolonial Practice Offerings
- Grief, rage, anxiety, etc. look different for everyone; therefore, invite your participant to play a game where you name a word or emotion or psychological term and they tell you the first thing that comes to mind.
- Asking for your therapy participant's definition or perspective on an emotional state is healthy and shows a capacity to be curious and not all-knowing.
- Providing many sessions/hours just to unpack and resource rage and/or

grief is to be expected. These emotions are often responsible for individuals feeling shame. Therefore, more space = more well-being long term.
- There is no getting over grief. Therefore, what would it be like to support the participant through ritual or ceremony? You could find a common place or space—or support the person through the process before, after, and during your time together.
- Bring in the cultural, historical, and ancestral when speaking about grief and rage.
- What are ways that you have noticed that grief has been affected by historical experiences?
- What is your relationship to grief?
- Who has modeled or shown sadness, or rage in your family/at school/in your friend circle? Why? How do you feel about that?
- How have you as MHPs been taught to engage with or "treat" grief (if at all)?
- What are your culture's beliefs about grieving?
- Is there anything that you may want to grieve or release as a practitioner; if so, can you allow yourself to share that and feel that?
- Is there anything in your personal life that you are avoiding grieving?
- Provide healthy education and outlets for participants' rage.
- Discuss rage disguises, their purposes, and new ways to direct the natural rage responses.

Affirmations
- Sacred Rage and Collective Grief are the embodiments of colonization.
- I am an embodiment of my lineage.
- I allow myself to feel my raw and unfiltered feelings.
- My body holds what I cannot process, what I cannot metabolize, and what I cannot release.
- I am a sacred reflection of my People.
- I create space to contain and release big emotions that scare me/scare others.
- Shadow work is psychological work.

- Spiritual work and spiritual reclamation can be trauma work.
- I trust what my body tells me.
- Boundaries are meant to be fluid, not stationary.
- It is okay and safe to be seen.
- I honor my "BIG" emotions.
- I honor my vulnerability and invite intimacy.
- I am not "out of control" so I don't need to gain "control."
- I have everything I need at the moment.
- *Journal Prompts:* Please be sure to take care of yourselves. These journal questions can be unpacked in TIME. No rush. Ease into it, and receive support. What our Sacred Inner Child often needs more than anything is to rest and to receive. This can feel scary.

Flight Types: Distraction and Devotion
- Where are you distracted, fuzzy, or confused in your life?
- Where are you overly committed, devoted, or attached to in your life?
- What does *distraction* teach you about your Ancestral Grief and Sacred Rage?
- Are there any ancestral experiences or events that may be driving you to *distraction*?
- Are there any places and spaces in your life where you are using *devotion* and *distraction* disguises as a shield?

Freeze Types: Dependence and Depression
- Where are you fearful, insecure, or dependent in your life?
- Where are you inaccessible, unnoticeable, or hiding in your life?
- What does *dependence* teach you about rage and the need to heal?
- Are there any people or places in your life where you are giving away your power? If so, why?
- Where may you be avoiding the journey of grieving? Who might support you?
- Where is there room for your "Bigness"?

Fight Types: Dominance and Defiance

These questions are inspired by journaling prompts by Ruth King in *Healing Rage*:
- Where are you distrustful, entitled, or overly defiant in your life?
- Where are you controlling, unforgiving, righteous, and overly dominant in your life?
- Who or what requires or expects your silence or "smallness"?
- What is your relationship to trust?
- What happens in your body when you let go of control?
- What happens in your body when you soften and receive?

Ways to Work With Our Rage-Grief Axis

1. Ancestral Inheritance
   a. What is your ancestral inheritance to grief and/or rage, and what does it look like for you?
      i. (Suggestion: Try to be specific. For some it is control and competition, for others it can look like "Pull up your bootstraps and handle everything yourself." Focus on the primary inheritance.)
   b. What are your family's views of grief and or rage? Are they separate? Similar? Of the same seed? Frowned upon? Expressed openly for a period of time?
2. Survival
   a. What role does survival play in your communication? In your relationships? In your defense mechanisms?
3. Grief Expression
   a. How have people in your family and the environment expressed grief?
4. Rage Expression
   a. Was rage or anger commonly expressed in your home(s)? What did that look or feel like?

5. Who?
    a. Who expressed rage or anger most frequently in your life as a youth and adult?
    b. How did you feel about them?
    c. What did society ask you to feel/believe about them?
6. Your Rage Relationship
    a. What is your relationship to rage at this moment?
    b. Are you aware of a relationship with rage at this time?
    c. Does rage terrify you? Why?
    d. What do you do with it?
    e. Does that feel good to you?
    f. Does it intimidate or embarrass you (or something else)?
    g. Are you willing to have another relationship to rage?
7. Holding Rage[25]
    a. Who can hold the rage in your life?
    b. Who has held rage for you?
    c. Who has reminded you that it's "okay" to feel super angry and enraged?
        i. (Reminder: Rage is not just "aggressive raging.")
8. Relationship
    a. What would you *like* your relationship to rage to look/feel more like?
    b. Has anyone role modeled that relationship for you?
9. Naming[26]
    a. What might your Inner Rage Child's name be?
    b. What might your Inner Rage Child need/desire/want?
    c. What might your Inner Rage Child be holding?
        i. (i.e., secret, pain, creativity, worries, etc.)
10. Space
    a. Who does your Inner Rage Child need space from?
    b. Can you honor that, just for a month or so?
    c. If not, what arises for you in your body considering this space?

---

25 To understand Rage Disguises and how they protect you, see Ruth King's work.
26 Please see Ruth King's work around our Inner Rage Child to learn more.

Gentle reminder #1: We always need to check one another's capacity and consent to contain your rage. It is essential to be clear and up front about what that could look like for us.

Gentle reminder #2: Your relationship, or lack of relationship to rage, will intensify, expand, or be nonexistent depending on your current needs, history of trauma, environment, childhood adverse experiences, health, relationships, culture, and capacity. Please be kind to yourself. This is rooted in lifelong work.

May We Create More of a Relationship to Our Collective Grief and Sacred Rage

Should you feel a disconnect or a lack of a relationship between you and your Inner Sacred Child, here are some loving suggestions . . .

1. **Honor**
   Create a space where your Inner Sacred Child is honored. A shelf or small table or corner of your desk. Add a picture of a younger you.[27] Add small items you would desire.

2. **Acknowledge**
   Talk/address/acknowledge your Inner Sacred Child daily. What do they desire, need more of, or dislike? What creates distress, joy, pleasure, irritability? Does this have a connection to a caregiver, ancestor, cultural belief, attitude, or norm?

3. **Listen**
   Listen when your Inner Sacred Child begins to tantrum. This may look like people-pleasing/fawning; crying a great deal so others acknowledge your pain; yearning to be seen, but having an immense

---

27 Ruth King's *Healing Rage: Women Making Inner Peace Possible* and Luisah Teish's *Jambalaya: The Natural Woman's Book of Personal Charms and Practical Rituals* have lovely sections on this process.

fear of showing up; lying excessively, even about little things; creating small fires; "knowing it all"; needing to be in a relationship/adored/wanted constantly; making decisions that don't feel good to you; becoming aggressive often; not speaking the truth when it is in your mouth; staying passive and numb.

4. **Be Curious**

   Begin to notice when your Inner Sacred Child likes and has an affinity to someone, and just be curious as to why. As well as the opposite.

5. **Energy**

   Consider adding a small energy medicine practice to your daily routine. EFT Tapping, the four thumps, or energy retrieval short meditations.

*Feel free to check out medicines and practices from your lineage traditions; or be sure to acknowledge, thank, and honor those traditions for a moment before your practice.

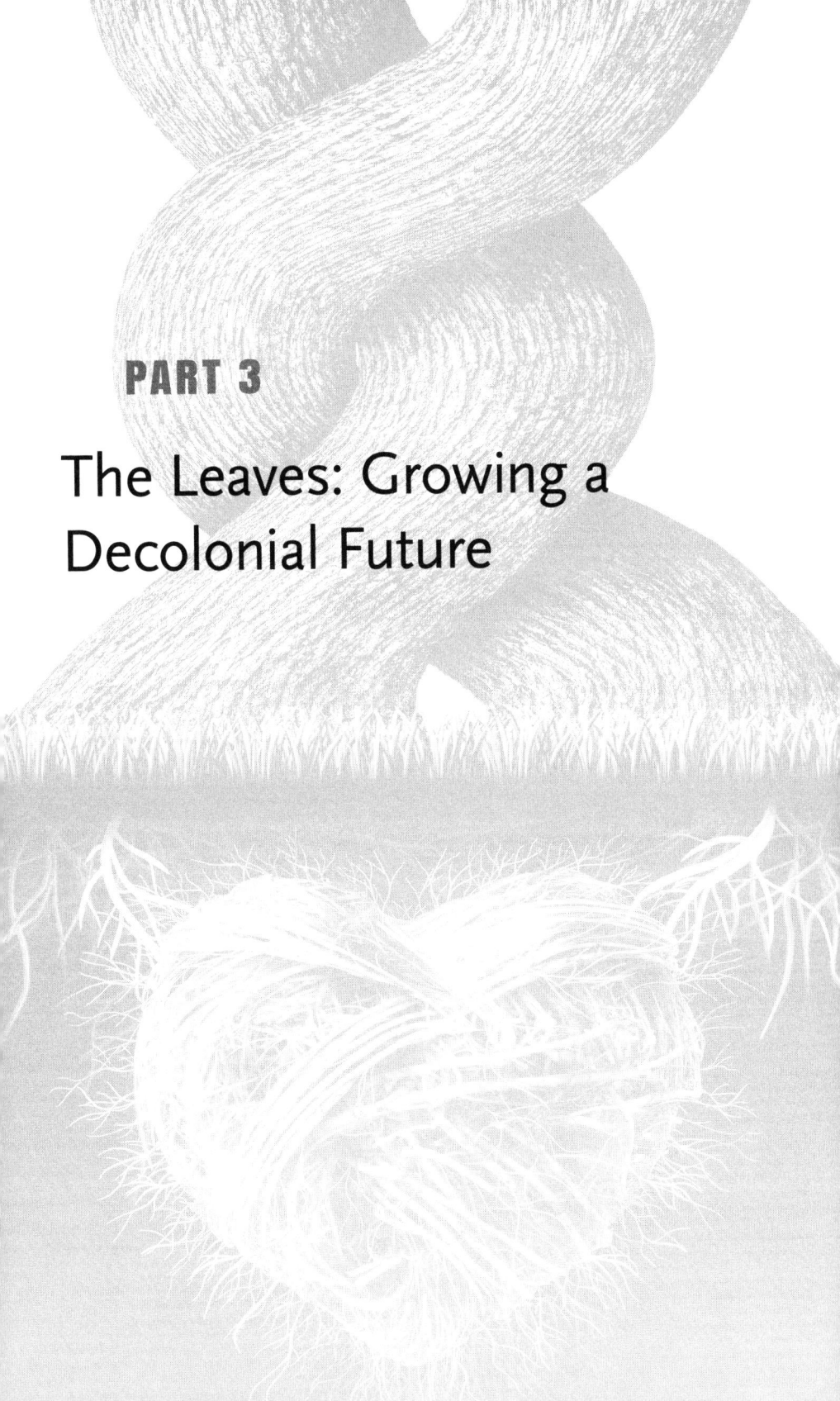

PART 3

The Leaves: Growing a Decolonial Future

CHAPTER 9

From the Inside Out: Energetic Boundaries

Energy boundaries allow connection without toxic merging and enmeshment. This is the beginning of emotional liberation.
—Maryam Hasnaa (2020)

Trauma clients have often lost touch with their bodies. For many, the body is not a safe place to go anymore, so they lose the valuable cues that come from these vital evolved pathways.
—Deb Dana (2019)

The spirit wants truth, understanding and compassion, we are finding that is what brings healing.
—Wendy Hill, member of the Cayuga Nation in an interview by Colin Graf published by *Anishinabek News* (2016)

I believe we are standing at planetary crossroads, where we can either continue on a path of destruction, or consciously choose a new way. . . . From political tensions to abuse of power, and the environmental crisis, looking at the chaos of the world around us, you can say that the planet is undergoing its own Spiritual Reactivation, as the shadow parts of our collective are being brought up to be healed. . . . As the patterns of our past crumble so that we can all transform, it [working with your

intuition] will become your guiding light. . . . When we truly work with our intuition, we can anchor into our bodies for grounding and reclaim our Energetic Self-Sovereignty.
—Natalie Miles, *You Are Intuitive: Trust Your Truth. Take Back Your Power.* (2020)

Decolonizing Therapy is born out of the burnout of therapists, the tears of early-career social workers as they sit in their car eating whatever they can afford to have for lunch in between home visits, out of the insanity that is hundreds of thousands of dollars in student loan debt. It is born of shifting the heavily white supremacist gaze back to equity and decolonial conversations; back to healing-centered services that highlight the humanity, relationship, and energetic synthesis between a "space holder" and the community and culture they serve.

Mental health professionals have become quite skilled at digging into the deeper emotions. Emotional heavy lifting, that is. It is our responsibility to create a sanctuary, with as much safety and intention as possible, where a person or people can arrive and unload their burdens, inadequacies, fears, traumas, and shame.

Energetic boundaries differ from physical boundaries in the fact that energetic boundaries can move far and wide from one's physical structure. When creating a safe space one puts out signposts around the space they occupy. This could be illustrated as an artwork, a style, a personality—an energetic signature that communicates nonverbally someone's energetic boundaries. Energetic boundaries are an extension of one's own style and energy that can be as close or as far as an individual is willing to project.

One can sense a welcoming and healthy, or unsavory or chaotic, energy around a person or place. A wonderful thing about these energetic boundaries is that they are coming into contact with each other all the time. Our energetic boundaries have a tendency to raise or lower others' energetic boundaries as we come into contact with each other. It could be said that one's smile lights up a room. In the inverse, one's energetic boundary could bump up against tens of thousands and millions of others sending many into dwindling spirals of blame, shame, and/or hate. You can say that one's energetic boundaries could be fueled by light or dark; love or hate.

We are evolving our energetic signature all the time. These signatures can evolve in a destructive or a creative way, due to familial, environmental, societal, and cultural energetic patterns. These patterns of energy in particular are either flowing in a constructive or destructive way. Patterns that encourage peace, cultural upliftment, love, collaboration, and creativity are constructive. Patterns that encourage separation, singular-minded thought, the minimization or dissolution of basic human rights, and the rights to express oneself are destructive. Acknowledging a pattern or behavior of energy that both a family member and we hold, while stepping into curiosity, and also receiving experienced and safe support, can allow us to expand the inquiry and honor that maybe this energy and pattern had been stuck. It is possible for energy to lay stagnant or dormant until there is "room to explore." When I think of many of our ancestors, I think of the Industrial Revolution and punching a clock. Working hard physical labor until we could not—there was not much space for the poor and the working poor to dawdle or be in leisure. It can make us curious to what sort of energy patterns, behaviors, belief, and practices have embedded themselves into our energetic bodies. Our energy system holds the emotional patterns, memories, pain, health problems, and even proclivity to addictions from our ancestors and our experiences. *The trauma of colonization is also quite energetic, and biological.*

Dr. Irvin D. Yalom (2002, p. 256), psychiatrist, professor, and author of existential and group psychotherapy, wrote:

> Life as a therapist is a life of service in which we daily transcend our personal wishes and turn our gaze toward the needs and growth of the other. We take pleasure not only in the growth of our patients but also in the ripple effect—the salutary influence our patients have upon those whom they touch in life.

Although this is a statement that rings true to so many therapists, there is also an unsaid meta meaning underneath those words that suggest that we are . . . well, *receptacles*. That we can hold and hold and hold and contain and contain limitlessly. That we are an amorphous, amalgamous, apolitical blank slate that has no personal life, preferences, style, or horrible habits (of course we do; we "should just never talk about them" *side-eye*).

Yalom (2002, p. 251) also noted that "psychotherapy is a demanding vocation, and the successful therapist must be able to tolerate the isolation, anxiety, and frustration that are inevitable in the work," in *The Gift of Therapy: Reflections on Being a Therapist*.

Phew. That is a great deal to expect of a person. If we consider the level of isolation that many therapists already experience as we are essentially hazed throughout graduate school—from student loan debt, to a lack of emotional support, to the assumption that all students have family members or loved ones who can support them throughout low-paying internships (including Affordable Care Act and APA matches), to the forced labor in communities that they are guests within, to the disconnect between practice and the white elderly men who dominate the research and praxis of the helping professional fields.

This chapter is merely a small synthesis and introduction to Energetic Boundary Work, as a form of decolonial practice. It is my opinion that we cannot begin to decolonize anything without first investigating our beliefs, honoring the misconceptions we've had, and creating new pathways; that is creating new ways of being WITH THE WORK and with the ways that we hold space. Too often both the recipients of therapy and the providers are deeply burned out and exhausted not just by the content, but by the energetics. Here are some comments to me, or in the chat, during a series I provide to mental health institutions, schools, hospitals, organizations, and practices called Politicizing Your Practice: The Road to Decolonizing Therapy.

When the term energetic boundary is introduced, I often receive or hear a barrage of elated comments:

- "Please say more—yes, finally someone gets it!"
- "YES! How can we decolonize these fields, if we don't shift how we are treated as therapists?"
- "I need an entire course—maybe a year—just on this."

- "I LITERALLY got a write-up for telling my supervisor about a vital session I had with a student regarding energy and Spirit hygiene."
- "Dr. M., please speak to my professors. All they talk about are physical and emotional boundaries. Yawn."
- "Our People knew this—and healing was therapy and therapy was healing—thank you. This is Decolonial!"
- "I need to know more—I feel like so many therapists and social workers ARE intuitive and are drained energetically by trauma!!!"
- "I don't know what you mean by this, but there is something here. After 25 years of providing therapy, energetic boundaries are a definite thing."

The important thing about our energetic boundaries is understanding that they are always bumping up against and relating to others' energetic boundaries. In regards to your energetic boundaries, it's important to hold onto your individual truth, perspectives, experiences, light, and love. Those with disruptive and/or deeply traumatized energetic fields can upset the energetic boundaries of others. We all evolve and expand when we can hold one's own distinct energy with love, compassion, honesty, authenticity, and move from a place of healed truth.

Of course, the 'Gram and TikTok are truly shifting the discourse, opinions, and engagement of mental health professionals. One of the gifts that social media gives is that of humanizing therapists. We see therapists with varying degrees of specializations, perspectives, religious and spiritual orientations, as well as with lives, outfits, co-occurring talents, and opinions outside of the classroom or therapy room.

Throughout my years as a student, and practitioner, I have heard multiple phrases to describe the work that mental health professionals engage in; however, the main phrases that stand out are: "Holding Space" and being a "Container." Although these phrases are overutilized and yet strangely (in embodiment) underrepresented, I find that they do capture the therapeutic frame beautifully. How do we give vocabulary to the practices of maintaining a therapeutic frame (invisible), listening with compassion and interest (invisible), creating an environment that allows individuals to openly share their deepest trauma and shame (mostly invisible), and creating the ideal conditions for often difficult feedback and conversations (invisible)? This does not include the relational dynamics between practitioner and participant that allow true change to begin to occur, within both individuals. These "invisible" dynamics are the crux of psychotherapy and mental health. The very fabric of therapy and clinical practice rests on *energy*.

Energy AND Therapy, You Say?

For those who may be uncomfortable with the term or use of the word **energy** in therapy, it is helpful to often look back at psychotherapy's forefathers (however problematic they are, as I have stated throughout this book). I mention these individuals as a way to anchor any readers who are still struggling to understand the correlations between energy and the roots of psychotherapy. Many may have forgotten that good ol' Sigmund Freud believed that people continuously generate "psychic energy," but only a certain amount is available for use at any point in time (Cherry, 2020). He contended that this psychic energy is then used by the three components of personality: the id, the ego, and the superego. The *id* is the first location where all of this psychic energy can be found. Freud's infamous psychoanalytic theory notes that "the *id* is the primitive and instinctual part of the mind that contains sexual and aggressive drives and hidden memories, the *supergo* operates as a moral conscience, and the *ego* is the realistic part that mediates between the desires of the id and the superego" (McLeod, 2021).

Energy is a concept in some psychological theories or models that is an unconscious mental function between biology and consciousness. Energy Psychology (EP) is seen within traditional Western psychotherapy as a "mind–body approach to understanding and improving human functioning. It centers on the relationship between bioenergy systems, neuro- and electrophysiological processes, and mental functions involving thoughts, emotions, sensations, and behavior." (Wise, 2017). These systems and processes exist and interact within the individual and between people. Hence, when we state Collective Energy, or "the Collective," throughout this book, we speak of the systems and energy processes existing and interacting within and between people, influenced by cultural, historical, and environmental factors.

Within a Western EP framework, emotional and physical issues are reflected in bioenergetic patterns within and around the mind–body–energy system. Many techniques were first popularized in the 1980s by Roger Callahan, PhD, under the name of "thought field therapy." David Feinstein, PhD, a clinical psychologist, has developed an energy psychology program that provides training for mental health professionals and nonprofessionals (Holmes, 2021). In Western Energy Psychology the mind and body are considered part of a holistic system along with energetic components of living. The mind–body–energy system communicates through "neurobiological processes, electrophysiology, psychoneroimmunology (PNI), consciousness [and subconsciousness], and cognitive-behavioral patterns" (Faherty, n.d.). Through the development of EP more methods for treatment in a healing, counseling, or therapeutic context have arisen within integrative health spheres. Energy psychology often uses cultural methods (such as meridians, chakras, qi) and bodily processes (such as "electromagnetic activity of the body, nervous system, and heart") to explain the applications (Faherty, n.d.).

Many "practitioners often combine cognitive, and physical interventions with activation of one or more of the human bioenergy systems" (Association for Comprehensive Energy Psychology [ACEP], n.d.). Other "practitioners focus upon the way in which thought and intention are expressed in the bioenergy system, and explore the therapeutic value of the . . . use of language and congruent intention" (ACEP, n.d.). EP approaches are often seen as easily adapted and integrated into most psychotherapy models and health care orientations, and are seen as "rapid, have little to no adverse effects, and are usually experienced as self-empowering by clients." Likewise in the medical model clinical world, these models have been beneficially applied to the assessment and treatment of trauma, anxiety, depression, pain, stress, psychophysiological issues, and self-sabotaging behaviors by a broad range of health care providers to regulate, effect, and promote emotional and physical health. There are over 100 research studies, including 51 randomized controlled trials published in professional and refereed journals, confirming the treatment value. These findings suggest that EP meets the criteria for evidenced-based treatment (Feinstein, 2019).

The ACEP describes the historical use of EP methods:

> Historically, EP methods integrate concepts and techniques from related fields, including acupuncture meridian theory, neuroscience, physics/quantum mechanics, biology, medicine, chiropractic, and psychology to facilitate change. For example, EP methods have been beneficially integrated into the psychotherapy process, nursing, medicine, coaching, athletics, and education. (ACEP, 2016)

There are multiple beneficial uses for forms of EP and other holistic-integrative methods entering Western mental health. For instance, after a heart-centered therapy training, overtaxed and under-resourced counseling center staff are able to provide groups for anxiety management and alleviating triggering symptoms related to PTSD experiences and diagnoses for underserved college students. This is beneficial as students do not have to necessarily share, understand their root cause issue or "presenting problem," nor commit to counseling. It also begins to expose the student to the counseling center staff, allowing them to become familiar with the center and explore the possibility of counseling.

The Origins of Burnout

Burnout is almost seen as an initiation into the health and wellness fields. This unsaid belief permeates much of supervision and coursework, "when you start to burnout . . ." MHPs are told, yet there is little to no prevention, as is common among the MHIC. Burnout consists of three components: emotional exhaustion, depersonalization of clients, and feelings of ineffectiveness or lack of personal accomplishment (Maslach, Jackson, & Lieter, 1997). Burnout is often seen as the fault or problem of an individual: "You aren't getting enough rest," or "You are managing your time poorly." In fact, burnout is a result of the colonial capitalistic conditioning imparted on a person as soon as they begin school. The common knowledge tells people to work hard, complain little, put in extra efforts, do not make a fuss, make your boss or teacher happy, and then you will get far. This is not a diss to hard work. Frankly, working consistently in a disciplined state toward a short-term goal, project, or creative endeavor can be deeply satisfying and beneficial to a person and a community. These feelings of unworthiness and ineffectiveness reach their pinnacle when practitioners have also been taught to place a large amount of their self-concept and well-being in their work. It is quite easy to do so when (a) the people and communities a practitioner works with reflect their culture, ethnicity, or race; (b) they are one of few (or any) persons of color; and (c) if the practitioner is living with disabilities and often feels (unconsciously or not) that they need to prove themselves or try harder. This makes sense when you juxtapose this within the context of living within late-stage capitalism, where healing practices have been co-opted and exploited for financial gain. The current system of mental health is unreasonable for many practitioners. Studies estimate that anywhere between 21% to 61% of MHPs experience signs of burnout (Morse et al., 2012), likely much more.

Thousands of early-career MHPs are often told:

- "Well, I had to struggle throughout my internship too. I was barely paid and I made it, you will find a way. You have to just separate it in your mind."
- "You need to toughen up, you are going to hear a lot of intense trauma-filled stories. You can't let it get to you."
- "Develop thicker skin."
- "You will get used to it. You have to."
- "You need better boundaries."
- "You are too sensitive."

What is ironic is that thousands of MHPs flock to psychology, social work, counseling, and psychiatry in order to find a way to channel their human service-oriented energy and worldview. The belief is that we will be held, contained, and educated in a manner that will support our growth as a sensitive community or science-based individual who seeks to provide lasting change to people in a variety of pain. The stark reality is that many of our institutional educational programs fall short. This is why countless early-career therapists and students across the globe flock to Insta-therapists and TikTok therapists asking for support, feedback on managing their programs, and wanting to be mentored by these Instagram and TikTok "therapy influencers."

Of course, there are and have been countless wonderful supervisors, faculty members, therapists, and adjunct instructors who have supported students and changed lives. Often these mentors not only humanize themselves to their students; they teach beyond the margins. They create a relationship with students, when appropriate and mutually supportive, and they often have the disapproving gaze of other colleagues on their backs. Historically, we've been beholden to traditional Eurocentric systems of teaching, thought, and behavior. This means that we have been expecting new generations of therapists—many of whom are NOT white—to continue to utilize the master's theories and techniques.

Almost every mental health professional in the States is familiar with "The Three Greats": Freud, Rogers, and Jung. Not to mention: Ellis, Skinner, Piaget, Bandura, Pavlov, Charcot, Erikson, Vygotsky, Bowlby, Fromm, and others. The list is extensive. Modern psychotherapy has primarily been built upon mental health perspectives of cisgendered, heterosexual men of European descent (as far as history can tell). However, there is another list that is also extensive and often underrepresented—the number of mental health workers who are not white across the globe who have innovated and continue to challenge the idea of the white, heteronormative cisgender gaze. What is clear is that we have missed: Dr. Inez Beverly Prosser, Mamie Phipps Clark, Dr. Nancy Boyd-Franklin, Dr. Robert Carter, Dr. Michael Yellow Bird, Dr. Maria Yellow Horse Brave Heart, Dr. Madonna Constantine, and Dr. Frederick W. Hickling.

For example, I taught a group therapy course for graduate students for a number of years. As the class became more comfortable and connected, student after student discussed how difficult it was to identify as Black/Latinx/Filipinx, Arab, etc. and to work in the community they were raised in; yet during staff and team meetings, their (generally white) supervisors and directors never asked their perspectives on what the communities may need or who the community leaders were. They noted feeling silenced, confused, and "put in their place." One graduate student, who was exiting a 12-year career in teaching noted, "It was like waking up on Christmas day and suddenly realizing no one cared for your gifts. Ignored. Overlooked. I felt lied to about the field I was entering. Even with theories and justice work . . . there was no true justice. Not for the clients, not for the care workers."

There is a paucity of true reeducation throughout social work, counseling, psychology, and psychiatry. Many institutions of higher education have begun to teach A COURSE related to diversity and equity. However, diversity, equity, and inclusion is not decolonization, as we have established in prior chapters. What therapy professionals desire is access to an education that will actually prepare them for the intersectional nature of the systems, cultures, and barriers they will have to navigate.

Energetics and Mental Health

Energy is political.
 Energy work is decolonial.
 Energy patterns are intergenerational.
 Energy is rooted in the ancestral.

Ancestor healing is a powerful and deeply spiritual way that many of us come to (a) know our kin and ancestry; (b) begin to explore our histories; (c) better understand generational patterns, karma, and beliefs; and (d) clear our karma/beliefs and patterns by healing the inherited energy patterns using energy, ritual, and sound. This may look quite different for every individual, community, culture, family, and generation.

For example, when holding space/doing therapy with a 24-year-old person practicing Santeria, their belief systems, ways of practicing, rituals, and even initiations may be very different than that of their grandparents or great-aunts. This could cause disconnection and discord within the individual, the family system, and in the spiritual community.

But make no mistake about it, energetic work is deeply rooted in the bones of many of our cultural and ethnic identities. Ritual is how many people have historically come together to grieve, celebrate, and be healed. Because there has been an increasing interest in people researching their family history to see how their lives have been shaped by previous generations, as well as ancestral veneration and energy work; it is often dismissed as "a trend." Many elders, religious and spiritual texts, prophecies, and healers would say that this "trend," is more of an Awakening.

The '60s and '70s began with a collective shift—an awakening. A political (rise of feminism and awareness of racism and integration) and spiritual (John Lennon and others popularized "spiritual quests" and normalized gurus, meditation, and *satsang*) awakening. Bringing into the forefront of collective mainstream media the exotification of Eastern beliefs and cultures. There also needed to be a shift in humanity's relationship to capitalism—in how people worked, who worked in the home, and a belief in increased productivity and hours away from the home.

In this same way, a shift in perspective, politics, beliefs, gender roles and the presence of individuals in the open fighting for freedom for all created a collective shift. Of course, not everyone was on board. Of course, there was a great deal of disagreement and strife; yet the youth of the '70s made space for the evolution into the '80s and beyond.

However, rather than dismiss the interest in ancestry, historical trauma, astrology, and energy work as a "trend," perhaps we can lend ourselves to notice the growth and shift of the collective unconscious. Psychiatrist Carl Jung used this term to "represent a form of the unconscious (that part of the mind containing memories and impulses of which the individual is not aware) common to humankind, as a whole, and originating in the inherited structure of the brain" (Encyclopaedia Britannica, 2020b). He believed that "human beings are connected to one another and their ancestors through a shared set of experiences. We use this collective consciousness to give meaning to the world" (Gimbel, 2020). Practitioners of energy medicine believe that the human energy field contains and reflects each individual's energy.

Some experiences that carry emotional energy in our energy systems include:

In *Anatomy of the Spirit* (2011, p. 34) Dr. Caroline Myss states that "this field of energy surrounds and carries us with the emotional energy created by our internal and external experiences—both positive and negative." She goes on to say "this emotional force influences the physical tissue within our bodies." Most famously, she argues that "your biography—that is, the experiences that make up your life—becomes your biology." The list below identifies some experiences as noted by Dr. Myss that carry emotional energy in our physical system.

- Traumatic experiences and memories
- Intergenerationally inherited traumatic experiences and memories
- Belief patterns and attitudes
- Inherited belief patterns and cultural norms
- Past-life experiences
- Past and present relationships (personal and professional)

Elsewhere in her book (p. 36), Myss describes emotional energy:

> Our emotional energy is converted into biological matter through a highly complex process. Just as radio stations operate according to specific wavelengths, each organ and system in the body is calibrated to absorb and process specific emotional and psychological energies. Each area of the body transmits energy on a specific, detailed frequency . . . an area of the body that is not transmitting at its normal frequency INDICATES the location of a problem . . . this way of interpreting the body's energy is sometimes called "vibrational MEDICINE," and is most akin to ancient medical practices and beliefs, from Chinese medicine to indigenous shamanic practices, to virtually every folk or alternative therapy.

Maintaining Your Energetic Boundary Makes All the Difference

Your energetic boundaries and other energetic boundaries are like bubbles bumping up against each other. Gaslighting happens when one's energetic boundary is overbearing and overloading other boundaries. When we do not trust ourselves, or if we have a history of deep trauma experiences, we may have a hard time maintaining our own truth. Part of healthy energy boundaries is being a clear conduit of our truth and not immediately becoming defensive or acting from a place of ego. Holding one's own comes down to being comfortable in who you are, including your idiosyncrasies and quirks. Those with histories of violence and trauma may inadvertently pick up or absorb another's feelings—this often occurs because of our own porous boundaries. Porous boundaries can occur because we are burned out, stressed, exhausted, or overworked. It is crucial to be compassionate with ourselves and get into the habit of checking our energetic capacities.

Emotions and Boundaries

Boundaries help us **be aware of ourselves, and our relationships**. They're important for self-care and making yourself a priority. MHPs actually see boundaries as "a crucial component of healthy relationships. Having clear boundaries in all relationships allows people to care for themselves psychologically, which is not selfish but an essential aspect of well-being" (GoodTherapy, 2017).

Therapist Nedra Tawwab (2021) wrote that:

> When we think about boundaries, we think about them as something with someone else. . . . A boundary could be a morning routine . . . having some quiet time after lunch. That's a personal boundary that you honor for yourself . . . so that does bring you a lot of peace.

There are many different types of boundaries—emotional, physical, and energetic are just a few. This is especially essential for individuals who "feel deeply." Where sensitivity and feeling what another feels begin to have an impact on one's life and well-being. Energetic boundaries can be especially useful to those who tend to struggle with people-pleasing, are empaths, or are highly sensitive people.

Dr. Elaine Aron began researching high sensitivity in 1991 and continues to do research on it today. The trait's scientific term is called Sensory-Processing Sensitivity. In Dr. Aron's best-selling book *The Highly Sensitive Person*, she beautifully asserts the following:

- Being highly sensitive is more average than it seems.
- It is innate. "In fact, biologists have found it in over 100 species (and probably there are many more) from fruit flies, birds, and fish to dogs, cats, horses, and primates. This trait reflects a certain type of survival strategy, being observant before acting. The brains of highly sensitive persons (HSPs) actually work a little differently than others." (Aron, 1991)
- You are more aware than others of subtleties.
- You are also more easily overwhelmed.
- This trait is not a new discovery, but it has been misunderstood.
- Sensitivity is valued differently in different cultures.

This is not to say that every MHP or clinician is highly sensitive. However, I will assert that we are all intuitive. We all have an innate sense, whether or not we care to note our energy bodies. Natalie Miles (2020) discusses how the intuitive body is a highly complex system where the energy body is connected to the intuitive body, and how they communicate with one another impacts how we feel and engage with the outside world. She notes that since energy is porous and undefined, it can be easy for our energy to become enmeshed with the world around us.

In other words, it may be crucial for a profession that involves entering peoples' homes; sitting with multiple family members and their discord; helping people process their personal, historical, and intergenerational trauma histories—as well as holding space for crisis and experiences of deep violence—to create "emotional boundaries that protect [one's] energy and help us preserve our sense of self, rather than becoming entangled in other people's beliefs, feelings, and problems" (Habash, 2017).

With that said, it is also worth acknowledging that this can get murky if a practitioner is not held accountable. In any support, affinity, or mentorship/teacher spaces, a practitioner will bring in (as they would in any therapies) their own bias. This chapter is not a permission to bring one's own bias or agenda to a person they're working with under the auspices of "intuition." Rather, it is acknowledging what many providers of care already hold and have, likely due to their ancestry that is often misunderstood, pathologized, and even seen as "unprofessional." This chapter is not permission to "say whatever you want in sessions." Rather it is in the service of discerning and distinguishing—always—our material from that of what the participant may need to hear. One of my favorite practices is to simply ask the participant if they would like to hear/know some insights that are arising. It is crucial that we are mindful of covert colonial impulses under the auspices of energetics.

I believe it is important to decolonize our relationship and understanding of "energy" as something "woo-woo" and separate it from mental and emotional wellness. It seems that when cisgender white people write and speak about mindfulness or spirit-centered energy work, this lands quite differently than a disabled Black body speaking about spirit and energy or an Indigenous-identified person speaking of how Spirit has called them to do important work. As we have discussed in Part 1 of this book, the roots of emotional–colonization are deep. Therefore, our work is bound to be deep, and the excavation of the level of our colonial mentality and belief systems need to be thorough as well.

> **JOURNAL PROMPT**
>
> We are wired and waiting for connection. It is in our blood and it is a biological imperative.
>
> - Where in your life is your energy being leaked or drained?
> - What is your role in this/these energy drains?

- What energy patterns still have authority in your behaviors and thinking that no longer feel valid?
- Have you ever compromised your sense of honor or personal ethics? When? Why? Have you made an effort to heal it?
- What superstitions have you grown up with? How do they still impact you today?
- List all the blessings and good energy that have come from your family.
- List any generational and familial curses you have heard of or experienced.
- What cultural or tribal traditions would you like to continue with your family and in your own life? Are there any you wish to stop completely?

Energetic Boundaries in Mental Health

The first course I took as a doctoral student was called Transpersonal Psychology. The Association for Transpersonal Psychology describes the field as a "school of thought in psychology centered on the spiritual aspects of human life. . . . The field utilizes psychological methods and theories to examine the spiritual subject matter" (Association for Transpersonal Psychology, 2021). Although I saw myself as a fairly spiritual person with a growing and robust spiritual life, I did not quite yet understand how decolonial theory came together with spirituality and energy science.

One of the first things that we did in the course was to read work from Stan Grof and Ken Wilber. We discussed meditation and the energy bodies, and above all we learned about the felt sense. The felt sense in focusing therapy centers on vague bodily feelings that are thought to correspond to unresolved emotional conflicts, which tend to resolve when one allows themselves to feel it.

Schmit defines energetic boundaries as "subtle, invisible, and profoundly felt. Losing them happens when you merge with other people's feelings and you lose your sense of self" (Schmit, 2017). The study of energetic boundaries is a vital and emerging field of understanding. It is scientifically understood that all living things have a field of energy that can be analyzed and detected. All humans, animals, and plants have this energy, and interrelate with each other. Vital research has been done on forest bathing, which is a healing relationship between humans and all plant and animal life. There can be a symbiotic relationship between our energetic boundaries when we relate to each other with peace, compassion, understanding, and love.

Energy Medicine in Our Cultures

Energy medicine has been a part of indigenous and cultural healing for thousands of years. In fact, just the action of holding and cradling one's newborn child is energetic in nature. Cultures and societies have danced and chanted around the fire as flames energized their purposes and brought their consciousness to higher states of awareness and peace. Western medicine colonized this historic and ancient healing practice by categorizing energetic work and healing as "alternative medicine," when, in fact, energetic medicine predates current medical practice. Loving hugs, healing touch, tapping, cupping, somatic work, Reiki, and others have been practiced by tribal healers from the beginning of time. The flow and movement of healing energy through the body was known to comfort the soul, relieve stress, and promote healing. Decolonial work comprises energy medicine, spiritual medicine, and tribal ritual, which promotes healing in many cultures. Colonial capitalist rhetoric recategorized ancient ritual and medicine as "woo woo." Decolonial practices and movements are recategorizing these methods as the healing practices they've always been. We are coming back to the root—back home to what we know heals.

In Indian yogic tradition, the *subtle body* is defined through chakras; depending on the system one follows, there are variations in the number of them (Sebastian, n.d.). Typically, there are seven major chakras and 21 minor ones. This system originated in Hindu culture and is most accepted. The seven major chakras are the Root, Sacral, Solar Plexus, Heart, Throat, Third Eye, and Crown Chakras. They can be described as "centers of transformation" that change energy as it passes through them and into the body (Sebastian, n.d.).

In Traditional Chinese Medicine the *subtle body* is defined through the *dantian* (or dan tian), which can be translated as "field of elixir" (Quinn,

2020) and can be described as the source of life force energy. Dantian is related to Taoist and Buddhist ideas of higher consciousness and, similar to the energy chakras, are thought of as "energy centers" (Quinn, 2020). However, they are different in that the dantian is more of a "storehouse" whereas a "chakra is a gateway" (Chong, n.d.). In addition to dantian being used in Traditional Chinese Medicine, it is also manipulated through tai chi, qigong, Reiki, and traditional martial arts.

According to Dr. Jason Chong, the dantian holds the "three treasures of the body" and represents three of five elements (heaven/fire, earth/water, and man/earth): Jing (lower dantian), Qi (middle dantian), and Shen (upper dantian).

It is helpful and normalizing for all MHPs to step outside of the therapy room and connect with what our communities and clients are connecting with, and perhaps needing more of.

Energetic boundaries not only benefit us—the space holders and MHPs—but benefits the people and communities we engage with and serve. Whether or not we are conscious or attuned to it, our clients, our youth, the people we are in relationship with SEE us and often model what we do. Therapists are firmly rooted in positions of privilege and power, even many therapists of color. Education, emotional intelligence, and a level of resilience are privileges that many of our communities do not yet realize they possess or cannot access. Therefore, it is important that we honor how we role model energy boundary setting and when it arises that we speak to it.

I think it is vital to note that boundaries, as a whole, are often spoken about and communicated in very masculine-centered ways. They are spoken and written about in very direct, assertive, and aggressive ways with little to no wiggle room. There is usually one direct line from "I need . . ." to "The end." Boundaries, especially energetic ones, do not always have to feel so rigid and inflexible; this can negatively impact oneself, and our relationships. Hence understanding our own energy bodies first is essential to energetic boundaries and, unfortunately, is a lesson that is beyond the scope of this book. However, there are a multitude of teachers and skilled energy workers who have written many texts around energy and mental health.

Roots of Energy Medicine

Traditionally, elders and healers have approached the person as an integrated whole, and more so, as a part and piece of a larger whole. Health is restored through restoring balance among mind, body, spirit, and community. Many elders focus more on the person, their environment, and any dis-ease or imbalances. The role of the external supporter—the "healer"—is usually to draw out the answers for the individual, rather than "prescribe" a particular theory or formula for healing. Psychiatrist and trauma therapist Bessel van der Kolk (2006) was able to note the similarities in healing ceremonies, music, and singing that "was communal . . . and restored an inner equilibrium once disturbed by trauma," (p. 225) between peoples of African and Native communities in the southwest United States and Southeast Asia. Restoring harmony and balance is not just spiritual; it is essential for connection and a positive sense of self. Working with a person as a whole being allows for integration; working with a person as part of a collective—as a global citizen rather than in separate parts—helps us break free from the chains of "disease," as it is defined by Western biomedicine.

The omission of the history, culture, and roots of the techniques and theories are forms of colonial harm. Energy psychology, felt sense, heart-assisted therapy, emotional freedom techniques (EFT tapping), and thought field therapy often fail to credit the cultures, countries, tribes, villages, healers, and countless spiritual Indigenous practitioners who have passed on the energy medicine and ancestral knowledge. As we have expanded upon in Chapter 7, Ancestral Roots in Mental Health "From Root to Bone," much of modern Western mental health care practices derive FROM our kin. Practices for hundreds of years have not been credited to many Indigenous and displaced people around the globe. This is another form of harm and intellectual–emotional colonization; as it harms the People, financially impacts generations, degrades the cultural fabric, and minimizes the true ritual and root of the practice. *Western adaptations of Indigenous practices omit the medicine and focus on the outcome.* We also see this in how many people who have come to be known as white have profited greatly from the fashions, scholarship, ideas, techniques, and styles of PoGM around the globe; however, many of us of the global majority are not compensated financially, intellectually, or emotionally. We also see this play out when oppressive energy is internalized by racialized peoples. As an example, the acupoint and EFT tapping protocols draw from the ancient Chinese healing system of acupuncture. The perception of acupuncture in the West has been mixed, with strong opinions from Western traditional models of health. People who have been educated in the biomedical approach to health are frequently asked how traditional healers "treat specific diseases," and interrogate practices while inquiring about clinical trials, N samples, and efficacy. This is not to say that there is not a place for traditional Eurocentric quantitative or qualitative research methods. However, research, in general, is deeply biased. To minimize cultural bias, we are told that researchers must "move toward cultural relativism by showing unconditional positive regard and being cognizant of their own cultural assumptions" (Levesque, 2011). Yet, we also are clear that cultural relativism is never 100% achievable. Research is as much a part of the colonial assault as asylums throughout psychology and psychiatry have been to Indigenous and Black people across the globe and throughout the past hundred years.

> It is important to note that this chapter may not speak to all practitioners nor participants of healing work; however, the topic of energetic boundaries has arisen so often, in so many settings, and so deeply impacted my own life that it felt necessary to include ways that we can support our authentic selves. As sensitives and as a culture who is collectively honoring sensitivity as a strength rather than a weakness, this is also mutually beneficial for the therapeutic relationship, in that participants get to express themselves more fully as we role model this behavior. Additionally, energy medicine/work/experiences are quite common in many Indigenous cultures around the globe. Many Indigenous tribes and people regularly make decisions based on specific beliefs, the behavior of animals, the

> flow and fullness of a river, etc. All things are alive with energy. This is decolonial in its very root.

Prompts to Support Incorporating Energy Medicine Into Your Practices
- Consider the person's relationships and community systems. *"Where are you held in your relationships?"*
- Consider the person's health. Should there be pain in various parts of the body, ask: "What are your hips carrying that may need to be put down?" "Where does your sexual abuse land on your body?"
- Consider the person's energy levels. "Are there tasks and activities you are engaging in that drain your energy?"
- Consider the person's support system. "Where do you feel most supported in your life?"
- Consider a person's points of energetic oppression. "Where is your gender/body/thinking/ability level most celebrated? Where is it most overlooked? Where is it most minimized?"
- Consider a person's spirit. "Could there be other reasons (besides mental health issues) for your disconnect with your mind?" Fill in appropriate inquiries and areas.
- One of my favorite ways to follow up is by asking: "And what do you feel capable and willing to do about this?"

Mental Health Professionals and Energy Work

Energetic boundaries have been beautifully spoken of in a myriad of ways and through a variety of professionals and practitioners. Therefore, as someone who practiced and facilitated psychotherapy for the past 18 years, and who has always been highly sensitive, intuitive, and deeply connected to my ancestors, it was an exercise in humility to have heard past therapists and supervisors tell me that psychology—a field I loved so deeply—and spirituality did not mix. It hurt me even deeper to be told by a possible dissertation chair that psychology and politics do not mix.

Therefore, this entire book, but especially this chapter, is dedicated to those of us who feel we need to fragment ourselves even further in order to fit into a narrow definition of what a therapist, mental health worker, or a healer IS. Thank goodness years later I landed upon Dr. C. who was not only an amazing, competent, and ethical psychologist, but also a deeply spiritual human and energy worker. She was able to weave psychology and spirituality together and be a teacher, mentor, and space holder. Through her container for 10 years, I was able to not feel "broken," and I was able to better honor my People, our history, our spiritual practices, and be an even better, more present, and less afraid psychotherapist.

Making the Work Come Alive Example
Swathiti,[28] a 19-year-old South Asian, nonbinary, goth-identified person came into session directly asking me, their possible therapist, the following:

- Do you know anything about empaths?
- What are your thoughts about people who have visions/hear things?
- Would you hospitalize someone who said they see the dead and are often provided advice from the dead?
- Do you have a relationship with your culture, culture's practices, and/or your ancestors?
- How do you identify?
- What are your Sun, Rising, and Moon signs?

My responses were as follows:

- I do in fact, quite a bit. I walk in the world as an empath, and my work and relationships are influenced by this.
- I think context is key. I would be open to hearing about how this person hears and sees things—how long, often, and when (if ever) do they feel fearful. I might ask about how it shows up and when (voices) show up,

---

28 All the names of individuals mentioned have been changed to protect their privacy.

and whether they feel the information is useful and whether there are boundaries.
- I aim to never hospitalize anyone. However hospitalization—or rather escort to a hospital, plus psychiatric evaluation—is reserved for a deep conversation between myself and the person I am holding space for. Should I/we decide it is essential for their safety and well-being or that of others—then yes. However, my preference is that early on in this container we create strong plans involving the support of others should the need for safe containment and support ever be needed, as to avoid any hospitalizations. However, the majority of the time, unless the advice is about harming oneself or others, then absolutely not. The hospital is no place for a medium.
- I have a robust relationship to my ancestors, spirit team, and culture. It is by no means complete, but my practices are important to me and help me be well.
- In summary, this is by no means the entirety of my identity, but I identify as a cis, fluid oriented, Black Panamanian woman of mixed heritage, who lives with disabilities. One or two which may impact our work together. Should you decide to work together, I would be happy to share more about my identities, if and when we formulate a mutual trusting relationship together.
- Cancer Sun, Virgo Rising, and Capricorn Moon.

I am happy to report that we worked together for over two years. They are now in graduate school for mechanical engineering and provides tarot and astrology sessions on the weekends. They no longer feels they are "insane," "broken," "cursed," or "bad" for not ascribing to the religion, cultural norms, and spiritual beliefs of their family (Punjabi Hindu). By no means does anyone need to respond in the manner in which I have. However, there is something to be said about meeting people where they are; and being reflected and seen by the people we hold space for. Part of energetic boundary work is allowing there to be a fair exchange of energy between client and provider. This does not mean that I processed my personal material and became their "spiritual teacher." Rather I made space for all of who they were, and allowed a reciprocal inquiry that allowed for us both to feel "full and grateful" for our therapeutic relationship after every session.

There is also something to be said about declining a potential therapy participant, and deciding mutually that it will not be a solid match. There is also something to be said about asking ourselves about what we think we know about what a therapist and clinician is, and whom we serve. Part of decolonizing therapy is having internal clarity that we do not have to serve institutions (although we may be technically), but clarifying the love for serving and working with mutual respect.

Side note, there is also something to be said about knowing your Sun, Moon, and rising signs. Optional, but highly encouraged.

I believe it is essential to all clinical staff out there who identify as deeply sensitive/intuitive/empath/highly sensitive to know that there are other MHPs who have been speaking about energetic boundaries. It helps to know that we are not alone.

It is also essential to note that many, many of our elders, family members, and cultures have been practicing and speaking with energy and Spirit for hundreds of years. Mental health was born OF the healing work of our grandmothers and our great-great-grandmothers. Contemporary proponents of energetic boundaries are more prevalent as more therapists embrace the impact and experiences of the mind–body–spirit connections (their own and those they hold space for).

Dr. Elaine Aron has facilitated numerous points of research and written *The Highly Sensitive Person*. One of my favorites, and the psychiatrist whose book, *Second Sight* made me weep, is practicing psychiatrist, empath, author, and UCLA Psychiatric Clinical Faculty, Dr. Judith Orloff. Dr Clarissa Pinkola Estés has written *Women Who Run with Wolves*; Dr. Gabor Maté wrote *When The Body Says No*; and Dr. Brian Weiss wrote *Many Lives, Many Masters*, just to name a few.

Energetic Boundaries and the Impact of Colonialism

The reality is that many of us who have been reared in traumatic environments, and many of us who have been raised (unconsciously or not) in societies with a great deal of systemic and structural oppression with big consequences for simply BEING who we are, can create this (understandable and normal) anxiety within us, making energetic boundaries even more difficult to set, primarily with ourselves. When we step back for a moment and consider how anti-Black racism affects those who walk in the world as visibly Black, when we think about how "everyday" ableism (from inoperable elevators in schools to the transportation system) continues to affect those who cannot access the world with the same ease as able-bodied folks, when we think about the ways in which trauma has been intergenerationally passed down and forms a level of healthy dissociation, yet that level of dissociation creates barriers to work, mental health issues, and an inability to not only ask for what one needs, but to protect one's ideas, time, and energy—white supremacy impacts all of our energetic boundaries.

Ways That White Supremacy (or Colonization) Impacts BIPOC's/PoGM's Energetic Boundaries

1. It makes it difficult *not* to experience a great deal of internal and external responsibility for the betterment of our communities/workplaces/students/family members to the detriment of one's health. It is hard to balance the love for one's community or culture and one's capacity. Many BIPOC/PoGM living and working in close communities have never become conscious of the cycle of being a present-day community healer, shaman, or *curanderx*, and the energetic essentials of having the same support poured back into one's cup (i.e., support, payment, child care assistance, etc.).
2. Feeling responsible and often absorbing the anxiety of white people and people with a great deal of privilege when there is discord in an environment.
3. Minimizing one's needs, because it feels as though one's safety is threatened. Therefore, allowing negative or minimizing treatment in order to "just get by." This can create a variety of energy and emotional dis-eases.
4. Fearful of "taking up space" or asking for what one needs for fear of appearing too much; therefore, one's energy is weak and dim.

Ways That White Supremacy (or Colonization) Impacts White People's Energetic Boundaries
1. Unconsciously taking up a great deal of space energetically. Making assumptions that one's way of creating boundaries is THE way.
2. Asking for and expecting that exceptions be made for one's distress and needs, regardless of how it impacts others around them. This can drain the energy of the people around them.
3. Expectations that others can and should set (all types of) boundaries with ease, and that there are no deeper consequences for others with identities that do not benefit from white privilege.
4. Consciously or not placing emotional labor on non-white peoples.

CAN YOU BRAINSTORM WAYS THAT WHITE SUPREMACY (OR COLONIZATION) HAS IMPACTED YOUR ENERGETIC BOUNDARIES?

REFLECTION
- In what ways and spaces might you give too much of yourself?
- In what ways were you conditioned/trained to give "too much" of yourself?
- In what ways has your field promoted porous boundaries?
- In what ways have you cut yourself off from experiencing what life has to offer because trauma caused you to create big, strong boundaries?
- In what ways have the structures, policies, and systems that make up mental health impacted your boundaries?
- In what ways has colonization impacted your boundaries? Energetically? Physically? Emotionally? Financially?

Having an embodied sense of a boundary will help your nervous system feel protected and safe. Most people feel calm and relaxed once they see or feel the boundary. The boundary gives us our space, and gives us a buffer with which to engage the world. This space is yours, and when you have a boundary you have the ability to say, "This is my boundary; you can't come in unless I invite you."

1. **Feel the 360-degree space around you.** Yes, you read that right. Take a moment to sit quietly, maybe during a walk outside or after exercising. Then see if you can feel the air that is around you extending about 1–3 feet. You can extend your arms and stretch into that space, moving your arms above your head, to the sides, and to the front. Then stop and notice how it feels to become aware of the space around you.

2. **Place a physical boundary.** You can do this with a six-foot piece of string or yarn, a couple of shawls, towels, or a sheet. Place the boundary around you; make it as close or as far as you feel is just right. You may notice that a boundary placed too close will feel tight or it might feel secure. Experiment and let yourself notice how different boundaries feel.

3. **Clear your space.** Now that you are feeling your space you might feel that there are thoughts, situations, feelings that are "too close." Maybe it's something you're worried about or are thinking about a lot. Place your hands right in front of your chest with your palms facing out, take a deep breath and as you exhale slowly though your mouth, push out with your hands and imagine pushing that thing that is too close to the outside of your boundary. Notice how you feel with a little more space away from it. Do you now have space to consider it in a different way?

If you feel the boundary is triggering or activating, then stop. You might explore what this **boundary** means to you. If it means disconnection and isolation, see if you can frame it as "this is space for me to feel myself and to know what I need." If you want to revisit this exploration, do only one of these steps at a time, and see what works for you.

Aspects of Emotional–Decolonial Unlearning

1. Energetic boundaries differ from physical boundaries, but they are not necessarily distinct, instead they overlap.
2. The trauma of colonization is also quite energetic, biological, and for many, even spiritual.
3. We each have an energy field. We can pick up on other people's subtle energy, and it can have an effect on us by penetrating our personal energy field.

4. It is irresponsible to be a container for suffering and overwhelm, without also ensuring you are tending to your own energy.
5. *Energy* is a concept in some psychological theories or models that is an unconscious mental function between biology and consciousness.
6. EP is seen within traditional Western psychotherapy as a mind–body approach to understanding and improving human functioning. It centers on the relationship between bioenergy systems, neuro- and electrophysiological processes, and mental functions involving thoughts, emotions, sensations, and behaviors and has been co-opted from other collectivistic and animistic cultures, such as Peruvian, Japanese, Chinese, Haitian, etc.
7. The Collective, is short for Collective Energy. These systems and processes exist and interact within the individual and between people. It is like a central hive mind.
8. The Collective is the systems and energy processes existing and interacting within and between Peoples, influenced by cultural, historical, and environmental factors.
9. Burnout is minimized and often seen as a badge of honor throughout the helping professions, and it is spurred on by capitalism.
10. Energy is political.
11. Energy work is decolonial.
12. Energy patterns are intergenerational.
13. Energy is rooted in the ancestral and is seen as normal and healthy.
14. Boundaries help us be aware of ourselves and our relationships with others.
15. Highly sensitive people make up more than 20% of our population.
16. Some mental health diagnoses are incorrectly diagnosing energetically sensitive, highly sensitive, or intuitive people. This further vilifies extrasensory capabilities that have been generationally passed down.
17. White supremacy impacts BIPOC's energetic boundaries.

Emo–Decolonial Practice Offerings

- Reflect on how energy is understood in our respective cultures; this includes that of the therapy participant and your own.
- Learn, introduce, or play around with concepts such as muscle testing and bioenergetics, which are also often used in heart-centered therapy work.
- Inward first! What are your own experiences and perceptions of energy boundaries?
- Help participants to connect their cultures and beliefs to new practices to "cleanse their energy or field," especially after coming into contact with large groups of people, family and friends, conflict, or public spaces.
- Support participants to better understand how their mood or behaviors may rapidly or slowly shift around certain people, places, and/or spaces.
- Inquire "Where or with whom in your life might you feel alive, well, situated? Where or with whom do you feel antsy, overwhelmed, agitated, or unclear? Are there patterns?" Of course, we always want to assess for harm and abuse of any sort.
- Engage participants in simple exercises like washing hands with cold water after a heavy class or meeting.
- Taking deep breaths before and after meetings or showering or bathing post difficult moments.

Affirmations for Your Energy Boundaries

- My body is wise.
- I honor my energetic sovereignty.
- I can listen and not absorb.
- I honor my energy body and soul.
- I trust the discernment I feel in my body and take action according to what I need in the moment.
- I can speak freely about energy and my beliefs about boundaries, without fear of judgment.
- I am allowed to release or put down what I cannot hold for the moment.
- It is OK for me to teach myself about energetic boundaries.
- It is safe for me to speak to my clients/students/family members about energy.

- I am willing to honor that my personal power is necessary for my emotional and physical health.
- I am capable of integrating the knowledge of what weakens my body and energy.
- I honor my family's belief systems.
- I feel safe in my heart.
- I honor the space to rest as an empath/intuitive.
- Showing up for my Self is safe.
- I break the cycle of self-sabotage and burnout in the name of "helping and saving" others.
- Lack of boundaries invites disrespect.
- You promote what you permit.
- I am entitled to step away from my family's superstition(s).
- I am learning to discern the difference between the collective and individual energy in my body.
- I can create new ways of honoring my energy and capacity.
- I can facilitate deep healing without taking on someone's pain by practicing empathy, not sympathy.
- It is safe to honor my culture's views regarding energy AND practice therapy.
- I am allowed to be a caregiver (clinician, parent, teacher, etc.) AND be loyal to myself.

CHAPTER 10

Politicizing Your Practice (Is How We Begin to Decolonize Therapy)

Revolution does not always move like wildfire. Sometimes it is a slow moss, blooming on trees. Patience and endurance are sacred tactics. In time, they overtake the forest, bringing softness back into the world.
—Jaiya John, Freedom: Medicine Words for
Your Brave Revolution (2020)

BIPOC need systemic and structural change, more than individual healing. Therapy alone will not liberate.
—Ji-Youn Kim (2021, April 15) [Instagram]

The conflict between the will to deny horrible events and the will to proclaim them aloud is the central dialectic of psychological trauma.
—Judith Lewis Herman, Trauma and Recovery: The Aftermath
of Violence–from Domestic Abuse to Political Terror (1993)

This chapter is an offering to the practitioners and providers of the globe: It is the Call to Action. This chapter will offer a commitment to Love. A commitment to the love that is present in helping others, healing ourselves,

D is for Decolonize.
Source: Anarchists (2019)

and helping to create a more internally and externally safe world for our generations to come. For the purpose of this book, the love is also offered back to a field that has asked for and taken a great deal from many, including practitioners: the love between a helper/supporter, practitioner/therapist/social worker/clinician, and participant/client of therapy.

This chapter will offer insight-oriented inquiries that are suggested to be done in community, a coalition, a collective, and/or an affinity space. Yet, **we have to be willing to learn to unlearn.** That begins with self-inquiry. **Question everything.** Emo–decolonial work is a verb, inviting insightful political inquiry and using history as a tool to shift from pathology to healing, to Unlearn, to Relearn in community, to see the political in the personal and social, to Resist, in order to REBUILD. These inquiries will be an eclectic array of reflection questions, insights, practices, and exercises to assist the process of politicizing as we crawl out of the current mental health biomedical complex.

The revolution is in the small baby steps forward, and the painful and informative ones as we look back.

Over the past 10 years, my decolonization was a word many of us with Indigenous ancestries globally, spoke of . . . fought for . . . and sang of. However, for much of traditional Western psychotherapy this is not the case. Political groups abhor human care workers using decolonization as a term, thinking it is being minimized. Yet, decolonizing does have a space and place in emotional work. Our own internalized decoloniality shows up in many spaces, places, and definitely, cases. Although, much like modern care workers and practitioners, the emotional aspects of decolonization are often overlooked and assumed. The emotional evolutionary component to land decolonization is essential. Without the emotional component, in addition to the return of land, the movements have a danger of staying a theory or the action of a small select few. To many mental health providers and those who are choosing to leave licensed care work it is clear that we must help bring an emotional and loving collective energy TO SOCIAL JUSTICE WORK. So many groups and individuals already have! This work rests upon and honors those elders' and ancestors' shoulders with deep clarity for mental health's evolution and grace.

This work has a dual process: (a) it highlights the need to transform the current MHIC, and its relationship to white supremacy, ableism, heterosexism, and classicism. It highlights the inadequacies in the mental health system as it currently stands, particularly for those who rely on community mental health like those living at and below poverty level, and (b) this work also highlights the need to return back Home: to our ancestry, to many of our practices, our medicines, our native tongues, and our communal ways of thriving, while reconfiguring and integrating these practices into the present and future. It also highlights the need to return back Home. For some people, this is a literal return to visit, live, or sit with elders in their villages. For others, this is a journey inward toward our past ancestries and experiences. This process is both internal and external. It is cyclical and flowing.

It will offer the essentialness of living—not doing—by **embodying** an **emotional evolution**. Highlighting the vitalness of emotional self-inquiry for those seeking to continue to hold space for others. Appreciating the values of transparency, accountability, and vulnerability (when appropriate).

Here are the co-occurring practices of emo–decolonial engagement:

POLITICAL: Politicizing Our Practices
SELF/PSYCHE: Emotional Evolution, Including the Body, Spirit, and Mind
COLLECTIVE: Cocreating Decolonial Pathways in Emotional (Mental) Health
ANCESTRAL: Communing and Getting to Know Our Ancestors and Ancestry

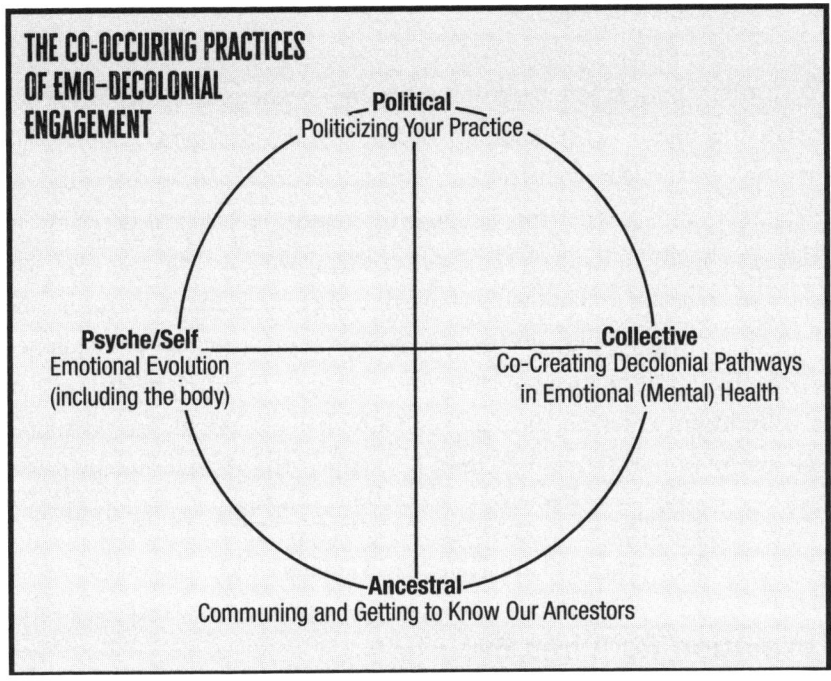

FIGURE 10.1 The Co-Occurring Practices of Emo–Decolonial Engagement

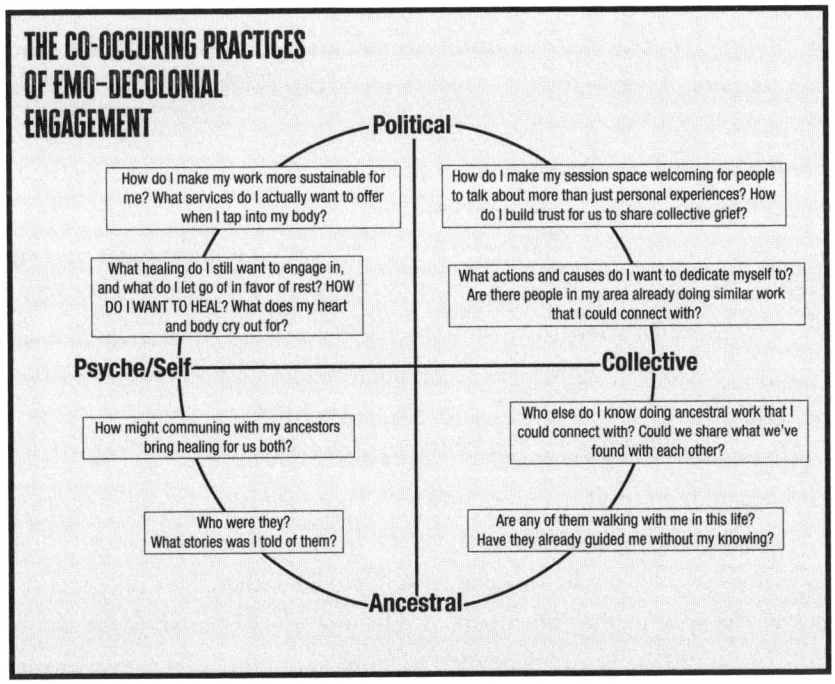

FIGURE 10.2 The Co-Occurring Practices of Emo–Decolonial Engagement Part 2

These arenas coexist in relationship with one another simultaneously. They are circular, in and out of colonial concepts of time, and personal, political, ancestral, and collective. Increasing one's emotional landscape can improve relationship and partnership building in creating decolonial pathways in emotional health. Equally, understanding one's own ancestral history; harm that your ancestors or family may have directly caused and/or received; and processing this guilt, rage, and grief with appropriate practitioners equipped to hold that frame can lead to better self-concept, emotional health, and an increase in joy. Likewise, partnering in a multigenerational, multidynamic community working toward cocreation of new pathways and therapy evolutions can lead to greater insight into one's intergenerational family current patterns and patterns we may need to shift and break.

Revolution Requires Evolution

Revolution requires evolution, as well as opportunity to shift the mental and behavioral health paradigms we are currently drowning within. An evolution **in relationship** to **our big** emotions. An evolution in reoccupying our bodies, specifically if the historical and ancestral trauma have created a disconnect. An evolution in how we teach our youth, reteach ourselves, in how we teach one another. It requires an evolution in how we engage in self-inquiry, and the importance of plugging self-inquiry in with embodiment and community.

Revolution requires evolution. One where emotional awareness is centered and not swept under the rug within education. It requires the divesting from colonial education and colonial consciousness. This will require, once again, self-inquiry, insight, the acceptance that we all evolve at different paces, and that the educators are reeducated.

Revolution requires that our therapy evolve. Parts 1 and 2 of this book has been an invitation to rework and reexamine our internal belief systems, slowing down in order to notice where practitioners have been covertly (and sometimes overtly) invited to blame individuals, rather than take a closer look at the systems they are a part of. This book has been an invitation to notice how the medicalization and "treating of symptoms" has felt so very uncomfortable and done so much harm; yet many in the helping fields have continued to stand by "how things have always been done."

Mental and behavioral health has overlooked and chosen to ignore the soul wounding of historical, ancestral, and intergenerational trauma—all emotional aspects of colonization.

This has led us here. To soaring substance-abuse-related deaths, increasing child and adolescent suicide rates, an increase in unhoused people and unemployment, global mass resignations, massive global displacement and forced migration of people from their lands, ecocide, environmental racism, pipelines on Indigenous sacred land, just to name a few. Humanity is bone-tired.

As the human barometers of emotional wellness, it is our responsibility to also collectively gauge and advocate for those who are unable to do so for a multitude of reasons. white supremacy, including its cousins of patriarchy, transphobia, ableism, xenophobia, racism, homophobia, and classicism, has ensured that MHPs stand down and slow down. But no longer. We cannot in good conscience continue to "treat" individuals in the school/office/hospital and not be proactive conscientious stewards of the collective. We cannot stay in our exhausting positions—whether in group, private, or community orgs and practices—keeping our heads down and the money barely flowing well enough for our basic needs. People need us. Frankly, we need us. **The entire emotional well-being of the globe, as we transition into new ways of living, requires us.**

Hence, we land here at the end of this book, hopefully having a better, deeper understanding of how focusing only on the individual, family, or even community/cultural group without the full panoramic view/lens of history and ancestry cheats us all. The seeds from the root are still required to plant new trees. We cannot just leap from where we currently are to where we want to be. That IS magical thinking.[29] We also cannot continue to sit on our hands, shrug our shoulders, and assume the massive pivot necessary in mental health will land in someone else's inbox. The time is now.

---

29 Note that this is being utilized as a play on words by utilizing psychotherapy's terminology against itself. "In psychotherapy, Magical Thinking can be treated with Cognitive-Behavioral Therapy (CBT), and is usually associated with OCD" (The Gateway Institute, n.d.).

Therapy participants are hungry for more. We are hungry for more, and hundreds of thousands of providers are literally sick, tired, dying, caged, and uninspired. We as providers of quality care desire to show up more fully—with our quirks, kinks, gifts, possibilities, and creativities WITHIN the frame of helping and giving therapeutic care.

This final chapter is an invitation. We are in privileged positions within our practices, nonprofits, graduate schools, institutions, detention centers, hospitalization programs, residentials, group homes, and outpatient centers. Our privilege gives us the ability to look inward. This chapter invites the "Knowers and Problem Solvers" to be seen . . . to be vulnerable. It is an invitation to deeply engage in your own work. Creating less harm, inviting in more space . . . more restful, less activated space to process; eventually having the capacity to create again.

The goal is for practitioners to be so healthy, present, nondefensive, and deeply rested that there will be space to form interdisciplinary coalitions, where our perspectives and feedback need to be welcomed. As a new Earth grows new skin, our emotionally conscious perspectives must include the participants AND have our own collective mental and emotional health knowledge.

Revolution cannot happen without insight and the presence of sound, healing, and community-based emotional and mental health initiatives. It is our job to ensure we maintain and embody clear healthy channels for these spaces. **You Are Important.**

In order to move into **decolonizing our therapy practices**, we would benefit from acknowledging that there are stages to this evolution of a very old school paradigm of therapy.

POLITICAL: Politicizing Your Practice

Part 1: *Politicize Your Practice*, today. Shifting from less pathology to more wellness and healing. This requires understanding the systems, the structures, and the people that continue to benefit from keeping the MHIC the way it is, snuggly under the arm of the MIC. This requires:

- Self-Inquiry and inquiry of Ancestral, Land, and Family. (More on this form of inquiry below.)

- Understanding the "root," the history, and role of colonization and historical and intergenerational legacies and transmissions of trauma.
- What are the expressions of these big "root level" forms of suffering/trauma? In other words how exactly and specifically does colonization show up in our lineages and people?
- Protect and provide accessible services for people on the ground.

That means the individuals who are most affected by capitalism, those living at the poverty level, those with less accessibility, those living under the boot of ableism and racism. Those who struggle to have accessible and consistent medication, support, and services for their emotional health. As noted prior, the cause for pause when dismantling archaic systems involves the knowledge that poor people will always be most affected. As the world crumbles and shifts and new ways are reborn, what happens to those most needing the mental health systems and support?

COLLECTIVE: Cocreating Decolonial Pathways in Emotional (Mental) Health

Part 2: *Cocreating New Pathways for Healing*—arranging an emotionally centered and decolonial lens on all we cocreate.

We will require **Emotional Think Collectives**. Spaces to convene by country, by city, by identity, by need (or whatever else you like; be creative). Group by group, like a web we come together to:

- Identify the need of those most affected by harm.
- Identify our shared focus and shared goal.
- Identify what is being done.
- Identify what folks need (key: to include community members and those with least accessibility in order to move our Emotional Think Tank conversations).
- Build community together. Meet one another's children. Share stories. Have outings and cookouts not related to "the work" because building relationships is the core of the emotional revolution.
- Relearn and understand how the MHIC has harmed people. Take time to understand how it affects self, family, ancestry, and community.

- Look at what is occurring globally—we do not need to recreate or to compete! We want to create together . . . what has worked? What is working now?
- Bring in folks who are in expressive arts, somatics, community health, students, traditional Western therapists, activists, writers, youths, school counselors, artists, lawyers, and so on. Our communities need to be robust with various perspectives and insights.

ANCESTRAL: Communing and Getting to Know Our Ancestors and Ancestry

Wolynn describes the effect of our ancestors in the following way:

> The history we share with our family begins before we are conceived. You already share a cellular environment with your mother and grandmother. When our grandmother was five months pregnant with your mother, the precursor cell of the egg you developed from was already present in your mother's ovaries. This means that before you were even born, your mother, grandmother, and the earliest traces of you were all in the same body = three generations; sharing the same biological environment. . . . [Similarly,] your inception can be traced to your paternal line through the precursor of the sperm you developed from that was present in your father when he was a fetus in his mother's womb. (Wolynn, 2016)

"We can begin to map out how the biological residue of traumas your grandmother experienced can be passed down with far-reaching consequences" (Wolynn, 2016; Yehuda & Lehrner; Danieli, 1998), as well as the strengths, capacities, artistic abilities, and otherwise. Intergenerational and ancestral connection is not all "heavy"; it can also be a beautiful reminder, and a return to natural ways of being with nature and one another. Decolonization is REVITALIZING.

ANCESTRAL INQUIRY

As always, allow yourself to be resourced and take your time. There is no rush to any of this work; it is a journey, a process—excavation.

If you are aware of your birth kin and ancestors:

- Where are your ancestors from?
- What was their experience(s) with colonization?
- Have your people ever experienced harm?
  — If so, by whom?
- Have your people caused harm?
  — If so, to whom?
- Can you repair, amend, work toward healing and engaging in giving land back, or giving monthly reparation checks, and so forth?
- How have expressions of historical trauma been transmitted?
  — (child rearing practices, starvation/hunger, lack of resources, engaging in harm and abusive cycles, working as a means of survival without rest, activism/advocating/fighting/justice-centered work without taking care of the physical body, martyr energy, etc.)
- What were the rituals of your people, if any?
- What was, or currently are, the spiritual or religious beliefs of your People? Do you subscribe to these beliefs and practices?
- Have your ancestors ever harmed others due to their spiritual, religious, or political beliefs? How does this make you feel?
- How was song used in your culture?
- How was movement or dance used in your culture?
- How were people living in alternate realities or with "differences" from the majority of the community treated?
- How does (has) colonization impact(ed) your people?
- Do your people have histories of forced displacement and migration?
- Where did your people(s) most commonly spend their time (i.e., farm, coastal areas, river, desert, mountains, etc.)?
- Did your ancestors wear specific clothing, colors, hair styles, facial markings, piercings, jewelry, etc.?
- Did your ancestors engage in or specialize in any specific healing?
- Did your ancestors engage in or specialize in any specific physical training (i.e., sword fighting, martial arts, etc.)?
- Are you connected to anyone in the present-day who is from your ancestry?

- How does this make you feel?
- When you think of your ancestors, how does your body feel?

> If you have no direct knowledge of your ancestors or cultural identity—if, for instance, you have not met, have grown apart, or have needed to separate from your biological family or culture—consider investing in DNA testing, simply as a means to find out more about a land, region, culture, or people. We know that there are many cultures who do not have sufficient DNA information, and there are many valid concerns about DNA testing. However, in the case of not being knowledgeable of the birth family, this can be helpful.

Land Inquiry

Part of the ancestral inquiry is communicating and connecting with the land. Some of our ancestors, if they were indigenous to the land, were and are stewards of the Earth. They have an intimate and likely healthy reciprocal relationship with waterways, trees, animals, the cosmos, weather, and what is built, destroyed, and utilized. Many of our ancestors experienced a connection with the land. Many elders pass on the wisdom that in listening to the land, you are in turn listening to oneself, and the entire web of the world. This is part of the type of wisdom that is innately part of ourselves, and in the politicizing and decolonial journey we are invited to re-remember and to reignite.

- What is the original name of that land?
- Write or talk about the land. Is it rocky, dry, hot? What color is the ground? Is it a rainy climate? Are monsoons, hurricanes, or tsunamis common? Has there ever been a drought?
- Have you ever set your physical body onto that land?
- Is the land of your ancestors still there?
- Has the land experienced any trauma/suffering?
- What are your People(s) relationship to the land?
- Has the land experienced a disconnect from its people?

- How have your People treated the Land, then and now?
- Does a person or people "control" the land now?
- How does this make you feel?
- Have you ever dreamed of the land? If so, in what way?
- When you imagine visiting there, or when you have visited, how have you felt?
- Are you allowed to return to your ancestral lands with ease?
- What does this mean to you?
- Do you feel connected to the Land?
- Is there something that your Land desires at this time?
- When was the first time you considered your "relationship to the Land" of your ancestors?

SELF/PSYCHE: Emotional Evolution, Including the Body and Relationships
INTERPERSONAL AND FAMILIAL

- If you have the privilege and access, what are the names of your parents, grandparents, and great-grandparents?
- What work/labor did your family engage in?
- Is there anyone your family does not speak about? Why is that?
- What was the health or vitality of your family members? What did you notice about the adults in your family growing up?
- What were relationships like in your family (i.e., love, sibling, caregiver, etc.)?
- Did your family have friends, not family?
- Did your family have pacts or secrets? Are there any you are aware of?
- What was the socioeconomic story of your family? Has it changed due to colonization, war, or displacement in any way?
- Has your family ever experienced displacement?
- Has your family experienced or caused attempted genocide or historical trauma? What did you grow up knowing or believing about the historical trauma if so?
- Do you utilize your native tongue or know it?
- Do you feel connected to your body in the country in which you live? Why or why not?

- Where globally, if you have had the privilege to travel outside of your resident country, do you feel most "at home"? Why might that be?
- What is your relationship to support and caregiving?

These questions are meant to be a helpful guide into your process. As always, resourcing one's self with nourishment, healthy movement, and connection often helps ground us after exercises such as these. It is important not to feel rushed or hurried while completing these.

For individuals who may be finding some of these questions painful or triggering, they may not know where to go from here. It may be helpful to engage in this section with a Guide. This can look like an affinity group, a collective, a practitioner, a spiritual teacher, or a close friend group. The decolonial journey is not an individual one. It may also help if you are white, to engage with a group of other white folks who are at various levels of their unpacking process. Shame and guilt are not useful emotions where we are headed as a global people! Everyone is welcomed; yet the entrance requires a willingness to be uncomfortable, work through conflict (interpersonally, historically, and personally), accept accountability (historically and personally), and have the willingness to not know. It's hard, I know; have compassion with yourself!

As an example, you may have done personal internal healing work from abuse; however, perhaps you have not quite known or been supported in knowing how to heal your relationship with earlier generations of family members who have perpetuated it. This is very common and such a large piece of this journey. One that care workers, practitioners, and politicized healers are quite skilled at. This is where you are invited to slow down, notice whether you are able to proceed, and resource yourself before continuing. This is not a race, contrary to colonial conditioning.

History Is a Tool

> *Healing trauma, making ourselves more whole again, and changing society and the economy, are distinct yet interdependent processes. They can work powerfully for and towards each other, or they can be at odds.*
> —Staci K. Haines (2019) *The Politics of Trauma*

Many of us wish to see the planet become a more balanced and peaceful place. However, there is no magical movement into balance without looking at the entire truth of a situation. The general public usually is not aware of the full truth of a situation. What is potent and difficult at this time on Earth is that we are at the breaking point of the polarities of systemic oppression. We are seeing a rise of control, division, and enslavement. Over the past 20 years, we are seeing a steady increase of consciousness. Humanity is questioning everything inherently taken for granted in the system (i.e., systems of government, boards, schools, licensing, etc.).

This is healthy. Our deep rage, grief, anxiety, and feelings of fear are healthy and understandable. We continue to attempt to evolve.

The increase in awareness and consciousness, as well as interest in culture and ancestry, has given rise to remembering. We are hurting as a collective. The needless suffering and destructive intent of people on the planet is breaking our hearts. We are also having a somatic bodily remembering of ancestral times of war, separation, and colonial violence. The power system has been able to oppress and control for decades. We need a different consciousness from the inside to the outside—from within ourselves, out to the policies and practices.

From the inside out, we must emotionally and physically politicize the practices and therapies we provide. It is and has been the colonial setup for practitioners of therapy to fall for the lie that "There is nothing that we can do," that we do not have Power. We have Power. We are being called to gather, to process, to admit . . . to do it differently. We have the power to disassemble and recreate new ways of working. We have the power to take what we hear from our therapy participants and make it better, more sustainable, and healing for participants as well as practitioners.

A gift of social media is being able to communicate with one another around the ways that we're not receiving what we need, as global citizens. When we don't get our needs fully met, we can see this show up in the anxious attachment many of us have toward governments that we once believed would care for us. Truly, it is gaslighting.

This section is a love letter to our nervous systems. It involves some inquiry that may take some time, space, and energy. It is my way of taking care of caretakers. As that is what practitioners of mental health practices are. Caretakers. I recall watching a clip of Ai-jen Poo advocating for domestic workers,[30] and I was struck by the question: "What a child care worker produces is human potential. What a home care worker produces is dignity and quality of life for the people who raised us. What can be more valuable?" (CBS Interactive, 2022).

How do we begin to create new ways? We get curious, and we move to a place of embodiment—resilient embodiment. We engage in active decolonial work—scaffolding what we learn as a way to maintain our sovereignty and identities, allowing many PGM to stay connected to our roots.

Decolonizing Is a Verb

Mainstream society continues to be designed to deny and minimize current and historical systemic violence that has led to the multigenerational traumas. The avoidance of the truth continues to deeply impact everyone.

Decolonizing therapy, as a verb and a practice, emerged over 15 years ago as I facilitated a university student peer education retreat. I witnessed the massive shifts in self-trust, cultural identity, and the willingness to embark on releasing some of the weight associated with intergenerational traumas and beliefs. I realized how incomplete and wrong mainstream clinical mental health had it.

Having taught graduate and undergraduate courses; provided psychotherapy, hospital clinical treatment, and crisis management; provided neuropsychological assessments, treatment plans, countless hours of Association of Psychology Postdoctoral–approved internships, group supervisions, process groups, EMDR certifications, EFT energy psychology trainings, and Jungian analysis; facilitated both weekend retreats each semester unpacking deep ancestral, racial, and familial trauma, and Undoing Racism workshops; community organizing with youth and migrant folks; unionizing;

---

30 I think it is also important to note that domestic workers are often subject to multiple forms of emotional, physical, and emotional abuse (including less pay) and are often seen as less valuable and/or intelligent than therapists. None of this is true. Nevertheless, the commonality and point being: Caretakers, including MHPs, are valuable.

counseling across multiple systems; and studying for licensure for months on end . . . around 2015 something inside of me and around me popped. I no longer could sit with a student seeking support and NOT see systemic oppression. I no longer engaged with my amazing long-term psychotherapist feeling fed. I was angry that she had to hide her spiritual gifts and teachings to be seen as "ethical." I could no longer silently simmer in rage, while nodding in a Student Affairs meeting at the hypocrisy of *campus compact* "creating communities on campus." We had communities, community builders, and liaisons. . . . No one really wanted to ask and listen to the community though. Our community was not "academic and professional looking" enough. I could no longer listen to our queer community in support group cry about being unhoused, unfed, unloved without wanting to activate and do something about it. **The personal was an embodied political.**

It did not happen all at once; it was not "magic." It was not "something special about me." It was years on end of asking myself some key questions that, no doubt, many community leaders, elders, organizers, and trainers had asked before. It can and often does take time for these questions to become more integrated and urgent within ourselves.

Metabolizing big ideas and emotional realities doesn't necessarily happen all at once; but, when we honor the process and make it our practice to continually ask these questions over and over again, change inevitably happens within and around us.

- How am I blocking access/gatekeeping?
- How can I provide more access?
- Whose voice/vote is not in the room?
- Is this personal, structural, ancestral, or all three?
- Who is harmed if we do not take this action?
- Where did I learn that (choose a belief) from? From whom?
- Who gains if we take this action?
- How am I profiting off people's pain?
- How does this make me feel?
- Am I triggered or at my growth point?
- How does my privilege show up here?

- How is whiteness showing itself right now?
- Who is not being heard in this conversation, and how can I be a better accomplice?
- Are community members, youths, elders, students, workers, stakeholders at the meeting/table/in the conversation? Why or why not?
- Am I currently IN my body? Why or why not?
- Who, not in this space, may have solutions? How can we cocreate solutions here?

The questions may sound like simple inquiries, but the journey and the moment-by-moment/meeting-by-meeting internal and external struggles were all growth points. They all led to an emotional evolution and deconstruction. It was deeply political and decolonial. As I unlearned systemic whiteness and understood that professionalism was code for white, I began to remember more and more, learn more and more, and push back calmly more and more. I was unliked a bit more. This is the role that I believe many MHPs are not always comfortable with—not "fixing and being good."

> **SELF-INQUIRY: DEFENSIVENESS AS A DECOLONIAL PRACTICE**
>
> 1. Do you feel defensive when others point out harmful aspects of your training/education/treatment approach?
> 2. Do you feel anger/resentment toward people further along in their decolonizing practice? If so, why?
> 3. Do you struggle with pleasing people? If so, does this make your requests for change or activism more difficult? What can be done to mitigate and work through this?
> 4. Do your boundaries suffer due to your practice/profession?
> 5. How does whiteness silence you, regardless of your race?
> 6. How has your internalization of Eurocentric values impacted your ability to form healthy relationships?
> 7. Are you uncomfortable with sitting in the uncomfortable?
> 8. Are you better at helping others, than helping yourself? If so, what does this show you about where you might need to heal?

Along with grieving, there is the process of removing the veil of niceness for the sake of being nice. As I slowly shifted into spaces that were more politicized, and spaces where others were doing their own work in order to support the community (granted this is not always seen in the same places), I felt less defensive, agitated, and a bit safer. In coalitions, groups, and community meetings with a like-minded purpose forward, for once in my life, I could feel hope and possibility for future creations and the dismantling of the current mental health systems. Words cannot adequately describe the sensation of safety. It had not begun with political work. Nor even some fancy therapeutic technique. It had not begun with the word "decolonizing" nor "politicizing." It began with truly *humanizing*. Seeing one another's needs, obstacles, illnesses—all as human . . . part of our ecosystem . . . part of our issue too. It felt amazing to be held and hold in return.

Peer Support: Our Relationships Are Political

One of the spaces and places where the seeds of the emotional, political, psychological, and collective came together for me—and hundreds of others—involved a student peer organization group called Peers Educating Peers (PEP). PEP changed me as a participant at 20 years old, and saved my life. Peer education, mixed with social justice; facilitating and creating interactive presentations; engaging in group psychotherapy, semester retreats, outings to NYC; and a chosen family—it exposed me to LOVE. True love. It was a form of community organizing before I understood what activism truly was.

Years later, after facilitating and coordinating PEP for 13 years AND having been a product of this very group, I can attest that relationships and the power of a healing justice–oriented group with a strong therapeutic frame . . . is healing.

The PEP program created space for self-inquiry and the inner work that consisted of group accountability. Our work ranged from psychodrama to somatic work, to attachment theories, to parts work, nervous system regulation, art therapy, drama therapy, astrology, dance, ball competitions,[31] and karaoke.

Many of us learned how to BE in a family for the first time in our lives. Others of us learned that family is a choice, and a verb. Others of us learned that family is not where we want to be (and that is okay). Mostly, many of us learned how to receive, give support, and love someone despite their "imperfections"—humanizing the fact that school and an education means nothing without health. For PEP, that meant mental, social, emotional, and basic-needs health. Honest, reciprocal, justice-minded, intergenerationally focused, therapeutic groups bring healing.

Peer Support IS Therapeutic

People who have experience with mental health issues, disability, trauma, and/or neurodivergence can offer a specific, unique, culturally and socially responsive, and accessible type of mental health care, known as peer support. The beauty of peer support is that it does not happen on a hierarchical level. It began with consistently having a place, space, and frame week by week, providing each person with a task, a role, an expectation. Sometimes they didn't meet them. Some folks just showed up every few months or weeks. Some people came to a Wednesday meeting, released and shared, and never returned—but we were there. Every Wednesday 3–5 p.m. Holding the belief that each person was contributing to the whole—even if they were too unwell to show up, or did not have money or a dish for the potluck. It is important to note that safety and accountability were paramount. The safety of the group (emotionally, physically, sexually, spiritually, etc.) was centered constantly—before the needs or beliefs of an individual. If someone or something became unsafe, they were not able to return until specific steps occurred. Even if they were rejected by other groups, as a structure . . .

---

31 Ball competitions refers to queer ballroom, also known as queer ball culture. It started in the 1970s as an underground "safe haven for Black and Brown young people" (Chakrabarti & Bauman, 2019).

as a community . . . we showed up. When caregivers didn't. When professors wouldn't. When mental health professionals couldn't.

When I ask the prior participants of this peer group what was the most healing part of their lives, they say PEP (peer group). When I ask why, I received so many answers such as:

- "I was able to safely talk about childhood/family stuff. That wasn't allowed growing up. We don't talk about it. We did in PEP, always. I survived. I am a better parent because of it."
- "I started to trust people. I do not recall ever trusting anyone. Ever."
- "I couldn't lie to myself, AND be in a relationship with people who knew me and saw me and loved me."
- "People held space for me. Strangers—but it felt so contained—so good."
- "I spoke up after a while about what I did not like. I wasn't kicked out. I was so confused and liberated."
- "I learned how to deal and be in conflict without hurting someone or being hurt."
- "I learned about how my ancestors and great-great-grandparents affect me today. Phew. School never taught us this!"
- "I learned about trauma—not like a therapist's explanation either, like a human . . . and I watched others before me work theirs out. That was hopeful."
- "I looked up to people. Some people were younger than me. They were doing THE WORK. Counseling, spiritual work, healing family work. Forgiveness and inner child work. Rage work. I wanted to be them; they were my new heroes."
- "I learned about myself. I had to face conflict head-on, in order to stay; elephants needed to be addressed."
- "It was safe for me to be queer, dark-skinned, loud, and angry. Period."
- "It was family. A family I didn't have growing up in foster care and with foster parents."
- "I grieved so hard when my dad died. They were there. They didn't treat me like I was fragile. They didn't fix it for me. They held me though."

- "My rage was allowed. I wasn't kicked out because I yelled. I didn't have to get arrested. That is a lot as a Black man."
- "I was happy as soon as I walked into our meetings, office, or room. Even if I know we were gonna talk about some deep stuff or people were having an issue that needed to be cleared up, it was the best part of my day and life. The time I spent with you all, it was a gift, an incredible gift being loved for who I am."
- "I never ever have been a part of a group of people that are from around my way, sort of look like me, and I wasn't being made fun of or judged. That is life changing. No individual therapy has ever done that for me so deeply. A therapist like you is one thing; a whole group of people who could easily take you out . . . them loving you is an entirely different healing energy. My whole lineage needed this."
- "The time spent with them has given me love, vulnerability, awareness of self, awareness of the world around me and how it operates, truth, growth, accountability, and so much more. I have also learned to be more honest with myself."
- "I learned to tolerate myself, then like myself, then eventually start to love myself."

For me, these qualitative comments are worth more than any study or z score. These are individuals who bring to life and humanize the work conveyed in the rest of this book. Healing does not happen in isolation.

Judith Herman stated that "Recovery can only take place within the context of relationships; it cannot occur in isolation." This can translate in a sociopolitical frame to our relationships being our politics. It's essential to allow ourselves to see love, vulnerability, and the possibility of trust as part of a decolonial frame. Choosing to engage in trust, after centuries of ancestral gaslighting and deep harm takes courage. Who and what do we regard as worthy of care, of love? The land? Animals? Students? Participants of therapy? Again, the personal is political and essential to our health.

Who Heals the Healers?

As mentioned prior, part of the emo–decolonial journey is the awareness and acknowledgment that we are still firmly embedded within the MHIC as practitioners, whether or not we are in private, institutional, in-home, school, nonprofit, or group practice. When making this statement in workshops, an energy of defensiveness, and then for some sadness, arises in a large wave. There is a loss in realizing that the systems, structures, governments, and/or theories that we have deeply believed in and pledged our lives and energy toward may not have been the treatment we hoped for as it pertains to mental and emotional health. There is a deep loss in truly recognizing that the mental and behavioral health care systems are incapable of creating and maintaining systems of health for our clients.

Furthermore, they are incapable of supporting the health and mental well-being of practitioners as well. There are layers to the process of acceptance. MHPs are immersed, whether we admit it or not, in colluding with all forms of supremacy. This is difficult to swallow. For practitioners who have long understood this, a disconnection and numbing often arises—a metaphorical shrug indicating "Doing the best I can, at least I am not THEM." The dividing, finger-pointing, and minimizing of one's own role continue to affect MHPs emotional health and professional healing work. The difficult truth is that the mental health fields are at best helpful and healing for those who have the intellectual[32] and financial capacity to consistently receive healing informed, culturally relevant, trauma conscious, intersectional, and nonexploitative support. Yet, what about everyone else? What about migrant mothers, Indigenous grandmothers, trans women reporting assault,

---

32 Intellect, like many things, is a social construct that is often used to determine who gets access (and how) based on how intelligent one might be labeled by those around them. This is an ableist practice, and therapy is often guilty of that same ableism. Therapy requires a certain degree of long-term focus and dedication even outside of the sessions in which we see the people we work with, and this can be a struggle for various neurodivergent and disabled people once they leave the one-hour blocks we have with them. Thus, access relating to someone's intellectual capacity becomes another level of our practices that we need to reexamine and get creative with alongside folks we work with. Ensuring they have the support they need outside of session as well. See the glossary entry on "Intelligence" for more.

and physically disabled veterans? What about caregivers living paycheck to paycheck who become quite ill? What about an older sibling managing their younger sibling's emotional and mental health crises? What about our domestic workers? Again, the pulse on the efficacy of mental health is at best measured by the ruler of class. If you cannot afford a "solid therapist," the likelihood is that your great intern or social worker may not be there when you return to the office.

> **ANONYMOUS COMMENTS FROM MHPs IN THE FIELDS OF SOCIAL WORK, COUNSELING, PSYCHOLOGY, AND PSYCHIATRY: NO ONE IS GOING TO SAVE US, BUT US.**
> - "I have 89 clients ('cases') I am to see. Weekly, monthly—there is no stipulation, but can you imagine attempting to see, support, uplift, hold space for, while managing and providing wraparound services for this many individuals. I started eating lunch with my 1 p.m. client. I could not hold my hunger anymore. The client said to me last week, 'Doc, I think we should stop seeing each other; you seem overwhelmed, man.' The coldest part is that he is so correct. I cried for 10 minutes straight afterward. I had to pull it together for my next client."
> - "I am three years into the field and I am working towards leaving. It is exhausting. Thousands of dollars on loans, and I am so irritated daily. What am I doing wrong? How do people give and give for years without proper support, salary, or mental wellness days? I asked for three days off due to the death of my aunt, and my supervisor said, 'If you don't show up, your aunt may not be the only one dead.' I cried and cried and cried, and finally showed up for the kids I work with, not my crappy boss."
> - "The availability of mental health care in our country needs a total reevaluation, with available, sustainable, accessible, universal care for all! Social workers provide the majority of mental health services in our country. We should be present in all schools, coordination services for our most vulnerable children and families, and our salaries wherever we work should reflect our arduous training, academically and in the field."
> - "I was so burned out at my last job that I violated the Ethical Standard of Dignity and Worth of the person. I feel so ashamed, I don't even know

why I am sharing this here. I lost my job because of it and was reprimanded by my school. I am committed to learning self-care skills and actually using them. I guess this is a warning to all therapists what can happen if you are severely burned out."
- "I left the field two years ago. I miss the youth I worked with. I miss the stories, the mutual growth. I miss feeling useful in this world. After leaving, I was depressed for a year; maybe I still am. I could barely clean my apartment or care for myself. I could not understand why! I thought I would be traveling and dating; instead I was dealing with years of burnout. The worst part is that other professionals make you feel badly about yourself; like it's your fault for being so good at your job, and so burned out. It is so sick, all of it."
- "I had a heart attack in my office in between my clients. It is not their fault. I thought it was my fault. I changed my diet, worked out more. Went back to work, had panic attacks now in between clients. My supervisor told me 'You need more rest, are you sleeping, seeing a therapist of your own?' No self-care is gonna fix my heart and my anxiety and my nervous system. This system is messed up, and it is killing Black and Brown social workers and therapists fast. Maybe that's the plan."

MHPs are riddled with burnout. Burnout can impair a MHP's ability to fulfill their ethical responsibility to their therapy participants, affects their emotional and physical health, and is characterized by emotional exhaustion, depersonalization, and reduced personal feelings of joy. Burnout creates difficulties thinking clearly and disconnection with colleagues and other MHPs. Practitioners experiencing burnout can be less attuned and less sensitive to themselves and others. Working within the MHIC places MHPs firmly in a capitalistic field, dealing with *Capitalism Fatigue*, attempting to do more with little. This further intensifies the gaslighting and emotional violence that MHPs experience working within the fields. This vicious cycle perpetuates itself through us all and leads to this kind of exhaustion and disconnection.

Any individual taking the full brunt of that load will experience deep fatigue and become unwell. The burdens of capitalism, poverty, racial trauma, ancestral trauma, etc. cannot be just on the shoulders of practitioners. MHPs are the only solution offered to people in crisis brought on by the very thing that is simultaneously burning out practitioners and participants. As I have stated prior, colonialism is cunning and purposeful—it wants us to be so weighed down by the burdens it puts on us, so that we can't raise our heads to look at the true cause of that weight. This is why having another person raise our chin up when we are feeling down is the medicine. Healing happens in community. Disconnection and suffering in isolation is the opposite of healing, ensuring that the participants trying to help others have resources for their own mental health or well-being is essential. This is why this work needs to evolve and transform.

We may instinctively realize that therapeutic work is "grueling and demanding" with "moderate depression, mild anxiety, emotional exhaustion, and disrupted relationships" as some of its frequent, yet common, effects (Norcross, 2000). Many MHPs have become numb to some of the key areas promoting burnout such as "inadequate supervision and mentorship, glamorized expectations . . . and acute performance anxiety" (Skovholt, Grier, & Hanson, 2001). Yet, as MHPs, we may not provide adequate attention to the long-term effects of burnout until suddenly everything seems overwhelming and has to stop. Ironically, researchers (MHIC) have found it useful to create and name syndromes—specifically compassion fatigue, vicarious trauma, and secondary traumatic stress, even imposter syndrome—to vaguely nod to the inherent problems within the field, while predominantly pointing to the practitioner's practices or lack of self-care as the culprit behind burnout.

> **IDEA**
>
> - What would it be like to have a group or team of consistent individuals supporting a person? What if these pods included a MHP, peer support, holistic support, spiritual support, somatic support, and, if needed, psychiatric support or plant medicine supervised support, case management support, and artistic support?
> - What if "teamwork really does help make the dreamwork work"? What if

> what we need is right there the whole time, which is an active case management wraparound services team approach for each person?
> - What if the next collective global action (across all systems and professions) IS to advocate for more politicized, decolonial healing, and engaged emotional support? Everywhere. Every government office, every classroom (not just one MHP per school), in every transportation hub, in every tourist attraction, in every astronomy classroom?

This model also acknowledges the reality that people have diverse needs—that the solution for one person may not necessarily help another, and therefore, multidisciplinary approaches and modalities are needed to accommodate and nourish the complexity of human experience.

MHPs, in the truest sense, are alone—we are the givers. If you identify as a woman of color, the chances of you giving in many other areas of your life is sky-high. Who heals the healer? Who takes care of the caretaker? How do we begin to engage in vulnerability as a person, when we are taught how to emotionally zip it up, push it down, and are generally never encouraged to work through our own caretaker intergenerational patterns?[33] Many times people equate making more money with less burnout, but the reality is that burnout is an expression of capitalism and colonization. It is what occurs when the body and mind is emotionally exhausted and pushed beyond capacity. Burnout is not "normal"; it is indeed violent.

Koeske and Koeske (1989) found that in addition to demanding workloads, one of the causes for burnout was low social support, particularly low coworker support. Research that identifies self-care as the antidote to burnout and notes that "adjustments in self-care are needed" are problematic and violent toward MHPs. No amount of vacation, spa, rest, singing, or regulating assisted my body after returning to "the trenches." My colleagues and I would (sadly) ask how one felt after returning from vacation. The vacationer would state, "Great, refreshed. Feeling ready!" Sarcastically and sadly the

---

[33] It is important to note that these patterns exist as a survival mechanism. Feel free to check out Chapters 5 and 6 for more on intergenerational trauma patterns.

non-vacationer who'd "held down the fort" would state, "Let's check back in and see if that lasts by tomorrow!" With a laugh and saunter away, the truth was enraging and disheartening. Nothing is wrong with you for loving the good work you try to do AND feeling disgusted and enraged by it.

The invitation to emo–decolonial work is to acknowledge the deep grief and rage, as we discussed in Chapter 10, and how this shows up for *practitioners*, not just participants of therapy. All practitioners, moving forward, would benefit from having an in-depth awareness of how gaslighting is present in our practices, where we collude, and how it impacts our practices. Practitioners have been and continue to be deceived by the mental, medical, educational, and behavioral health fields. This deception will desire to be processed. It is healthy to experience a range of feelings from denial, bargaining (yes, Kübler-Ross's Stages of Grief are appropriate here), rage, confusion, and grief to name a few.

For years, I assumed if I received "enough" training, more "cutting-edge" therapeutic intervention certificates, ticked off more competencies, obtained my license, joined a different therapist support circle, organized "better, more" on the side, and just "did things differently" in my sphere of influence, then it would be "enough." For a year or two, the guilt and gnawing nausea would be assuaged. I would speak to other practitioners, and close friends who reminded me of the many, many people I was helping. This is certain. I am grateful for a profession that for many years allowed me to utilize what I innately do best, to hold a sturdy, nonjudgmental, conscious container for really big difficult experiences of hideous trauma, to facilitate healing-oriented therapeutic groups with joy, and to support people during intense crises.

What increased with every training, certificate, technique, competency, circle, and organizing meeting was the sense that MHPs as a whole were conveniently leaving themselves out of the gatekeeper[34] role and conversa-

---

34 Gatekeeping: We recognize that persons who work in institutions often function as gatekeepers who ensure that the institution perpetuates itself. Gatekeepers who operate with anti-racist values and who maintain an accountable relationship with the community can help to generate institutional transformation rather than perpetuate an unjust status quo (The People's Institute for Survival and Beyond, n.d.).

tion, and often out of the cross-movement building. Yes, we are so busy being "good at crisis," and handling the emotional health of hundreds of people (all valid and vicariously intense) that we never stopped to look down the river and ask, "Why on earth are there so many babies in the water?" Why are our children drowning? Why is mental health plummeting?

A study in the January 2022 issue of *Child and Adolescent Psychiatric Clinics of North America* found that, overall, 21.8% of U.S. children ages three to 17 have been assessed for one or more health conditions (Bethell et al., 2022, as cited in Kempler & Benham, 2022). The study notes that the sheer prevalence of mental health problems across the United States for children ranged from about 15 to 60%, and that the risk increased with the particular type of adverse childhood experience (social, relational, or both). Children had been exposed to many hardships and adverse childhood experiences (ACEs), such as food scarcity and racism, as well as conflict with caregivers due to the caregiver's mental health or aggression toward the child (Kempler & Benham, 2022). The study coauthor, Dr. Tamar Mendelson, Bloomberg Professor of American Health in the Bloomberg School's Department of Mental Health contended:

> There is a mental, emotional, and behavioral health crisis for children in our country . . . we need to address the structural and systemic issues that threaten young people's well-being; at the same time, there is a lot we can be doing to decrease risk factors for families.

The call to action, to politicize, to decolonize is vital. Our children need us. We need each other. We need to be better role models, and activate the knowledge we have to do better. What will we do about it, not individually but collectively, cross-sectionally, multiculturally, and multigenerationally?

Repetition and Themes Intergenerationally

Patterns showing up across and within families, communities, countries, and cultures are common. Intergenerational trauma transmission methods, both direct and indirect, play a large role in this process. We see this from an Indigenous lens in the ancestors living with the effects of specific ailments, ghosts, or medicines over the course of seven generations. It is helpful to also consider what questions or themes may assist the individual in highlighting various beliefs, relationships, histories, and such.

These questions are intended to provoke general reflections, and can be an excellent precursor in service of the SSTTs we will be discussing.

Some questions to consider:

- Are there themes of trauma in your life that you see in previous generations?
- Are there any beliefs that have been carried from generation to generation?
- Have any political events coincided with events that have impacted your life/your culture/your family/any salient identities?
- Are there any themes related to emotional and mental health that you would like to include (it's important to note that it is often common for people to leave out big emotions like struggles accessing or healthily engaging with grief, rage, anxiety, and mental health diagnoses)?
- Do you notice any correlations between your struggles and _____ (parent/caregiver/uncle etc.)?
- How does your relationship to _____ (i.e., alcohol, binging, self-harming, fighting, dating, grief, etc.) show up in the timeline?
- Who or what stories were omitted, and why?
- What have you learned about your own story? Your own parts?
- What aspects of you are still deeply suffering?
- What aspects of you feel present, somatically resilient, and certain?
- Where do you feel separate from yourself, inaccessible, or lacking access from parts of the world?
- Are there any places where you might be blocking access to others in the world? Consciously or not.
- Are there spaces where you are avoiding your joy/purpose/intuition? What reasons are arising?

It is important to note that there is privilege when it comes to individual insight-oriented therapy, especially compared to our grandparents' generation whose primary concern was very likely keeping the family together, placing food on the table, escaping persecution, and finding solid work. However, these are entirely different times.

It is to be understood that decolonial work may bring up elements of resistance and tension in organizations, health care agencies, and practices. This is to be expected, and welcome. Resistance is not "bad or good." (Down with binaries!) Resistance lets us know that we are struggling up against parts of ourselves, and others, that are calling out for us to change, readjust our view, or acknowledge what feels impossible.

We cannot decolonize organizations, structures, and systems that are inherently violent. Racism is rampant. Thousands of diversity, equity, and inclusion and anti-racism educators globally work tirelessly with managers, directors, HR staff, employees, deans, residents and others to create more equity. To provide education about how implicit bias and racism affect people. Whether we call white people fighting for liberation accomplices, allies, or note that folks have privilege or that they are "advantaged"—regardless it is important . . . needed. This recognition is often a really solid start for schools, organizations, practices, hospitals, and businesses that are oblivious to discrimination, prejudice, and anti-Black racism.

Yet what has always concerned me is the harm for so many Indigenous, Black, and Brown racialized (IBBR) people sitting "at work" while also exposed to the microaggressions in the unconscious comments of their white or white-passing colleagues and, sometimes, bosses.

How infuriating that it is mostly IBBR people who continue to organize, advocate, activate, and essentially die of exhaustion as well as deal with violence impacting their mental and emotional health. How infuriating that many "allies" get to say "I don't have time for this," or "This is too much," or just disappear. It is confusing to see signatures on emails with #fightingracism or #decolonialwarrior or #blacklivesmatter when in actuality it is a farce, another form of gaslighting, and one that leads to so much racial trauma and internalized deep hatred.

During the summer of 2020, amid the pandemic, amid Black lynchings and the public murders of George Floyd, Breonna Taylor, Ahmaud Arbery, many Black people's nervous systems went into overdrive. It was of course witnessing, publicly, a murder of another human, but it was also the bodily, somatic memory of what some of our ancestors had experienced publicly.

It was the realization that we still aren't safe: not in public, in our bed, or jogging, minding our business. A reminder that we are only hired, highlighted, and wanted when our pain and intergenerational suffering is on display. A reminder that we have to say yes to as many jobs, interviews, presentations, events, and white people as possible because we do not know when we will get this attention and support again. A reminder that a lot of loved ones who walk in the world as white weren't really listening prior, because during the summer of 2020, suddenly everyone was crying, donating, sharing articles, studying, and joining groups. It was fear, not just performative. I felt the fear and ancestral guilt. I felt empathy and rage. I felt grief and isolation. I have no doubt Asian kin and First Nations Canadian kin felt the same as the violence and the pandemic literally excavated the shadow collectively. Skeletons were coming and continue to come out of every closet.

This is why *Decolonizing Therapy* invites us to engage in inquiry in the four arenas:

> Ancestral (Historical/Land)
> Community/Collective (Political)
> Family (Intergenerational)
> Individual (Self-Awareness)

We are deeply interconnected, but the root holds the medicine. The roots hold experience, wisdom, and literal embodied (in our telomeres and DNA) possibility for change—for evolution. I think we desire an embodied evolution, that allows mental health to extend beyond pathology and treatment into active healing—a revitalization and resurrection with a dose of restitution.

Healing can serve and inform social change. Mental and emotional health fields are part of this process.

The invitation is for practitioners to:

1. Work on oneself—not just in traditional talk therapy. This includes working on our prejudices: anti-blackness, anti-fatness, internalized ableism, perfectionism, xenophobia, and so forth.
2. Grow and get uncomfortable in the community. Attend multigenerational gatherings with various ages, identities, bodies, abilities, and cultures but sharing a common focus often work best.
3. Engage in advocacy, activism, and support work where you are the learner and listener. Not the martyr and academic or teacher. Join a grassroots organization without doing harm.

Why We Must Politicize Our Practices

A professor in my graduate program pulled me aside one weekend after class. He said to me, "Jennifer. You are good at what you do. This comes easy to you. But don't let the field take away the richness of your life." Years later, a supervisor in partial care commented as we wrapped up supervision, "What is your joy outside of working with trauma? Because you'll need that always to survive this field. When we are solid at what we do, no boundary is enough." Years later, a holistic practitioner noted to me as I sat there exhausted, sad, irritable and stated, "Do you know what happens when too much milk is removed from cows?" I shook my head no. "They express blood Jennifer, blood. That's where you are."

We are not martyrs. We are not "sin-eaters." We are not cows. We are not mammies. We are not victims. We are not perpetrators. Fellow colonized therapists, we are products of our environment. So, the invitation is to **politicize. To galvanize. To be part of the evolutionary process of change** and **transformation.** That we, as MHPs, **alchemize** our pain, overwhelm, burnout, discontent, secondary and vicarious trauma experiences, and our rage to shift our practices. To get reeducated, to unpack our own histories, to be conscious of our privilege, to get honest about how the fields have dehumanized us all. To get honest about how our beloved fields have euthanized our deeply empathic energies and emotions, asking us to be a blank, distant, neutral slate always. We have become weapons of the licensing boards, our graduate programs, our mental and medical health industrial complex. Politicizing our practice is an invitation to create personal, systemic, and global change in mental and behavioral health, and to invite the uninvited voices to the table. We do not have the answers alone.

We are all needed. Yet could we imagine a new capacity? A new frame, a new form of exchange and consistent, accessible care. There is a need for MHPs and emotional care workers who carry strengths in identifying the desire for harm of self and others. There is a need for emotional care workers who have strengths in transformational and healing-justice circles to assist with conflict and serious harm. There is a need for emotional care workers who have specialties in supporting people through sexual harm, substance abuse, identity, ancestry, grief, rage, the soma, nervous system regulation, and ecological trauma. Peer support is also deeply necessary. Coaching and further deepening into any one or more of these areas are necessary. Surface psycho-educational educators on social media providing weaving consciousness, evolution, poetry, and the universality of human emotional suffering are needed. Community crisis emotional support teams are needed. Social work that is actually socially conscious, and responds to contemporary challenges is essential.

We are a global people born of abuse.

We have been abused by systems, structures, and corrupt governments. Research tells us that abused children have an innate belief that love can coexist with abuse. This is where MHPs are at this time in history. Many practitioners are still deeply hoping that something will magically change (again with magical thinking), without really changing our practices or ourselves. An elevation in psychological, social, psychiatric consciousness is among us, whether we feel good about it or not.

Thousands of therapy providers (i.e., social workers, counselors, marriage and family therapists, psychologists, psychiatrists) are shifting into coaching with the hope of having more autonomy, making more money, and having more space "to do good work." Yet, this still does not assist or include those who are the working poor, or who are drowning in systemic poverty. This does not include or provide solid emotional health care to so many people. Although the mass exodus out of therapy practices and institutions frees practitioners momentarily, it still continues to feed capitalism and leave thousands if not millions of people emotionally starving. The system is set up in a way that causes therapists with the privilege of choice to believe that the only way they can create a practice that supports their own well-being is by excluding the people who need help the most. This is the artifice of self-care under capitalism—somehow the most vulnerable are always the ones to pay the price.

Some practitioners genuinely do not feel exploited, and do not believe they have anything to grieve. Others believe that more culturally competent interventions will help. Others believe one field or another within mental health has the answer. Others believe smashing the *DSM* and removing pathology and the medical model from within our work will be the answer. Others believe that improvements to their one-to-one practices will be the answer. Others believe in burning it all down, in having no therapy at all, and that community care is the answer. Others believe that ceremonial circles and healing focused engagement is the answer.

What is clear is that there is no singular one answer. Practitioners require more collectives, more processing, more brainstorming. Yet there is vast knowledge among us to recreate new ways of helping, supporting, ensuring people are kept safe. Yet the current structures and industrial complexes are made to make money while treating the infection, not healing the soul wound.

Decolonizing therapy engages in psychopolitical reeducation, collective building, and ancestral elevation work in order to begin to change the narratives around what is therapy. What is truly decolonial, and quite political, is knowing that there will always be an evolution of our fields, and that the decolonial process is a journey that is deeply intertwined with our therapy participants, the decimation of other systems, and people globally of all identities being WELL.

As a psychotherapist, I recognized the ways in which mental health oppression, and the larger net of ableism was foundational to colonialism, white supremacy, gendered oppression, capitalism, imperialism, and to all forms of oppression. I understood and heard other psychotherapists acknowledge how mental, emotional, and disability "issues" were also Indigenous sovereignty issues, immigration issues, trans and nonbinary justice issues, police brutality issues, etc. That is what white supremacy and oppression does. It creates an aura of gaslighting and confusion.

For MHPs, the violence is further exacerbated by the deeply emotional nature of our craft. Therapy is an art. There is personality, technique, communication skills, container styles, years of experience, types of experience, prior supervisors, theoretical conceptualizations, identity, culture, belief systems, practice configurations, and emotional factors, just to name a few. I have sought ways of combating disconnection and isolation to allow people to find healing and communal connection. Communal connection may look different for everyone.

Cocreating New Timelines

We cannot be pioneers of change on this planet if we feel completely comfortable in the level of consciousness and types of practices that already exist around us.

In many Indigenous cultures globally, traditional storytelling is a significant way of expressing Indigenous knowledge, culture, and oral traditions. Traditional storytelling provides holistic interconnectedness, collaboration, reciprocity, spirituality, and humility; more importantly, it impacts positively on the community. Oral traditions are the backbone of Indigenous knowledge transfer, and storytelling is the method by which much is shared. **Storytelling serves to connect individuals and communities to their place and time, as well as to one another.** Stories are also used to teach history, cultural etiquette, and spiritual beliefs. Additionally, I have heard elders speak about the healing nature of storytelling in terms of what it provides: stories of resilience, strength, and strategy; it educates and draws in younger generations; it is a symbol of survival, as many Indigenous people's practices have faced attempted extermination or been forced into deep hiding, as we have seen in Santeria, mysticism, occultism, Theosophical Society, modern astrology, neo-paganism, and the New Age movements, which would be known as syncretism.

On the psychological, theoretical side, narrative therapy supports storytelling and notes that it allows people to not only find their voice, but to use their voice for good, helping them to become experts in their own lives and to live in a way that reflects their goals and values (Rivera, 2020). Additionally, it can allow for participants of therapy to adjust their lens and speak of their experiences in the third person or the first. It allows space to tell alternative stories about their lives, so they better match who and what they want to be, leading to positive change. Narrative therapy is nonpathologizing, nonblaming, and sees participants as experts on their own.

A family systems perspective views "family members as inextricably intertwined in their lives and in death, and views all family members of society as ultimately interconnected" (McGoldrick et al., 2008). Family are those who are tied together through common legal, biological, cultural, emotional, physical, spiritual, and social history. The fabric of families are interrelated, interdependent, interwoven, where changes in one part of the system leads to change in another. Family interactions, relationships, and stories tend to be "repetitive, reciprocal, and patterned" (McGoldrick et al., 2008). Families repeat themselves. Although the behavior and personality may shapeshift and transform, often, yet not always, similar themes will recycle unconsciously from one generation to the next. Bowen, Brave Heart, Danieli, DeGruy, Duran, and other scholars, practitioners, researchers, and healers call this intergenerational or multigenerational trauma, as we discussed at length in Chapter 6.

Recently, I discovered that SSTTs are used in a myriad of ways in order to look at themes in individuals' lives and families—themes such as substance abuse, intimate partner violence, family roles, and so forth. However, when beginning SSTTs with my former clients, the process was clinically intuitive, not taught. Below is an explanation of the ways in which the timeline addresses places of hope, and people of hope and support, as well as instances of hurt, pain, and struggle, including historical experiences. The SSTT is an intergenerational framework for understanding personal, familial, political, global, and ancestral themes. It can focus on intergenerational patterns, experiences of cultural violence or attempted genocide, attachment, legacies, migration patterns, familial events interweaving with global political events and tragedies, as well as patterns and themes of emotional, physical, spiritual, and ancestral health. It can be utilized by any of us. The

SSTT focuses on historical patterns within the family system, including chosen family, and how this may impact, impair, or bring clarity to their present-day experiences.

The timeline practice can be utilized with anyone, anywhere, although it is ideal to be utilized in conjunction with insight-oriented support, having emotional resources, a community or group format, and access to coping mechanisms. This would allow for relief should the material discovered elicit an emotional reaction. Please see our Resources section for a timeline example!

In the interest of bringing people to wellness, and meeting practitioners and participants where they are now, the SSTT can begin to allow us to conceptualize "What else is possible?" We can begin to imagine creating new ways of relating to individuals, families, and collectives seeking support. The SSTT invites us to coinvestigate themes and areas of consistent confusion and frustration, in a disarming manner: with timeline art. It centers the healing benefits of writing, art, making meaning of memory, finding sociocultural material, global connections to our lives, cocreation, and coworking with another.

The SSTT can also be utilized with organizations, community grassroots groups, extended family, relationships, etc. It is a tool for thematic expansion that allows us to notice how and why our present-day emotional material may be activated and exacerbated. I like to think that it highlights our triggers and our tools.

The timeline can also identify forms of abuse (i.e., economic, political, mental, emotional, sexual, and physical); microaggressions; threats; abuse of elders, land, resources, and children; abuse of privilege (i.e., light-skinned, male, cisgender, white, able-bodied, etc.); migration patterns; spiritual and religious beliefs; practices; caretaking roles; medical history; education; experiences with law enforcement; political activism; and even emotional patterns (i.e., fear, being silenced, isolation, self-injury, avoidance, rage, grief, expressions of anxiety, depression and hyperactivity, insomnia, etc.).

The following sections cover quick insights and inquiries for various practitioners who are still immersed in structures and systems, while attempting to maintain a politicized and historically conscientious framework. It is my hope that some of these inquiries become second nature and eventually are inconsequential, because they are so embedded in our fields.

These are organized individually, collectively, and historically for ease—however they can and often do overlap.

Organizational Shifts in Real Time
Here's a framework for MHPs when working with individuals, families, and communities that may help them conceptualize how historical trauma may show up in the present-day.

INDIVIDUAL
- How has this child/adolescent/caregiver/person/couple/family been impacted (from a exo-systemic lens) by colonization and/or (attempted) cultural genocide?
- Is there possible historical trauma in this child/caregiver/person/family's life?
- Is there unresolved grief and/or rage affecting their well-being?
- What themes are present in this person's life that have impacted their ancestors? Have these themes evolved, expanded, or contracted?

COLLECTIVE
- How has historical trauma affected their relationships?
- How has historical trauma affected how they see themselves (i.e., worthlessness, vacant esteem, etc.)?
- How has it affected how they have been parented, and/or parent?
- Where does white-bodied supremacy and oppression show up in how they (unconsciously) engage with children?

HISTORICAL
- What did our elders and ancestors KNOW that we may have forgotten?
- Where is there resilience and strength in the individual, community, and system?
- Will learning/talking more about their history and forms of collective trauma and triumphs strengthen them?
- Will it lessen over-responsibility, guilt, and shame?

Taking Steps Toward Liberation

QUESTIONS TO ASK

- Who is teaching us?
- Who do we accept education from?
- What are we learning?
- What techniques are really client-centered?
- What techniques are imbued with healing, rather than dependency on the MHIC?

STEPS TO TAKE

- Allow accountability.
- Compassion . . . compassion.
- Center action around people with least access.
- Be willing to learn from organizations based in the community, as much as academics.
- Create NETS that WORK. (The People's Institute for Survival and Beyond, personal communication, 2012)
- Learn about your People's history.
- Ask for help.
- Be honest about what you are not willing to risk, such as your privilege, and why . . . with one's self first.

Question Everything

- Who is your practice NOT trauma-informed for?
- What does actively being trauma informed look like in this moment?
- How does late-stage capitalism affect your practice, well-being, and relationships?
- How does society reinforce messages that amplify our psychological distress?
- How can we heal in an environment without feeling like WE are wrong?
- Whose voice, perspective, and opinion am I not really listening to? Why?

Unlearn
- Move away from pathologizing.
- Practice energetic boundaries, not just physical and emotional ones.
- Honor righteous rage *within mental health.*
- Question professionalism.
- Hold more spaces for queerness, especially nonbinary and trans folks.
- Bring all of your own identities into the room when appropriate.
- Chew on the difference between therapy and healing.
- Learn your history and the history of the land you are occupying.
- Understand how environmental factors, such as racism, sexism, fatphobia, classism, ableism, etc. affect a person's emotional health—and their coins!
- Be aware that therapists were trained under white supremacy (consciously or not).
- Be aware that as professionals, healers, and helpers we have an obligation and the propensity to unlearn these ways.

Steps to Take in the Community

five · love languages
reclaiming as a love language.
unlearning as a love language.
reparations as a love language.
accountability as a love language.
decolonization as a love language.
 —Jacquelyn Ogorchukwu (2021, October 13) *Instagram*

I do not want to be fixed. I want to change the world. I want to be alive, awake, grieving, and full of joy. And I am.
 —Leah Lakshmi Piepzna-Samarasinha, Care Work: Dreaming Disability Justice (2019)

What if instead of guilting yourself for not working hard enough on your creative projects, you ask yourself: What would make this so

> *exciting and compelling that I can't wait to play and create and build on these ideas?*
> —Yumi Sakugawa (2021, May 14) *Instagram*

I could write an entire separate book on cross-movement building in alignment with disability justice. There is so much to say about the intersections between disability justice, educational systems, healing in emotional health, the carceral system, and mutual aid. For the purposes of this book, the list titled "Acts of Resistance" provides essential pieces to the evolution for the revolution within emotional and mental health care, and supports and is vital to the emo–decolonial process. Together.

Resist
We can resist daily. Resistance is often seen as such a "dirty word," but truly we can resist in a multitude of ways. From deciding how to view and engage with unhoused people in our community to engaging with other parents, caregivers, and loved ones who may be exhausted with more compassion. We can resist "grind" culture, and the need to "be perfect and have it all under control." We can resist structurally by choosing NOT to just teach the *DSM*, or focus on its updates and additions as "adequate change." We can resist over pathologizing angry, scared, and anxious children and have conversations about the contexts in which they are living and how this is impacting their ability to regulate their big feelings; rather than provide a "case example." Sometimes slowing down is resisting. **At other times vulnerability in highly intellectual spaces is resisting.** Disagreeing can be a form of resistance. Compassion with another's shadow can be resistance.

> **ACTS OF RESISTANCE: WAYS PRACTITIONERS CAN OPPOSE THE MHIC[35]**
> - Acknowledge the sociodemographic, social, political, and health factors that are known to be risk factors for certain mental health problems.

---

[35] Inspired by the literature review titled *The Impact of Spirituality and Mental Health* by Dr. Deborah Cornah.

- Ensure that the methodologies employed are those most appropriate to answer the questions being addressed.
- Consider not creating theories, methods, or skill sharing without the consent and lead guidance of original descendants of the practice.
- Include community members who are often the service users, wherever possible, in the design, conduct, and analysis of research projects.
- Consider using spiritual or religious activity as an outcome measure and to explore the impact of mental health on different expressions of spirituality.
- Be sufficiently designed to identify factors that are exclusive to spiritual or religious activity and how they relate to other dimensions of being human (emotional, psychological, social, intellectual).
- Take into account the range of demographic variables that could moderate or mediate the relationship between spirituality and mental health.
- Develop measures of religion and spirituality that cut across a range of religious traditions without robbing those traditions of their distinctive and substantive characteristics.
- Explore the impact and effectiveness of the "healing" dimensions of different spiritual activities.
- Define and clarify for consumers and practitioners the differences between treatment and healing.
- Identify the role of the soul wound or soul loss within the context of healing and intergenerational trauma transmission.

Cocreating New Pathways

> *We often tell people that they have imposter syndrome when people are correctly identifying: "Oh, I don't belong here." The system is not built for them. And that's correct. There is some fundamental sense in which you do not belong.*
> —Chanda Prescod-Weinstein in Neel Dhanesha's (2022) article "A Physicist's Lessons About Race, Power, and the Universe" for *Vox*

So much of our world and existence is organized around the frameworks put in place by a few white men. Designed to consolidate their power and forced upon us without our consent. It's no wonder many of us get the message that we're not meant to be centered. We feel it in our bodies. We fully understand that we're meant to stand on the sidelines. Not taking space. But we do not have to stop existing or codreaming.

There are other ways to be. We don't need to exist in their spaces, with their rules, with their structures and guidelines. New spaces require more inclusion, accessibility, emotional evolution, rest, collective-directed-by-those-most-affected action, and safety that is transformative and abolitionist in response. Chanda Prescod-Weinstein noted that the gaslighting that many people experience when assessing that they *do not feel safe or belong* suggests that one's capacity for analysis is working, and notes it's a sign of competency to identify that. This de-centers a deficit model, and helps individuals to not feel so alone and absurd in their line of thinking.

(Re)Education is essential. People tend to mobilize and take accountability when they are informed. This includes information around one's history, ancestry, harm, emotional and mental health, healthy expressions of emotional harm, community building, activism, ancestral and holistic healing, and politics among others.

Prevention is essential. People globally desire, and need more accessible emotional and mental health. If systems and policies won't provide what is needed, people-power must create and establish this. This is where you readers/practitioners come in.

Intervention is essential. There need to be people, practitioners, spaces, and ways of engaging that allow safe intervention when harm is occurring. This includes mental and emotional health, harm to self or others, situational violence, systemic and structural state-sanctioned violence, as well as racial, gender-based violence, among others.

Radical and healing-based responding is essential. We are taught to react, not respond. Responding to a crisis is entirely different than reacting to it. Responses ideally would be radical, in that they are grounded in politicized collective people-power, trauma-harm conscious theory, and have a strong focus on decolonial healing. People who have lived through and survived harm require support, consistently and long-term. There also need to be spaces for people who have been harmed to process, relearn, unlearn, and heal. This may look different depending on the harm.

Politicized and insight-oriented collective accountability is essential. To decolonize is quite different from the action and journey of decolonization. Less metaphor and much more accountable, community-oriented action. Providers of healing need accountability.

This is liberation. Their way isn't the only way, and it can be so freeing to realize that. Whole new worlds open outside of our world structure, and then we begin to **see** each other. We begin to learn from each other, sharing these lives we were living on the margins.

Breathe and Release

Many of our cultures, certainly Western culture, do not provide the space, nor instructions of how to sit with uncomfortable emotions. Big emotions like grief and rage are so healthy. What is deeply necessary is release. May we normalize the experiencing of big emotions, and the releasing. This is an entire encyclopedia on its own. I could write for hours on the importance of big emotions. Chapter 8 focused on the Grief-Rage Axis as expressions of colonial pain and suffering. Part of politicizing ourselves and our work, are allowing the true space and time (very hard under late-stage capitalism) to:

A. Be supported and held in community (or with a teacher and guide),
B. Create space for grief and rage (big emotion) to be experienced. Sadness is normal and healthy!
C. Make time to connect to your body and breathe.
D. Make time for yourself.
E. Receive support as practitioners.

> What conditioned response do we hold that needs to be observed, and cleared in order to allow ourselves to receive and give in healthy reciprocity?
> Who are we ethically obligated to: A licensing board of examiners? Ancestors? Community? Clients? Our culture?

> I had a Post-It note on my computer while working at a residential center and deciding whether I wanted to sit for my licensing exam:
> Boards do not have a monopoly on ethics.
> What are daily small practices that you we can engage in together that reflect the future we desire?
> What obstacles are preventing the collective from thriving? What obstacles are preventing expansive systems from taking root in our current collective gardens?
> What would it look like to share rituals and practices that reflect the future we desire? (Note this is very different from appropriating.)

Planning as a Form of Prevention

I have a not-so-secret aversion to the act of planning, and yet it is exactly what my easily excitable neurodivergent brain and recovering, highly sensitive body requires and thrives in. I used to understand planning as punishment, because that is what it felt like as a child who was frequently told in mean ways to "calm down, slow down, sit down, stop talking," all in one breath. However, through some deep ancestral, spiritual, personal, and group-supported excavations over the years, I discovered that in fact I needed to see how much planning and care I utilized when I created plans of support and preparation with the people I worked with therapeutically. Many of the people I have had the privilege to engage in therapy with over the last 20 years could not afford, literally and figuratively, to think about planning for much of anything. Usually because urgency was chasing them: a sick child to be picked up from school, an expensive car repair, debilitating pain, legal fees, etc. I understand this because I grew up like that: Watching adults barely make ends meet.

I started to create a "Just in Case Shit Pops Off Escape Plan" with people I engaged in therapy with (we literally called it that). Call the plan whatever you like, but based on a person's capacity (mentally, physically, financially, mentally, emotionally, relationally, and energetically) we would create a plan for each of these arenas if possible—meaning they did not enter our therapeutic relationship already in a state of crisis. Part of politicizing ourselves and our work is allowing the space and time to engage in creativity related to our areas of specialization. Use what we have and what we are good at to help make others safe! Here is a very small, condensed list of possibilities:

- During the "getting to know you" period (sometimes within first contact with a family, person, or group) become comfortable talking about their worst case scenarios, what has occurred that could reoccur and may need support, and even what the reality of a situation could be. Then prepare for that, together, or with your team/crew/family/peers.
- Include peer support, politicized abolitionists comrades/compañeros, social workers, healers, folks in their spiritual communities, whoever they cosign as "safe." This list can change at any time and should be updated regularly. Mia Mingus has created magical Pod Mapping Worksheets that are magnificent as resources—I wish I had those years ago! But Venn diagrams on cardboard, paper, or on the computer would do too!
- How would they like things to be handled and who would they like for me to contact if they become ill, are unable to relate to you or others in a safe manner, or if they lose contact with this reality—and for what period of time? Who might they want contacted for specific concerns or care needs? For example, if I was experiencing a break with reality I would want "X" to be called. If I was experiencing a health issue I would want "X" contacted.
- Explicitly ask whether they would be open to the involvement of the police, paramedics, EMTs, spiritual advisors, religious items, family, partners, peer support, psychiatric facilities, and others. When would calling them be appropriate?
- Inquire their interest sooner rather than later regarding group support and peer support.
- Inquire how they would like to be notified if something were to happen to you, or if you could not be reached due to your own personal emergencies.

Dr. Nadine Burke Harris, the first surgeon general of California and author of *The Deepest Well* (2018), wrote in her book that:

The revolution is in the creative application of knowledge to mitigate harm whenever it pops up. Because when you know the mechanism, you can use that understanding in countless ways to drastically improve the human condition. This is how you spark a revolution. You shift the frame, you change the lens, and all at once the world is revealed, and nothing is the same.

Practice is how we transform.

We are the HOW TO. The call to action is that all mental health professionals decide to get vulnerable. Decide to form better relationships. Decide to teach and call one another in. Decide how to do this together.

> **WAYS THAT PRACTITIONERS CAN CREATE SPACES OF DECOLONIAL CREATIVITY AND JOY**
>
> - Love on your human self. Remember that we are not expected to KNOW everything. It is impossible and unhealthy. Honor what you have yet to understand and know, all while getting there with grace.
> - Give yourself a ton of compassion. Once again the process of setting boundaries WHILE maintaining a sense of fluidity for what we have yet to cocreate as a collective is jarring. Especially for those of us who set out with a clear vision of "how we will help people who are in suffering." Keep in mind the emotional–decolonial process is a work in progress within each of us, within the collective global circuit.
> - Allow your mission to be one of love and joy. Setting energetic and emotional boundaries should not mean that we intend to harm others with our boundaries. Instead, it is our role to create more space to daydream, inquire, investigate, wonder, and play.
> - Love ourselves despite what we think we can change and improve!
> - Learn how to be in balance and stand in our power when connecting to others.
> - Rather than fix ourselves, we just need to know ourselves and accept ourselves more.

Recovery from colonization is political. Decolonizing is political.
Recovery from colonization is ancestral. Decolonizing is spiritual and energetic.
Recovery from colonization is emotional. Decolonizing is healing.

Aspects of Emotional–Decolonial Unlearning
1. Part of the emotional–decolonial journey involves being willing to unlearn that which feels comfortable and familiar; relearning stories and histories; being willing not to know everything; slowing down; being willing to initially question everything (internally at first then gently outward); and to slowly (re)build: community, faith in humanity, faith in people-power, etc.
2. Be willing to honor the embodied experiences, as much as the intellectualized perspective.
3. Co-occurring practices of emo–decolonial engagement:

    POLITICAL: Politicizing Your Practice
    SELF/PSYCHE: Emotional Evolution, Including the Body
    COLLECTIVE: Cocreating Decolonial Pathways in Emotional Health
    ANCESTRAL: Communing and Getting to Know Our Ancestry

4. It takes practices to honor the play between political, self, collective, and ancestral emo–decolonial engagement.
5. Therapy has evolved, and we believe it will continue to evolve.
6. The Land has a history, story, and an energy; you are invited to form a relationship to the land you are on—if you have the capacity and privilege, as well as the Land you are from (if you are not already residing on it).
7. All revolutions require first an internal evolution.
8. Practitioners are allowed to have fun in therapeutic spaces.
9. Decolonization is a verb and the emotional has a role in the process.
10. Curiosity is a really spacious place to be!
11. Take your time metabolizing new paradigms and ideas.

12. Peer support supports both participant and practitioner.
13. Group helping/healing work is reflective of collectivistic cultures.
14. Being well can really only happen when embedded in a nest of relationships. We encourage group healing/helping spaces.
15. Practitioners are sick and dying. We will no longer stand for this abuse.
16. Intergenerational patterns/themes as timelines that affect our current life.
17. Storytelling and creating our own stories as healing.
18. Healing can serve and inform social change. Mental and emotional health fields are part of this process.
19. Practitioners MUST continuously process, embody and deal with their own material, and politicize themselves.
20. Mental health oppression, and the larger net of ableism, was and is foundational to colonialism, white supremacy, gendered oppression, capitalism, imperialism, and to all forms of oppression.
21. Consider not creating theories, methods, or skill sharing without the consent and lead guidance of original descendants of the practice.
22. Include community members who are often the service users, wherever possible, in the design, conduct, and analysis of research projects.
23. Engage with joy as much as possible.
24. It is not YOU. You did not cause yourself to get sick. The colonial capitalism spoon fed you the poison.

Emo–Decolonial Practice Offerings
- Part of the journey is the joy and connection of cocreating a healing/wellness/therapeutic map together. Honor that the journey may be unlike anything you have experienced.
- What would it look like to allow your therapeutic participants to change you?
- Invite in storytelling, art, poetry, and dance into the container!
- Build community together. Cocreate together. I have seen this look like student groups, or a Board, or a food drive, or even a small workshop at a local church on emotional health.

- Invite in the therapy participant's support group when appropriate, including extended family; extended family is family.
- Should a person require more support as they are transitioning through a serious experience of pain or harm or emotional pain, consider weaving into the container solid peer support.
- Processing any internal shame around not being "Indian enough. Black enough. Puerto Rican enough . . . because . . ." is a beautiful introduction into the schisms in their world. Allow these conversations to be explored.
- Consider what you might like to bring into helping/healing spaces that you have not already. Why not? What would this feel like to do so? Who can support you in bringing this work in? Who can you consult with?
- Frequently ask yourself or others in this work, "Whose voice or body is not in the room?" Then do something about it.
- When conflict arises in group spaces invite inquiry around what is being absorbed in this space/group that is happening collectively or in the world?
- Invite narrative therapeutic work into spaces. Invite storytelling. Invite learning to trust each other (particularly in group spaces).
- Work from a historical generational wound lens, not just a childhood trauma lens.
- Reestablish a slow and kind relationship to our own physical bodies.
- Create circles and spaces for colonized peoples to begin to reform trusting relationships with one another, one's ancestry, and the Land.
- Make space for fluidity, neoexpansive abilities, and queerness with the self and with nature.
- Find ways to disrupt, organize, paradigm shift, and undo harm.

CONCLUSION

Call to Action

What else is possible?
 The call is to not just loosen the straightjackets, nor just change and alter the types of treatments that MHPs offer to the people we serve, but to look at what deinstitutionalizing and depathologizing mental and behavioral health in and out of therapy rooms would look like.

What else is possible?
 It is a question I frequently ask myself and share with my students. What would feel good or better than X feeling, in this moment? And of course, what connections between science, health, emotional wellness, politics, the body, and the humanity of a person and a situation are we missing?

What else is possible?
 When people ask what we collectively need more of, I usually say art, connection, vulnerability, and a hell of a lot of self-reflection and compassion. People are often surprised at the art aspect of my response. Whether in my peer education group, engaging in psychodrama work, narrative therapy, child and adolescent therapy, rituals related to death, EMDR, tapping (EFT), crisis management, or energy work, no matter what, the practice of creativity was present. I have witnessed more shifts in the spontaneous places in between pain and reconciliation; forgiveness and fear; trauma and resilience within an artistic container.

How could art and peer support; how could culture, ritual, and bookstores; how could rap battles and circles of vulnerability; give people more power over their mental and emotional health? And in turn, the experiences and energetic ancestral power over their histories?

What else is possible?
Frantz Fanon, a psychiatrist and philosopher, was born in Martinique in 1925 under French colonialism. He submitted *Black Skin, White Masks* as his medical thesis at the University of Lyon (Fanon, 1967/1952). It was rejected. Fanon came to see colonial violence as embedded within the institution, the hospital itself, not just the people inside the walls. He too understood that the institution could not help those under colonialism's boot. But he soon gave his patients space to create. To make art. To write. They saw a major decline in psychiatric symptomatology and asylum incarceration.

What else is possible?
Dr. Frederick W. Hickling was a professor emeritus in psychiatry and Executive Director of the Caribbean Institute of Mental Health and Substance Abuse at the University of West Indies at Mona, Jamaica (Gudzer & Walcott, 2021). Dr. Hickling understood that Jamaicans' greatest mental health challenge had been to counter the psychological impact of more than 500 years of European racism and colonial oppression. He strongly saw the correlation between the descendants of African people enslaved in Jamaica and the internal dismantling of colonial structures and policies that incarcerated thousands of Jamaicans in mental asylums. He sought to heal the historical legacy of sustained structural violence that was a potent cause of modern mental illness. Dr. Hickling included psycho-historiographic cultural therapy as a form of intervention and part of his approach to decolonizing and deinstitutionalizing Jamaica's large asylum system. These practices are taught and used today in large group spaces.

What else is possible?
Patients in these and many other hospitals were humanized, seen, and given their own innate possibility and internal power back. Not one of them. Not ten of them. A community of them. It was not a magical phenomenon.

Rather, I believe that Fanon, Hickling, and others realized decolonization is the "meeting of two forces," as Fanon has written. He understood the importance of honoring the historical process, and healing in a dynamic interaction of systems within systems.

What else is possible?

This to me sounds like a call to action. To investigate somatically and ancestrally what has worked, what may need leaving behind, what our elders may have to say, what ritual prescriptions are at our service, what plant medicines have healed for centuries, what healing we may need to slow down and engage in—and how to do it. Can our movements and medicine build in abolition and struggle against multiple forms of social and political division? How can our therapeutic healing have roots in resistance? How can those of us helping to facilitate and guide that healing be rooted in consciousness and anti-oppressive resistance while remaining open and loving and hopeful?

What else is possible?

I share these experiences because there is hope. We can change. Things can be different. And sometimes putting down the constant frenzied crisis energy, to fill our own reservoir, to go downriver to see "why are so many of our children drowning in the water."

What else is possible once we discover some of the historical horrors over the centuries?

We organize, we rest, we wail and weep, we honor our sacred rage, we speak and share, we take turns tending to the fire, we make art, we make love, we dance our asses off, we care for the children, we safely use plant medicines, we chant, we pray, we engage in ritual, we start getting comfortable with being outrageously creative and messy and spectacular. We do it differently. We keep one another safe.

These might be some of the most healing things we can do. Together.

Practitioner Resources

CONTENTS

FOR SUPPORT AS YOU READ THROUGH CHAPTER 8

Plant Allies for Rage and Grief Work From a Mixed Indigenous (Yakama, Irish, and Eastern European) Perspective *by Jacqui Wilkins*   371

Questions to Consider Asking Oneself and People You Support   375

Somatic Soul Trauma Timelines   376

FOR SUPPORT AS YOU READ THROUGH CHAPTER 9

Backpack Exercises   387

FOR SUPPORT AS YOU MOVE FORWARD

10 Energetic Boundary-Setting Techniques and Ways to Restore Them   391

For Support As You Read Through Chapter 8

I have asked Dr. Jacqui to share about plant allies as a remembering and honoring of many of the extremely accessible, natural methods of being WITH our bigger—and sometimes scarier—emotions. Dr. Jacqui's Plant Allies for Rage and Grief work provides space for possibility, and continuing to commune, heal and liberate—along with the land.

Plant Allies for Rage and Grief Work From a Mixed Indigenous (Yakama, Irish, and Eastern European) Perspective

Shared by Dr. Jacqui Wilkins, ND of Xálish Medicines, 2020, with permission

This share is meant to offer inspiration. It does not cover dosage, duration, contraindications, interactions, preparations, part of Plant worked with, and so forth. Each Plant kin is a multifaceted and expansive being with multiple ways of healing, balancing physiology, and offering support. These are just a few. Please ensure you are working with each Plant relative in a respectful and sustainable way which includes knowing how and when (or when not) to work with them, for you and your unique being. Please seek guidance when working with a new Plant.

To soothe our hearts during grief, and rage:

- Hawthorn is a quintessential heart Medicine. Deeply comforting, and healing to our heart. They also may help us hold boundaries with their sharp thorns and offer protection especially around our hearts if we are feeling tender.
- Rose is another beautiful heart and grief Medicine. They may connect us to our maternal lineages for deep healing. Many of our Ancestors looked to Rose for healing, especially if we hold grief and rage within those lineages or relationships or need support with boundaries.
- Linden is also sweet heart Medicine that is moistening rather than drying. They may be calming to the nervous system, and a soothing heart ally for folks with drier constitutions.

To balance Fire, so that we don't burn out, we may look toward moistening, and cooling Plants:

- Marshmallow leaf, flower, and root are typically soothing, as well as moistening. They help call in Water and rooted Earth Elements for grounding.
- Mullein leaves may be cooling, soothing, and reduce excess inflammation. They may offer grief support as the lung is associated with grief in Traditional Chinese Medicine. I find they are also a Plant kin that helps us connect and hear our Ancestors guiding us when we may feel unsure of next steps.
- Lemon Balm is another cooling Plant ally. They are also calming, potentially reduce anxiety, and act as a restorative for the nervous system.

For moving anger if we find ourselves stuck in it, so that we can create change:

- Mugwort (*Artemisia vulgaris*) may help to move stagnant energy, while also helping us vision and dream new ways forward.
- Vervain is another Plant ally that may help to support energy flow in the body, as well as uncovering truths held within that we may have hidden from ourselves. Supporting us in living our most authentic way of being

our most aligned selves. They may be drying, so use caution internally if there is a lot of heat.
- Ginger is another warming and moving Plant kin, along with other warming spices like Cinnamon, Clove, and others.
- Mints, like Spearmint and Peppermint, may gently offer movement with some cooling energy. They may help balance energetics with warmer Plants.
- Lymphatic moving Plants like Cleavers, Calendula, or Dandelion may also sometimes help us move stuck energy and support flow and detoxification pathways. Connecting us to the Earth, and our Earth elements, for grounding and rooting into our being.

For embodiment, and coming back into our being, flower essences may be supportive:

- Shooting Star is one of my favorite essences for embodiment and integrating Star wisdom, while remembering our purpose, gifts, and path here. Helpful when there is a lack of clarity and sense of belonging.
- California poppy flower essence may be acutely helpful during times of intense anger. They may help repattern energies, traumas, emotional patterns, and behaviors, so that we can remain embodied and take action from this aligned place.

Coming back into our bodies in ways that feel safe, supportive, and nourishing may be helpful. Any Plant ally that helps us remember this embodiment in an accessible way may also be supportive. For example, through scent or textures. Of course, this may be different for each of us depending on our Ancestral Plant connections, Plants that grow in our environment, and those we already have relationship with.

Working with Ancestral Plant Medicines, whether consciously known or not, may also be supportive. They may help remind us of the Medicine we carry within and the wisdom that our Ancestors share with us. Getting to know the Plants that grow in our bio-region (community) and working with them in a good way may also be supportive. They may help us remember our connection to the Land, to the Plants and to all of Creation.

If accessible, returning to the Land, the Sun, Air, Stars and Water, to the Elements, may also feel nourishing and soothe our nervous system. Connecting this way, even if just on the sidewalk or a nearby park, may help to create some space to drop into the body while also rooting to the Earth and Cosmos. Just being with the Plants, Trees, and Sun, can sometimes help attune our breath, Spirit, and physiology. Knowing we are the Land embodied.

Remembering to also honor our relationships and responsibilities with the Earth. Things such as: asking permission, harvesting in a reverent way, making offerings, giving gratitude, and honoring protocols, which are beyond the scope of this guide. Gratitude and intention are vital when working with our Plant kin. Please keep in mind that this is a *very* simplified/brief overview of just a few Plants that came forward in speaking and connecting to our grief and rage. There are many, many more facets and healing aspects, and personality to each one of these Plants than what is shared here. As well as which parts of the Plants to work with, preparations, dosages, interactions, and health contraindications. There are many more Plants that may be supportive as well. Please get to know them in their wholeness, as deepening these relationships offers healing as well.

*As always, please consult your health care practitioner/naturopathic doctor/herbalist/medicine folks/Elders first. These Plants are starting points, or suggestions, and may not align with everyone. Please follow up with those cautions with trusted Medicine folks, or your health practitioners.

Questions to Consider Asking Oneself and People You Support

- Whose grief/anger/depression is this?
- Where have I felt/seen/engaged like this before?
- Has anyone on either side of your family suffered from a trauma that involved (insert presenting issue here)? To utilize my example, "Has anyone on either side of your family, to your knowledge suffered from a trauma that involved feeling responsible to *protect others*, feels as though they have been identified as feeling like a trapped cat, or have been *violated or harmed by men?*"
- Where do you notice this (insert word/feeling) arise in your family system?
- Where have you seen (insert word/feeling) arise in your (insert ethnic/religious community, etc.)?

For example, during my tenure as a psychologist at a university counseling center I worked with a student who displayed intense experiences of leaving her body, frequent insomnia, "dark spirits attempting to drag her to bad places during the evening," and sudden nose bleeds.

Each time that we would unpack an event or situation, we would be drawn back to the here and now. After months of work together, I invited the student to talk about her experience migrating from Haiti. She appeared confused, and stated, "Dr. Mullan, but I am here to talk about why I am waking up screaming, with a bloody nose every night, not my country." I nodded and we spoke about the bloody nose and screaming in various forms, as per her request for a few more sessions.

However, after weeks, she walked into the office, appearing visibly concerned and flatly stated, "Part of me died when I left my homeland of Haiti; part of me is still dead. I was asleep and I do not recall much, but my grandmother was in the house with me alone that day. Political unrest was occurring and our family attempted to get us out as efficiently as possible. I was recently told the story. They said that they took me first from my bed in the middle of the night, but my grandmother did not know the kidnappers were my uncles. So she began to scream and shout; they banged her head accidentally against the doorframe because she was scared, screaming, and struggling until we were both placed in a small boat together with eight other strangers. I didn't know she had broken her nose or that she was screaming . . . but now I physically and literally do."

It was important for me to educate myself on the island of Hispaniola, the tenuous relationship between Haitians and Dominicans of the island, as well as the pervasive and deep anti-Blackness and religious shame Haitians endured. I learned about the immense amount of trauma, including the 2010 earthquake and daily traumas resulting from poverty, economic disparity, and political unrest. I also learned about the high levels of resilience and hope, the concept of survival being a prominent theme for many Haitians, and the strength in religious coping, along with many people experiencing religious shame, perhaps due to the negative perception of Haitian Vodou. I also learned through reading, friendships, documentaries, and the woman I was working with about the limited research in Haiti by examining the trauma the country has experienced, as well as the role that resilience, hope, and religious coping play in the Haitian experience.

This is just one example of the ways in which trauma transmission shows itself in our therapeutic containers, and role modeling of the importance of mental health providers "doing the work." Politicization and decolonization are verbs, not metaphors.

Somatic Soul Trauma Timelines (SSTT)

When looking at psychotherapeutic theory and interventions, the narrative, somatic, liberation, feminist, and (psycho)drama therapy movements have conveyed the most interest in the histories and stories of family members of society who have been marginalized. A cousin of the genogram, the Somatic Soul Trauma Timelines (SSTT) came about in my practice as a result of requests from therapy participants who sought out a physical, tangible, at times colorful, interactive (includes practitioner participation), artistic, and creative way of visually seeing and working through historical and intergenerational themes—especially traumas—in their lineage. What happened naturally in this process with participants, was an addition of looking at the community (when relevant), and the political (it is almost always relevant). Together, with therapeutic participants, we cocreated an intervention that was (their words not mine) *"dope, decolonial, and embodied."* I named it "Somatic Soul Trauma Timelines" because it blends interaction from the Soul, the nontangible parts of our being, the imprints from our ancestral lines, our character, and somatics, as in the Greek word for body (soma). It is a tool that celebrates honoring what additions are a full-bodied "YES" and those that are a visceral "NO." By laying familial, political, cultural, and individual histories into this visual receptacle, we weave a compassionate story of trauma.

Paulo Freire (1994, p. 31, as cited in McGoldrick et al., 2008, p. 14) contended, "that no one goes anywhere alone, even those who arrive physically alone . . . we carry with us the memory of many fabrics, a self-soaked in our history and our culture." This is the fabric of emo–decolonial work in the present. Weaving the threads of memory of the past, with the fabric of the present, imagining a more embodied healing-centered future.

Political (Global)—This SSTT could include what may have been happening politically in the world/in their life that had or could have impacted the individual. This may or may not include the individual's personal family if it has relevance for them, or impacted the family for various reasons.

It is best to allow people to share what comes up for them, rather than rummage through each global event or year throughout history. Sometimes individuals only note one, two, or more global events, and none that they believe have impacted the family (i.e., leaving other family members in Italy, arriving through Ellis Island; escaping genocide; arriving in Canada without citizenship and being part of a mass migration, country accepted refugees, etc.).

Collective (Identity/Culture/Social)—This SSTT focus could include any given characteristic or combination of characteristics—such as race, economic status, class, ethnicity, gender, sexual orientation, or religion—and events or experiences that may have affected and impacted the individuals, or their family systems (including school, friendship circle, etc.) worldview.

Ancestral/Intergenerational—This SSTT could include family history, and experiences that were shared, seen, or whispered about that had an impact or left an impression on the individual. It does not need to be accurate. As with expressions of traumatic material, it matters how we perceive it to have impacted us. Individuals can also utilize their chosen family or collective community.

Overlapping historical events with family situations are not seen as random happenings but as occurrences that may be interconnected systematically, though the connections may be hidden from view (McGoldrick, 1995). We know that there are many relationship patterns in families. This timeline could include ancestral experiences (i.e., of grandparents, great-grandparents, uncles, aunts, unknown ancestors connected through stories or shared cultural experiences), events, stories that have been personally witnessed, heard, read about, or passed down.

Individual (Self-Insight and Experiences)—The Individual SSTT can include any salient experiences, events, or memories that arise for the individual in relation to a specific theme that has been discussed and decided upon prior (i.e., struggles with emotional health, sexual harm, etc.). It can also be extremely general and identify various forms of traumas (Big and small "t" traumas) along the way (i.e., death of an elder aunt, death of a cousin next to an individual, death of a beloved pet, etc.).

Preparing for Resourced Somatic Soul Trauma Timelines

What may be needed to embark on the timeline journey varies per individual, organization, and culture. Our identities, accessibility needs, comfort levels, and stage of processing our experiences of trauma and suffering will all vary, and impact the process. One of the primary preparatory needs necessary to embark on the process is a commitment and preparation from the practitioner. This involves some art, prior genogram understanding would be helpful, as having experience understanding trauma expressions, and nervous system regulation (McGoldrick et al., 2008). Above all, have a clear understanding, and structure for your participant's window of tolerance.

From the participant, there should have been already established a peaceful or safe place prior to the start of the SSTTs. A healthy connected relationship with the participant, consent, and also a healthy relationship where "pause; stop; let's proceed" can and has been verbalized.

Frequently my practice focused upon one specific theme at once, so as not to overwhelm a person. You would be surprised how often a person resourced and armed with markers, oak tag or cardboard, laying in a comfortable position, music in the background, with a support care person can witness their experiences or family's experiences and not become deeply overwhelmed with the experiences. Rather, the timelines offer distance, a shift in perspective, and the gift of narrating their stories.

Somatic Soul Trauma Timeline Example: Jarod would consistently note in therapy that he felt "not Black enough." Having grown up in New Hampshire in the States, he had grown up in a very middle-class neighborhood. His mother is a doctor in a large teaching hospital, and his father works in business. His two younger sisters, he would note in sessions, had grown to be fearful of him—his behavior. They called his "other side," "Simon." He would laugh and feel strong, powerful that people feared him, because at school no one took him seriously—not the Black kids or the white kids. They called him an "Uncle Tom," and he would often note in sessions, "Might as well capitalize on it. I can make white people feel safe around me, which in turn keeps me safe and moving up the ladder. And my skin color and body immediately make me fit in as long as I don't speak." A year or so into our collaborative therapeutic work, he slowly began to unravel this identity as a person with "mental health issues." In fact, he would say this on dates or in disagreements, as a way to "unconsciously push people away."

One fall afternoon he came into the room completely emotional and disoriented. He noted, "It didn't work. My mask—the facade, didn't work." He went on to note that he had tried within a very large work board meeting to ask for equitable and diverse hiring practices, citing himself as an example. Unfortunately, the chair flippantly cut him off two minutes into his presentation saying, "Why would we need another African American, if we have one as savvy and sharp as you, Jarod?" Everyone in the room agreed, with the exception of another colleague of color who looked down and appeared uncomfortable and upset. He fled the meeting, slammed the door, and began screaming down the hallway to the elevator. Jarod was faced with the reality of how history, identity, and beliefs, all crumbled around him. The structural racism, the blatant racism, microaggression, the anti-Blackness—it was all present. For months, we gently unpacked the event. He left his job, involved HR, and felt "safer," yet he noted he would never again "be safe," because his bubble of security had burst. Almost six months later, we came to his family history. We arrived at the banks of his memories of his family, his diagnoses of ADHD, bipolar disorder, and prior to 12 years old, oppositional defiant disorder, conduct disorder, and even psychotic disorders.

As we created a Somatic Soul Trauma Timeline together, we were able to highlight various themes, areas, and beliefs that arose throughout his familial, ancestral, and personal fabric that was directly linked to the effects of colonization, and possibly (we did not want to assume for his ancestors) trauma. He consequently began to feel lighter. A few months later he would leave a session and say, "I spent years talking about my behaviors, and what was wrong with my brain, and it was hell having my body not listen to me. Doc, I could have done some seriously good work if all of my expensive social workers, psychiatrists, and therapists slowed down. If they helped me connect with some deeply old family lines, and even some wounds from family having been transplanted to the antebellum South. I do not want to wear a mask anymore—I literally do not WANT ONE anymore." Important to note, I cried after he left my room because a deep part of me was also healing through his work on himself. In turn, he WAS engaging in clearing up and out the resounding effects of intergenerational and historical trauma.

During our last correspondence a year ago, he has stopped all psychotropic medications (with his psychiatrist's support) and is solely taking appropriate supplements; engaging in MMA and martial arts, a strong morning ritual practice, and in a Black Men's Support Circle; and during winter taking a mild antidepressant, which he seeks to be off of in the next few years. But above all, he is beginning to like himself, and is creating healthy relationships in the world, is taking a trip Down South with his father to visit his grandfather he had never met, and is mentoring youth. Consequently, months after we stopped our work together, he shared that he had been learning more about his ancestry, and his grandfather had provided information into his experiences growing up as a butler for "a nice white family." He later realized what this may have meant; he and his mother inferred that

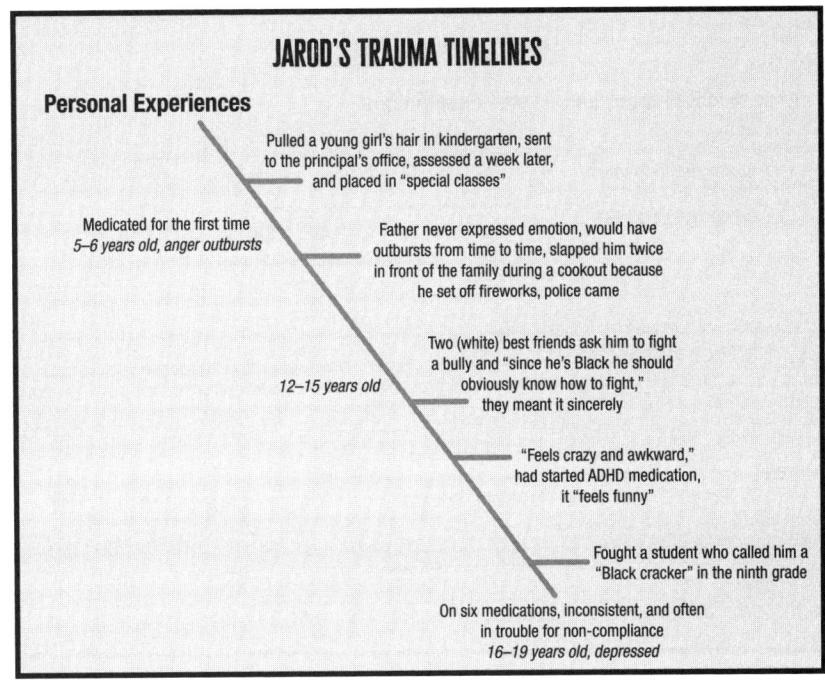

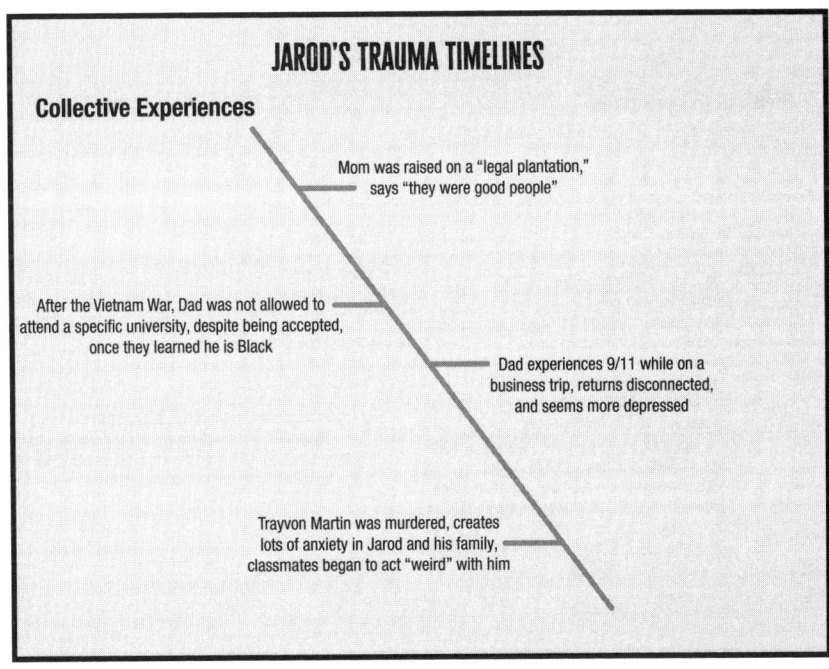

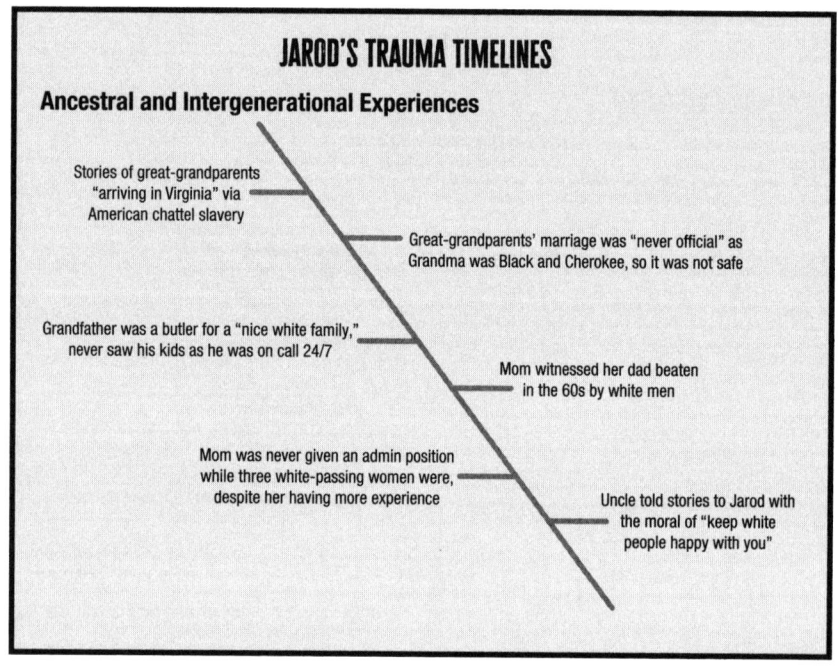

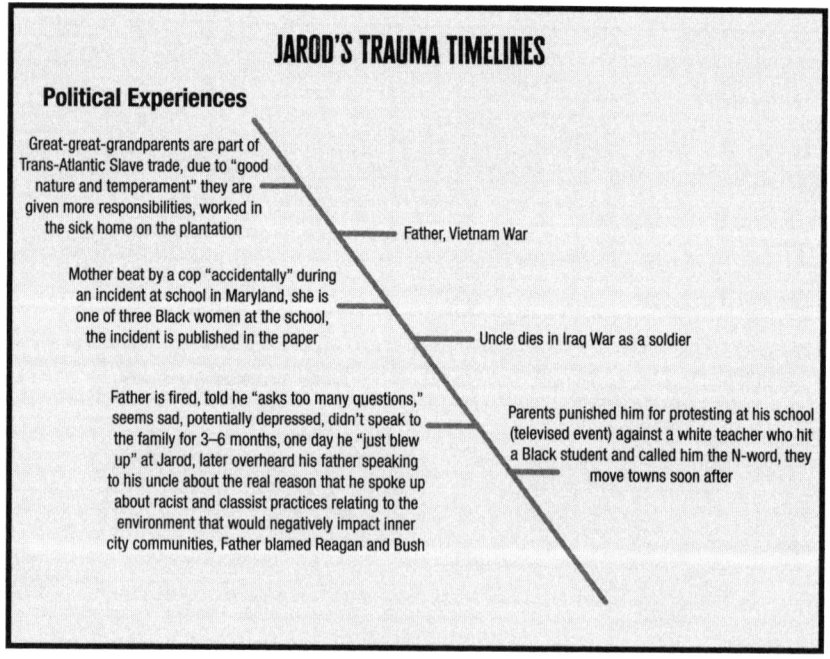

the family owned a plantation and were his grandfather's family's "masters," based on history and placement. Likely there were shifts in laws and regulations related to slavery at the time of his rearing. As we know, the institution of slavery did not end in 1865.

This is an internal process of decolonization. It is an essential part of the emo–decolonial journey, as our ego mind can trick us into believing that we are to immediately begin community organizing (I am not against this choice) or immediately begin to engage in group work or excavating ancestral trauma. In my experience, it is not ideal to jump into deeper work related to ancestry without a firm base, support, and the nervous system elasticity needed to safely do so; as we can never be sure what may arise. See Jarod's SSTT opposite:

The SSTT can also be utilized to identify specific areas and is even more effective when less general. I have supported therapy participants in using themes such as the effects of colorism, substance dependence and addiction, sexual harm (those harming, as well as those having been harmed), dis-ease (from emotional and mental to physical imbalances), rage, expressions of depression and grief, self-harm, gender identity, sexual orientation and expression, religious trauma and abuse, expressions of anxiety, familial abuse, partner abuse, systemic racism, sexism, classism, among others. Each time, even if an individual or group were unaware of the details of their family lineage ancestry, and a form of colonial violence arose, creating connections for the person.

Lifelines

One area of inquiry that is useful to add, especially if someone is feeling overcome with emotion, is *Lifelines*. Spending time on Lifelines allows for glimmers of hope and a reminder that many of us pushed through violent and difficult experiences with support. Whether a beloved pet, a support group online, gardening, bird-watching, sleeping, a caregiver, music, movement, or television shows! For Jarod, for example, his Lifelines included areas that brought out his somatic resilience, as somatic therapy would identify his shape. The places where he felt a lifeline, a hand, resilience, hope, joy, connection, and help. How he remembered how it made him feel and where it

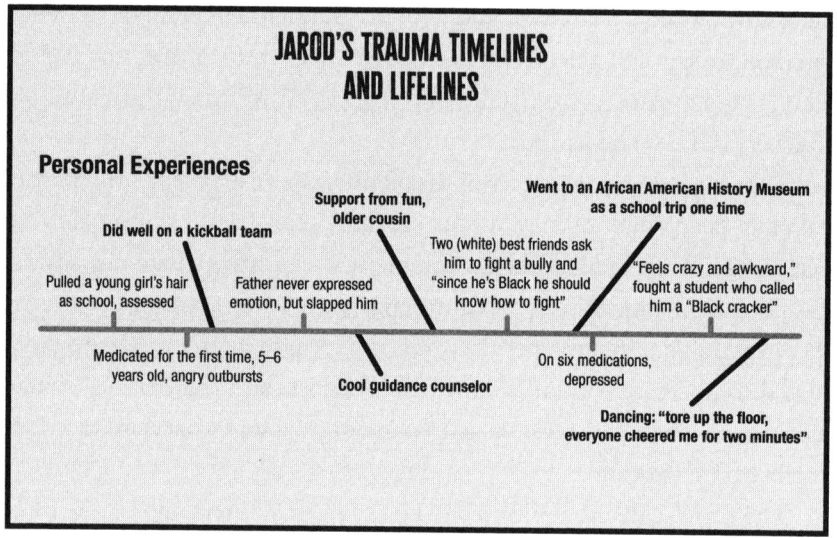

arose in his body. For Jarod, he recalled: connecting with a fun older cousin who was supportive, talking to a cool guidance counselor, being a part of a kickball team and doing quite well, a trip to a museum that mirrored his own identity, a school dance, where he had a moment of feeling on top of the world where his peers cheered him on. Lifelines are an essential part of the Somatic Soul Trauma Timeline process and can also be utilized on every single timeline.

> *The ordinary response to atrocities is to banish them from consciousness. Certain violations of the social compact are too terrible to utter aloud: this is the meaning of the word unspeakable.*
> —Judith Herman

Many people living with trauma histories and legacies of big suffering have come into contact with the mental health and psychiatric systems . . . and many individuals are never offered trauma education, peer support or therapy that is safe, culturally relevant, and cost-effective.

By exploring trauma in a collaborative, artistic, and truly client-led way (such as in Somatic Soul Trauma Timelines) space is created for the participant to use the method as they wish. SSTTs are expansive and rooted in many ways of healing that were indigenous to our people before the imposition of Western therapy.

So, as anti-oppression and decolonizing become common terms, it is important that these frameworks do not merely become buzzwords: They should be backed by actions. Decolonizing practices, including how we do therapy, is a complete shift from Eurocentric teachings. There are actions we can take, words we can say, and ideas we can unlearn/relearn/learn to transform colonial engagement. In offering Somatic Soul Trauma Timelines to you, my hope is that you are able to further expand on this method to decolonize your own therapy practice.

For Support As You Read Through Chapter 9

Backpack Exercises

One of the most essential ways that therapists can remain firmly in their power and reground themselves is to ensure that there is a disconnection to any energies you may have picked up, before and after a person you are working with. I know firsthand how difficult it can be to find the space and time to disconnect, or "clear your energy bodies," especially when the window between the person leaving and the person arriving is minute. Here are three small easy exercises that can be done within 30 seconds, when you are running short on time, and are attempting to return an email, use the restroom, and respond to a loved one's text all within a six-minute window.

Additionally, this simple technique ensures that no lingering energy is sucking at your own, and you are practicing beautiful energetic hygiene by ensuring that you are not passing anyone else's energy to anyone else you engage with.

1. Rub your hands together with the intention to break up and release any energies you no longer need, and to break connection with any person you have come into contact with. Open your hands. Blow on and wiggle fingers.
2. a. Spray an energy clearing spray or burn a plant or herb that has a connection to cleansing within your lineage and people.

b. Say aloud or to yourself "Any energies that are not mine, that do not serve my highest purpose and path, I command you to leave and send you to _____ (e.g., the light, the earth)." Fill in the blank with your own choice of wording that fits your lineage and or spiritual traditions.

3. Close your eyes, or focus your gaze on something comforting in the room and soften your gaze. Imagine a white small light in the center of your chest. As you breathe in and out, allow it to expand. Allow the white light to cover your entire body in a silvery glowy egg. Then, imagine thick roots growing from your base or feet and extending into the earth with each breath. Feeling centered and strong, receive anything that is needed from your roots and earth. Then allow a beautiful white light from above to come down and course through your body (at the same time that the roots are expanding and unfurling below) let it clear what is not needed. Place a large bubble of violet purple light around you, protecting you. Imagine it being reinforced by images/beings that feel supportive.

4. During a Trauma and the Body weekend workshop with Jane Clapp, I learned about the paper plate exercise. It is a somatic exercise that also soothes the nervous system and involves a form of bilateral stimulation. Grab a paper plate (a regular one, not the fancy strong ones). Grab a tennis ball or other light bouncy ball. With your nondominant hand, first hold the paper plate upside down on top of your open hand. If walking is accessible to you, stand and walk after adding the ball on top of the upside down paper plate with your focus purely on keeping the ball steady and ON THE PLATE. Notice your breath. It is perfectly fine for the ball to keep falling. Play. Have fun. Allow yourself space and time to reorient yourself and be with the process. Also notice if your perfectionism is creeping in saying things like, "Why can't you do this? What is wrong with me?!" Nothing is wrong with you. The more relaxed and present you are, the more steady your hand. Once you feel pretty good at

the process, try to sit, then stand, then get onto the floor, squat, all while balancing the plate and the ball. Youth also love to engage in these practices with us.

You're also welcome to engage in all four in between groups, meetings, and sessions if you like.

For Support As You Move Forward

10 Energetic Boundary-Setting Techniques and Ways to Restore Them

1. Take a moment and stop what you're doing. Allow yourself a breath and disengage energetically from what you're doing. This can be done by taking several deep breaths and saying a word that is helpful to you. I use the word "CENTERED." I know people who say, "ground," "focus," "here now," and "I'm back." Even naming a person or place that grounds and centers you would work, "9th St. Park at sunset during a jog," "Niagara Falls," "Abuela's casita," "LBI beach at dawn." Anything that helps bring you into the present time and into your own body, allowing you to separate from whatever it is that is occurring in the moment.
2. Name 5–10 differences between you and the other people you're with. For example, "I have curly hair, I am not 6' 5", I am wearing peach and orange, I am nonbinary, I am drinking grape juice, etc." This will further help you:
    a. Bring you back into your body.
    b. Separate you from the person you are merging with.
    c. Ground your energy.
3. Say your name aloud, to assist in bringing you back into your own body and experience.
4. Ask yourself: "Is this my problem, feeling, anxiety, worry, or emo-

tion?" If not, ask if you would like, "Whose is it?" Feel free to return the energy to the Earth, dissipate it, in a way that feels best to you.
5. Work to name what happened. For example, "My supervisor just had an exchange with my coworker; it was an uncomfortable exchange filled with passive–aggressive tones and my coworker angrily walked out of the meeting. I did not feel good, my stomach hurts watching this. I felt confused and my mouth was dry."
6. If this is pleasant, helpful and not activating for you, gently begin to pat your body. Gently pat all over your body while breathing and blowing out any intense emotions or feelings inside of you in a big "whooshing breath."
7. When and if you feel overwhelmed, take three deep breaths. Name one feeling that is predominant in how you are feeling. Example: I am feeling embarrassed. Breathe into the embarrassed feeling 100%. Allow yourself to feel the feeling 100% for exactly 45 seconds. Set a time. Know that it is JUST a feeling. Continue to repeat this and allow yourself to breathe through and feel the feeling. Please note this may require more space to move, unwind, and breathe post feeling.
8. Emotional Freedom Technique (EFT) Tapping: Tapping derives from our Indigenous people, most notably Eastern philosophies and spirituality such as acupuncture and acupressure. These practices focus on qi in the body and blockages to energy meridians. However, there are spoken words that support that Indigenous peoples throughout the Amazon and South America have utilized energy tapping for thousands of years. Recently, a client shared that when upset or unwell, her family members in the Amazon in Peru have gently tapped on body parts with rocks to help them center and become more connected to Earth. She called it tierra magic—Earth magic.
9. Breathwork. Breathwork has been a part of many cultures the world over, either as a religious/spiritual practice or to aid in movement. Our breathing speeds up when we are activated and slows or deepens when we our nervous systems are calmed. To use our breath as a way to be with the body is to add a reminder that we are alive in

the present moment. Breathwork can be the pathway to feeling our feelings, to uncovering what our bodies need from us, and to much more. Experiment with breathing deeper, slower, faster. Try lying down and placing your hands on your body. Remember, by virtue of having a body you are qualified to work with it.

10. Meditation. There are numerous forms of meditation across the planet. I truly believe it is essential to find a way to be in our body and find a place to land. That can look like walking meditation, dancing, traditional meditation, visualization exercises, and so forth. Dr. Bruce Lipton, pioneer of epigenetics, has discussed the violence of stress. Stress hormones are the #1 killer. If your immune system is working properly, it will suppress parasites and germs. When the immune system shuts down, we are under stress; then we get the dis-ease called "opportunistic infections." Stress shuts down our immune system. How do we treat the stress of late-stage capitalism and honor our energetic boundaries is the question. My favorite meditation involves a slow walk and listening to music that transports me, or guided meditations to help me sleep. Please note that silent meditations do not always feel good for colonized peoples.

11. Once you've identified the source of the energy, first, visualize it leaving by sending it away. Then, invoke love and compassion for yourself and the other people, to make the transition back into your own truth easier and without blame.

Energetic Boundary Setting, like anything else, gets easier with practice, and it is truly a practice, much like meditation. It is actually akin to a branch of mindfulness. So energetic boundaries are not tangible, but for human service workers (whether someone is in sales or hospitality or a therapist) when they are put in place, they change how we move through the world and our energy levels.

Glossary/Terms to Chew On

The glossary of terms is here to support your reeducation process. So often I have been midway through a book when I have forgotten the definition outlined earlier in the text. These definitions are fluid and ever changing, much like this work. I would be kind to yourself around remembering and learning these terms or committing them to memory. *Part of colonial conditioning is the process of socializing us as a people to consistently forget.* Many of us may be more familiar with the therapeutic and psychological terms, as opposed to the more political or social justice terms (or vice versa). I hope this glossary is yet another resource for your relearning, teaching, and sharing.

Ableism (aka disability oppression)   The systemic discrimination and exclusion of disabled people while privileging those who are temporarily able-bodied (T. Smith, 2012).

Abolition   Defined as the act of abolishing or removing systems, practices, or institutions. Generally used in prison abolition as a movement, but can also refer to mental health industrial complex abolition as the two are closely related. Historically, abolitionism, or the abolitionist movement, was the movement to end slavery largely by those currently enslaved and those who had been recently "freed." In Western Europe and the Americas, abolitionism was a historic movement that sought to end the Atlantic Slave Trade and liberate the enslaved African people.

Aboriginal People or Aboriginal   Existing (in a place) from the beginning or from earliest days. Of or relating to the Indigenous peoples of Australia, as well as Métis, Inuit, and First Nations identified people, regardless of where they live in Canada and the United States, *regardless* of whether they are registered under the *Indian Act* of Canada, or are enrolled as one of the 573 federally recognized tribes in the United States.

Allochronism   Coined by Johannes Fabian, this term refers to practices in anthropology and other cultural studies (Raja, 2019; J. Smith, 2012). It describes the process through which the European researcher observes those they are studying (non-Europeans) in colonized spaces. From that observation, the European researched positions the object of study as having existed in the past, whereas Europe is in the present (Raja, 2019). This creates false ideas of modernity versus primitive.

Anti-Black Racism   The specific practices or structural policies that institutions create to further discriminate and stereotype people of Black African descent. The term "Anti-Black Racism" was first expressed by Dr. Akua Benjamin, a Ryerson Social Work Professor (Black Health Alliance, n.d., paras. 1–2).

Anticipatory-racism reaction   A reaction that POC may develop as a defense mechanism that anticipates future discrimination or racism because of their past experiences of it (DeArth-Pendley, 2012). This reaction can be expressed as fear, paranoia, distrust, anger, hypervigilance, anxiety, disengagement from others, interpersonal difficulties, hostility, sadness, defeatism, and oppositionality.

Assimilation   How one cultural group absorbs another socially, and often forcefully.

Bicultural Production   When something produced by a creator has influences from both their own/original culture and others (J. Smith, 2012).

Binary   Something made of or based on two things or parts. Gender binary is the classification of gender into two distinct, opposite forms of masculine and feminine, whether by social system or cultural belief. Most cultures use a gender binary today, having two genders, due to colonial impact.

Capitalism   An economic system in which a country's trade, industry, and profits are controlled by private companies, instead of by the people whose time and labor powers those companies (Kelly, 2020). The United States and many other nations around the world are capitalist countries. Capitalism is one of the roots of PoGM's oppression, and it prioritizes accumulation of wealth via competition of market prices and wages.

Capitalism Fatigue   Related to late-stage capitalism, sometimes called *burnout* or *chronic fatigue*. Where existing under capitalism causes marked tiredness and exhaustion as a result of the impossible productivity standards placed upon a person trying to survive.

Cisgender Someone who is not transgender, identifying with the gender they are assigned at birth.

Collective Energy Systems and energy processes existing and interacting within and between people, influenced by cultural, historical, and environmental factors.

Colonialism How nations continue their control over other countries and the Indigenous people there that have been made dependent on them in some way (J. Smith, 2012).

Colonial subjugation How foreign lands that are already occupied are dominated with force and social control.

Colonization The establishment of settlements.

Colonize The creation of a colony for persons to either settle in or be confined to, thus subjugating the original population to colonial government and rule (J. Smith, 2012).

Colorism Also known as skin color stratification, colorism is a product of racism. It describes how people with lighter skin colors are privileged over those with darker skin colors in all areas of life (Hunter, 2007).

Contagions Contagious diseases.

Crip A reclaimed word and thus used as an identity by some disabled people, has expanded to be inclusive of those with physical impairments and sensory impairments (T. Smith 2012).

Decolonization More than just independence from a colony/colonial power, decolonization has become the process by which we heal the society, systems, and political frameworks we live within so that we may achieve true healing for our communities and selves. It is a return to the ancestral wisdom.

Dialectic Stemming from Greek philosophers such as Socrates and Plato, this is a form of logic that seeks to resolve contradictions between seemingly opposing ideas (J. Smith, 2012).

Dialogic/Dialogism A theory from Mikhail Bakhtin, a Soviet critic, that poses that by having various people engage in dialogue with each other it disrupts authoritarianism (J. Smith, 2012).

Disability Can be physical, mental, cognitive, sensory, emotional, or developmental and includes many types of chronic illness. It is ever changing and expansive with much variance within how it affects someone, when it shows up, who it commonly affects, and how visible it is to others.

Disability Justice A liberatory framework that intersects equity, access, and freedom for all people with disabilities to social and economic justice for all people. The framework was created by Patti Bern and Sins Invalid.

Disenfranchised Grief Grief that a person experiences when a loss cannot be openly acknowledged or publicly mourned. Native American have been portrayed by the dominant culture as stoic and without feelings, incapable of grief. There has been little recognition of their sense of loss, need to mourn, or ability to do so. The message is that they have no need or right to grieve.

Dis-ease A lack of being at ease or in alignment with the self, Louise Hay talked about this as a main cause of illness in her book *You Can Heal Your Life*.

Dysaesthesia Aethiopica The supposed mental illness that Cartwright proposed as the reason for why enslaved Africans did not want to work, caused supposed "mischief," caused disturbances among others, and did not feel pain from punishment. An example of scientific racism.

Emotional–Decolonial (Emo–Decolonial) Process A decolonial framework that intersects political, emotional health, ancestral, and intergenerational process of remembering, unlearning, honoring, and relearning the root of disconnection for colonized peoples globally. It is the process of emotionally creating individual and collective equity, access, and freedom for all colonized peoples.

Epigenetics An emerging field of science that studies heritable changes caused by the activation and deactivation of genes without any change in the underlying DNA sequence of the organism.

Ethnographic Relating to the study and recording of human cultures.

Eurocentrism Centering European/Western ways of thinking, being, and societal norms in general, when viewing the history or culture of a non-European/Western culture.

Execrable Of very poor quality or condition.

Expressions A reframing of what we are taught to label as "symptoms." By using expressions, we aim to humanize the responses people have to life events.

Extirpate To destroy completely; wipe out.

Forced Migration Also known as forced displacement, describing how a person or group of people are coerced in some way to move from their home/place of origin (usually as a result of violence or persecution of some kind). Usually the "forced" aspect is unconscious, as it is embedded in imperialism, capitalism, and other systemic and global doing.

Gaslighting Coined from the 1944 film *Gaslight* in which the woman-lead starts to question her sanity because of how her new husband manipulates her and their environment to deny her reality and undermine her. Gaslighting as a verb refers to this similar manner of manipulation and abuse in relationships today.

Gatekeepers Are people who work inside of institutions, and often have access to specific services. Gatekeepers, when unconscious, often function as those "who ensure that the institution perpetuates itself" (The People's Institute for Survival and Beyond [PISAB], n.d.). Gatekeepers who operate with anti-racist values and who maintain an accountable relationship with the community can help to generate institutional transformation rather than perpetuate an unjust status quo.

Gender Nonconforming A spectrum of self-identification that is used to illustrate that all people are oppressed by the gender binary, pressured to fit into societal categories (Sennott & Smith, 2011 as cited in T. Smith, 2012). It includes people who are differently gendered while understanding that not all trans folks identify as differently gendered and not all differently gendered folks identify as trans.

Genocide The purposeful and systematic murder of a people (ethnic, national, racial, religious, or other oppressed identity), the intent can be to murder the whole group or a significant number.

Genogram A practical framework for understanding family patterns. They allow you to map the family structure clearly and to note and update the map of family patterns of relationship and functioning as they emerge.

Heterosexism Illustrates the systemic advantages of heterosexuals through norms and privileges awarded to them by society (Blumenfeld, 2007; Pharr, 1988; Herek, 2004; as cited in T. Smith, 2012). Through fear, hatred, and exclusion, LGBTQ people and their needs are either ignored, hidden, or silenced through this oppression. Can also be used to describe how homophobia shows up in institutions and in displays of power from the practices, policies, and cultural norms that view heterosexuality as the only natural expression.

Historical Trauma The collective emotional and psychological injury both over the life span and across generations, resulting from a cataclysmic history of genocide.

Historical Trauma Response A theory explaining the intergenerational trauma that Indigenous peoples of so-called North America experienced surrounding colonialism. It has now expanded to explain other peoples historical traumas as well (J. Smith, 2012).

Historical Unresolved Grief Grief resulting from the historical trauma of genocide; grief that has not been expressed, acknowledged, and resolved. Like trauma, it can span across generations, originally coined by Dr. Maria Yellow Horse Brave Heart.

Homophobia Originally coined by George Weinberg in the 1960s to describe a clinical condition of people who expressed irrational fear and hatred of those who are attracted to the same sex (T. Smith, 2012). Now it is used to describe all discrimination, violence, prejudice, and harassment toward LGB people. However, those more commonly targeted are those whose gender expression is viewed as in opposition to what heteronormativity would demand of them (i.e., men who are viewed as feminine and women who are viewed as masculine by the cultures surrounding them).

Humanism The belief that even without higher powers, afterlife, or the belief in other supernatural presences, that humans can desire and act to give their lives meaning and aspire to a greater good.

Humorism (or humoralism) A belief held by ancient Greek and Roman physicians (and until the 19th century) that an excess or deficiency in any of the four bodily fluids or humors—blood, black bile, yellow bile, and phlegm—directly affected their health and temperament.

Individual Capitalists Are typically wealthy people who have a large amount of capital (money or other financial assets) invested in business, and who benefit from the system of capitalism by making increased profits and thereby adding to their wealth (Kelly, 2020).

Internalized Oppression The ways in which victims of oppression begin to believe in the so-called absolute power of the oppressor, and deny the power they have within (J. Smith, 2012). Their self-worth transforms into self-hatred, which can then be further internalized or placed on other people marginalized by society, continuing the cycle. Within internalized oppression is "internalized racial inferiority" displayed by BIPOC and "internalized racial superiority" displayed by white people.

Intelligence A social construct used as a measure of someone's mental aptitude. It can encapsulate ability to learn, applying one's knowledge to the environment (like on tests), ability to reason/skilled application of reason, comprehension and mental acuity. Intelligence often fails to recognize that one can excel in certain areas and need more supports in others. Someone might be labeled intelligent by others in recognition for their ability to learn many things quickly, and in the same breath, be dismissed when that person struggles to apply the skills/knowledge they've gained.

Imperialism A nation's or state's policy and practice of extending dominion through land and territory taking, or gaining economic and political control over other areas and peoples (Haines, 2019). This always involves the use of power and force—military or economic. Most imperialist nations, including the United States, deny their use of imperialism, and instead find or create an enemy to justify their tactics by saying it is in the name of freedom. Imperial powers often competed with each other for the best potential resources, markets, and trade.

Imperialist Nostalgia A form of racism disguised as nostalgia that poses the bygone eras or events as something aspirational. By purposefully hiding the horrors of those eras it makes the mourning seem innocent in nature (J. Smith, 2012).

Intergenerational Trauma The concept of intergenerational trauma was introduced in psychiatric literature through descriptions of behavioral and clinical problems in offspring of Holocaust survivors. Intergenerational trauma is also known as inherited family trauma, transgenerational trauma, or multigenerational trauma. They are seen in psychology as the psychological effects (that the collective trauma) experienced by a group of people has on subsequent generations in that cultural group. The theory states that trauma can be inherited because there are genetic changes in a person's DNA. The changes from trauma do not damage the gene (genetic change). Instead, they alter how the gene functions (epigenetic change).

Lakota Takini Network, Inc. A native nonprofit collective of traditionalists, helping professionals and service providers, that is recognized for its research in historic trauma.

Medical Industrial Complex The medical industrial complex is a term coined in 1971 by Barbara Ehrenreich in her book *The American Health Empire Power, Profits, and Politics*. The term *medical industrial complex* refers to the multibillion-dollar health industry composed of doctors, psychiatrists, hospitals, nursing homes, insurance companies, drug manufacturers, hospital supply and equipment companies, real estate and construction businesses, health systems, consulting and accounting firms, and banks (Ehrenreich, 1971). As defined by Ehrenreich, the concept of a medical industrial complex conveys the idea that an important and primary function of the health care system in the United States is to make a profit. Making patient care, efficacy, and self-management a sideline to the bigger motive of money. Another critique of the profit driven motives of the medical industrial complex is that this system does not look at the contributions of social factors such as environmental degradation, war, poverty, racism, and other forms of oppression to illness (Jones & Rainey, 2006; Kurtz, 2009).

Medicalization The process by which nonmedical problems become defined and treated as medical problems often requiring medical treatment ("Medicalization," 2022). For example, behaviors (like one's sexuality), beliefs, appearance, and normal life events or processes (aging, birth, death, and grief) (T. Smith, 2012). Also inclusive of those who reject treatments from the MIC/MHIC, such as medications of any kind, surgeries that are cosmetic but presented as "corrective" (such as those intersex folks are subjected to) and anything that would make one "more acceptable" according to standards of beauty or health that the MIC puts forward.

Mental Health Industrial Complex Refers to the multibillion-dollar health industry composed of psychiatrists (clinical and nonclinical), social workers, psychologists, marriage and family therapists, psychoanalysts, Jungian analysts, counselors, licensing boards, ethics boards, associations, universities, hospitals, group homes, outpatient, partial care, day treatment and residential programs, therapeutic schools, insurance companies, drug manufacturers, and consulting firms. Often the MHIC seeks to explain suffering through biomedical means. Attributing things to inherent problems in the brain when it is caused by social or political factors that affect a person's life. Overall, this leads to more medication prescriptions and more revenue for an industry that is not set up to heal or solve these systemic issues because it treats them as individual (Greene, 2019).

Neoliberalism Ideology where deregulation, reduction in government spending, and (generally 19th century ideals of) free-market capitalism are prioritized (Oxford Languages, 2022).

Oppression The systematic subjugation of one social group by a more powerful social group for the social, economic, and political benefit of the more powerful social group.

Pandemic An epidemic that is geographically widespread.

Politicization An encompassing process by which an individual or group becomes aware of all dimensions of their existence, including oppressive conditions, social forces, economic circumstances, and cultural repression with particular attention to the political forces (Linklater, 2014).

Politicized Healers Practitioners who have an analysis of structural power, colonization, social change, and intersectionality who have been trained in a variety of ancestral-healing traditions (Haines, 2019). Politicized healing disrupts the individualism of mainstream therapeutic approaches. These practitioners bring an understanding of the ancestral, power, trauma, healing, oppression, and privilege, and have the means to transform these into collective well-being, love, action, and emotional and physical health.

Posttraumatic Slave Syndrome A term coined by Dr. Joy DeGruy, that speaks to the ongoing and festering wound that African Americans, in particular, experience in the absence of healing alongside continued oppression. Behaviors that tend to arise with PTSS are ever-present anger, racist socialization, and a vacant self-esteem.

Power Access to resources, the ability to influence others, access to decision-makers to get what you want done, and the ability to define reality.

Prejudice To prejudge, often based on stereotypes; could be positive or negative.

Privilege A privilege is a special advantage not enjoyed by everyone. A benefit enjoyed by an individual or group that is beyond what's available to others. Access that others do not have.

Psychogenic Mental or emotional rather than physiological in origin.

Psychohistory Is an amalgam of psychology, history, and related social sciences and the humanities. It examines the "why" of history, especially the difference between stated intention and actual behavior.

Psychological Pathology The study of the causes, components, course, and consequences of psychological disorders, characterized by what is "abnormal" or "dysfunctional" (Holmqvist, 2013).

Queer A reclaimed word and identity that can go beyond sexuality and gender. It can be used to express how someone exists among binary ideas and the ways they don't align with binarism and monolithic societal pressures (T. Smith, 2012).

Racial Discrimination A source of trauma that creates economic insecurity from a lack of employment, housing, health care, food, and access to public spaces. It exacerbates cycles of trauma and poor health leading to more difficulty in accessing resources (Drexel University Center for Hunger-Free Communities [DU CHFC], 2019, para. 1).

Racism A specious classification of humans codified by North Americans in 17th–18th Century, using "white" as the model of humanity, for the purpose of establishing and maintaining social status and privilege, and a legitimate relationship to power (PISAB & Dr. Maulana Karenga, personal communication as part of their Undoing Racism workshop). *Racial prejudice + power = racism.*

Racism-Related Fatigue The tremendous psychological and physiological exhaustion that POC experience as a result of, and in response to, chronic exposure to racism and oppression in multiple social systems with which they interact regularly (DeArth-Pendley, 2012).

Racism-Related Stress/Distress Chronic exposure to racism and oppression can compromise an individual's psychological and physical well-being. Stress can be expressed as tension headaches, muscle tightness, inability to concentrate, intrusive thoughts, and a general sense of anxiety and tension that eventually can impair and weaken the immune system leading to a greater susceptibility to minor and major illnesses (DeArth-Pendley, 2012).

Rage The emotion is often identified as uncontrollable anger, and has historically been seen as problematic and violent. It is often confused with anger; however, it is the accumulation of ancestral emotion, including but not limited to anger. It can be accumulated within our own lifetime, from childhood, or throughout the histories of our ancestors and communities. Ruth King identified six disguises of rage: depression, dependence, distraction, devotion, defiance and dominance. It is seen as the love child of ancestral trauma and shame. (See Chapter 8 for more.)

Rage-Grief Axis The combination of rage and grief expressions, derived from collective historical trauma and intergenerational trauma transmission. Including both the conscious and unconscious aspects of our emotions. Grief and rage are identified as an axis because they are two sides of the same coin; it is impossible to have one without the other. (See Chapter 8 for more information; coined by Dr. Jennifer Mullan.)

Residential Schools Sponsored by the government, these religious schools forced Indigenous children to assimilate into Euro-Candian culture through loss of community, abuse, and isolation.

Scientific Racism A specific form of racism that used pseudoscientific methods to prove the suppose superiority of whiteness and white people to keep Black people enslaved and justify the reasoning for why they were enslaved (Harvard Library, n.d.).

Self-Determination Regarding government, the right for a group, nation, or community to form their own systems, future, and goals (J. Smith, 2012).

Sovereignty An inherent right all nations hold that cannot be transferred between nations. In the U.S. there are three forms, one being tribal, showing that Indigenous peoples have been recognized as a sovereign body through policy (J. Smith, 2012).

SSTT Inspired by the genogram, SSTTs encapsulate the political, collective, ancestral/intergenerational, and individual levels of trauma in a person's life. It allows the person opportunity to explore not only their own history, but that of the world and family unit they grew up in, providing context for what they and their family experience.

Survivance Coined by Gerald Vizenor (Anishinaabe) to describe the ways Indigenous people write contemporary literature and tell stories in a modern context (J. Smith, 2012). A mix of survival, endurance, and firm rejection of colonial oppression.

Syncretism The combination of two or more belief systems into a single, integrated system.

System(s) An interlocking set of parts that together make a whole; an established way of doing something.

Systematic As relating to or consisting of a system; methodical in procedure of plan; marked by thoroughness and regularity (Merriam-Webster, n.d.).

Systemic Oppression Violence that creates structural disadvantage through incarceration, over-policing, lack of food or housing that leads to poverty in communities of POC (DU CHFC, 2019, para. 1).

Temporarily able-bodied A phrase used by disability theorists to illustrate that disability is a part of the human experience and will affect everyone at some point in their life. Either through their own aging, illness, or war (T. Smith, 2012).

Therapist or Mental Health Practitioner/Provider (MHP) A provider that has been trained within the MHIC and sanctioned to provide medicalized treatment under ethics boards local to their state, country, and/ or province to "treat the pathology in an individual, community, culture or identity" as categorized by the *DSM*'s most current version, and Eurocentric cultural norms. They works as a service based provider for the system, although the intention is to work as a support to the individual seeking support.

Transgender A gender identity (often has little relationship to sexuality) that describes how one doesn't align with what they were designated at birth (T. Smith, 2012). Can describe a wide range of people that self-identify with it, where sexuality also broadly ranges, independent of the gender they identify with or express.

Transgender Oppression Societal oppression of those who express their gender (or are of a gender/sex identity) that challenges the norms set out by society (T. Smith, 2012). This may be intentional or not and these people may or may not identify with transness in some way. It privileges cisgender people over trans and gender-nonconforming folks.

Transphobia Discrimination through fear or hatred that targets expressions of gender that are unconventional (T. Smith, 2012).

Trauma-Informed Involves the prevention and recognition of trauma while responding to it in ways that understand it is multi- and intergenerational in nature. Trauma-informed work also involves understanding how oppression and systems that exploit or discriminate are also traumatic (DU CHFC, 2019, para. 6).

Trauma-Informed and Trauma Responsive Approaches To be trauma-informed or present one's work/self as trauma-informed means they acknowledge how trauma is ongoing and seek to understand the signs and symptoms of trauma in those they work with. There is intention and praxis in place to avoid re-traumatizing/creating new traumas in all people involved (DU CHFC, 2019, para. 7).

White-Bodied Supremacy A term coming from the works of Resmaa Menakem to describe the kind of trauma response coming from "intergenerational transmission of oppressive race-based biases and fears held in the body" (Complex Trauma, 2021). It is these reactionary responses and unconscious biases that keep racism alive. Menakem asserts that these patterns cannot be changed through cognition alone and that they must be addressed somatically.

White Supremacist Racism System(s) of power that enforce the supposed supremacy and dominance of "white" people and "whiteness" based on the political and scientifically racist preposition that developed in the 17th and 18th centuries. It is still upheld by people through their engagement with and belief in systems of power (McLean, 2014).

References

Abdullah, S. (1994). Posttraumatic stress disorder: A diagnosis for the victims of the African-American holocaust in the United States of America component. In A. Thompson (Ed.), *The African principle* (pp. 1–19). African World Community Press.

Aborignal Healing Foundation. (2004). *Historic trauma and Aboriginal healing.* Anishinabe Printing.

Actually Jamie. (2014, March 25). *As the lights wink out.* That Jamie. http://thatjamie.com/2014/03/lights-wink/

Adamec, R. (1997). Transmitter systems involved in neural plasticity underlying increased anxiety and defense: Implications for understanding anxiety following traumatic stress. *Neuroscience & Biobehavioral Reviews, 21*(6), 755–765. https://Doi.org/10.1016/s0149-7634(96)00055-3

Adler, A. (2021, September 2). In *Wikipedia.* https://en.wikipedia.org/w/index.php?title=Alfred_Adler&oldid=1041947569

Akbar, N. (1998). Afrocentricity: The Challenge of Implementation. In J. D. Hamlet (Ed.), *Afrocentric visions: Studies in culture and communication* (pp. 247–250). SAGE Publications.

Akbar, N. (1991). Mental disorder among African Americans. In R. L. Jones (Ed.), *Black psychology* (pp. 339–352). Cobb & Henry Publishers.

Akbar, N. (1996). *Breaking the chains of psychological slavery.* Mind Productions and Associates.

Akili, Y [@YoloAkili]. (2022, June 27). *Replacing "marginalized communities" with "intentionally exploited communities."* [Tweet]. Twitter. https://twitter.com/YoloAkili/status/1541531283058151426

Allan, R. (2019, June 20). *The demonization of African spirituality in the church is antithetical to the history of Black Christianity*. RaceBaitr. https://racebaitr.com/2019/06/20/the-demonization-of-african-spirituality-in-the-church-is-antithetical-to-the-history-black-christianity/

Allione, T. (2008). *Feeding your demons: Ancient wisdom for resolving inner conflict*. Little, Brown. Spark.

American Psychiatric Association (1994). *Diagnostic and statistical manual of mental disorders*. (4th edition). Washington, DC: Author.

American Psychiatric Association. (2000). *Diagnostic and statistical manual of mental disorders* (4th ed., text rev.).

American Psychiatric Association. (2013). *Diagnostic and statistical manual of mental disorders* (5th ed.). https://doi.org/10.1176/appi.books.9780890425596

American Psychiatric Association. (2021, December). *Apology to people of color for APA's role in promoting, perpetuating, and failing to challenge racism, racial discrimination, and human hierarchy in U.S.* https://www.apa.org/about/policy/racism-apology

Anderson, C. (2016). *White rage: The unspoken truth of our racial divide*. Bloomsbury Publishing.

Annenberg Learner. (n.d.). Native voices. In *American passages: A literary study*. https://www.learner.org/series/american-passages-a-literary-survey/native-voices-video/#:~:text=bicultural%20production%20%E2%80%93%20A%20text%20or,as%20influences%20from%20other%20cultures

Appiah, K. A. (1990). Racisms. In David Goldberg (ed.), *Anatomy of Racism*. University of Minnesota Press. pp. 3–17.

Aron, E. N. (2013). *The highly sensitive person: How to thrive when the world overwhelms you*. Kensington Publishing Corp.

Association for Comprehensive Energy Psychology. (n.d.). Applications of energy psychology. [Webpage]. https://www.ep-conference.org/about-acep

Association for Transpersonal Psychology. (2021). *What is Transpersonal Psychology*. https://www.transpersonalcommunity.org/

Attachment Trauma Network. (2017, January 27). *Neurosequential model of therapeutics (NMT)*. https://www.attachmenttraumanetwork.org/neuro-sequential-model-of-therapeutics-nmt/

Auerhahn, N. C. & Laub, D. (1998). Intergenerational memory of the Holocaust. In Y. Danieli (Ed.), *Intergenerational handbook of multigenerational legacies of trauma* (pp. 21–41). Plenum.

Auguste, E., Nobles, W., & Rowe, D. (2021, November 21). *Why the APA's apology for promoting white supremacy falls short*. NBC News. https://www.nbcnews.com/think/opinion/why-apa-s-apology-promoting-white-supremacy-falls-short-ncna1284229

Avila, E., & Parker, J. (1999). *Woman who glows in the dark: A curandera reveals traditional Aztec secrets of physical and spiritual health*. Perigee.

Barocas, H. A., & Barocas, C. B. (1979). Wounds of the fathers: The next generation of Holocaust victims. *International Review of Psycho-Analysis, 6*(3), 331–340.

Baranowsky, A. B., Young, M., Johnson-Douglas, S., Williams-Keeler, L., & McCarrey, M. (1998). PTSD transmission: A review of secondary traumatization in Holocaust survivor families. *Canadian Psychology/Psychologie canadienne, 39*(4), 247–256.

Bascom, W. R. (1969). *Ifa divination: Communication between gods and men in West Africa*. Indiana University Press.

Battiste, M. (2010). Nourishing the learning spirit. *Education Canada, 50*(1), 14–18. https://www.edcan.ca/wp-content/uploads/EdCan-2010-v50-n1-Battiste.pdf

Bauer, N. M. (2022). The devil and the doctor: The (de)medicalization of exorcism in the Roman Catholic Church. *Religions, 13*(2), 87 (article number 87). https://doi.org/10.3390/rel13020087

Bby Anarchists [@bbyanarchists]. (2019, October 23). *The children will know about our peoples forceful displacement. How the colonizers brought violence to our homelands and inflicted pain* [Digital artwork]. Instagram. https://www.instagram.com/p/B394K5dg8i7/

Bekoff, M. (2000). Animal emotions: Exploring passionate natures: Current interdisciplinary research provides compelling evidence that many animals experience such emotions as joy, fear, love, despair, and grief—we are not alone. *BioScience, 50*(10), 861–870. https://doi.org/10.1641/0006-3568(2000)050[0861:AEEPN]2.0.CO;2

Bernock, D. (2014). *Emerging with wings: A true story of lies, pain, and the love that heals*. 4f Media.

Bhattacharya, S., Fontaine, A., MacCallum, P. E., Drover, J., & Blundell, J. (2019). Stress across generations: DNA methylation as a potential mechanism underlying intergenerational effects of stress in both post-traumatic stress disorder and pre-clinical predator stress rodent models. *Frontiers in Behavioral Neuroscience, 13*(113). https://doi.org/10.3389/fnbeh.2019.00113

Bhopal, R. (2007). The beautiful skull and Blumenbach's errors: The birth of the scientific concept of race. *BMJ (Clinical Research Ed.), 335*(7633), 1308–1309. https://doi.org/10.1136/bmj.39413.463958.80

Bioneers. [Username] (2018). *Rupa Marya—Health and justice: The path of liberation through medicine* [Video]. YouTube. https://www.youtube.com/watch?v =GyymzSE0VE8[36]

Bishop. A. (2018, January 19). *Becoming an ally: breaking the cycle of oppression* .http://web.archive.org/web/20180119171330mp_/http://www.becominganally .ca/Becoming_an_Ally/Educating_Allies__Ch.html

Black Health Alliance. (n.d.). *Anti-Black racism*. https://blackhealthalliance.ca/ home/antiblack-racism/

Blanchett, W. J., Klingner, J. K., & Harry, B. (2009). The intersection of race, culture, language, and disability: Implications for urban education. *Urban Education, 44*(4), 389–409. https://doi.org/10.1177%2F0042085909338686

Blumenfeld, W. J. (2007). Heterosexism: Introduction. In M. Adams, W. Blumenfeld, C. Cateaneda, H. W. Hackman, M. L. Peters, & X. Zuniga (Eds.), *Readings for diversity and social justice*, 371–376. Routledge.

Bragin, L. (2021, March 31). *Black women's eloquent rage: A lecture from Brittney Cooper*. Vanderbilt Political Review. https://vanderbiltpoliticalreview.com/10446/ campus/black-womens-eloquent-rage-a-lecture-from-brittney-cooper/

Brave Heart, M. Y. H. (2003). The historical trauma response among Natives and its relationship to substance abuse: A Lakota illustration. *Journal of Psychoactive Drugs, 35*(1), 7–13. https://doi.org/10.1080/02791072.2003.10399988

Brave Heart, M. Y. H. (2005, April 22). *From intergenerational trauma to intergenerational healing*. [Keynote address]. Fifth Annual Wellbriety Conference, Denver, CO, United States of America.

Brave Heart, M. Y. H., & DeBruyn, L. M. (1998). The American Indian holocaust: Healing historical unresolved grief. *American Indian and Alaska Native Mental Health Research, 8*(2), 60–82. https://doi.org/10.5820/aian.0802.1998.60

British Columbia Ministry of Education. (2017). *Aboriginal Report 2011/12 - 2015/16: How are we doing?* http://www.bced.gov.bc.ca/reports/pdfs/ab_hawd/ Public.pdf

Britton, A. M. (2016). *Lucumi & the children of cotton: Gender, race, and ethnicity in*

---

36 The original website accessed became inactive during the course of writing this book. As a result, the link refers to an archived version of the site as it existed at the original time of accessing.

the mapping of a Black Atlantic politics of religion. [Doctoral dissertation, City University of New York]. CUNY Academic Works.

Burstow, B. (1992). *Radical feminist therapy: Working in the context of violence.* SAGE Publications. https://doi.org/10.4135/9781483326092

Cajete, G. (2000). *Native science. Natural laws of interdependence.* Clear Light.

Caldwell, C., & Leighton, L. B. (Eds.). (2018). *Oppression and the body: Roots, resistance, and resolutions.* North Atlantic Books.

Canadian Association of College and University Student Services. (2017). *Student Affairs and Services Competency Model.* CACUSS. https://www.utm.utoronto.ca/slp/sites/files/slp/public/shared/CACUSS_Student_Affairs_and_Services_Competency_Model_FINAL.pdf

Canadian Council on Learning. (2009). *The state of Aboriginal learning in Canada: A holistic approach to measuring success.* http://www.afn.ca/uploads/files/education2/state_of_aboriginal_learning_in_canada-final_report,_ccl,_2009.pdf

Carl Jung. (2021, September 2). In *Wikipedia.* https://en.wikipedia.org/w/index.php?title=Carl_Jung&oldid=1042019232

Caroll, S. (n.d.). *Effects of the French Revolution.* Rewordify.com. https://rewordify.com/index.php?u=np9jdtgngt7mq8

Carr, R. (2022, January 25). *With the transfer, tribal consortium returns Indigenous guardianship to Sinkyone Lands on Mendocino Coast.* Save the Redwoods. https://www.savetheredwoods.org/press-releases/523-acres-of-forestland-donated-to-intertribal-sinkyone-wilderness-council/

Carrington, P. (n.d.). *History of meridian tapping and EFT.* Pat Carrington. https://patcarrington.com/about-eft/history-of-eft/

Carter, R. (2007). Racism and psychological and emotional injury: Recognizing and assessing race-based traumatic stress. *The Counseling Psychologist, 35*(1), 13–105. https://doi.org/10.1177%2F0011000006292033

Cartwright, S. A. (1851). *Diseases and peculiarities of the negro race.* Africans in America. https://www.pbs.org/wgbh/aia/part4/4h3106t.html

CBS Interactive. (2022, March 10). Melinda French Gates and Ai-Jen Poo advocate for "invisible" domestic labor and care workers [TV series episode]. In *Changing the Game.* CBS News. https://www.cbsnews.com/video/melinda-french-gates-and-ai-jen-poo-advocate-for-invisible-domestic-labor-and-care-workers/

Center on the Developing Child. (n.d.). *Epigenetics and child development: How children's experiences affect their genes.* Harvard University. https://developingchild.harvard.edu/resources/what-is-epigenetics-and-how-does-it-relate-to-child-development/

Centers for Disease Control and Prevention. (2021, April 6). *Violence prevention: About the CDC-Kaiser ACE Study.* https://www.cdc.gov/violenceprevention/aces/about.html

Chakrabarti, M., & Bauman, A. (2019, December 11). *The growth (and new contexts) of LGBTQ ball culture.* On Point. WBUR Boston. https://www.wbur.org/onpoint/2019/12/11/ballroom-scene-lgbtq-ball-culture-vogue

Cherry, K. (2020, March 12). *Cathexis and anticathexis according to Freudian theory: According to the Freudian theory of drives.* Verywell Mind. https://www.verywellmind.com/cathexis-and-anticathexis-2795843

Cherry, K. (2020, April 28). *Wilhelm Wundt Biography.* VeryWell Mind. https://www.verywellmind.com/who-is-the-father-of-psychology-2795249

Chong, J. (n.d.). *What is the dantian? Why is lower dantian breathing important?* Dantian Health. https://dantianhealth.com.au/what-is-the-dantian/

Cleveland Clinic. (2019, December 9). *What happens to your body during the fight-or-flight response?* https://health.clevelandclinic.org/what-happens-to-your-body-during-the-fight-or-flight-response/

Coates, T.-N. (2010, October 20). A culture of poverty. *The Atlantic.* https://www.theatlantic.com/personal/archive/2010/10/a-culture-of-poverty/64854/

Coates, T.-N. (2015). *Between the world and me.* Spiegel & Grau.

Colonization. (2022, January 24). In *Wikipedia.* https://en.wikipedia.org/w/index.php?title=Colonization&oldid=1067737877

Complex Trauma. (2021). *White body supremacy.* https://www.complextrauma.org/glossary/white-body-supremacy/

Cooper, B. (2018). *Eloquent rage: A black feminist discovers her superpower.* St. Martin's Press.

Cornah, D. (2006). *The impact of spirituality on mental health: A review of the literature.* Mental Health Foundation. https://www.mentalhealth.org.uk/sites/default/files/impact-spirituality.pdf

Council for the Advancement of Standards in Higher Education. (2015). *CAS Professional Standards for Higher Education* (9th ed.).

Cowan, E. (2014). *Plant spirit medicine: A journey into the healing wisdom of plants* (2nd ed.). Sounds True.

Crowther, L. (2019, August 6). *What is disenfranchised grief?* Legacy. https://www.legacy.com/advice/what-is-disenfranchised-grief/

Dana, D. (2018). *Polyvagal theory in therapy.* Norton.

Dana, D. (2019, September 9). *Engaging the rhythm of regulation: A polyvagal theory guide to safety and connection* [Pre-conference workshop]. DDP International Conference, Kansas City, U.S. https://ddpnetwork.org/usa-canada/conferences/registration-open-for-2019-ddp-international-conference-kansas-city-usa/

Dana, R. H. (2005). *Multicultural assessment: Principles, applications, and examples.* Routledge.

Danieli, Y. (1998). Introduction. In Y. Danieli. (Ed.), *International handbook of multigenerational legacies of trauma* (pp. 1–17). Springer U.S. https://doi.org/10.1007/978-1-4757-5567-1

Darkmatter. (2015, September 5). *Poet duo Darkmatter on how "Transmisogyny is the afterlife of colonialism," and more.* Medium. https://medium.com/the-cake/poet-duo-darkmatter-on-how-transmisogyny-is-the-afterlife-of-colonialism-and-more-d8997df8e2b5

Daut, M. (2020, June 30). *When France extorted Haiti: The greatest heist in history.* The Conversation. https://theconversation.com/when-france-extorted-haiti-the-greatest-heist-in-history-137949

de Arellano, M. A. R., Lyman, D. R., Jobe-Shields, L., George, P., Dougherty, R. H., Daniels, A. S., Ghose, S. S., Huang, L., & Delphin-Rittmon, M. E. (2014). Trauma-focused cognitive behavioral therapy for children and adolescents: Assessing the evidence. *Psychiatric Services, 65*(5), 591–602. https://doi.org/10.1176%2Fappi.ps.201300255

DeArth-Pendley, G. (2012). *Racial disparity and the pathologizing of People of Color in mental health diagnoses and psychological assessment.* Research Gate. https://www.researchgate.net/publication/293653360_Racial_Disparity_and_the_Pathologizing_of_People_of_Color_in_Mental_Health_Diagnoses_and_Psychological_Assessment

DeGruy, J. (n.d.) *Post Traumatic Slave Syndrome.* JoyDeGruy.com. https://www.joydegruy.com/post-traumatic-slave-syndrome

DeGruy, J. (2005). *Post-traumatic slave syndrome: America's legacy of enduring injury and healing.* Uptone Press.

Dein, S. (2010). Religion, spirituality, and mental health. *Psychiatric Times, 27*(1). https://www.psychiatrictimes.com/view/religion-spirituality-and-mental-health

Dhanesha, N. (2022, January 17). *A physicist's lessons about race, power, and the universe.* Vox. https://www.vox.com/22880089/physics-race-chanda-prescod-weinstein-disordered-cosmos

Dobkin de Rios, M. (2002). What we can learn from shamanic healing: Brief psychotherapy with Latino immigrant clients. *American Journal of Public Health*, 92(10), 1576–1582. https://doi.org/10.2105%2Fajph.92.10.1576

Donegan, M. (2020). How Bertha Pappenheim cured herself. In J. Valenti & J. Friedman (Eds.), *Believe me: How trusting women can change the world* (pp. 16–22). Seal Press.

Donovan, M. S., & Cross, C. T. (Eds.). (2002). *Minority students in special and gifted education*. National Research Council.

Douglass, F. (1894/n.d.). *The Civil Rights Case* [Speech transcript]. Civil Rights Mass Meeting, Washington, DC, United States. (1883). https://teachingamericanhistory.org/document/the-civil-rights-case/

Drescher, J. (2015). Out of DSM: Depathologizing homosexuality. *Behavioral Sciences*, 5(4), 565–575. https://doi.org/10.3390%2Fbs5040565

Drexel University: Center for Hunger-Free Communities. (2019). *Systemic oppression and trauma: Why healing-centered, two-generation approaches are crucial to poverty alleviation*. https://drexel.edu/hunger-free-center/research/briefs-and-reports/systemic-oppression-and-trauma/

Du Bois, W. E. B. (1903). *The souls of black folk: Essays and sketches*. A. C. McClurg & Co., Chicago.

Duran, E. (2006). *Healing the soul wound: Counseling with American Indians and other Native peoples*. Teachers College Press.

Duran, E. (1995). *Native American Postcolonial Psychology*. State University of New York Press.

Ehrenreich, B. (1971). *The American health empire: Power, profits, and politics*. Random House.

Elliot, G. (2016, July 21). *10 ways white supremacy wounds White people: A tale of mutuality*. American Friends Service Committee. https://www.afsc.org/blogs/acting-in-faith/10-ways-white-supremacy-wounds-white-people-tale-mutuality

EMDR International Association. (n.d.). *About EMDR therapy*. https://www.emdria.org/about-emdr-therapy/

Encyclopaedia Britannica. (n.d.). Toussaint Louverture's achievements. In *Encyclopaedia Britannica*. Retrieved August 28, 2020, from https://www.britannica.com/summary/Toussaint-Louvertures-Achievements

Encyclopaedia Britannica. (2020, February 28). Collective unconscious. In *Encyclopaedia Britannica*. https://www.britannica.com/science/collective-unconscious

Equal Justice Initiative. (2014, September 1). *"Cultural genocide" and Native American children.* https://eji.org/news/history-racial-injustice-cultural-genocide/

Estés, C. P. (1995). *Women who run with the wolves: Myths and stories of the wild woman archetype.* Ballantine Books.

Eyerman, R. (2002). *Cultural Trauma: Slavery and the Formation of African American Identity.* Cambridge University Press.

Faherty, K. (n.d.). *Energy psychology.* Red Bank Counselling. https://redbankcounseling.com/energy-psychology/

Fanon, F. (1967). *Black skin, white masks* (C. L. Markmann, Trans.). Grove Press. (Original work published 1952)

Farreras, I. (2013). *History of mental illness.* Noba textbook series: Psychology. Noba Project.

Feinstein, D. (2019). Energy psychology: Efficacy, speed, mechanisms. *Explore, 15*(5), 340–351. https://doi.org/10.1016/j.explore.2018.11.003

Fenton, L. W. (2020, July 17). *Take note: Dr. Tashel Bordere on suffocated grief.* WPSU. https://radio.wpsu.org/education/2020-07-17/take-note-dr-tashel-bordere-on-suffocated-grief

Ferguson, I. (2017). *Politics of the mind: Marxism and mental distress.* Bookmarks Publications.

Findlay, D. (2021, October 1). *Weekly tip: Define lateral violence* [Video]. https://www.dfindlay.ca/2012/10/01/weekly-tip-define-lateral-violence/

Fitzsimons, T. (2018, June 20). *'Transsexualism' removed from World Health Organization's disease manual.* NBC News. https://www.nbcnews.com/feature/nbc-out/transsexualism-removed-world-health-organization-s-disease-manual-n885141

Flaherty, S. C., & Sadler, L. S. (2011). A review of attachment theory in the context of adolescent parenting. *Journal of Pediatric Health Care, 25*(2), 114–121. https://doi.org/10.1016%2Fj.pedhc.2010.02.005

Foor, D. (2017). *Ancestral medicine: Rituals for personal and family healing.* Simon and Schuster.

Ford, A., Blanchett, W. J., & Brown, L. (2006). *Teacher education and students with significant disabilities: Revisiting essential elements.* Center on Personnel Studies in Special Education. http://copsse.education.ufl.edu/copsse/docs/IB-11E/1/IB-11E.pdf

Forneret, A. (n.d.). [Website homepage]. Alica Forneret. https://alicaforneret.com/

Fowers, A., & Wan, W. (2020, June 12). Depression and anxiety spiked among

Black Americans after George Floyd's death. *The Washington Post.* https://www.washingtonpost.com/health/2020/06/12/mental-health-george-floyd-census/

Fraley, R. C. (2018). *Adult attachment theory and research: A brief overview.* Psychology Illinois Labs. http://labs.psychology.illinois.edu/~rcfraley/attachment.htm

Freire, P. (2018). *Pedagogy of the oppressed: 50th-anniversary edition.* (D. Macedo, Trans.). Bloomsbury Publishing. (Original work published 1968)

Fuentes, A., Ackermann, R. R., Athreya, S., et al. (2019). AAPA Statement on Race and Racism. *Am J Phys Anthropol.* 169, 400–402. https://doi.org/10.1002/ajpa.23882

Gaelic Matters. (n.d.). *Celtic Religion and Beliefs.* https://www.gaelicmatters.com/celtic-religion.html

Galindo, D. L. (2016). *Trauma, resilience, hope, and religious coping in Haiti* (Publication No. 55195958) [Doctoral dissertation, George Fox University]. Semantic Scholar.

Gallagher, R. (2016, July 1). As a psychiatrist, I diagnose mental illness. Also, I help spot demonic possession. *The Washington Post.* https://www.washingtonpost.com/posteverything/wp/2016/07/01/as-a-psychiatrist-i-diagnose-mental-illness-and-sometimes-demonic-possession/

Gardner, F. (1999). Transgenerational processes and the trauma of sexual abuse. *The European Journal of Psychotherapy, Counselling & Health, 2*(3), 297–308.

The Gateway Institute. (n.d.). *Magical thinking: OCD symptoms and treatment.* https://www.gatewayocd.com/magical-thinking-ocd-symptoms-and-treatment/

Gimbel, S. (2020, October 14). *Carl Jung and the concept of collective consciousness.* Wondrium Daily. https://www.wondriumdaily.com/carl-jung-and-the-concept-of-collective-consciousness/

Ginwright, S. (2018, May 31). *The future of healing: Shifting from trauma-informed care to healing centered engagement.* Medium. https://ginwright.medium.com/the-future-of-healing-shifting-from-trauma-informed-care-to-healing-centered-engagement-634f557ce69c

Ginzburg, R. (1988). *100 years of lynching.* Baltimore, MD: Black Classic.

Giordan, G., & Possamai, A. (2016). The over-policing of the devil: A sociology of exorcism. *Social Compass, 63*(4), 444–460. https://doi.org/10.1177%2F0037768616663982

GoodTherapy. (2016, January, 8). *Stockholm Syndrome.* https://www.goodtherapy.org/blog/psychpedia/stockholm-syndrome

GoodTherapy. (2018, June 22). *Breathwork.* https://www.goodtherapy.org/learn-about-therapy/types/breathwork

GoodTherapy. (2017, June 27). *Boundaries*. https://www.goodtherapy.org/blog/psychpedia/boundaries

Graf, C. (2016, August 23). Wendy Hill: Second chance at life gives greater purpose of healing others. *Anishinabek News*. http://anishinabeknews.ca/2016/08/23/wendy-hill-second-chance-at-life-gives-greater-purpose-of-healing-others/

Greene, E. M. (2023). The mental health industrial complex: A study in three cases. *Journal of Humanistic Psychology, 63*(1), 84–102. https://doi.org/10.1177%2F00221 67819830516

Grob, G. N. (1972). *Mental institutions in America*. Transaction Publishers.

Gudzer, J., & Walcott, G. (2021, November 5). *Psycho-historiographic cultural therapy and its emergence in Jamaica*. Harvard Medical School. https://ghsm.hms.harvard.edu/ghsm-events/friday-morning-seminars/psycho-historiographic-cultural-therapy-and-its-emergence

Gutman, H. G. (1976). *The Black family in slavery and freedom 1750–1925*. New York, NY: Vintage.

Habash, C. L. (2017). *How to set energetic boundaries and stay true to yourself*. PsychCentral. https://psychcentral.com/blog/imperfect/2018/01/how-to-set-energetic-boundaries-and-stay-true-to-yourself

Haines, S. K. (2019). *The politics of trauma: Somatics, healing, and social justice*. North Atlantic Books.

Haiti Outreach Ministries. (2020). *Haitian health care beliefs and Voodoo (Voudou)*. https://www.haitiom.org/wp-content/uploads/2021/05/Health-care-beliefs-and-Voodoo-rev-2020.pdf

Hancock, R. L. A. (2017). "We know who our relatives are": Métis identities in historical, political, and legal contexts. In J. Carrière & C. Richardson (Eds.), *Calling our families home: Métis peoples' experiences with child welfare* (pp. 9–30). JCharlton Publishing.

Harris House. (2016, April 11). *How trauma affects the brain*. https://www.harrishousestl.org/primer-trauma-affects-brain/

Harris, A. (2021, April 26). The burden of being 'on point.' *The Atlantic*. https://www.theatlantic.com/politics/archive/2021/04/black-boys-traumamisunderstood-behavior/618684/

Harris, N. B. (2018). *The deepest well: Healing the long-term effects of childhood adversity*. Houghton Mifflin Harcourt.

Harry, B., & Klingner, J. (2006). *Why are so many minority students in special education?: Understanding race & disability in schools*. Teachers College Press.

Hart, T. (2010). *The secret spiritual world of children: The breakthrough discovery that profoundly alters our conventional view of children's mystical experiences*. New World Library.

Harvard Library. (n.d.). *Scientific racism*. https://library.harvard.edu/confronting-anti-black-racism/scientific-racism

Hasnaa, M [@Maryamhasnaa]. (2020, June 20). *Energy boundaries allow connection without toxic merging and enmeshment. This is the beginning of emotional liberation. Where you begin to* [Tweet]. Twitter. https://twitter.com/maryamhasnaa/status/1274208996014977024

Hay House Incorporated. (2021, January 5). *Spirit junkie card deck* [Mobile app]. *Apple App Store*. https://apps.apple.com/us/app/spirit-junkie-card-deck/id1532996434?mt=8

Heldke, L. M. & O'Connor, P. (Eds.). (2003). *Oppression, privilege & resistance: Theoretical perspectives on racism, sexism, and heterosexism*. McGraw Hill.

Herek, G. M. (2004). Beyond homophobia: Thinking about sexual prejudice and stigma in the twenty first century. *Sexuality Research & Social Policy, 1*(2), 6–24.

Herman, J. L. (1992). *Trauma and recovery: The aftermath of violence—from domestic abuse to political terror*. Basic Books.

Hickling, F. W. (2009). The European-American psychosis: Psychohistoriographic perspective of contemporary Western civilization. *The Journal of Psychohistory, 37*(1), 67–81. https://pubmed.ncbi.nlm.nih.gov/19852241/

Hickling, F. W. (2020). Owning our madness: Contributions of Jamaican psychiatry to decolonizing global mental health. *Transcultural Psychiatry, 57*(1), 19–31. https://doi.org/10.1177/1363461519893142

A history of mental institutions in the United States [Timeline]. (2012). Tiki-Toki. http://www.tiki-toki.com/timeline/entry/37146/A-History-of-Mental-Institutions-in-the-United-States/#vars!date=1807-11-11_09:09:40!

History of York. (n.d.). *Georgian: The Retreat*. http://www.historyofyork.org.uk/themes/georgian/the-retreat

Holmes, L. (2021, August 18). *What is energy psychology?* Verywell Mind. https://www.verywellmind.com/is-energy-psychology-for-real-2330736

Holmqvist, M. (2013). Psychological Pathology. In M. D. Gellman & J. R. Turner (Eds.), *Encyclopedia of Behavioral Medicine* (pp. 1559–1560). Springer. https://doi.org/10.1007/978-1-4419-1005-9_1174

Homer, B. (2011). Freire, teaching, and learning: Culture circles across contexts by Mariana Souto-Manning. *Journal of Latinos and Education*, 10(3), 277–279. https://doi.org/10.1080/15348431.2011.581116

hooks, b. (1996). *killing rage: ending racism*. Henry Holt & Company.

hooks, b. (2004). *The will to change: men, masculinity, and love*. Atria Books.

Horne, G. (2018). *The apocalypse of settler colonialism: The roots of slavery, white supremacy, and capitalism in 17th century North America and the Caribbean*. NYU Press.

Hughes, L. (1995). *The collected poems of Langston Hughes*. Vintage.

Human Rights Campaign Foundation. (n.d.). *The lies and dangers of efforts to change sexual orientation or gender identity*. https://www.hrc.org/resources/the-lies-and-dangers-of-reparative-therapy

Hunter, M. (2007). The persistent problem of colorism: Skin tone, status, and inequality. *Sociology Compass* 1(1), 237–254. https://doi.org/10.1111/j.1751-9020.2007.00006

Hypnosis Motivation Institute. (2022). 1850 – The Nancy School. In *Hypnosis in History*. Hypnosis Motivation Institute: College of Hypnotherapy. https://hypnosis.edu/history/the-nancy-school

Immigration Act of 1882. (1882).

Immigration Act of 1907. (1907).

Ina, S. (1999). *Children of the camps: Viewer's guide*. Children of the Camps Documentary. http://www.children-of-the-camps.org/documentary/viewguide2.html

Infoplease. (2017, February 11). *How many countries?* https://www.infoplease.com/world/diplomacy/how-many-countries

Ingerman, S. (1991). *Soul retrieval: mending the fragmented self through shamanic practice*. HarperSanFransico.

Jaenisch, R., & Bird, A. (2003). Epigenetic regulation of gene expression: How the genome integrates intrinsic and environmental signals. *Nature Genetics, 33*, 245–254. https://doi.org/10.1038/ng1089

James, B. (1994). *Handbook for treatment of attachment trauma problems in children*. Free Press.

Jean-Martin Charcot. (2021, September 10). In *Wikipedia*. https://en.wikipedia.org/w/index.php?title=Jean-Martin_Charcot&oldid=1043510933

Jiang, S., Postovit, L., Cattaneo, A., Binder, E. B., & Aitchison, K. J. (2019). Epigenetic modifications in stress response genes associated with childhood trauma. *Front Psychiatry, 10*, 808. https://doi.org/10.3389%2Ffpsyt.2019.00808

Johann Friedrich Blumenbach. (2022, January 28). In *Wikipedia*. https://en.wikipedia.org/w/index.php?title=Johann_Friedrich_Blumenbach&oldid=1068370912

John, J. (2020). *Freedom: Medicine words for your brave revolution*. Soul Water Rising.

Johnson, J. (2012). *TLC 023—American Indian literature: Resistance and renewal* [Syllabus]. English/American Indian Studies Program, University of Idaho. https://www.webpages.uidaho.edu/engl484jj/Historical_Trauma.htm

Kanji, K. (2020, July 3). *The 'benevolent' policing of social work and mental health*. Rabble. https://rabble.ca/anti-racism/benevolent-policing-social-work-and-mental-health/

Kellerman, N. P. F. (2001). Transmission of Holocaust trauma—An integrative view. *Psychiatry, 64*(3), 256–267

Kelly, K. (2020, August 25). What 'capitalism' is and how it affects people. *Teen Vogue*. https://www.teenvogue.com/story/what-capitalism-is

Kempler, C., & Benham, B. (2022, January 25). *Study reveals fourfold range in rates of mental health problems among U.S. children based on relational and social risks*. John Hopkins Bloomberg School of Public Health. https://publichealth.jhu.edu/2022/study-reveals-fourfold-range-in-rates-of-mental-health-problems-among-us-children-based-on-relational-and-social-risks

Kessler, D. (2019). *Finding meaning: The sixth stage of grief*. Scribner.

Khan, A., & Meadows, J. [@wokescientist & @jessiethesluggish]. (2021, December 2). *A series breaking down capitalist psych & it's impact on our collective mental health* [Carousel]. Instagram. https://www.instagram.com/p/CW_UpftPgoA/

Kim, J.-Y. [@itsjiyounkim]. (2020, August 7). *Therapy is supposed to be a safe(r), healing space but I have witnessed and heard of too many instances of* [Carousel]. Instagram. https://www.instagram.com/p/CDmbnk4hZLy/

Kim, J. K. (2020, August 10). *Eight ways that therapists can perpetuate white supremacy*. ItsJiYounKim. https://www.itsjiyounkim.com/blog/8-ways-that-therapists-can-perpetuate-white-supremacy

Kim, J.-Y. [@itsjiyounkim]. (2021, April 15). *I'm fed up with witnessing my BIPOC clients being directed towards more therapy when their workplaces are the ones harming* [Carousel]. Instagram. https://www.instagram.com/p/CNsXb4osR_e/

King, R. (2004). *Healing rage: Women making inner peace possible*. Gotham.

Koeske, G. F., & Koeske, R. D. (1989). Work load and burnout: Can social support and perceived accomplishment help? *Social Work, 24*(3), 243–248. https://www.jstor.org/stable/23715305

Kohout, E., & Brainin, E. (2004). How is trauma transmitted? *International Journal of Psychoanalysis, 84*, 1261–1264

La Guardia, F. H. (1961). *The making of an insurgent: An autobiography 1882–1919*. Capricorn Books. (Original work published ca. 1948)

Lacal, I., & Ventura, R. (2018). Epigenetic inheritance: Concepts, mechanisms and perspectives. *Frontiers in Molecular Neuroscience, 11*(292). https://doi.org/10.3389/fnmol.2018.00292

Lehrner, A., & Yehuda, R. (2018). Cultural trauma and epigenetic inheritance. *Development and Psychopathology, 20*(5), 1763–1777. https://doi.org/10.1017/s0954579418001153

Lenin, V. I. (2008). *Imperialism, the highest stage of Capitalism*. [eBook edition]. Marxists Internet Archive https://www.marxists.org/archive/lenin/works/1916/imp-hsc/index.htm

Levant, E. (2014, Aug 25). A tragedy that doesn't cry for an inquiry. *Toronto Sun*. https://www.torontosun.com/2014/08/25/a-tragedy-that-doesnt-cry-for-an-inquiry

Levesque, R. J. R. (2011). Cultural Biases in Research. In: Levesque R. J. R. (Ed.) *Encyclopedia of Adolescence* (pp. 583–584). Springer. https://doi.org/10.1007/978-1-4419-1695-2_632

Levine, P. A., & Frederick, A. (1997). *Waking the tiger: Healing trauma: The innate capacity to transform overwhelming experiences*. North Atlantic Books.

Lichtman, H. (1984). Parental communication of Holocaust experiences and personality characteristics among second-generation survivors. *Journal of Clinical Psychology, 40*(4), 914–924.

Linklater, R. (2014). *Decolonizing trauma work: Indigenous stories and strategies*. Fernwood Publishing.

Lumen Learning. (2022). History of mental illness from the Stone Age to the 20th century. In *Abnormal Psychology*. https://courses.lumenlearning.com/hvcc-abnormalpsychology/chapter/1-5-prominent-themes-in-abnormal-psychology-throughout-history/

Maker, A. H., & Buttenheim, M. (2000). Parenting difficulties in sexual-abuse survivors: A theoretical framework with dual psychodynamic and cognitive-behavioral strategies for intervention. *Psychotherapy, 37* (2), 159–170.

Manke, K. (2020, February 17). *Historian uncovers gynecology's brutal roots in slavery*. Berkeley News. https://news.berkeley.edu/2020/02/17/historian-uncovers-gynecologys-brutal-roots-in-slavery/

Marya. R. (2018). Colonialism Diagram [Infographic]. https://www.youtube.com/watch?v=GyymzSE0VE8&t=3s

Marya, R., & Patel, R. (2021). *Inflamed: Deep medicine and the anatomy of injustice.* Farrar, Straus and Giroux.

Maslach, C., Jackson, S. E., & Leiter, M. P. (1997). Maslach burnout inventory: Third edition. In C. P. Zalaquett & R. J. Wood (Eds.), *Evaluating stress: A book of resources* (pp. 191–218). Scarecrow Education.

Matthews, D. (2019). Capitalism and mental health. *Monthly Review, 70*(8), 49–62. https://doi.org/10.14452/MR-070-08-2019-01

McCoy, B. (2021, December 20). How your brain copes with grief, and why it takes time to heal. NPR. https://www.npr.org/sections/health-shots/2021/12/20/1056741090/grief-loss-holiday-brain-healing

McGoldrick, M., Gerson, R., & Petry, S. (2008). *Genograms: Assessment and intervention* (3rd ed.). W. W. Norton.

McLean, S.-A. (2014, December 14). *Glossary: White supremacist racism.* Decolonize ALL The Things. https://decolonizeallthethings.com/learning-tools/glossary-of-key-terms/

McLean, S.-A. (2017, May 30). *Decolonization: What ought to be.* Decolonize ALL The Things. https://decolonizeallthethings.com/2017/05/30/what-is-what-ought-to-be/

McLeod, S. (2021). *Freud's id, ego, and superego.* SimplyPsychology. https://www.simplypsychology.org/psyche.html

McMurdock, M. (2022, February 20). *School leader crisis: Overwhelmed by mounting mental health issues and public distrust, a 'mass exodus' of principals could be coming.* The 74. https://www.the74million.org/article/school-leaders-crisis-overwhelmed-by-mounting-mental-health-issues-public-distrust-mass-exodus-of-principals-could-be-coming/

Mead, E. (2021, December 14). *The history and origin of meditation.* PositivePsychology.com https://positivepsychology.com/history-of-meditation/

Medicalization. (2022, January 19). In *Wikipedia.* https://en.wikipedia.org/w/index.php?title=Medicalization&oldid=1066581573

Mehl-Madrona, L. (2019, March 1). What can Western medicine learn from Indigenous healing traditions? *The Positive Side: Freedom Fighter, 21*(1), 18–21. https://www.catie.ca/positive-side/what-can-western-medicine-learn-from-indigenous-healing-traditions

Menakem, R. (2017). *My grandmother's hands: Racialized trauma and the pathway to mending our hearts and bodies.* Central Recovery Press.

Mental Health America. (n.d.). *Black and African American communities and mental health.* https://www.mhanational.org/issues/black-and-african-american-communities-and-mental-health

Mentally Fit Pro. (n.d.). *The big list of burnout resources for mental health professionals.* https://www.mentallyfitpro.com/c/share-a-resource/the-big-list-of-burnout-resources-for-therapists

Merriam-Webster. (n.d.). Alienist. In *Merriam-Webster.com dictionary*. Retrieved October 4, 2021 from https://www.merriam-webster.com/dictionary/alienist

Merriam-Webster. (n.d.). Systematic. In *Merriam-Webster.com dictionary*. Retrieved January 15, 2022. https://www.merriam-webster.com/dictionary/systematic

Metzl, J. M. (2010). *The protest psychosis: How schizophrenia became a Black disease.* Beacon Press.

Miles, N. (2020). *You are intuitive: Trust your truth. Take back your power.* Numinous Books.

Milgram, N. A. (1978). Psychological stress and adjustment in time of war and peace: The Israeli experience as presented in two conferences. *Israel Annals of Psychiatry & Related Disciplines, 16*(4), 327–338.

Miller, P. S., & Levine, R. L. (2012). Avoiding genetic genocide: Understanding good intentions and eugenics in the complex dialogue between the medical and disability communities. *Genetics in Medicine, 15*(2), 95-102. https://doi.org/10.1038%2Fgim.2012.102

Mingus, M. (2015, February 6). *Medical industrial complex visual.* Leaving Evidence. https://leavingevidence.wordpress.com/2015/02/06/medical-industrial-complex-visual/

Miu, A. S., & Moore, J. R. (2021). Behind the masks: Experiences of mental health practitioners of color during the COVID-19 pandemic. *Academic Psychiatry, 45*, 539–544. https://doi.org/10.1007/s40596-021-01427-w

Miyoshi, N. (1978). *Identity Crisis of the Sansei and the Concentration Camp.* Children of the Camps Internment History. http://www.pbs.org/childofcamp/history/health.html

Mongiovi, J. (n.d.). *A history of hypnosis: From ancient times to modern psychology.* https://johnmongiovi.com/history-hypnosis

Moran, M. (2020, October 14). Activist Angela Davis addresses economic, racial inequalities in annual Hesburgh lecture. *The Observer.* https://ndsmcobserver.com/2020/10/activist-angela-davis-addresses-economic-racial-inequalities-in-virtual-lecture/

Morse, G., Salyers, M. P., Rollins, A. L., Monroe-DeVita, M., & Pfahler, C. (2012).

Burnout in mental health services: a review of the problem and its remediation. Administration and policy in mental health, 39(5), 341–352. https://doi.org/10.1007/s10488-011-0352-1

Mullan-Gonzalez, J. (2012). *Slavery and the intergenerational transmission of trauma in inner city African American male youth: A model program—from the cotton fields to the the concrete jungle.* (Publication No. 3539806) [Doctoral dissertation, California Institute of Integral Studies]. ProQuest Dissertations Publishing.

Mullan, J [@decolonizingtherapy]. (2019, January 9). *This letter is wrapped in deep love and compassion. It's not just limited to therapists, but body workers, social workers* [Photograph]. Instagram. https://www.instagram.com/p/BsbNQPtBiR9/

Mullan, J [@decolonizingtherapy]. (2019, September 13). *We can tend to our emotional mental health and hold systemic oppression accountable. But many social service groups do not. I want to know if you're down for the struggle* [Photograph]. Instagram. https://www.instagram.com/p/B2W7tMVAp_F/

Myers, B. E., II. (2014). *"Drapetomania": Rebellion, defiance and free Black insanity in the Antebellum United States* (ProQuest ID: Myers_ucla_0031D_13159) [Doctoral dissertation, University of California, Los Angeles]. eScholarship. https://escholarship.org/uc/item/9dc055h5

Myss, C. (2011). *Anatomy of the spirit: The seven stages of power and healing.* Penguin Random House Australia.

Nagata, D. K. (1993). *Legacy of injustice: Exploring the cross-generational impact of the Japanese American internment.* Plenum Press. https://doi.org/10.1007/978-1-4899-1118-6

Nagata, D. K., Trierweiler, S. J., & Talbot, R. (1999). Long-term effects of internment during early childhood on third-generation Japanese Americans. *American Journal of Orthopsychiatry, 69*(1), 19–29. https://psycnet.apa.org/doi/10.1037/h0080378

National Indian Brotherhood, Canada, Indian, & Northern Affairs. (1972). *Indian Control of Indian Education.* National Indian Brotherhood.

National Institutes of Health. (2007). *Information about mental illness and the brain.* NIH National Library of Medicine. https://www.ncbi.nlm.nih.gov/books/NBK20369/

Negroid. (2022, February 17). In *Wikipedia.* https://en.wikipedia.org/w/index.php?title=Negroid&oldid=1072348756

Niederland, W. G. (1964). Psychiatric disorders among persecution victims: A Contribution to the understanding of concentration camp pathology and its afteraffects. *Journal of Nervous and Mental Diseases, 139,* 458–474.

Norcross, J. C. (2000). Here comes the self-help revolution in mental health. *Psy-*

chotherapy: Theory, Research, Practice, Training 37(4), 370–377. https://psycnet.apa.org/doiLanding?doi=10.1037%2F0033-3204.37.4.370

Novic, E. (2016). *The concept of cultural genocide: An international law perspective.* Oxford University Press. http://dx.doi.org/10.1093/acprof:oso/9780198787167.001.0001

O'Connor, E. M. (2001). An 'American psychologist.' *Monitor on Psychology, 32*(10). https://www.apa.org/monitor/nov01/american

Ogorchukwu, J. (2018). *The geometry of being Black.* CreateSpace Independent Publishing Platform.

Ogorchukwu, J. [@ogorchukwuu]. (2021, October 13). *A tender reminder* [Photograph]. Instagram. https://www.instagram.com/p/CU-5bPYBp-m/

Ó Gráda, C. (1993). *Ireland before and after the famine: Explorations in economic history, 1800–1925.* St. Martin's Press.

Olivera, L. (2022). *Already enough: A path to self-acceptance.* Simon & Schuster.

Orloff, J. (2008). *Second sight: An intuitive psychiatrist tells her extraordinary story and shows you how to tap your own inner wisdom.* Grand Central Publishing.

Osman, J. (2020, October 11). What is colonialism? A history of violence, control and exploitation. *Teen Vogue.* https://www.teenvogue.com/story/colonialism-explained

Ott, T. O. (1973). *The Haitian revolution: 1789–1804.* University of Tennessee Press.

Owens, D. C. (2017). *Medical bondage: Race, gender, and the origins of American gynecology.* University of Georgia Press.

Owens, L. R. (2020). *Love and rage: The path of liberation through anger.* North Atlantic Books.

Oxford Languages. (2022). Colonialism. In *Oxford Languages Online English Dictionary.* Oxford University Press. https://www.oed.com/

Oxford Languages. (2022). Colonization. In *Oxford Languages Online English Dictionary.* Oxford University Press. https://www.oed.com/

Oxford Languages. (2022). Neoliberalism. In *Oxford Languages Online English Dictionary.* Oxford University Press. https://www.oed.com/

Patel, B. (2020, April 23). *The brain under conflict.* Mediate. https://www.mediate.com/articles/patel-brain-conflict.cfm

Peer, A. (2020, October 16). *Global poverty: Facts, FAQs, and how to help.* World Vision. https://www.worldvision.org/sponsorship-news-stories/global-poverty-facts

The People's Institute for Survival and Beyond. (n.d.). [Website homepage]. https://pisab.org/

The People's Institute for Survival and Beyond. (n.d.). *Our principles*. https://pisab.org/our-principles/

Pérez, E. (2013). Willful spirits and weakened flesh: Historicizing the initiation narrative in Afro-Cuban religions. *Journal of Africana Religions, 1*(2), 151–193. https://doi.org/10.5325/jafrireli.1.2.0151

Pete, S. (2016). 100 Ways: Indigenizing and decolonizing academic programs. *Aboriginal Policy Studies, 6*(1), 81–89. https://doi.org/10.5663/aps.v6i1.27455

Pharr, S. (1988). *Homophobia: A weapon of sexism*. Inverness, CA: Chardon Press.

Piastrelli, B. (2021). *Root and ritual: Timeless ways to connect to land, lineage, community, and the self*. Sounds True.

Pidgeon, M. (2008). Pushing against the margins: Indigenous theorizing of "success" and retention in higher education. *Journal of College Student Retention: Research, Theory & Practice, 10*(3), 339–360. https://doi.org/10.2190%2FCS.10.3.e

Pidgeon, M. (2012). Transformation and Indigenous interconnections: Indigeneity, leadership, and higher education. In C. Kenny & T. N. Fraser (Eds.), *Living Indigenous leadership: Native narratives on building strong communities* (pp. 136–149). UBC Press.

Piepzna-Samarasinha, L. L. (2018). *Care work: Dreaming disability justice*. Arsenal Pulp Press.

Pilgrim, D. (2005, November). *Drapetomania*. Ferris State University. https://www.ferris.edu/HTMLS/news/jimcrow/question/2005/november.htm

Pinderhughes, E. (1989). *Understanding race, ethnicity and power: The key to efficacy in clinical practice*. New York, NY: Free Press.

Pinker, S. (2019, February 21). Inheriting the trauma of genocide. *The Wall Street Journal*. https://www.wsj.com/articles/inheriting-the-trauma-of-genocide-11550761430

Psychotherapy Networker. (2020, August 11). *Gabor Maté on understanding grief as an antidote to trauma* [Video]. YouTube. https://www.youtube.com/watch?v=x_oo8yFj9h0

Quinn, D. (2020, December 28). *What are dantian? The energy centers of Chinese Medicine*. Healthline. https://www.healthline.com/health/dantian#what-are-dantian

Raja, M. (2019, December 4). *Allochronic discourse*. Postcolonial Space. https://postcolonial.net/glossary/allochronic-discourse/

Ravilochan, T. (2021, July 17). *The Blackfoot origins of Maslow's hierarchy of needs*. Buffalo's Fire. https://www.buffalosfire.com/the-blackfoot-origins-of-maslows-hierarchy-of-needs/

Reardon, D. J. (1997, September 27). The Irish Famine: Complicity in murder. *The Washington Post.* https://www.washingtonpost.com/archive/opinions/1997/09/27/the-irish-famine-complicity-in-murder/5a155118-3620-4145-951e-0dc46933b84a/

Rege, S. (2021, March 3). *Epigenetic mechanisms in psychiatric disorders—major depression, psychosis, and addiction.* Psych Scene Hub. https://psychscenehub.com/psychinsights/epigenetic-mechanisms-in-psychiatric-disorders-major-depression-psychosis-and-addiction/

Reid, J. (2019). Reclaiming possession: A critique of the discourse of dispossession in Indigenous studies (corrected version). *On Culture.* https://doi.org/10.22029/oc.2018.1145

Restak, R. (2000). *Mysteries of the mind.* National Geographic Society.

Rhodes, R. (1990). *A hole in the world: An American boyhood.* Simon and Schuster.

Rivera, A., Jr. (2020, March 21). *What is narrative therapy and why does it work?* BeatBullying https://www.beatbullying.org/narrative-therapy/

Roberts, S. O., Bareket-Shavit, C., Dollins, F. A., Goldie, P. D., & Mortenson, E. (2020). Racial inequality in psychological research: Trends of the past and recommendations for the future. *Perspectives on Psychological Science, 15*(6), 1295–1309. https://doi.org/10.1177%2F1745691620927709

Rodney, W. (1981). *How Europe underdeveloped Africa* (3rd ed.). Howard University Press.

Rosenthal, S. (2016, February 19). Marxism and psychology. *Socialist Worker,* (410). https://socialistworker.co.uk/socialist-review-archive/marxism-and-psychology/

Roth, J. A. (n.d.). *Ireland's troubling history: British colonialism's effect on Irish research.* Irish Sig. https://irishsig.wordpress.com/research/general-ireland-research/irelands-troubling-history-british-colonialisms-effect-on-irish-research/

Rowland-Klein, D., & Dunlop, R. (1998). The transmission of trauma across generations: Identification with parental trauma in children of Holocaust survivors. *Australian & New Zealand Journal of Psychiatry, 32*(3), 358–369.

Ruane, M. E. (2019, April 30). A brief history of the enduring phony science that perpetuates White supremacy. *The Washington Post.* https://www.washingtonpost.com/local/a-brief-history-of-the-enduring-phony-science-that-perpetuates-white-supremacy/2019/04/29/20e6aef0-5aeb-11e9-a00e-050dc7b82693_story.html

Said, E. (2003, July 20). Blind imperial ignorance. Los Angeles Times. https://www.latimes.com/archives/la-xpm-2003-jul-20-oe-said20-story.html

Sakugawa, Y. [@yumisakugawa]. (2021, May 14). *A reminder to myself. Sometimes the answer is not work harder but make it more exciting. And rest more! Slow* [Photograph]. Instagram. https://www.instagram.com/p/CO3ndSxg6ig/

Samara, M., Hammuda, S., Vostanis, P., El- Khodary, B., & Al- Dewik, N. (2020). Children's prolonged exposure to the toxic stress of war trauma in the Middle East. *BMJ, 371*, 8–13. https://doi.org/10 1136/bmj.m3155

Sandoval, M. C. (1979). Santeria as a mental health care system: An historical overview. *Social Science & Medicine: Part B: Medical Anthropology, 13*(2), 137–151. https://doi.org/10.1016/0160-7987(79)90009-7

Sandy, N. [@rehumanizingourselves]. (2021, May 25). *Learnings from the frontlines of anti-colonial, rehumanizing, trauma care work: Moving away from oppressive, inaccurate, victim-blaming mental health language* [Photograph]. Instagram. https://www.instagram.com/p/CPTk1WSjcaQ/

Sandy, N. [@rehumanizingourselves]. (2022, February 28). *A revised slide from my previous post. Thank you @shea.sandy for the important additions of forced removal/relocation and disinformation.* [Photograph]. Instagram. https://www.instagram.com/p/CahLXYuu1xl/

Santiago-Irizarry, V. (2001). *Medicalizing ethnicity: The construction of Lation identity in a psychiatric setting.* Cornell University Press.

Saul, J. (2013). *Collective trauma, collective healing: Promoting community resilience in the aftermath of disaster.* Routledge.

Schiebinger, L. (2017). *Secret cures of slaves: People, plants, and medicine in the eighteenth-century Atlantic world.* Stanford University Press.

Schmit, J. (2017). *Energetic boundaries: 5 boundary setting tricks.* Wild Tree Wellness. https://wildtreewellness.com/energetic-boundaries/

Schwartz, R. C., & Blankenship, D. M. (2014). Racial disparities in psychotic disorder diagnosis: A review of empirical literature. *World Journal of Psychiatry, 4*(4), 133–140. https://doi.org/10.5498%2Fwjp.v4.i4.133

Scientific racism. (2022, March 1). In *Wikipedia.* https://en.wikipedia.org/w/index.php?title=Scientific_racism&oldid=1074666456

Scott, K. L., & Copping, V. E. (2008). Promising directions for the treatment of complex childhood trauma: The intergenerational trauma treatment model. *The Journal of Behavior Analysis of Offender and Victim Treatment and Prevention, 1*(3), 273–283. http://doi.org/10.1037/h0100449

Sebastian, S. (n.d.). *Chakra questions and answers.* Chakra Anatomy. https://www.chakra-anatomy.com/chakra-questions.html

Sejpal, A., & Roy, A. (2019, January 3). *How to think about empire*. Boston Review. https://bostonreview.net/articles/arundhati-roy-thinking-about-empire/

Shamdasani, S. (2005). 'Psychotherapy': The invention of a word. *History of Human Sciences, 18*(1), 1–22. https://doi.org/10.1177/0952695105051123

Sharfstein, S. S. (2005, Aug 19). Big pharma and American psychiatry: The good, the bad, and the ugly. *American Psychiatric Association: Psychiatric News*. https://doi.org/10.1176/pn.40.16.00400003

Shepherd, K. (2021, January 8). *How images of White terrorism impact Black bodies*. Common Justice. https://blog.commonjustice.org/blog/how-images-of-white-terrorism-impact-black-bodies

Shrira, A., Mollov, B., & Mudahogora, C. (2019). Complex PTSD and intergenerational transmission of distress and resilience among Tutsi genocide survivors and their offspring: A preliminary report. *Psychiatry Research 271*, 121–123. https://doi.org/10.1016/j.psychres.2018.11.040

Shontz, F. C. (1968). Somatopsychological aspects of mental health. *The High School Journal, 51*(7), 294–300. https://www.jstor.org/stable/40366820

Shosan, T. (1989). Mourning and longing from generation to generation. *American Journal of Psychotherapy, 43*(2), 193–207.

Shulman, L. M. (2018). *Before and after loss: A neurologist's perspective on loss, grief, and our brain*. JHU Press.

Sigmund Freud. (2021, September 9). In *Wikipedia*. https://en.wikipedia.org/w/index.php?title=Sigmund_Freud&oldid=1043308915

Sills, R. (Host). (2020, September 6). *Embodied Astrology with Renee Sills* [Audio podcast]. https://www.embodiedastrology.com/ea-astro-updates/guest-episode-liberatory-disruption-sacred-rage-in-conversation-with-dr-jennifer-mullan

Skovholt, T. M., Grier, T. L., & Hanson, M. R. (2001). Career counseling for longevity: Self-care and burnout prevention strategies for counselor resilience. *Journal of Career Development, 27*(3), 167–176. https://doi.org/10.1177%2F089484530102700303

Smith, F. M. (2010). Possession, embodiment, and ritual in mental health care in India. *Journal of Ritual Studies, 24*(2), 21–35. https://www.jstor.org/stable/44368826

Smith, T. (2012). *Pathology, bias and queer diagnosis: A crip queer consciousness*. [Master's thesis, Smith College]. Smith Scholar Works. https://scholarworks.smith.edu/theses/1074

Social History for Every Classroom [SHEC]. (n.d.). *Boston abolitionists warn of slave catchers*. https://shec.ashp.cuny.edu/items/show/1213

Soco Rey Therapy. (n.d.). *The space*. https://www.socorey.com/the-space

Soicher, R. (2023). Vocabulary. In R. Biswas-Diener & E. Diener (Eds.), *Noba textbook series: Psychology*. DEF publishers. http://noba.to/65w3s7ex

Sorsdahl, K., Stein, D. J., Grimsrud, A., Seedat, S., Flisher, A. J., Williams, D. R., & Myer, L. (2009). Traditional healers in the treatment of common mental disorders in South Africa. *The Journal of Nervous and Mental Disease, 197*(6), 434–441. https://doi.org/10.1097/NMD.0b013e3181a61dbc

Sotero, M. (2006). A conceptual model of historical trauma: Implications for public health practice and research. *Journal of Health Disparities Research and Practice, 1*(1), 93–108.

Spinazzola, J., Blaustein, M., & van der Kolk, B. A. (2005). Posttraumatic stress disorder treatment outcome research: The study of unrepresentative samples? *Journal of Traumatic Stress, 18*(5), 425–436. https://doi.org/10.1002/jts.20050

Starks, A [@MelaninMvskoke]. (2021, October 14). *African Americans are the displaced descendants of Indigenous Africans. We never relinquished our relationship to the land of our ancestors* [Tweet]. Twitter. https://twitter.com/MelaninMvskoke/status/1448506670812778497

Strobel, L. M. (2016). *Coming full circle: The process of decolonization among post-1965 Filipino Americans*. CreateSpace Independent Publishing Platform.

Sutherland, C. (2007, July 16). *Haitian Revolution (1791–1804)*. BlackPast. https://www.blackpast.org/global-african-history/haitian-revolution-1791-1804/

Suzuki, L. A., Prendes-Lintel, M., Wertlieb, L., & Stallings, A. (1999). Exploring multicultural issues using qualitative methods. In M. Kopala & L. A. Suzuki (Eds.), *Using qualitative methods in psychology* (pp. 123–133). SAGE Publications, https://doi.org/10.4135/9781452225487.n10

Tagaq, T. [@tagaq]. (2017, June 20). *Not only are indigenous people forced to shoulder the burden of colonialism; we are expected to celebrate it. #Canada150* [Tweet]. Twitter. https://twitter.com/tagaq/status/877219670184656897?s=20

Talbot, I. A. (2007). The Punjab under colonialism: Order and transformation in British India. *Journal of Punjab Studies, 14*, 3–10. https://punjab.global.ucsb.edu/research/journal/volume-14

Tawwab, N. (Guest). (2021, March 17). *Create personal freedom, set boundaries, and improve your relationship* (1085) [Audio podcast episode].

In *The School of Greatness*. https://lewishowes.com/podcast/create-personal-freedom-set-boundaries-improve-your-relationship-with-nedra-tawwab/

Teish, L. (2021). *Jambalaya: The natural woman's book of personal charms and practical rituals*. HarperOne.

Timeline of psychotherapy. (2021, October 18). In *Wikipedia*. https://en.wikipedia.org/w/index.php?title=Timeline_of_psychotherapy&oldid=1050515855

Torres, G. [@gabestorres]. (2022, January 4). *I'm looking forward for the time ahead when we learn all the more that our experiences of de-conditioning and change* [Carousel]. Instagram. https://www.instagram.com/p/CYT5euTvI5Q/

Toth, K. (2020). *Effects of intergenerational trauma on attitudes toward reconciliation among genocide survivors in Rwanda*. [Undergraduate honors thesis, Ohio State University]. Knowledge Bank. http://hdl.handle.net/1811/91753

Truth and Reconciliation Commission of Canada. (2015). *What we have learned: Principles of truth and reconciliation*. http://www.trc.ca/websites/trcinstitution/File/2015/Findings/Principles_2015_05_31_web_o.pdf

Tseng, W.-S. (1973). The development of psychiatric concepts in traditional Chinese medicine. *Archives of General Psychiatry, 29*(4), 569–575. https://doi.org/10.1001/archpsyc.1973.04200040109018

Tuck, E., & Yang, K. W. (2012). Decolonization is not a metaphor. *Decolonization: Indigeneity, Education & Society, 1*(1), 1–40.

Unite for Sight. (n.d.). *Module 2: A brief history of mental illness and the U.S. mental health care system*. https://www.uniteforsight.org/mental-health/module2

Universities Canada. (2015, June 29). *Universities Canada principles on Indigenous education*. https://www.univcan.ca/media-room/media-releases/universities-canada-principles-on-indigenous-education/

University of Texas at Austin Liberal Arts Instructional Technology Services. (n.d.). *African Americans may still be experiencing the effects of slavery, concluded Joy DeGruy Leary*. https://laits.utexas.edu/africa/ads/503.html

Valeii, K. (2021, September 4). *How does intergenerational trauma work?* VeryWellHealth. https://www.verywellhealth.com/intergenerational-trauma-5191638

van der Kolk, B. (2006). Clinical Implications of Neuroscience Research in PTSD. *Psychobiology of Posttraumatic Stress Disorder: A Decade of Progress, 1071*(1), 277–293.

van der Kolk, B. (2014). *The body keeps the score: Brain, mind, and body in the healing of trauma*. Viking.

van der Kolk, B. (2021). *Exploring intergenerational trauma*. The Master Series.

https://themasterseries.com/wp-content/uploads/2021/05/Asset-03-Exploring-Intergenerational-Trauma-with-Dr.-Bessel-van-der-Kolk.pdf

van Dijk, W., Faber, M. J., Tanke, M. A. C., Jeurissen, P. P. T., & Westert, G. P. (2016). Medicalisation and overdiagnosis: What society does to medicine. *International Journal of Health Policy and Management, 5*(11), 619–622. https://doi.org/10.15171%2Fijhpm.2016.121

Vedantam, S. (2005, June 28). Racial disparities found in pinpointing mental illness. *The Washington Post.* https://www.washingtonpost.com/archive/politics/2005/06/28/racial-disparities-found-in-pinpointing-mental-illness/938a6081-b46c-4b7c-a4c9-4fd831670ec9/

Villoldo, A. (2000). *Shaman, healer, sage: How to heal yourself and others with the energy medicine of the Americas.* Harmony Books.

Wade, B. (2021). *Grieving while Black: An antiracist take on oppression and sorrow.* North Atlantic Books.

Walinga, J., & Stangor, C. (2020). 15.2 Insanity: A history of mental illness. In S. Walters (Ed.), *Psychology: 1st Canadian Edition.* https://psychology.pressbooks.tru.ca/chapter/15-2-insanity-a-history-of-mental-illness/

Walker, M. (1999). The inter-generational transmission of trauma: The survivor's relationship with their children and on the children themselves. *The European Journal of Psychotherapy, Counseling & Health, 2*(3), 281–296.

Ward, M., & Lebowitz, S. (2022, January 12). More leaders are scrapping the 40-hour workweek. Here's how it became so popular in the first place. Business Insider. https://www.businessinsider.com/history-of-the-40-hour-workweek-2015-10

Washington, J. R., Jr. (1981). The religion of Antiblackness. *Theology Today, 38*(2), 146–151. https://doi.org/10.1177%2F004057368103800203

Watanabe, H. (2002). The transgenerational transmission of abandonment. In *Infant and toddler mental health: Models of clinical intervention with infants and their families.* American Psychiatric Publishing, Inc., 187–205.

Waxman, O. B. (2019, August 20). The first Africans in Virginia landed in 1619. It was a turning point for slavery in American history—but not the beginning. *Time.* https://time.com/5653369/august-1619-jamestown-history/

Weiss, M., & Weiss, S. (2000). Second generation to Holocaust survivors: Enhanced differentiation of trauma transmission. *American Journal of Psychotherapy, 54*(3), 372–385.

Weingarten, K. (2003). *The blindness of one's heart.* Penguin.

Weingarten, K. (2004). Witnessing the effects of political violence in families:

Mechanisms of intergenerational transmissions and clinical interventions. *Journal of Marital and Family Therapy, 30*(1), 45–59.

Weiss, B. L. (1988). *Many lives, many masters: The true story of a prominent psychiatrist, his young patient, and the past-life therapy that changed both their lives.* Touchstone.

Wesley-Esquimaux, C. C. & Smolewski, M. (2004). *Historic trauma and aboriginal healing.* Aboriginal Healing Foundation.

WGBH Interactive. (1998). *The Haitian revolution: 1794–1804.* Africans in America. http://www.pbs.org/wgbh/aia/part3/3p2990.html

White, T. J. (2010). The impact of British colonialism on Irish Catholicism and national identity: Repression, reemergence, and divergence. *Etudes Irlandaises, 35*(1), 21–37. https://doi.org/10.4000/etudesirlandaises.1743

Wise, E. (2017, March 15). *What is energy psychology?* Wise Mindbody Healing. http://www.wisemindbodyhealing.com/articles/approaches-healing-modalities/traditional-chinese-medicine-tcm/qigong/what-is-energy-psychology/

Wolynn, M. (2016). *It didn't start with you: How inherited family trauma shapes who we are and how to end the cycle.* Penguin Life.

Yalom, I. D. (2002). *The gift of therapy: An open letter to a new generation of therapists and their patients.* Harper Collins Publishers.

Yalom, I. D. (1995). *The gift of therapy: Reflections on being a therapist.* Piatkus.

Yao, Y., Robinson, A. M., Zucchi, F. C., Robbins, J. C., Babenko, O., Kovalchuk, O., Kovalchuk, I., Olson, D. M., & Metz, G. A. S. (2014). Ancestral exposure to stress epigenetically programs preterm birth risk and adverse maternal and newborn outcomes. *BMC Medicine, 12*(121) https://doi.org/10.1186/s12916-014-0121-6

Yehuda, R., & Lehrner, A. (2018). Intergenerational transmission of trauma effects: Putative role of epigenetic mechanisms. *World Psychiatry, 17*(3), 243–257. https://doi.org/10.1002/wps.20568

Yellow Bird, M. (2014). *Decolonizing the Mind: Healing Through Neurodecolonization and Mindfulness* [speech audio recording]. Vimeo. https://vimeo.com/86995336

Yoshikawa, L. E. M. (2005). The legacy continues after 60 years: The transgenerational effects of the Japanese-American WWII incarceration on third generation males. *Dissertation Abstracts International: Section B. Sciences and Engineering, 66*(2), 1190. Retrieved from ProQuest Dissertations and Theses database. (Publication No. 3164913)

Young, I. M. (1990). *Justice and the politics of difference.* Princeton University Press.

Index

Note: Italicized page locators refer to figures; tables are noted with *t*.

A
Abdullah, S., 198
ableism (aka disability oppression), 9, 45, 97, 105, 121, 144, 152, 310, 318, 321, 349, 364, 395
abnormal behavior, supernatural view of, 224
Abnormal Psychology online course (Lumen Learning), 224
abolition, 33, 395–96
abolitionists, 105
Aboriginal Healing Foundation
　Historic Trauma and Aboriginal Healing report, 202
　on unresolved trauma, 180
Aboriginal People, 180, 395
ABPsi. *see* Association of Black Psychologists (ABPsi)
accountability, 28
Achenbach, T., 163*t*
acupuncture, 222, 305
addiction
　epigenetics and role in, 152
　generational patterns of, 95
　recovery spaces, gatekeeping and, 225
ADHD, 149, 380
ADHD medications, adverse effects of, 152
adverse childhood experiences (ACEs), 143, 343
　health and well-being through lifespan influenced by, *144*
affirmations
　for countering diagnostic enslavement, 166
　for grieving and reclamation, 98
　for holding our histories, 67
　for intergenerational self-inquiry, 212–13
　offerings of, 64
　for reclaiming equitable healing, 123–24
　for Sacred Rage and Collective Grief, 277–78
　for your energy boundaries, 314–15
African Americans
　four distinct periods of trauma faced by, 200
　soul wound in experience of, 177
　students classified as having an intellectual disability, 161
　see also Black Indigenous People of Color (BIPOC)
African Diaspora, multigenerational trauma and, 179
African Holocaust, 81
African spirituality, anti-Black racism and, 227
Ainsworth, M., 162*t*
Akbar, N., 78

Akili, Y., 130
Alcoholics Anonymous, 225
alienist, derivation of word for, 119–20
Allione, T., 34
allochronism, 393
American Association of Biological Anthropologists, 111–12
American Health Empire, The (Ehrenreich), 401
American Psychological Association, 198
amygdala, 241, 242
analytic psychology, 161t
Anatomy of the Spirit (Myss), 230, 297
ancestors and ancestry
  ancestral support, 228–29
  communing and getting to know, 318, 319, 324–27, 363
  inquiring about, 166, 324–26
  land inquiry, 326–27
  power of ancestor healing, 295
Ancestral Plant Medicines, 373
ancestral roots in mental health, "from root to bone," 214–37
  aspects of emotional-decolonial unlearning, 235–36
  blood and earth, 233–35
  emo–decolonial practice offerings, 236–37
  grief rituals and ancestral-healing inquiries, 233
  the people's stories, 231–33
  spiritual roots, 215–31
ancestral strengths, recentering, 34
ancestral trauma, dysregulated states and, 241. *see also* historical trauma; intergenerational trauma; multigenerational trauma
Anderson, C., 269n24
anger, rage *vs.*, 266–67
anger management classes, 151, 275
Answering the Call of the Ancestors (Collado), 225
anti-Black racism, 310, 345, 380, 396
anticipatory racism reaction, 141, 396
antidepressant medications
  adverse effects of, 152
  pharmaceutical sales and classification of, 146
antipsychotic medications, 107
  adverse effects of, 152
  pharmaceutical revenues and, 146
APA Council of Representatives, need for actions over apologies by, 141–45
Appiah, K. A., 109
Arbery, A., 55, 158, 239, 345
Archives of General Psychiatry, 106
Armenian Genocide, 90, 176
Army Alpha and Beta Intelligence Tests, 162t
Aron, E., 299, 309
art and creativity, need for, 366, 367. *see also* affirmations; ceremony; storytelling
Assembly of First Nations, 82
assessments, creating alternatives to, 166
assimilation, 393. *see also* forced migration (or forced displacement)
Association for Transpersonal Psychology, 301
Association of Black Psychologists (ABPsi), 142
astrology, 350
asylum management, plantation management themes and tenets of, 116–18
asylums
  establishment and mission of, 103
  pathology of moral treatment and, 115–16
  plantations, policing, and, 114–15, 118–19
attachment
  concerns, emo–decolonial practice offerings and, 122
  four main types of, 204
  mechanisms of trauma transmission and, 204–5, 211
attachment theory, 162t
Auerhahn, N. C., 201
Auguste, E., 142
Australia, colonies or territories maintained by, 51
Avila, E., 230

awakening, collective shift in the '60s and '70s and, 296. *see also* Woke

B
babalawos, 6, 236
"babies in the water" metaphor
   getting real and, 170
   questions attached to, 25, 343
backpack exercises, 369, 385–87
Bajon, B., 104
Bakhtin, M., 394
Balasubramanian, J., 99
ball competitions, 334n31
Bandura, A., 178, 294
Bayley, N., 163t
Beck, A., 161t, 162t
Beck Depression and Anxiety Inventories, 162t
Before and After Loss (Shulman), 249
behavior, challenging pathologization of, 123
behaviorism, 161t
Bekoff, M., 249
Belgium, "Scramble for Africa" and, 43
Bengali Babas, 6
Bernstein, G., 239
bias
   in creation of diagnostic categories, 146
   in MHIC and MIC, 151–52
bicultural production, 396
Big Pharma, 146, 152
binary, 396
bioenergetics, 314
BIPOC. *see* Black Indigenous People of Color (BIPOC)
bipolar disorder, 266, 380
Black Indigenous People of Color (BIPOC)
   addiction cycles and, 86
   backend learning and, 245
   disenfranchised grief and, 254
   emotional–decolonial unlearning and, 97
   global colonization and lived experiences of, 50
   psychological tools not accurate with, 140–41
   ways white supremacy impacts energetic boundaries of, 310–11, 314
   Western frameworks of mental health system and, 122
   see also First Nation Indigenous People; People of Global Majority (PoGM)
Black Lives Matter, 200
Black Muslims, 106
Black people, four categories of mental disorders among, 78. *See also* African Americans; Black Indigenous People of Color (BIPOC)
Black Power Movement, 200
Black rage, seen as an affliction, 151
Black Skin, White Masks (Fanon), 367
Black women, medical racism and, 104
Black youth, Suffocated Grief among, 252
Bland, S., 55
Blood, N., 222
"blood memory," historical violence and, 187
Blumenbach, J. F., 112, 113, 114
boarding schools, 175–76, 256
body, history written within, 240–42
Booker, M., 55
Bordere, T., 252, 253
Boston Tea Party, 223–24
boundaries
   emotions and, 298–300
   in families with traumatized parents, 207
   having embodied sense of, 312
   setting, for people of colonized backgrounds, 220
   types of, 299
   see also energetic boundaries
bounds of "therapy," changing, 164–65
Bowen, M., 162t, 178
Bowen Family Systems Theory, 178
Bowlby, J., 204, 211, 294
Boyd-Franklin, N., 294
brain fog, 241

Brave Heart, M. Y. H., 9, 80, 81, 169, 174, 176, 208, 256, 259, 294
breathe and release, allowing true space and time for, 359
breathwork, 393–94
Britain, 47
  "Scramble for Africa" and, 43
British Parliament, Irish Potato Famine created by, 52
Brown v. Board of Education, 50
"Burden of Being 'On Point,' The" (Harris), 160
burnout, 286
  early career clinicians and, 86, 293–94
  as expression of late-stage capitalism, 154, 313
  mental health practitioners and, 338, 339, 340, 341, 347
  origins of, 292–95
  three components of, 292
  see also Capitalism Fatigue
Burstow, B., 125
Butcher, J. N., 162t

C
California Genocide, 50
Callahan, R., 291
Call to Action, 101, 103, 316, 366–68
Campos, S., 163
Candomble, 223
capitalism, 49, 349, 364, 396
  shift in humanity's relationship to, 296
  suffering caused by, 139–45
Capitalism Fatigue, 396
  gaslighting and, 154–57
  mental health practitioners and, 339
care workers, small revolutions for, 92–93
Caribbean Institute of Mental Health and Substance Abuse (CARIMENSA), 184
Carroll, S., 60
Carter, R., 199, 294
Cartwright, S. A., 107, 108, 109, 110, 114, 115, 118, 398
Castile, P., 55
Cattell, J. M., 161t

Cattell, R. B., 162t
Cayman Islands, continued occupation of, 51
CBT. *see* cognitive–behavioral therapy (CBT)
Center for the Study of White American Culture, 48
Central Lunatic Asylum for the Colored Insane, 142
ceremony, 227–28, 236
chakras, 302–3
Challaie, S., 115
chanting, 226
Charcot, J. M., 178, 215, 294
Child and Adolescent Psychiatric Clinics of North America, 343
Child Behavior Checklist series, 163t
children
  mental health crisis for, in US, 343
  spiritual lives of, 229–31
Chinese Massacre of 1871, 50
Chisom, R., 112
Chong, J., 303
Christianity, colonizers and spread of, 47–48
cisgender, 148, 210, 397
cisnormativity, impact of, 148
Civil Rights Movement, 105, 106
Clapp, J., 240, 388
clarity, community and, as key, 159–61
Clark, M. P., 294
classism, 97, 152, 318, 321
clergy, 235
coaching, 348
Coates, T.-N., 160, 214
codependence, 94
Coffield, B., 9
coffin ships, Irish emigration to North America and, 52
Cofield, B., 193
cognitive–behavioral therapy (CBT), 321n29
cognitive development theory, 162t
cognitive theory, 161t
Collado, C., 225
collective-empowerment, new emerging field of, 137

Collective Energy (or "the Collective"), 290, 313, 397
collective grief, creating more of a relationship to, 281–82
collective healing, leaders of the movement toward, 182–85
collective trauma, 265
Collective Trauma, Collective Healing (Saul), 265
collective unconscious, 296
collusion, systemic, 132–33, 142, 143
colonialism, 47–48, 126, 397
  categories as tool of, 114
  definitions of, 41n8, 42
  diagram of, 49
  energetic boundaries and impact of, 287, 310–11
  as purposeful, subversive force, 44
  see also colonization
colonial subjugation, 397
colonization, 397
  ancestral/historical, 7–8
  attachment styles as a mechanism of trauma transmission and, 205–6, 211
  a blueprint, 65
  as a collective global Stockholm syndrome, 76–81
  as the core wound, 40
  expressions of trauma related to, 93–96
  forced migration as product of, 53–54, 66
  healing from effects of, 102
  language of, 53
  money making and, 111
  people's stories and legacy of, 56–58
  questions to ask individuals whose history is correlated with trauma of, 181
  racism as branch off of roots of, 113
  rationalizations of Western thoughts and violence of, 87–88
  reflection questions, 49
  at the root of our depression, 135–37
  tools of, 137–39
  as trauma, 42–43
  see also decolonization

colonized therapists, honoring the awakening of, 1–5
colorism, 45, 394
Columbus, C., 48, 50, 60
community, clarity and, as key, 159–61
community, steps to take in, 355–63
  breathe and release, 359
  cocreating new pathways, 357–59
  planning as a form of prevention, 360–63
  resist, 356–57
community healing spaces, 163
compassion fatigue, 340
complex trauma, varying degrees of severity in, 209
conduct disorder, 122, 134, 239, 266, 380
conformity
  comfort of, 224
  mental health oppression and, 9
Conolly, J., 115
Constantine, M., 294
contagions, 397
conversion disorder, 216n21
conversion therapy, 224
Cooper, B., 275
Cornah, D., 356n35
cortisol, 95, 241, 242
Cowan, E., 214
creativity and joy, decolonial, creating spaces of, 362. *see also* art and creativity
Crenshaw, K., 9
criminal justice system, mental health system informed by, 122
crip, 397
cultural competence, generalized treatment and, 259
cultural relativism, 305
cultural trauma, 179, 180, 210, 244
Cultural Trauma: Slavery and the Formation of the African American Identity (Eyerman), 179
culture-bound syndromes in the *DSM*, cautionary note about, 210
"Culture of Poverty, A" (Coates), 160
curanderas, 6, 24, 215, 226, 235
curiosity, cultivating, 170

Cushing, B. B., 49
"cycles of abuse," attachment relationships and, 205

D
DACA. *see* Deferred Action for Childhood Arrivals (DACA)
Dana, D., 69, 285
Danieli, Y., 180, 204, 206, 207
dantian ("field of elixir"), 303
darvish/a, 235
Daut, M., 61
Davis. A., 39
DeArth-Pendley, G., 141
death and dying, transition ceremonies for, 231–33. *see also* grief and grieving
de Beaumont, G., 114
DeBruyn, L. M., 256
decolonization
    as an awakening, 192
    definition of, 81, 394
    emotional aspects of, 317–18
    healing and wellness as huge part of, 23–24
    internal process of, 383
    learning, 44–47
    longitudinal process of, 170, 187
    as a metaphor, going beyond, 88
    multifaceted political work of, 183–85
    reclaiming ourselves from exploitation through, 87
    requirements of, 91
    as a return, 44
    revitalizing nature of, 324
    unsettling nature of, 23, 81–84
    as a verb, 330–33, 363, 376
    see also colonization
Decolonization is not a metaphor (Tuck & Yang), 22
Decolonize First, 184
Decolonizing Fitness, LLC, 184
Decolonizing Trauma Work: Indigenous Stories and Strategies (Linklater), 23
Deepest Well, The (Harris), 361
defensiveness, as a decolonial practice, 332

Deferred Action for Childhood Arrivals (DACA), 56
DeGruy, J., 9, 80, 81, 179, 181, 255, 402
Dein, S., 216
demonic possession, 224, 225
Denmark, colonies or territories maintained by, 51
deportation, fear of, 56
depression, colonization at root of, 135–37
depressive disorder, epigenetics and role in, 152
dervish/a, 215
Dessalines, J-J., 60
de Tocqueville, A., 114
deviance vs.normal, on the binary of, 165
Dewey, J., 161*t*
Dhanesha, N., 357
diagnosis
    creating allowance for insights related to, 95–96
    roots of, 126–28
    as tool of subversion and control, 273
    violence of, 133–35
    see also diagnostic enslavement
Diagnostic and Statistical Manual, Fourth Edition (DSM-IV), 209, 216
Diagnostic and Statistical Manual of Mental Disorders, 5th edition (DSM-5), 70, 152, 184
diagnostic enslavement, 125–66
    aspects of emotional-decolonial unlearning, 164–65
    author care note, 125–26
    being part of the solution and the problem, 128–33
    capitalizing off suffering and sadness, 151–53
    colonization at root of our depression, 135–37
    countering, affirmations for, 166
    emo–decolonial practice offerings, 165–66
    founding white practitioners in psychology and their theoreti-

cal or assessment contributions, 161t–163t
gaslighting and Capitalism Fatigue, 154–57
grounding reflection questions, 131
resistance as insanity, 158–59
roots of diagnosis, 126–28
suffering caused by capitalism, 139–45
tools of colonization, 137–39
unpacking with reflection questions, 157–58
the violence of diagnosis, 133–35
the violence of individualism, 150–51
the violence of "normal," 145–49
see also psychological enslavement
Diagnostic Statistical Manual (DSM), 140, 143, 144, 147
on diagnosis, symptoms, and, 164
history of pathologization in, 145
Western "ideal" human and, 148
dialectic, 397
dialogic/dialogism, 397
Diddy, P., 46
difference, fear of, 224
dirt eating, 109–10
disability, 394
disability justice, 356, 397–98
disability rights movement, 1
dis-ease, 395
root of, 7–8
disenfranchised grief, 253–54, 262, 398
displacement, real-world effects of, 40. *see also* forced migration (or forced displacement)
dissociation, 241, 310
divine healthy action, being the change and, 29
DNA, trauma transmission and changes in, 195
Doka, K., 253
domestic workers, 330, 330n30
Dominican Republic, 60
dopamine, 152
Douglass, F., 190
Drapetomania, scientific racism and, 107–9, 121

Drapetomania: Rebellion, Defiance, and Free Black Insanity in the Antebellum United States (Myers), 110
dread, existential, statements around, 94
Du Bois, W. E. B., 223
Dunlop, R., 203
Duran, B., 176, 255
Duran, E., 174, 176, 208, 255
Dysaesthesia Aethiopica, 108, 121, 398
dysthymia, 239

E
early career clinicians, 84–87, 286, 293, 294. *see also* mental health practitioners/providers (MHPs)
ecocide, 49
education
decolonizing, call for, 82
as a form of colonization, 79–80
educational psychology, 161t
EFT tapping. *see* Emotional Freedom Technique (EFT) tapping
ego, 290
Ehrenreich, B., 398
elders, 226, 304, 350
Elliot, G., 171
Ellis, A., 178, 216, 294
Ellis Island, 136
embodied healing, inviting into your life, 31
EMDR. *see* Eye Movement Desensitization Reprocessing (EMDR)
emo–decolonial engagement, co-occurring practices of, 318, *319*
ancestral, communing and getting to know our ancestors and ancestry, 318, *319*, 324–27, 346, 363
collective, cocreating decolonial pathways in emotional (mental) health, 318, *319*, 323–24, 346, 363
political, politicizing our practices, 318, *319*, 322–23, 346, 363
self/psyche, emotional evolution, 318, *319*, 327–28, 346, 363
emo-decolonial work, as a verb, 317

emotional–decolonial healing, sacred responsibility attached to, 41
emotional–decolonial paradigm shift, journey within, 96
emotional–decolonial (emo–decolonial) practice offerings, 66–67, 98, 122–23, 165–66, 189, 211–12, 236–37, 276–77, 314, 364–65
emotional–decolonial (emo–decolonial) process, 398
  centering, 22
  tenets of, 32–34
emotional–decolonial unlearning, aspects of, 64–66, 97, 121–22, 164–65, 210–11, 235–36, 275–76, 313–14, 363–64
emotional decolonization, deprogramming necessary for, 77
emotional energy in our physical system, experiences that carry, 297
emotional evolution, embodying, 318
Emotional Freedom Technique (EFT) tapping, 304, 305, 366, 393
emotional (mental) health, co-creating decolonial pathways in, 318, *319*, 323–24, 363
Emotional Think Collectives, 323
emotional wellness, viewed through decolonial lens, 24
emotion and communication processing, considering multiple forms of, 123
emotions, boundaries and, 298–300
energetic boundaries, 285–315
  affirmations for, 314–15
  aspects of emotional–decolonial unlearning and, 313–14
  benefits of, 303
  definition of, 302
  emo-decolonial practice offerings, 314
  impact of colonialism and, 287, 310–11
  maintaining, 298
  in mental health, 301–2
  patterns within, 287
  physical boundaries *vs.*, 286, 313
  setting, 10 techniques and ways to restore them, 369, 391–94
  understanding, 288–89
  see also boundaries
energetics, mental health and, 295–96
energetic signatures, evolving, 286, 287
energy, therapy and, 290–92
energy medicine
  incorporating into your practices, 306
  in our cultures, 302–5
  roots of, 304–5
Energy Psychology (EP), 290, 291–92, 313
energy work
  coming alive, example of, 307–8
  mental health professionals and, 307–10
EP. *see* Energy Psychology (EP)
epigenetic inheritance, soul wound and, 81. *see also* intergenerational trauma
Epigenetic Modifications in Stress Response Genes Associated with Childhood Trauma, 203
epigenetics, 398
  intergenerational trauma and mechanisms of, 152, 203
  trauma transmission and, 195, 202–3
Equal Justice Initiative, 175, 176
equitable healing, reclaiming, affirmations for, 123–24
erasure, colonized education and, 223–24
Erikson, E., 69, 265, 294
Espiritismo, 226
Estés, C. P., 230, 310
ethnographic, 398
etiology, definition of, 209n20
eugenics movements, 137, 144
Eurocentric conceptual system, implosion of, 77
Eurocentrism, 398
Europe, Age of Discovery and, 47–48
evolution, required by revolution, 320–22, 363
existential anxiety, 94
existential psychology, 162*t*
exorcisms, 217
expressions, symptoms *vs.*, 128n14, 165, 398

Eye Movement Desensitization Reprocessing (EMDR), 218–19, 218n22, 366
Eyerman, R., 179

F
Falkland Islands, continued occupation of, 51
Family Systems Perspective, of trauma transmission, 206, 351
family systems theory, 162t, 178
Fanon, F., 9, 91, 367, 368
fatphobia, 9, 45, 184
Febo, D., 163
Feeding Your Demons (Allione), 34
Feinstein, D., 291
felt sense, 301, 304
femicide, 49
50 acres, 30 shillings, 10 bushels of corn, and a musket, 50
fight, flight, freeze, or fawn response, 240, 247, 269, 270, 276
financial instability, generational patterns of, 95
First Nation Indigenous People
    intergenerational trauma and descendants of, 200
    "Six Phases of Historical Unresolved Grief" for, 256
Fitz, P., 178
flight types
    distraction and devotion, 278
    dominance and defiance, 279
flogging, 217
Floyd, G., 55, 150, 158, 261, 345
forced migration (or forced displacement), 102, 126, 177, 398
    emotional-decolonial frame involving, 76
    as a form of trauma, 74
    grieving losses related to, 74
    as a product of colonization, 53–54, 66
    see also land inquiry; land theft
forest bathing, 302
Forneret, A., 251
foundationalism, 161t
France
    colonies or territories maintained by, 51
    Haiti's liberation from and extortion by, 59–61
    "Scramble for Africa" and, 43
Frank, V., 162t
freeze types, dependence and depression, 278
Freire, P., 9, 68, 99, 377
Freud, S., 161t, 178, 215, 290, 294
Fromm, E., 294
Fugitive Slave Act, 105
functionalism, 161t

G
Galápagos of the Philippines, continued colonization of, 51
Gallagher, R., 225
Galton, F., 161t
Gardner, H., 162t
Garner, E., 55
gaslighting, 9–10, 45, 144, 205, 298, 329, 339, 345, 350, 358, 398–99
    Capitalism Fatigue and, 154–57
    collective, 73
    psychological violence of colonization and, 105
gatekeepers, 342n34, 399
Gaylord-Harden, N., 160
gender binary, 149, 396
gendered oppression, 349, 364
gender nonconforming (GNC) persons, gender dysphoria and, 149
gender nonconforming spectrum of self-identity, 399
genocide, 40, 43, 49, 102, 126, 177, 256, 258, 399
    Armenian, 90, 176
    of Indigenous peoples on Turtle Island, 175n17
    Irish Potato Famine, 52
    settler colonialism and, 48
genograms, 3, 376, 396. *see also* Somatic Soul Trauma Timelines (SSTT)
Germany, "Scramble for Africa" and, 43
gestalt psychology, 162t
Gettysburg Address, 224

G.I. Bill, 50
Gibraltar, continued occupation of, 51
Gift of Therapy, The (Yalom), 288
"glimmers," in Polyvagal Theory, 263
global colonization 101, 50–53. *see also* colonization
Glossary of Terms, reeducation and use of, 28
"good-enough treatment," less acceptability of, 164
Gorman, R., 163
grief and grieving, 33, 175, 241, 359
  addressing root of the wound and, 260
  affirmations for, 98
  in animals, 249
  aspects of emotional–decolonial unlearning and, 275–76
  definition of, 249
  disenfranchised, 253–54, 262, 395
  emo-decolonial practice offerings for, 276–77
  generational patterns of, 95
  historical unresolved, healing and living with, 255–62
  misconceptions about, 250
  multiple impacts of, 249–50
  pathologizing, 239, 275
  the people's stories about, 248, 262–65
  plant allies for soothing our hearts during, 371–74
  public trauma and, 158, 159
  stages of, 248–51, 342
  suffocated, 252
Grief Brain, 249
grief rituals, 219, 233
Grof, S., 301
gurus, 226
gynecology, enslaved African people's bodies and founding of, 50, 104

H
Haines, S. K., 328
Haiti (*Ayiti*)
  colonization and attempted erasure of people in, 176
  derivation of name for, 60
  historical example related to, 59–61

Haitian earthquake of 2010, 376
Haitian-identified persons
  author reflection on, 62–63
  reflection exercise for, 61–62
Haitian Revolution, 59–61, 110
hajah, 215, 235
Haldol, 106
Hanwell Lunatic Asylum, 115
Harris, A., 160
Harris, N. B., 361
Hart, T., 229
Hasnaa, M., 285
Hay, L., 3n1
healers, 215, 235, 304
  commodification of, 6
  healing, who is responsible for, 337–43
  see also mental health practitioners/providers (MHPs)
healing
  ancestral support and, 228–29
  Call to Action for, 366–68
  ceremony and, 227–28
  collective, leaders of the movement toward, 182–85
  decolonization as integral part of, 23–24, 44, 83
  deep connection between religion and, 224
  from effects of colonization, 102
  equitable, affirmations for reclaiming, 123–24
  Indigenous *vs.* Western approaches to, 216–17, 236
  of multigenerational wounds, 201
  politicized decolonial work and journey toward, 201, 211
  from the root, 63, 66
  by shamans *vs.* by therapists, 223
  social change informed by, 346
  spiral staircase of, 80–81, 80n13
  stolen spirits of, 221–23
  see also affirmations; wellness
Healing Rage: Women Making Inner Peace Possible (King), 265, 281n27
healing spaces, therapeutic spaces and, 30
Healing the Soul Wound (Duran), 174

"Healing Through Neurodecolonization and Mindfulness" (Yellow Bird), 184
health disparities, for Black mothers, 104
hearing voices, asking clarifying questions about, 237
heart-assisted therapy, 304, 314
Heavy Head, R., 222
helpers, as source of suffering, 70–71
Henry VII, King of England, 51
Herman, J. L., 9, 14, 30, 316, 336, 384
Hersey, T., 185
heteronormativity, impact of, 148
heterosexism, 97, 318, 399
Hickling, F. W., 80, 182, 184, 256, 294, 367
highly sensitive people, 299, 309, 314
Highly Sensitive Person, The (Aron), 299, 309
Hill, W., 285
Hispaniola, 59, 60, 62, 376
historical emo–decolonial healing work, the people's stories related to, 185–87
historical trauma, 33, 210, 244, 321, 399
  ancestral support and, 228
  aspects of emotional–decolonial unlearning and, 187–88
  conceptualizing, organizational shifts in real time, 353–54
  cumulative effects of, 200–201
  definition of, 175
  emo–decolonial practice offerings, 189
  Holocaust survivors and Japanese internment survivors and, 196–97
  Human Services programs and tentacles of, 182
  impacts and symptoms of, 173
  within our bodies, 240
  question framework when looking at, 173–74
  soul wound as, 175, 188
  understanding, 171–74
  see also intergenerational trauma; multigenerational trauma
historical trauma response, 396
Historical Unresolved Grief, 399–400
  coining of term for, 258
  healing and living with, 255–62
history as a tool, 328–30
history/culture/identity, reasons clients/students/participants may choose not to discuss with you, 55
holding our histories, 63–67
  affirmations, 67
  aspects of emotional–decolonial unlearning, 64–66
  emo–decolonial practice offerings, 66–67
Holocaust survivors, historical trauma and, 196–97
Home
  ache for, 135
  colonization as separation from, 40
  reflection questions related to, 96–97
  safety and concept of, 68–69, 72–73
Homestead Act, 50
homophobia, 152, 400
homosexuality, removed from *DSM-I* and *DSM-II*, 224
honesty, 31–32
hooks, b., 9, 150, 238
Hôpital général de Paris, 103
hospitals, establishment and mission of, 103
How Europe Underdeveloped Africa (Rodney), 50
humanism, 397
humanistic psychology, 161t, 162t
humanization, practicing, 128
humility, 96, 247, 307
humorism (or humoralism), 400
hysteria, 216n21

I
ICD-9. *see* International Classification of Diseases, Ninth Revision (ICD-9)
íceach, 6
id, 290
Ifa, 223, 226
illness, conceptualized over person, 102
imams, 226
immigrants. in New York City Lunatic Asylum, 136–37
Immigration Act of 1924, 136

immigration and citizenship laws, various diagnoses and, 136
Impact of Spirituality and Mental Health, The (Cornah), 356n35
imperialism, 9, 349, 364, 401
imperialist nostalgia, 398
imposter syndrome, 94, 220, 340, 357
incarceration
    of Black men, "new version of schizophrenia" and, 106–7
    generational patterns of, 95
India, colonization of, 50
Indian Act of Canada, 395
Indian Removal Act, 49
Indigenous children, forced to attend boarding schools, 175–76
Indigenous healer identities, 6
Indigenous healing philosophies, wellness model as basis of, 102
Indigenous identities, span of, 43n9
Indigenous people
    disenfranchised grief and, 256
    institutionalization of, 107
    storytelling and, 350
    Western psychotherapy and roots/practices of, 222–23
    see also Black Indigenous People of Color (BIPOC); First Nation Indigenous People
individual capitalists, 397
individualism, violence of, 150–51
Industrial Revolution, 287
Infant Development Scales series, 163t
Inflamed (Patel), 91
inflammation, 270
    generational or historical trauma and, 195–96
    inflamed society and, 91
Inner Rage Child, 268, 269, 270, 280n26
Inner Sacred Child, loving suggestions for, 281–82
insanity
    effect of civilization and, 114–15
    resistance as, 158–59
insecure-avoidant attachment, 204

insecure-disorganized attachment, 204, 205, 211
insecure-resistant attachment, 204
Insight-Oriented Collective Accountability, essential need for, 359
Instagram @*decolonizingtherapy*, messages received in posts, 18–20
Insta-therapists, 294
institutionalized racism, 161, 177
Instituto Familiar de la Raza (Mission District, San Francisco), 163
intelligence, 337n32, 397
intelligence testing, 144
intelligence theory, 161t
"intentionally exploited communities," "marginalized communities" *vs.*, 130
intergenerational curses and traditions, gentle ways for healing, 199
Intergenerational Handbook of Multigenerational Legacies of Trauma (Danieli), 180
intergenerational trauma, 33, 80, 81, 186, 321, 351, 401
    ancestral support and, 228
    attachment mechanisms of, 204–5, 211
    attachment styles, trauma of colonization, and, 205–6, 211
    biological theories of, 202
    cumulative effects of, 200–201
    direct and indirect mechanisms of, 202, 203, 204, 207
    disenfranchised grief and, 254
    epigenetic mechanisms of, 202–3
    Family Systems Perspective of, 206
    intergenerational level of, 195, 210
    interpersonal level of, 195, 210
    intrapsychic mechanisms of, 203
    methylation and, 152, 203
    modes and mechanisms of, 201–8
    ongoing, 175
    parents with PTSD and, 208
    repetition compulsion and, 203–4
    social learning mechanisms of, 207–8
    social learning theory and, 206
    study of, 194–201

Index 447

varying degrees of severity in, 209
  see also historical trauma; multigenerational trauma
intergenerational trauma transmission, 262
  aspects of emotional-decolonial unlearning, 210–11
  patterns in, 343–44
  studying, 194–201
intergenerational tree of transmission, 92
intermittent explosive disorder, 122, 239, 266
internalized oppression, 397
International Center for Multigenerational Legacies of Trauma, 180
International Classification of Diseases, Ninth Revision (ICD-9), diagnoses, 88
interpersonal psychology, 161t
intervention, essential need for, 358
intrapsychic psychodynamic theory, 204
intuition, elevated, 95
intuitive body, 299
Ireland, history of British colonialism in, 51–53
Irish descent, working with people of, 53
Irish Potato Famine, 52, 59
isolation, as a tool, 153
iyanifa, 6

J
Jamaica
  Hickling's legacy of decolonial mental health activism in, 182, 184, 256–57, 367
  smallpox experiment on enslaved people in, 104
Jambalaya (Teish), 230, 281n27
James, W., 161t
Japanese internment survivors, effects of historical trauma on, 196–98, 200
John, J., 5, 191, 215, 316
Journal of Consulting and Clinical Psychology, 216
joy, creating spaces of decolonial creativity and, 362

Juneteenth, 200
Jung, C., 161t, 294, 296

K
kaiwhakaora, 6
Karenga, M., 113
Kaufman, A. S., 162t
Kaufman Intelligence and (K-BIT, K-SEALS, K-ABC, KAIT, K-TEA) series, 162t
Kayapo people of the Amazon, 224
Kendi, I. X., 119
Kessler, D., 239, 251
Khan, A., 153
Kim, J-K., 182, 316
King, R., 9, 169, 238, 265, 267, 269, 270, 271, 275, 279, 280n25, 280n26, 281n27, 401
Kingdom of Kush (Nubia), 224
Klein, M., 69, 162t, 178
"Know-Knows," 219
Koeske, G. F., 341
Koeske, R. D., 341
Kohut, H., 162t
Koval-Dhaliwal, A., 80n13
Kübler-Ross, E., 251, 342

L
Lakota people, massive group traumas experienced by, 175
Lakota Takini Network, Inc., 398
land decolonization, emotional evolutionary component of, 318
land displacement, forced Indigenous, 176. *see also* forced migration (or forced displacement); land theft
land inquiry, 326–27
Landry, A., 175n17
land theft, 40, 43
language
  limiting, misleading, and violent, 129–30
  oppressive, inaccurate, victim-blaming *vs.* anti-oppressive, trauma-informed, respectful, *138*
  psychological, divisiveness of, 146–47

language (*continued*)
  soul wound and use of, 177
  that polices, use of, 129
Laub, D., 201
learning
  to love the questions, 29
  to unlearn, 317, 355
learning theory, 161*t*
Lennon, J., 296
Levine, P., 69
liberation, 33, 354
Liberation Psychology, 9
Lifelines, Somatic Soul Trauma Timelines and, 383–84, *384*
limpias, 163, 163n16, 226
Linehan, M., 69, 178
Linklater, R., 23, 102, 169
Linnaeus, C., 113
Lipton, B., 80, 195, 394
lived experience, as vital wisdom, 210
Lopez, N., 163
Louisiana Medical Association, 107
L'ouverture, T., 60
love
  commitment to, 316–17
  peer education and, 333, 336
Lumad People, Philippines, militarized communities of, 176
Lumen, M., 83, 151
lynchings, 345

M
Magellan, F., 51, 53
magical thinking, 321n29
Mahler, M., 69, 178
major depressive disorder, 209, 239
maladaptive behaviors, defining, 208n19
Malcolm X, 106
maltreatment, cycles of, social learning theory and, 207–8
managed care, session limits and, 70
Mandela, N., 9
Manekem, R., 403
Many Lives, Many Masters (Weiss), 230, 310
"marginalized communities," "intentionally exploited communities" *vs.*, 130

martial arts, 303
Martin, T., 55
Martín-Baró, I., 8–9
Marya, R., 195
Maslow, A., 161*t*
Maslow's hierarchy of needs, appropriation of, 222
Maté, G., 261, 310
maternal mortality rates, for Black mothers, 104
McCoy, B., 249
McGoldrick, M., 377
MCMI personality test series, 162*t*
Meadows, J., 153
Medical Bondage: Race, Gender, and the Origins of American Gynecology (Owens), 104
medical industrial complex (MIC), 6, 7, 11, 12, 22, 84, 132, 151–52, 401
medicalization, 137, 150, 402
medical model, illness as basis of, 102
medical racism, 104, 105
meditation, 391
mediums, 226
Menakem, R., 190
Mendelson, T., 343
mental health
  ancestor healing work and, 309
  energetic boundaries in, 301–2
  energetics and, 295–96
  "invisible" dynamics of, 290
  religious involvement and, 216
mental health industrial complex (MHIC), 4, 5, 7, 8, 10, 11, 71, 84–91, 121, 171, 206, 224, 348, 402
  appropriation and co-optation by, 222, 223
  collusion with Big Pharma, 152
  connecting to our political work, 12
  early career clinicians in, 84–87
  expired nature of, 137
  interests of Big Pharma and, 146
  legacy of racism in psychiatry and, 105
  modern-day bias in, roots of, 151–52
  neutrality valued by, 151
  opposing, acts of resistance, 356–57
  outdated system of wellness and, 127

people exploited with "expired ointment" within, 140
transforming, 318
visualizing, 85
visualizing: stakeholders, 86
visualizing: tools/impact, 87
wriggling out from under, 130–31
mental health oppression, 9–10
mental health practitioners/providers (MHPs), 402
 anonymous comments from, 338–39
 asking essential questions, 42
 burnout and, 338, 339, 340, 341, 347
 Call to Action for, 101, 103, 316, 366–68
 creating spaces of decolonial creativity and joy, 362
 healing, 337–43
 as the HOW TO, 362
 origins of burnout in, 292–95
 sick and dying, 322, 364
 see also Mental Health Industrial Complex (MHIC); politicizing your practice; practitioner resources
mental health professionals, energy work and, 307–10
mental health systems
 co-optation of Indigenous practices and, 33
 informed by criminal justice system, 122
 who is your master in?, 119–21
meridian tapping, 222, 226
methylation, 152, 203
MHIC. *see* mental health industrial complex(MHIC)
MHPs. *see* mental health practitioners/providers (MHPs)
MIC. *see* medical industrial complex (MIC)
microaggressions, 245, 345, 380
migration experience, unfolding, therapeutic questions for, 74–75
Miles, N., 286, 299
Millon, T., 162t
mind–body–energy system, communication through, 290, 291

mind control, 9–10. *see also* gaslighting
mindfulness, 391
Mingus, M., 5, 361
minimal sharing about self, 70–71
Minuchin, S., 162t
Miyoshi, N., 197
MMPI Personality Tests, 162t
money making, colonization and, 111
Montgomery Bus Boycott, 200
moral treatment, pathology of, 115–19
Mott Hall Bridges Academy, 163
Mozambique, continued occupation of, 51
multigenerational trauma, 186–87, 188. *see also* intergenerational trauma
muscle testing, 314
Myers, C., 110, 111, 114, 116, 117, 118
My Good People, use of term, in Black and Brown communities, 26n5
Myss, C., 3n1, 230, 297

N
NAACP, 200
Nagata, D. K., 197
Nahanee, T., 184
Nap Ministry, 185
narrative therapy, 350–51, 366
National Indian Brotherhood, "Indian Control of Indian Education" by, 82
Native American Indian peoples, "Six Phases of Historical Unresolved Grief" for, 256. *see also* Black Indigenous People of Color (BIPOC)
Native American Postcolonial Psychology (Duran & Duran), 46, 176, 255
Naturalization Act, 50
ndi obi, 6
neoliberalism, 402
Netherlands, the
 colonies or territories maintained by, 51
 "Scramble for Africa" and, 43
neurodivergent identity, 94
New Age movements, 350
New Caledonia, continued occupation of, 51
New World, 50n11. *see also* Turtle Island

New York City Lunatic Asylum, percentage of immigrants forming population of, 136–37
New Zealand, colonies or territories maintained by, 51
niceness, removing the veil of, 333
Nisei, effects of historical trauma on, 196–97
"normal"
  capitalist values of Westernism and, 149
  unpacking exclusionary nature of, 147–48
  violence of, 145–49
normal *vs.* deviance, on the binary of, 165
Norway, colonies or territories maintained by, 51
note-taking during sessions, 71

O
object relations theory, 162t
obsessive–compulsive personality disorder, expressions of trauma and, 148–49
Ocoee Massacre, 50
ofrendas, 232
Ogorchukwu, J., 68, 355
O'Grada, C., 52
Olivera, L., 5
On the Natural Variety of Mankind (Blumenbach), 112
oppositional defiant disorder, 122, 134, 239, 266, 380
oppression, 349, 350, 364, 399
  institutionalizing resistance to, 103
  rage as response to, 210
  systematic, historical trauma and, 172
  systems of, 8
  transgender, 149
  see also resistance
Oquendo, A., 240
oral traditions, 350
Orloff, J., 230, 310
Osman, J., 48
overdiagnosis, 150
Owens, D. C., 104

Owens, L. R., 238, 275
"Owning our Madness" (Hickling), 257

P
pain, alchemizing, 347
Panama, Indigenous Kuna Yala and Maya people in, 43
pandemic, 402
  of 2020, racial trauma and, 200, 345–46
panic attacks, 95
papaloas, 235
paper plate exercise, 386–87
parasympathetic nervous system, 240, 276
Parker, I., 184
Parker, J., 230
past, the, present affected by, 55–56
Patel, B., 241
Patel, M., 91, 190
Patel, R., 91, 190
patient–provider relationship, absolute power in, examples of, 118
Pavlov, I., 69, 294
Peers Educating Peers (PEP), 333–34, 335
peer support, 364
  relationships as political in, 333–34
  therapeutic nature of, 334–36
people blaming, system blaming *vs.*, 10–13
People of Global Majority (PoGM), 177, 177n18
  ways white supremacy impacts energetic boundaries of, 310–11
  see also Black Indigenous People of Color (BIPOC); First Nation Indigenous People
People's Institute Survival and Beyond (PISAB), 25, 49
PEP. *see* Peers Educating Peers (PEP)
perfectionism, 94
personal failure, social failure considered as, 149
pharmaceutical industry
  financial ties between *DSM* members and, 146

revision process of *DSM-5* and, 145
Philippines, 52, 53, 56
   continued occupation of, 51
   Lumad People in, militarized communities of, 176
physical boundaries, energetic boundaries vs., 286, 313
"Physicist's Lessons About Race, Power, and the Universe, A" (Dhanesha), 357
Piaget, J., 162t, 294
Piastrelli, B., 230
Piepzna-Samarasinha, L. L., 355
Pinel, P., 115
PISAB. *see* People's Institute Survival and Beyond (PISAB)
planning, as a form of prevention, 360–62
Plant Allies for Rage and Grief work, 369, 371–74
   California poppy flower essence, 373
   ginger, 373
   hawthorn, 372
   lemon balm, 372
   linden, 372
   lymphatic moving plants, 373
   marshmallow leaf, flower, and root, 372
   mints, 373
   mugwort (*Artemisia vulgaris*), 372
   mullein leaves, 372
   rose, 372
   Shooting Star, 373
   vervain, 372–73
plantation management, themes of asylum management and tenets of, 116–18
plantations, policing, asylums, and, 114–15, 116, 118–19
plática, 163, 163n15, 228
Plato, 394
Pod Mapping Worksheets, 361
PoGM. *see* People of Global Majority (PoGM)
police brutality and violence, 180, 254, 350
policing, plantations, asylums, and, 114–15

politicization, as a verb, 376
politicization process, 403
politicized decolonial work, journey towards healing and, 201, 211
politicized framework for healing, 21–25
politicized healers, 403
politicizing your practice, 316–65
   aspects of emotional–decolonial unlearning and, 363–64
   cocreating new timelines and, 350–63
   decolonizing as a verb and, 330–33
   emo–decolonial engagement and, 318, 319, 363
   emo–decolonial practice offerings for, 364–65
   healing the healers and, 337–43
   history as a tool in, 328–30
   peer support and, 333–36
   question everything in, 317, 354
   reasons for doing, 347–50
   repetition and themes intergenerationally and, 343–47
   requirements of, 322–23
   revolution requires evolution for, 320–28
polygeny, 112
Poo, A-J., 330
porous boundaries, generational patterns of, 95
Portugal, 47
   "Scramble for Africa" and, 43
possession, of an individual, land or space, 215, 225–27, 235
Posttraumatic Slave Syndrome (PTSS), 81, 178–81, 255, 402
posttraumatic stress disorder (PTSD), 81, 198
   attachment styles and, 205
   DSM-IV criteria for, 209
   trauma transmission and parents with, 208
power, 403
   absolute, in patient–provider relationship, 118
   of ancestor healing, 295

practitioner resources
  for support as you move forward, 366, 391–94
  for support as you read through Chapter 8, 369, 371–84
  for support as you read through Chapter 9, 369, 387–89
prejudice, 403
Prescod-Weinstein, C., 357, 358
prevention, essential need for, 358
priestesses, 6
priests, 226
prison industrial complex, 116, 132
privilege, 69–70, 72–73, 400
productivity, traditional work week and, 157
profits, medical and mental health industrial complexes and, 12
projective identification, 203, 204
Prosser, I. B., 294
psychiatric disorders, pathologizing, over-medicalization of, 146
psychiatrist, roots of term, 119–20
psychiatry
  founded on punishment, 107
  modern, decolonized psychology vs., 153, 153t
psychic energy, 290
psychoanalysis, 161t
psychogenic, 403
psychohistory, 403
psychological enslavement, 45, 104–5
  moral treatment and, 115–19
  persistence of, 122
  plantations, policing, asylums, and, 114–15, 116, 118
  questioning who is your master?, 119–21
  unpacking 400 plus years of, 136
  violence and, 105
  see also diagnostic enslavement
psychological pathology, 403
"psychological terrorism," 150–51
psychology, decolonized, modern psychiatry vs., 153, 153t
psychometrics, 161t

psychosis, 152, 216
psychotherapy, "invisible" dynamics of, 290
PTSD. see posttraumatic stress disorder (PTSD)
PTSS. see Posttraumatic Slave Syndrome (PTSS)
Puerto Rico, continued occupation of, 51
punishment, psychiatry founded on, 122

Q
qigong, 303
quality therapy, 32, 32n7
queer, 403
queer ball culture, 334n31
quotation marks, use of, in text, 14n3

R
race, construct and creation of, 111–14, 121
race-based traumatic stress, 141, 199–200
racial discrimination, 403
racial profiling, 55
racial trauma, 140, 141, 201, 244
racism, 55, 97, 152, 257, 321, 345, 380, 403–404
  chronic, logical responses from living with, 141
  institutionalized, 161, 177
  internalized, 255
  medical, 104
  overlap of ableism and, 105, 121
  People's Institute definition of, 113
  scientific, 104, 107–9, 110, 111, 112, 118, 119, 122, 137, 149, 404
  see also white supremacy
racism-related fatigue, 141, 404
racism-related stress/distress, 141, 404
racist socialization, 255
Radical and Healing-Based Responding, essential need for, 358–59
Radical Therapy Center, Philadelphia, 184
rage, 33, 241, 245, 261, 359
  addressing root of the wound and, 260
  allowed feelings of, 259–60
  anger vs., 266–67

aspects of emotional–decolonial
  unlearning and, 275–76
diagnosing, psychology serving capitalism and, 269–70
Disguises of, 267, 269, 270–71, 272, 280n25, 404
emo–decolonial practice offerings for, 276–77
glorious righteous ancestral, necessity of, 265–75
intergenerational trauma and, 193–94
pathologizing, 239, 275
the people's stories about, 242–44, 262–65
plant allies for soothing our hearts during, 371–74
as response to oppression, 210
Rage-Grief Axis, 33, 404
  genesis of, 274
  ways to work with, 279–81
Rage Types, primary and salient, 271–72
Rank, O., 178
Rashatwar, S., 184
rational emotive therapy, 216
rebuilding, through emo-decolonial work, 317
reclamation, affirmations for, 98
reconvergence and reconnection, beginning process of, 7
(re)education, essential need for, 358
@rehumanizingourselves, 138
rehumanizing ourselves, decolonization and, 171
Reiki, 303
religion
  divide between mental health care and, 216
  healing deeply connected to, 224
relocation of Native peoples, disenfranchised grief and, 256. *see also* forced migration (or forced displacement); land theft
repetition compulsion, trauma transmission and, 203–4
Report on the Diseases and Physical Peculiarities of the Negro Race, A (Cartwright), 107

residential schools, 240, 404
resistance
  acts of, 356–57
  boarding schools and acts of, 176
  to decolonial work, 345
  as insanity, 158–59
  to oppression, institutionalizing, 103
resource exploitation, 48, 49, 52
Restak, R., 215
revolution, 234
  evolution required by, 320–22, 363
Reynoso, S., 163
Rhodes, R., 201
Rice, T., 55
Richards, K., 120
Rodney, W., 50
Roe, T., 268
Rogers, C., 69, 162t, 294
root, addressing, by digging deeper, 82–83
Root and Ritual (Piastrelli), 230
Root Workers, 5–6
Rorschach, H., 162t
Rorschach Inkblot Test, 162t
Rosenthal, S., 273
Rowland-Klein, D, 203
rugged individualism, late-stage capitalism and, 137
Rush, B., 116, 118

S
Sacred Inner Rage Child, 268, 270, 272, 278
Sacred Rage, 95, 275
sadness
  allowed feelings of, 259–60
  capitalizing off of suffering and, 151–53
safety
  concept of Home and, 68–69, 72–73
  decolonial journey and, 30
  micro decisions related to, 246
  privilege of, 69–70, 72–73
  true humanizing and, 333, 334, 335
Said, E. W., 39
Sakugawa, Y., 356
Sansei, effects of historical trauma on, 197

santera/o, 6, 24, 215, 235
Santeria, 223, 226, 295, 350
Santiago-Irizarry, V., 88
Santo Domingo (present-day Dominican Republic), 60
Saul, J., 265
schizophrenia, 273
    Civil Rights Era and reformulation of, 106
    incarceration of Black men and "new version of," 106–7
Schmit, J., 302
school-to-prison-nexus, 132
scientific racism, 104, 110, 111, 118, 119, 149, 401
    Drapetomania and, 107–9
    eugenics movements and, 137
    legacy of, 122
    rise of, 112
"Scramble for Africa," 43
secondary traumatic stress, 340
Second Sight (Orloff), 230, 309
Secret Spiritual World of Children, The (Hart), 229
secure attachment, 204
self-actualization theory (Maslow), appropriation of, 222
self-care, 120, 125–26, 156–57, 191, 298, 341, 349
self-determination, 401
self-hatred, 255
self-inquiry, learning to unlearn through, 317
self/psyche, emotional evolution, including the body and relationships, 318, 319, 327–28, 363
self-psychology, 162t
self-sovereignty, 41
sensation-perception theory, 162t
Sensory-Processing Sensitivity, 299
session limits, 70, 123
settler colonialism, 48–50, 66
sexism, 97, 152
shamanistic traditions, idea of soul loss in, 209–10
shamans, 6, 24, 215, 223, 226, 235

shame, unexamined, perpetuation of violence and, 106
Shosan, T., 196
Shulman, L., 249
Sitting Bull, assassination of, 175
16 PF personality test, 162t
Skinner, B. F., 161t, 294
slavery, 43, 49, 49, 50, 78, 126, 158, 159, 177, 383
    criteria for PTSD and survivors of, 198
    justifying, construct of race and, 111
    medical racism and, 104
    wealth of the United States and, 105–7
    see also Posttraumatic Slave Syndrome (PTSS); psychological enslavement
Slavery and Healing the Intergenerational Soul Wound in Inner City African American Male Youth of the African Diaspora (Mullan), 196
small revolutions, for care givers and space holders (practitioners), 92–93
Smith, T., 146, 147, 151, 260n23
social failure, considered as personal failure, 149
social justice work, bringing emotional, loving collective energy to, 318
social learning theory(ies)
    cycles of maltreatment and, 207–8
    trauma transmission and, 206
social media, 289, 329
Socrates, 394
Somatic Soul Trauma Timelines (SSTTs), 263, 344, 369, 376–84, 406
    Ancestral/Intergenerational focus, 377–78, 381
    Collective focus, 377, 381
    example of, 379–80, 381, 382
    focus and use of, 351–52
    Individual focus, 378, 381
    Lifelines and, 383–84, 384
    naming of, 377
    Political (global) focus, 377, 382
    resourced, preparing for, 378–79
    utilization of, 383

soul loss, symptoms and causes of, 209
Souls of Black Folk, The (Du Bois), 223
soul wound, 174–77, 180
  epigenetic inheritance and, 81
  as historical trauma, 174–75, 188
soul wounding, Indigenous communities and use of term, 208
sovereignty, 350, 401–2
space holders (practitioners), small revolutions for, 92–93
Spain, 47
  "Scramble for Africa" and, 43
"Spell of Capitalism, The" (Smith), 260n23
sperm, altered methylation patterns in, 203
spiral staircase, 80, 80n13
spiritual roots, 215–31
  ancestral support, 228–29
  ceremony, 227–28
  children and, 229–31
  possession, 215, 225–27
  stolen spirits of healing, 221–23
SSTTs. *see* Somatic Soul Trauma Timelines (SSTTs)
stakeholders, in MHIC, 86
Starks, A., 40
state murder, "psychological terrorism" and, 150–51
St. Croix, continued occupation of, 51
St. Mary of Bethlehem, London (Bedlam), 103
Stockholm syndrome
  collective global, colonization as, 76–81
  definition of, 76
  origin of name for, 77
  symptoms of, 77
storytelling, 350, 364
straight lines in school, asking students to walk in, 71
stress, violence of, 394
Strobel, L. M., 39
structuralism, 161t
structural violence, multigenerational wounds and, 201

students of color, percentage of diagnosed with disabilities, 161
subtle body, 302–3
suffering
  capitalist causes of, 139–45
  capitalizing off of sadness and, 151–53
  examining and honoring the root of, 139
Suffocated Grief, 252
suicidality, antidepressants and, 152
Sullivan, H. S., 161t
superego, 290
supervision, reciprocal and intergenerational, 247–48
supremacism, 49
survivance, 402
survivor syndrome, symptoms of, 196
Sutherland, C., 59, 60
sympathetic nervous system, 276
symptoms, expressions *vs.*, 128n14, 165
syncretism, 350, 405
synonyms that nurture wellness, finding, 130
system blaming, people blaming *vs.*, 10–13
systemic oppression, 405
system(s), 405
szeptunka, 6

T
Tagaq, T., 39
tai chi, 306
tapping (EFT). *see* Emotional Freedom Technique (EFT) tapping
Tawwab, N., 298
Taylor, B., 55, 158, 345
Teish, L., 9, 230, 281n27
temporarily able-bodied, 405
"Ten Ways White Supremacy Wounds White People: A Tale of Mutuality" (Elliot), 171
thalamus gland, 242
Theosophical Society, 350
The People's Institute for Survival and Beyond (PISAB), 112, 113
therapeutic container, safety within, 69

therapeutic privilege, giving up, 211
therapeutic spaces, healing spaces and, 30
therapists, 402
  perpetuation of white supremacy and, 183, 188
  ways people are policed by, 70–71
  see also mental health practitioners/providers (MHPs)
therapy, as an art, 350
Thorndike, E., 161*t*
thought field therapy, 291, 304
TikTok therapists, 294
Titchener, E., 161*t*
Torres, G., 5
Traditional Chinese Medicine, 303
Transatlantic Slave Trade, 179, 200
transgender, 405
transgender oppression, 149, 405
"transness," attempts to end pathologization of, 149
transpersonal psychology, 301
transphobia, 9, 406
trauma
  ancestral, 241
  collective, redressing, 206–7, 265
  of colonization, expressions of, 93–96
  cultural, 179, 180, 210, 244
  global and Indigenous perspectives on, 208–10
  intergenerational tree of transmission and, 92
  "managers" and coping with, 200
  multigenerational, 186–87, 188
  public, resistance as insanity and, 158–59
  racial, 140, 141, 201, 244
  root of, addressing, 82–83
  vicarious, 127, 340
  Western context for roots of word, 187, 189
  see also historical trauma; intergenerational trauma; multigenerational trauma; posttraumatic stress disorder (PTSD)
Trauma and Recovery (Herman), 30
Trauma Burger, example of, 89–90
trauma-informed, 406
trauma-informed and trauma responsive approaches, 406
trauma transmission, questions to ask oneself and people you support, 369, 375–76
treatment plans, 70
Treaty of Guadalupe Hidalgo, 50
trephination, 215, 217
Trujillo, R. L., 186
Trump, D., 150
trust
  difficulties with, 95
  in yourself, your intuition, and your fellow comrades, 30–31
Tuck, E., 22
Turtle Island, 50n11, 51, 111
  genocide of Indigenous peoples on, 175n17, 176
  settler-colonial context of, 22
Tuskegee experiment, 50, 104

U
"Understanding Grief as the Antidote to Trauma" (Maté), 261–62
United Kingdom, colonies or territories maintained by, 51
United Nations, 51
United States
  colonies or territories maintained by, 51
  slave labor and wealth of, 105–7

V
vacant esteem, 255
Vaid-Menon, A., 99
Valeii, K., 195
van der Kolk, B., 69, 200, 229, 304
Vespucci, A., 50
vicarious trauma, 127, 340
violence
  in clinical mental health initiation process, 192–93
  collective and cultural, soul wound and, 177
  deep, "in the name of science," 100

of diagnosis, 133–35
drivers of, understanding, 160
of individualism, 150–51
internalized or externalized self-hatred and, 255
of "normal," 145–49
police brutality, 180, 254, 350
psychological enslavement and, 105
race-based traumatic stress and, 199–200
of stress, 391
structural, multigenerational wounds and, 201
unexamined shame and, 106
see also colonialism; genocide; historical trauma
Vizenor, G., 405
Vodou, 223, 226, 227, 376
voluntold, 18n4
von Békésy, G., 162t
Vygotsky, L., 162t, 294

W
Wade, B., 238
Washington Post, 106, 119
Watson, J., 161t
Watters, W., 216
Waxman, O. B., 158
wealth
  on the backs of Black folks, 105–7
  settler colonialism and generation of, 48
Wechsler, D., 162t
Wechsler Memory Scales, 162t
Weiss, B., 230, 310
wellness
  cocreating plan for, 94
  as huge part of decolonization, 23–24
  inviting multiple forms of, 123
  MHIC and outdated system of, 127
  see also healing
Wertheimer, M., 162t
Western Energy Psychology (WEP), 291
Western mental health, roots of: a People's history, 101–3

When the Body Says No (Maté), 310
white-bodied supremacy, 406
whiteness
  pervasive situating of, 97
  as a Western wound, 91
white practitioners in psychology, founding, and their theoretical or assessment contributions, 161t–163t
White Rage (Anderson), 269n24
white supremacist racism, 406
white supremacy, 9, 11, 32, 97, 318, 349, 350, 364
  anti-Blackness against backdrop of, 223
  BIPOC's/PoGM's energetic boundaries impacted by, 310–11, 314
  check-in regarding, 78
  "divide and conquer" energy of, 177
  individual internalized, 7
  scientific racism and, 119
  therapists and perpetuation of, 183, 188
  as a virus and a plague, 82
  white culture informed by, 6–7
  white people's energetic boundaries and, 311
  white people wounded by, 171, 188
Wilber, K., 301
Wilkins, J., 371
Willie Lynch Letter and The Making of a Slave, The, 144
Willie Lynch letters, 108
Wilmington Massacre, 50
WISC and WAIS Intelligence Tests, 162t
wisdom
  global Indigenous, reviving, 231
  vital, lived experience as, 210
witches, 6, 226
Woke, being *vs.* staying, 192
Wolynn, M., 324
Woman Who Glows in the Dark (Avila & Parker), 230
Women Who Run with Wolves (Estés), 230, 310
Woodcock, R., 162t

Woodcock-Johnson Cognitive and Achievement Tests, 162t
workaholism, 149. *see also* burnout
work week, traditional, productivity limits and, 157
Wounded Knee Massacre, 175, 256
Wright, B., 142
Wundt, W., 161t

X
xenophobia, 97

Y
Yalom, I. D., 287, 288
Yang, K. W., 22
Yehuda, R., 80, 204, 206, 207, 254
Yellow Bird, M., 80, 184, 294
Yerkes, R., 162t

About the Author

Jennifer Mullan, PsyD, is a dynamic international speaker, professor, healer–spiritualist, and scholar–activist and is widely known as the "Rage Doctor." Trained as a clinical psychologist, Dr. Jennifer Mullan birthed Decolonizing Therapy—a psychological evolution that weaves together political, ancestral, therapeutic, and global well-being.

Dr. Mullan is a major disruptor in the mental health industrial complex. Her work is an urgent call to dive to the root of global and generational trauma to unlock the wisdom of our sacred rage.

She received ESSENCE Magazine's 2020 Essential Hero Award in mental health, and was featured on The Today Show, *Vox*, *Cosmopolitan*, *Allure*, GQ, and the *Calgary Journal*, among many others. She currently lives in Northern New Jersey on land that was stewarded by the Leni Lenape people.

Want to take your Decolonizing Therapy journey further? Visit www.decolonizingtherapy.com/bonus to access bonus resources.